the NEW cook's tour of
sonoma

the NEW cook's tour of sonoma

150 recipes and the

best of the region's

food and wine

michele anna jordan

photographs by faith echtermeyer

SASQUATCH BOOKS
SEATTLE

An earlier edition of this book was published in 1990 under the title *A Cook's Tour of Sonoma*.

Printed in the United States of America.
Distributed in Canada by Raincoast Books Ltd.
04 03 02 01 00   5 4 3 2 1

Cover and interior design: Kate Basart
Cover and interior photographs: Faith Echtermeyer
Food stylist: Michele Anna Jordan
Copy editor: Frances Bowles

Library of Congress Cataloging in Publication Data
Jordan, Michele Anna
The New Cook's Tour of Sonoma / Michele Anna Jordan.
        p.   cm.
    Includes bibliographical references and index.
    ISBN 1-57061-218-8 (alk. paper)
    Cookery. 2. Grocery trade—California—Sonoma County—Guidebooks. 3. Sonoma County
    (California)—Guidebooks. I. Title.
    TX714.J68 2000
    641.5—dc21   00-029652

SASQUATCH BOOKS
615 Second Avenue
Seattle, Washington 98104
(206) 467-4300
books@SasquatchBooks.com
www.SasquatchBooks.com

For Guy & Mary Duryee

For Lesa Tanner

And in memory of Luther Burbank & Kate Wolf

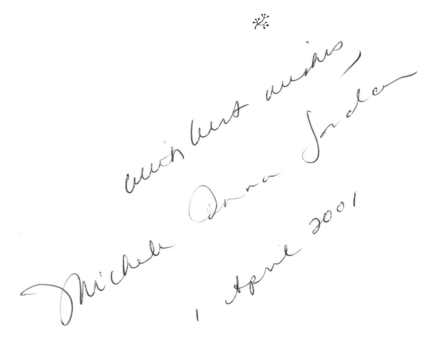

Contents

List of Recipes

Acknowledgments

MY EXPERIENCE OF SONOMA COUNTY has been shaped to a very large degree by the place where I have lived for more than a dozen years, a charming country cottage surrounded by meadows, apple trees, plum trees, olive trees, chestnuts, and berries, and overlooking Atascadero Creek, about a mile west of downtown Sebastopol. Vegetables, roses, lavender, and artemesia thrive in my garden. Mockingbirds serenade me, and bold little hummingbirds sip nectar from flowers outside the window of my study. In the summer, dozens of monarch butterflies live in the boudleahs near my front door. When winter storms recede, thousands of frogs join in a nighttime chorus that seeps through the very walls, a soundtrack of this time and this place. I cannot imagine living anywhere else. I am deeply grateful to Mary and Guy Duryee for inviting me to move into this sweet little house and for allowing me to stay, through the good times and the bad. Their kindness and generosity have made it possible for me to write. Guy and Mary, this book is for you. How could it be for anyone else?

Lesa Tanner, my assistant, continues to amaze me, not only with her calm attention to details that leave me flustered but also with her wisdom, humor, intelligence, grace, loyalty, and talent. I feel lucky to have met her, and even luckier that she is still with me. So thank you, Lesa, and good luck with your book (just don't abandon me when it's a bestseller).

Every writer should be blessed with a copyeditor as gifted, as kind, and as generous as Frances Bowles: thank you, a thousand times, for everything. And a big thank you to everyone at Sasquatch Books, especially Gary Luke and Jennie McDonald, for believing in the book, for hiring Frances, and for being so genuinely kind and enthusiastic (and patient). And to Faith Echtermeyer, thanks for understanding my Sonoma and capturing it in such fine photographs.

Mary Karlin, a dedicated cheerleader for Sonoma County food, wine, and agriculture, provided invaluable assistance, as did Roslyn Layton, whose timely question at the San Francisco farmers' market was the seed from which this book grew. Roslyn became an invaluable assistant and deserves the credit for the detailed listings of Sonoma County wineries. Merci, Roslyn. And merci beaucoup to Evelyn Anderson for keeping Sonoma Provence alive and thriving. Many, many thanks to Frédèrique Lavoipierre for producing my radio show, Mouthful, and to Ted Crimy, for engineering (and for listening to my stories). And to the entire gang at KRCB-FM, for keeping it all happening. Thanks to Dan Taylor, Diane Holt, and Diane Peterson of the Press Democrat, Robin Davis of the San Francisco Chronicle, and Mark Trautwein of KQED-FM for being such great colleagues. And thanks to Heidi Magnussen for being so much fun.

So many people helped with this book that I cannot possibly name them all. From writers such as Gaye LeBaron and Larry McDonald to restaurateurs such as Patrick Martin of the Healdsburg Charcuterie and cheesemakers such as Cindy Callahan, people were generous with their time, their talent, and their stories. Tim Tesconi, Dan Benedetti, John Ash, Mimi Luebberman, David Viviani, Newton Dal Pogetto, Linda Cornelius, Greg Reisinger, Ridgely Evers, Colleen McGlynn, Jennifer Bice, Gary Farrell, and dozens of others offered sage advice, encouragement, and material. And big thank-yous to Lou Preston of Preston of Dry Creek and George Rose of Clos du Bois Winery for their enthusiastic support of my books, and of me. Bill Traverso, Paul Root, Tony Marti, and Darryl Roberts offered wise advice and guidance about wine. And to Ray Tang and Shawn Kearny-Tang of Mariposa, thanks for the good food, laughs, and recipe.

Amy Rennert is more than just an agent; she is a friend and a source of wisdom and encouragement. Thanks for everything, Amy.

John Kramer, Nancy Dobbs, and Annie and Andrew Dobbs-Kramer continue to enrich my life with memorable hours in the kitchen and around the table. To them, and to my daughters Gina and Nicolle, my friends Ginny Stanford, Sid Nappi, Julieta Weiss, Michel Stong, John Boland, and James Carroll, thank you yet again.

Hayfields are cut, harvest has begun
Riding through the orchards in the morning sun
Good times in the country, can't you smell the air
Apples and apricots and plums to spare

Down gentle roads with no white line
Like a pathway to another time
Old houses passing, frontyards of flowers
I could ride in the country for hours and hours

—Kate Wolf, "Riding in the County," 1972

Introduction

I

IN MY EARLIEST MEMORY OF SONOMA COUNTY, I am wrapped in a beach blanket on the shore of the Russian River, gulping air and sobbing. I can hear the delighted shouts and squeals of my half-sister and her friends who had enticed me into following them off a pier into the shimmering emerald green water. I can see them leap, but I cannot recall my own jump.

I was not yet three years old and I couldn't swim. They were teenagers and in their exuberance had apparently forgotten their main responsibility, babysitting me. Oops. Eventually someone plucked me from the water and my memory coalesces with my first shore-side breath. It would be years before I would venture into the water again, but my baptism was complete. Sonoma County was a part of me, the connection visceral and binding.

I grew up in a small town in Solano County, about twenty miles east of here; trips to Sonoma County were a high point of my earliest years. During an elementary school flirtation with marine zoology, I visited the laboratories of the University of California at Dillon Beach and collected sea anemones, lichen, and limpets from the nearby tide pools. As a teenager, I lounged on the county's beaches and river banks and rode in a homecoming parade with a "Smash Santa Rosa" sign—our football teams were rivals—taped to a friend's copper-colored 1957 Chevy Impala. My boyfriend, whose sister lived in El Verano (adjacent to the town of Sonoma), and I spent hours hiking through the county's redwoods and driving its mountain roads in his vintage Austin Healy. A high school counselor suggested I consider attending Sonoma State University and, in spite of the distraction of an early marriage and two children born before I was of drinking age, it wasn't long before I moved to the lowlands of Lakeville east of Petaluma.

The girls and I lived in a little farmhouse built in the 1950s amidst large dairy farms, undulating hills and valleys of hay, and majestic corridors of eucalyptus trees planted a century earlier as windbreaks. The fragrance of new-mown hay mingled with warm spring rain and the slightly menthol scent of damp eucalyptus leaves remains a wildly intoxicating aroma, almost painfully evocative of this time, this place. In the summer, when the setting sun would backlight the splayed branches and bathe the landscape in an orange glow, the girls would giggle and point to the forest of giant broccoli. In the fall, the hunter's moon rose over the land, an enormous red sphere, haunting and eerily vivid, as if it were a sentient being. After the girls were asleep, I would go for long walks in its silvery blue light, making countless wishes on the night's stars, hoping we would never have to leave.

Although I had been intrigued by food and cooking since I was a little kid, my tastes and skills were shaped by our years in Lakeville. When our landlady, Dottie Henning, gave us milk from Mulie, the family cow, I spooned off the thick cream, saved a little for the coffee I had just learned to drink, and taught the girls to make butter with the rest of it. During a party one Easter, the girls and their friends found not only the six dozen eggs I had dyed the night before, but several dozen white ones, too, laid by an independent hen in the stump of an old eucalyptus tree behind the house. I learned to let myself be surprised by nature and to let our meals be shaped by its bounty. We grew a few things, mostly tomatoes, spinach, and broccoli, gathered blackberries along country roads, and shopped at farm stands, a butcher shop, and two local cheese factories. We drove to the coast for fresh salmon and bought milk at Miller's Drive-in Dairy in Petaluma, where everything came in glass bottles. In those days—idyllic in memory, but in reality fraught with all the challenges and mistakes of solo motherhood—I even cut and split our firewood.

These were my student years. I realize now that I cared more about day-to-day living, about friends and conversation, about cooking, eating, and the pleasures of the table than I did about getting a degree (which I did get, almost in spite of myself).

For me, college was more of a bridge to myself than it was a path to a career; it was how I found my way home.

I believe I can identify the exact moment when I knew I belonged in Sonoma County. A professor was offering me career advice and asked where I thought I might like to live. Would I be willing to move to the Midwest, he asked, or the East Coast, where there might be good job opportunities? I recall his exasperation when I refused even to consider living anywhere but here. I think he predicted that I would have a hard time of it. I left his office duly chastened but unshaken in my resolve to remain in Sonoma County. (It is a source of great pleasure that the school that once warned me of my imminent failure now trots me out regularly as one of its success stories.)

II

IT'S HARD NOT TO BE NOSTALGIC ABOUT THOSE DAYS. Sonoma County was a well-kept secret, a hidden jewel thirty-five minutes north of the Golden Gate Bridge but much farther away in most people's minds. I remember looking over my shoulder frequently back then, mindful that discovery was inevitable, aware that indeed it was already happening, unfolding slowly as others like me moved north.

When I think of this time, I am drawn to the opening lines of Madeleine Kamman's first book, *When French Women Cook*. "[T]he France I left, my France, does not exist anymore; it has disappeared, slowly receding into time past," she writes. "Where are you, my France," Madeleine asks as if it were a plea, a mantra, a prayer, "where women cooked, where the stars in cooking did not go to men anxious for publicity but to women with worn hands stained by vegetables peeled, parched by work in house, garden or fields, wrinkled by age and experience. Where are you? Nowhere but in the folds of my memory . . . I shall woo you and recreate you, bring back to life your women so that you know, dear readers, that there was once a civilization that was human, tender, enjoyable and lovable."

Sonoma County is not gone, but much of its rural character is ephemeral, a dream, a memory, a desire that fades a bit each day, an inevitable loss as our population swells and greed rather than family tradition inform too many decisions about the land. The changes began as people moved here not for the country life that it is still possible to live, but for the cheaper rent, lower housing prices, and easy commute to San Francisco. Many of these newcomers complain loudly about the messy realities of farming, and they spend four hours a day or more in their cars because, in fact, the commute to the city is no longer easy. Nor are rents and housing costs reasonable; in late 1999, the vacancy rate was hovering around 0 percent and homes were selling for 20 percent or more over the asking price. The cry to widen Highway 101

("Three lanes all the way!" they shout) is deafening and ubiquitous, a topic at every gathering and a guaranteed flash point if you suggest that perhaps it's not such a good idea after all. Yet on the narrow passage from Marin County to Sonoma County, a stretch of about eight miles, something incredible occurs. Business parks give way to dairies, a wetland, a rustic old house. You slow down, not just literally—traffic is often stopped along this stretch—but emotionally and spiritually, too. In an instant, the landscape, even the light, has changed, and you are in a different place. If we widen this slender artery, Sonoma County will no longer be the distinctly separate, pastoral province it still is, even now. The roads will still be congested, and we will look exactly like every other suburb of the Bay Area.

Yet even as this controversy threatens to eclipse all other concerns, I go to the farmers' market, linger in a new restaurant, or teach a class at Ramekins, our extraordinarily successful new cooking school, and realize that tremendous blessings have come with the discovery of my Sonoma. Our farmers, winemakers, cheesemakers, dairymen and -women, chefs, and shopkeepers greet a new century with a health and vitality I could not have predicted a decade ago. We are no longer a well-kept secret, we are no longer hidden, but the rough jewel that Luther Burbank discovered sparkles still, perhaps more brightly that it ever has.

III

AND WHAT OF OUR COOKING, how has it changed? Is there such a thing as Sonoma County cuisine? Is there a definitive wine-country style? The short answer is no, not in the true sense of the word. A cuisine has a long history. It is passed from generation to generation for decades and centuries. It evolves slowly, born of indigenous ingredients, geographic isolation, and age-old techniques; it is shaped by those charged with the responsibility of feeding their families, which is almost always to say, the women.

The original cooking of this place is, of course, that of the native tribes who first lived here, the Miwoks, Pomos, Kashayas, and Wappos, whose cuisines remained discrete and separate as wave after wave of immigrants displaced them from their land. The new cooking in Sonoma County became a microcosm of what it was in California, a patchwork quilt of influences, shaped by the classic dishes, tastes, prejudices, and traditions of European settlers, especially Spanish, Italian, German, French, Portuguese, and Basque. (Although Asians were among the early residents here, the cuisines of Asia would have little general influence until the late twentieth century.) The unifying thread and the golden needle, as it were, that stitched these influences together was the fertile land itself; the long growing season and remarkable bounty of California are reflected in miniature in Sonoma County.

During those early years, people raised much of what they ate and drank. Chickens provided eggs, a cow milk that was churned into butter and made into cheese, which lasted longer than the perishable liquid. The whey and leftover milk were fed to hogs that were slaughtered in the fall, their blood made into sausage, their legs cured for prosciutto. Farmers grew grapes to make wine for their own tables; women baked bread and made fresh pasta not because it was trendy but because it was all there was. Polenta—frequently topped with robins caught near creek beds and stewed in tomato sauce—was a staple.

Styles of eating and cooking changed here, as they did throughout the United States, with the rise of the automobile and the advent of the supermarket. Sonoma County did not escape the bland cooking of the 1950s and 1960s, yet as we awoke from that period, remarkable things happened that did not occur elsewhere. As the gourmet revolution of the 1970s progressed, restaurateurs—inspired by the success and innovation of Chez Panisse in Berkeley—turned to our small farmers, cheesemakers, and winemakers in search of the handcrafted ingredients that were to shape a new California culinary style, born in the restaurant rather than the home. This in turn inspired more small farmers, who now had a market for their harvest. (I featured a much more thorough exploration of the history and influences of cooking in the Golden State in a previous book, *California Home Cooking*, published in 1997.)

Sonoma County has played a pivotal role in the development of contemporary California cooking, and as our small farmers and winemakers have responded to the demand for artisan products, a style of sorts *has* emerged. You can call Sonoma County cooking—or wine-country cuisine, if you prefer—a cuisine of possibility, a style shaped by the seasons, by the land, and by the chefs who have been inspired by what the land can yield. There are few rules, and no classic mother recipes to which these chefs by tradition must adhere. In a very real sense, anything goes. As we enter a new century, it is impossible to know exactly how all of this will evolve. Restaurants are driven by trends, by a fickle public and an even more mercurial press that seems to require a continuous diet of fashionable new ingredients. A cuisine based as ours currently is on heirloom fruits and vegetables, handcrafted cheeses, delicate olive oils, and other foods that grow almost literally outside our front doors, is fragile, vulnerable to the whims and fashions of an increasingly global marketplace. Before we can declare Sonoma County cuisine a lasting tradition, it must take root and blossom in the home as well as in the restaurant and it must survive for a generation or two, a process inseparable from time itself. The final word will be written by others. It is my hope that *The New Cook's Tour of Sonoma* will shed light on this time and this place, Sonoma County on the cusp of the twenty-first century.

IV

I BEGAN WRITING ABOUT FOOD IN GENERAL, and Sonoma County's specifically, more by accident than design. Bruce Robinson, who is today the general manager of the radio station where I have two regular programs, asked me to write a food column for the newspaper he then edited, the *Sebastopol Times and News*. I was managing a restaurant and owned a catering business at the time, and it was easy to ignore his first request. When he called a few months later and said, "Just get me something by Friday, and include a recipe or two," I decided I had better seize the opportunity. When a reader called me after that first column appeared in March of 1986, I was hooked. Week after week, I turned to local markets, especially Fiesta in Sebastopol and Traverso's in Santa Rosa, for inspiration. Why would I look elsewhere? These many years later, my life remains organized around the rhythm of a weekly column, the visits with farmers and shopkeepers that inspire it still, and the slow unfolding of the seasons that shape it.

A Cook's Tour of Sonoma was my first book, and I approached it with tremendous exuberance, modest ambition, and a single goal, to share some of my favorite local foods and offer recipes that had been inspired by my years here and by those early columns. I thought of it as a love letter. After its publication (though not because of it), my life changed in ways I could not have foreseen. I began writing for the *Sonoma County Independent,* and under the wise guidance of James Carroll, the editor during my tenure, and John Boland, the publisher, I matured as a writer, honing my skills and developing a deeper understanding of the responsibilities any writer brings to her work.

At the *Independent*, I acquired a perspective I lacked as I wrote that first book; revisiting *A Cook's Tour* has been at times uncomfortable, its mistakes and indulgences frequently more apparent to me than any strengths it may have had. It's a glimpse at my younger self, eager yet naive, curious but a bit too breathless. Yet my motivation then was similar to my purpose now, to celebrate and honor this remarkable land and those who have made a commitment to nurturing it and preserving its bounty.

I wrote then that my purpose was political as well as a gastronomic; it remains so today and is informed by even greater urgency. The race towards a homogeneous culture continues at breakneck speed. Increasingly, we buy food in generic superstores, eat in national chain restaurants where regional character is nothing more than a caricature of the latest trend, purchase books anonymously over the Internet. Shopping malls are virtually identical the world around, only the faces of the shoppers vary. I fear that global consumerism, fueled by the World Trade Organization, and the siren song of advertising have lulled us into a dangerous trance.

For now it is entirely possible to travel an alternate route, to discover the shopkeeper who will remember not only your name but also your favorite cheese, to find the farmer who offers a wholesome harvest grown without a toxic soup of chemicals, to meet the bookseller who's in the business for the love of reading. That's what my Sonoma is all about, and I truly believe that, in nurturing it we will preserve it, rescue it from what sometimes seems an inevitable demise.

As I write the last few pages of this book, the afternoon light has turned golden; year, decade, and century are all drawing to a close. It is nearly ten years to the day since I finished the original *Cook's Tour of Sonoma*, and the memory of that time is palpable: the haunting autumn light, an identical morning chill, the same troubling concerns. Yet there is something more, too, a growing realization that the fruits of discovery are not at all bitter, but rather yield up a sweet nectar of success. At the window a hummingbird, its ruby neck feathers illuminated by the sun's rays, sips sugar water. Jamaica, curled on top of the monitor of my Macintosh, meows languidly, her hunting spirit subdued by months of frustration. Olive, cozy at my feet, purrs her approval.

—*Michele Anna Jordan*
November 1999

PART I

Cornucopia

LUTHER BURBANK'S FINGERPRINTS ARE ALL OVER SONOMA COUNTY, in the names of streets, businesses, and buildings, in fairs and festivals that honor him, at his home and garden in Santa Rosa and his experimental farm in Sebastopol, less than a quarter of a mile from my home. It's hard to imagine what we would be today if our young Luther hadn't headed west from his native Massachusetts, a journey inspired in part, his biographer Peter Dryer tells us, by a broken heart. With his three brothers already in California, cash from the sale of his Burbank potato in his pocket, and the pain of unrequited love in his veins, America's greatest gardener set out by train to meet his fate, and to shape ours. He arrived in Santa Rosa on October 31, 1875, and almost immediately began filling his letters home with the declarations that reverberate to this day, among them his most enduring words: "This is the chosen spot of all this earth as far as Nature is concerned."

During his lifetime Burbank, working at an astonishing pace and with an enviable intensity and focus, developed over eight hundred new varieties of plants. The selection of specific characteristics in plants—that is, the art of hybridization—is a slow process, born of both science and intuition. By all accounts, Burbank had an uncanny ability to select plants with desirable qualities. These plants he would then isolate from the others, pollinate by hand if necessary, select again from a new generation, and continue until he had the exact qualities he wanted. He developed new varieties of apples, berries, cactus, cherries, eggplants, figs, grapes, nectarines, peaches, pears, plumcots (pluots), quince, strawberries, almonds, chestnuts, pine nuts, barley, quinoa, oats, rye, wheat, elephant garlic, gladioli, marigolds, sweet peas, roses, the Shasta daisy, and over one hundred ten varieties of plums. The diversity and abundance of Sonoma County is reflected in Burbank's dizzying cornucopia of accomplishments. He was one of the most famous men of his day.

In Burbank's time, the process of hybridization was not entirely understood. He talked to his plants and believed that his ability to communicate with them went beyond mere intuition into a realm he described, for lack of a better term, as spiritual. This belief in himself as particularly, and specially, gifted, combined with a flair for self-promotion, brought him no end of trouble. He did not have a scientist's characteristic modesty (nor the discipline for meticulous documentation) and so was viewed with increasing skepticism by the academic community. The religious community was even more suspicious. The publication of the first edition of Burbank's catalogue, *New Creations in Fruits and Flowers*, in June of 1893, angered Christian fundamentalists of the day. The creation of new plants belonged solely to their God and they had little tolerance for one who claimed the ability for himself. Religious zealots picketed Burbank's home and held prayer vigils on his lawn. He appears to have been condemned as a heretic as frequently as he was lauded as a genius; the condemnations continued until the end of his life. Not long after delivering a lecture—a sermon, really—in defense of himself at the First Congregational Church in San Francisco, Luther Burbank suffered a heart attack and died on April 10, 1926.

Today, scientists can slice, dice, and splice the DNA of plants and animals (and humans, for that matter), eliminating unwanted attributes and creating desirable new ones: strawberries that don't freeze, tomatoes that don't rot, seeds that carry their own pesticides. It is a sophisticated endeavor—and, some would say, both ill conceived and dangerous—with implications as mysterious as Burbank's experiments were considered by some in his day. Yet there is a signal difference. Contemporary efforts alter genetic material at its most basic level by slicing off segments of DNA from one species and splicing them into the DNA of another, a process that does not and could not happen in the natural world. Burbank influenced a process that occurs all of the time without human intervention. Current efforts, regardless of how well-intentioned they might seem, circumvent the seasons, defy the earth's natural laws and rhythms, and disregard the harmony of its countless creatures. The principal harvest seems to be high profits for stockholders.

Luther Burbank, in contrast, talked of creating a vibration of love in which his plants would feel safe; he tried, it is said, to make a heaven on earth. There is a moment nearly every day when I look at this miraculous landscape, at the huge bowl of sky overhead with its horizon of trees as yet unobscured by the hand of man, and know that I am seeing exactly the same spectacular skyline he saw a century ago when he traveled from his home in Santa Rosa to his West County farm. Given this glorious sight and all the hidden treasures that I know are tucked here and there down country lanes and back roads, it's impossible to say he didn't succeed.

CHAPTER I

Abundance

Dairy Alchemy

*Dry Jack ❧ Teleme ❧ Camellia ❧ Crescenza ❧ Taupinière ❧ St. George ❧ Sonoma Jack
❧ Fromage Blanc ❧ Bellwether Blue ❧ Cheddar ❧ Goat Milk Soap ❧ Organic Milk ❧
Feta ❧ Pepato ❧ Carmody ❧ Jalapeño Jack ❧ Casero*

HAPPY, WELL-FED MOTHERS MAKE THE BEST MILK. This is as true of goats, sheep, and cows as it is of humans, and it is one of the reasons that both milk and cheese from Sonoma County are so good. Moderate temperatures, grassy pastures, and air cleansed by ocean breezes create an environment in which cows thrive. Compared with the large farms of California's Central Valley, where summer temperatures can be very high, dairy farms in Sonoma County offer an easy life. Overcrowding is not a problem; small herds are raised on small family farms, many in operation for decades. Most local dairies were members of the California Cooperative Creamery until December 1998, when the organization merged with the Dairy Farmers of America, the largest dairy co-op in the United States. Ninety-five percent of North Bay dairy farmers belong to the co-op, which distributes members' milk to the bottlers and cheesemakers.

In spite of Sonoma County's ideal climate, milk production is shifting to the large dairies of the Central Valley, where land is cheaper. On these vast farms, cows live in temperature-controlled barns with grain, hay, and water provided at individual stalls.

"What is better for a cow," Ralph Sartori, a manager with Dairy Farmers of America, asked as we discussed this geographic shift, "to walk the hillsides in the open air, chewing on grass and wearing out her legs, or to be inside a comfortable barn where everything she needs is right in front of her?" I vote for open air, sunshine, and the family farm.

Enormous corporate hog farms in the Midwest and Southeast have brought the family pig farm to the brink of extinction. Pigs are raised entirely indoors in crowded quarters; their natural life cycle is interrupted to produce meat with less fat. As a result American pork has lost much of its flavor—pigs are naturally fat creatures; altering this characteristic changes everything else—and the environment near the large farms is being compromised in devastating ways because these operations do not have an efficient method of handling the prodigious quantity of manure. I can't help but draw parallels between these hog farms and the huge dairy farms that raise cows away from their natural outdoor environment. I can't shake the suspicion that fresh air, exercise, and lolling in a pasture in the warm sun are essential elements in the alchemy of milk, just as a big ol' mud puddle—used by a pig to cool itself in hot weather—is crucial to the alchemy of pork.

Although there are fewer family dairies here than there were not so long ago, those that remain may find a stable niche that will insure their survival. What could make our dairy farmers unique in the twenty-first century is a growing commitment to organic milk and sustainable farming. Dairies, both new and existing, are converting to organic practices. Much of the interest in organic farming is centered in western Sonoma County and northern Marin County, where dairies provide organic milk for the fresh market as well as for butter and cheese.

Clover Stornetta Farms, Inc.

It is unusual when visibility, history, and quality intersect; add environmental sensitivity and you have a rare and precious convergence, expressed locally in Clover Stornetta Farms, Inc., one of the most successful agricultural enterprises in Sonoma County. All along Highway 101 are the now-famous billboards of Clover's mascot, Clo the Cow, in her various guises, as a judge ("Supreme Quart"), for example, and a dancer in a field of flowers ("Tip Clo through your two lips"). Clo first appeared in 1969, and today the company receives a steady flow of suggestions for new pun-driven scenes.

Clover's history stretches back to the early 1900s, when the Petaluma Cooperative Creamery distributed its dairy products—this was before refrigeration when the main product was Clover butter; milk was used to feed the pigs that produced much of a dairy's income. The creamery thrived until one night in 1975 when the building was destroyed by an enormous fire; I could see the smoke and the ominous orange glow from my cottage eight miles east of town. The loss of the co-op was devastating to the dairy farmers who relied upon it to sell their milk, but out of the ashes rose Clover Stornetta Farms. Gene Benedetti, his son Dante Benedetti, and four others purchased the co-op's distribution business and the old Stornetta Dairy in Sonoma. Since then, Clover Stornetta has built a shiny new plant, opened in 1991, and has been a good neighbor in countless ways, including environmentally.

In the early 1990s when the controversy over synthetic bovine growth hormone erupted, Clover Stornetta took the bold step of promising publicly, and in print, that the company would never sell milk or other products with the additive, viewed by many as potentially dangerous to human health, cruel to cows, and unnecessary, given that there is a surplus of milk in the United States. As pressure grew statewide and nationwide to use it and shut up—it is, after all, entirely legal to use the hormone and there is no requirement to inform consumers that a product contains it—Clover Stornetta held fast to its position. The company quietly developed a reputation for having the cleanest milk in the country.

As the decade drew to a close and the fervor over the hormone quieted, Clover Stornetta did an unusual thing. Instead of letting the issue drop, the company hired an independent auditor to certify its claims about the milk. Its North Coast Excellence Certified program has the strictest standards in the dairy industry, with guidelines that surpass those required by state and federal agencies. Milk is tested daily for antibiotics and pesticides (no trace of either is allowed), it is monitored for bacteria, and dairies that sell milk to Clover must sign contracts certifying that they do not and will not use rBST, the bovine growth hormone. Clover pays its farmers a premium and visits each farm—they are all family owned—every year.

In the spring of 1999, Clover introduced organic milk produced by a single farm in the Two Rock area west of Petaluma. St. Anthony's Farm, which is owned by the Franciscan Brothers, a Catholic service order in San Francisco, serves as a halfway house for recovering addicts that have gone through an initial treatment program in the city. Jim Kehoe, who oversees the farm, approached Dan with his idea for a separately labeled organic milk. "How can I tell my residents not to use drugs," he reasoned, "when I'm giving chemicals to my cows?" The organic program is remarkably successful; the demand for the milk almost immediately surpassed the supply, and Dan is assisting other dairies with the transition to organic farming. The primary difference between organic milk and Clover's already high-quality milk is what the cows eat; for milk to be certified as organic all of their feed must be organic, too.

Dan Benedetti and his father Gene are full of tales of farming life in early Petaluma, of a time when butter was hauled from Steamer Gold Landing on the Petaluma River down to the Bay Area. The family still makes its own wine—zinfandel—and Dan recalls one of his grandfather's favorite lunches, a big raw red onion dressed with oil, vinegar, salt, and pepper. As this life recedes into the past, people like the Benedettis and businesses like Clover offer an oasis of optimism, a reason to believe that family farms can and will survive.

Redwood Hill Farm Goat Dairy

Steven Schack always credited the comfortable environment of Green Valley with the success of his cheeses. "It really is a heavenly atmosphere," he liked to say. "There is something so special here, everyone who comes to see the goats mentions it."

I arrived at the farm one afternoon with a group of students from a class I was teaching at Santa Rosa Junior College. Jennifer Bice, Steve's wife, was walking down the hill with a newborn goat, just minutes old, in her arms. Another kid, this one born a few days earlier, was hopping along behind her, and when I leaned down to take a closer look, he almost leapt into my arms. For the rest of the tour, the little kid nestled against me, nuzzling my neck and cuddling contentedly.

Steven Schack and Jennifer Bice met in the 1970s while showing their prize-winning goats, a passion they shared throughout their life together. Jennifer's parents had operated a goat dairy in western Sonoma County since the late 1960s, and when they moved to Hawaii in 1978, Jennifer and Steve, married by this time, took over. In 1985, they added natural goat yogurt to the raw goat milk they sold in the health-food market. Soon after, they introduced feta, ricotta, and mozzarella, all made with goat's milk.

Today Redwood Hill produces Camellia, a Camembert-style goat cheese; crottin; two excellent fetas, one pasteurized and one using raw milk; aged cheddar; aged smoked cheddar; several fresh chèvres; and a selection of goat yogurts without the additives found in most commercial yogurts. Redwood Hill Farm's products are available throughout much of the United States, including in major natural foods markets, Zabar's and Dean & DeLuca in New York, and Zingerman's in Ann Arbor, Michigan. In the Bay Area, you'll find the cheeses at the Berkeley farmers' market. In southern California, Steven's parents sell the cheese at the Santa Monica farmers' market.

The dairy sits high on a ridge in the heart of Green Valley. A redwood deck surrounds the pretty red building and overlooks Iron Horse Vineyards with its manicured vines and signature palm trees; the Sonoma and Mayacamas Mountains and Mount Saint Helena glisten in the distance. On a clear day it seems as if you can see the entire world.

"I like seeing it every day," Steve always said about Mount St. Helena, where for more than two decades he welcomed each new year's sunrise. On August 5, 1999, shortly before his fiftieth birthday and just a few months after learning that he had advanced pancreatic cancer, Steven died. It is an inexpressibly sad loss, and now I think of goat heaven rather differently from the way in which Steve first described the dairy that Jennifer must now care for without him.

Sonoma Cheese Factory

"Dairymen love this tie," David Viviani says with a twinkle in his eye as he points out the brown and the black and white cows that adorn the deep blue silk, a mixing of breeds you rarely see on the farm. With his light-hearted style but remarkably effective business savvy, David rarely misses a detail, or an opportunity. David is a third-generation cheesemaker. His grandfather Ceslo arrived in California from northern Italy near Lucca in 1912 and soon began making cheese, both in partnership with Tom Vella and on his own. (For a detailed account of the cheesemaking ventures of both families, see *American County Cheese* by Laura Chenel.) By the late 1940s his sons had joined him.

In the late 1960s, milk prices were high, cheese prices were low, tourists were few and far between, and the Sonoma Cheese Factory was struggling. When David graduated from high school, he joined his father, Pete, by then the manager, bringing an infectious enthusiasm with him. Soon David was back at the high school, augmenting the family coffers by selling sandwiches to former classmates. Enlivened by David's verve, entrepreneurial acumen, and dedication, Sonoma Cheese Factory entered a new period of vitality that just happened to coincide with the rediscovery of Sonoma County as a tourist destination.

"The wine country was invented during the gas crisis," David likes to say. That's when people discovered that Sonoma County was geographically close to San Francisco yet far away in spirit and atmosphere. An hour's drive would transport you to another time, when life seemed much more appealing than it did in the city, where you might spend hours in line to buy gas. Our wineries, fruit stands, and cheese factories enjoyed a boom that has never slowed.

It was at this time that Christo Javacheff, a sculptor born in Bulgaria and known professionally simply as Christo, erected the Running Fence, an art installation that brought the first traffic snarls I can remember to Sonoma County. Made of white parachute cloth, the 18-foot-high fence wound westward through the undulating hillsides and dairy farms from Penngrove to Dillon Beach, where it plunged dramatically into the sea. Thousands of visitors came to see the fence, which was in place for two weeks in September 1976, and traffic on Highway 101 was often at a standstill.

With its location on the north side of Sonoma's downtown plaza, the Sonoma Cheese Factory is the most visible of all of the county's cheese companies. Through a large window near the back of the store visitors can look in on the workers as they cut warm curds and roll them into wheels of cheese. If you visit at the right time, you'll be invited to suit up and roll a wheel yourself. Sonoma Jack is the company's signature cheese. Among its other selections, my favorite is Sonoma Teleme with its voluptuous texture and mildly tangy flavor.

Vella Cheese Company

The historic Vella Cheese Company is a must-see destination if you're anywhere near Sonoma. Established in 1931 in a turn-of-the-century brick brewery that had closed after the enactment of the Eighteenth Amendment, it is a treasure chest of atmosphere, history, and some of the finest handcrafted cheeses in California. If you know you'll be in town, call and arrange for a tour; be sure to ask that Ig Vella be your guide. If your timing is right, workers will be rolling and pressing cheese in the main room with its comforting humidity and enticing aroma of sweet warm milk. You'll see the aging rooms, where wheels of the famous Bear Flag Dry Jack and California Gold Dry Jack sit on wooden shelves in their dark cloaks of cocoa and pepper, slowly developing the deep nutty flavors for which they are so widely praised, and all the while be entertained by Ig's colorful stories.

Upstairs, there are labyrinthian aging rooms with narrow passages through old wooden racks, relics of another time, stacked with cheese. It is a remarkable sight, and one I treasure, especially when I consider that county agencies would prefer every bit of wood be replaced by stainless steel and plastic. (Plastic was once thought to be more sanitary than wood, though studies in the late 1980s disproved the idea; stainless steel is, of course, fire resistant.)

The history of the Vellas and their cheesemaking in Sonoma County begins in 1906, when Joe Vella arrived from Sicily and soon established the Sonoma Mission Creamery. World War I made it difficult to import the Italian cheeses the company had been distributing and so Joe began making his own. He was joined by his brother Tom in 1923 and for a time formed a partnership with Celso Viviani, who also worked at the creamery. The company prospered through another world war and a lucrative partnership with Kraft Foods, but in 1948, when Celso Viviani wanted a business in which his children could be more involved, the partnership was dissolved. Tom reestablished Vella Cheese Factory, his son Ignazio working alongside him from the time he was a small boy. Various pursuits—including a degree in history, a year in Italy, and eleven years as a Sonoma County supervisor—took the young Ig far from his Sonoma County roots before he settled into his leadership role at the cheese factory in 1981.

Ig credits the quality of the Guernsey milk he gets from a nearby dairy with the consistently high quality of his cheeses. Dry Jack is Vella's most popular cheese, but the Monterey Jack, lower in salt and moisture than other jacks, Jalapeño Jack, raw milk jack, and cheddars are both popular and outstanding.

In 1998, Tom Vella, after having transferred ownership of the factory to Ig and his three sisters, died at the age of one hundred.

Laura Chenel Chèvre

Before Chez Panisse introduced its salad of field greens and chèvre, mainstream America knew little about goat cheese. Now it's everywhere. It was inevitable that a domestic industry would develop. With increased travel to Europe, where chèvre is ubiquitous, and a growing interest in artisan foods in general, it was just a matter of time. But someone had to be first, and it was a young woman from Sebastopol who loved goats.

Laura Chenel grew up in a farmhouse near Gravenstein Highway in Sebastopol, where she raised her first goats. When she found herself with an abundance of goat milk, she tried her hand at making cheese. Her success spawned an entire new industry. Today there are dozens of producers of goat cheese in the United States.

"When I was first making my cheese," she recalls, "I thought it would just go to retail stores. I couldn't imagine a restaurant wanting it. There was a wonderful wine and cheese shop in San Francisco, and the owner told me I must take my cheeses to Alice Waters. At the time, I had no idea who she was. So I took my cheese to Berkeley. I set them out on a counter and everyone tasted them. No one had ever come to Alice with little farm-made cheeses before; it fit right in with what she was doing. Alice had a big smile on her face and said, 'Oh, yeah, I'll take sixty of these a week.' That was a huge order for me at the time, and it's never stopped."

As Laurie's business grew, she stopped raising goats herself, built a factory, purchased milk, and introduced several new types of chèvre, including my favorites, Tome, an aged cheese perfect for grating, and Taupinière, a ripened cheese with enticingly complex flavors. For a time she had a mail-order catalogue and a small tasting room where visitors could buy cheese.

In the mid-1990s, Laura Chenel Chèvre moved into the old Stornetta dairy just east of the town of Sonoma in the Carneros viticultural area. Mail order was turned over to Williams-Sonoma, there is no tasting room, and Laurie has returned to her first love, raising goats.

Marin French Cheese Company

Southwest of Petaluma, just across the Marin County line, is the Marin French Cheese Company, where cheeses have been handcrafted since 1865, making it the oldest factory in the North Bay. It is also one of the best places in the south county for a picnic, especially in the spring when the hills are nearly neon green, the pond is high and full of ducks, and red-wing blackbirds are eager for crumbs from your French bread. You once needed to bring the bread and other picnic items to go with the cheese you could buy here, but today the deli has expanded and there's a good selection of wines, too.

The small company is best known for the cheeses sold under the Rouge et Noir label, Camembert, Brie, breakfast cheese, and the robust schloss, my favorite. In the mid-1990s, the company introduced flavored Brie cheeses, some under the Rouge et Noir label, others under a new brand, The Cheese Factory. These flavored cheeses may not appeal to traditionalists, but they have been quite popular.

Joe Matos Cheese Factory

When I first wrote about St. George cheese, it was available only at the tiny Joe Matos Cheese Factory in the flatlands of southwestern Santa Rosa. You had to know about it. Most of the cheese was sold to the Portuguese community of Northern California. Then Tomales Bay Foods, a small distribution company, discovered it; today you can buy St. George cheese in specialty stores throughout the Bay Area, and in a few locations around the country, such as Murray's Cheese Shop in New York City.

Joe Matos has tended the herd and Mary Matos has made the moderately sharp, semisoft cheese, named for their homeland, an island in the Azores, since the early 1980s. Initially, the cheese was made from unpasteurized milk, which gives any cheese greater depth of flavor and unique character, but strict health department regulations are increasingly discouraging. Today, most of the milk is pasteurized, though Mary does make a small quantity of cheese from raw milk.

The farm is tucked away off a lightly traveled country road down a long, pitted driveway full of mud puddles during the rainy season. The cows are often huddled along the fence and follow you with their big brown eyes as you walk to the tasting room, where you sometimes have to push the family sheep away from the front door.

Inside, the air is saturated with the earthy, nutty aroma of aging cheese. A bell rings as you open the door, announcing your arrival to Mary or one of her assistants, who appears quickly to offer you a sliver of tasty cheese to nibble as you decide how much to buy. My advice is to get more than you think you'll need. Not far away, in markets in Sebastopol, Santa Rosa, and Healdsburg, St. George cheese is sold for $12 a pound. Here at the factory, it still sells for $4, and the atmosphere is free.

Bellwether Farms

"Oh, you know that crazy woman from San Francisco, she thinks she's going to milk sheep," Cindy Callahan says with a laugh, explaining that that's what everyone said as word of her plans to start a sheep dairy near Valley Ford spread throughout the food community. I first heard about Cindy while I was staying in a small *podera* in

Tuscany just east of Siena in the spring of 1990. "Sonoma County?" someone said, "I think there's some nutty woman near there who's going to try to make cheese like this." I took another bite of the succulent fresh pecorino and made a mental note to track her down.

The farm was established in 1986 and for several years produced only premium baby lamb, most of it sold to a few Bay Area restaurants. During this time, the Callahans traveled to sheep dairies and cheese factories in Italy to study the process that so many people thought would never succeed in the United States. In 1992, the family enterprise released its first sheep's milk cheeses. Cindy's older son, Liam Callahan, is the cheesemaker. Her younger son Brett handles delivery and construction. Liam's wife, Diane Callahan, does the accounting and works in the cheese room one day a week.

The cheeses are made in the Italian style, similar to pecorino. There are four types, Toscano, aged at least three months; Pepato, with whole black peppercorns; Caciotta, a young and creamy Toscano; and the unique San Andreas, a smooth, flavorful cheese aged for a minimum of two months and named for the magnificent fault that runs along the coast.

Sheep's milk is richer than cow's milk, with more butterfat and more protein. But compared with cows, sheep produce little milk. The Callahans quickly realized they would never turn a profit with only sheep's milk cheeses. Because they are able to buy superior milk from a neighbor, Larry Peters, they developed several cow's milk cheeses. At his Spring Hill Ranch, Larry raises Jersey cows, which give a rich golden milk that produces outstanding cheese. (In 1998, Peters introduced Spring Hill Jersey Cheese, with jack, mozzarella, ricotta, quark, and cheddars among the selections, and he plans to make a European-style cultured butter.)

Bellwether's Carmody, an aged wheel, is a delicious, smooth-textured table cheese. The Crescenza, a cheese so luscious and creamy that in Northern Italy, its traditional home, it often replaces butter, is entirely worthy of its forebearer. Both the ricotta and *fromage blanc* are richly colored and wonderfully flavored.

Near the end of 1999, the farm released its first blue cheese, a deep yellow, blue-veined cheese, Bellwether Blue, that resembles Stilton in appearance and Gorgonzola in taste and texture. Plans are underway for a blue cheese made from sheep's milk and likely to be named Bodega Blue.

Bodega Goat Cheese

The success of Patti and Javier Salmon's Peruvian-style goat cheese is, at least in part, a testament to the power of salt. When I tasted the first cheeses in the early 1990s, I found them bland and flat. At that time, salt-free foods were enjoying a brief spike in popularity; the Salmons were making their cheeses to appeal to this market. Yet salt adds more than saltiness to foods; it also allows flavors to blossom into themselves. It is essential in cheesemaking. I truly wanted to like these cheeses—the Salmons have a passionate devotion to organic and sustainable farming—but each time I tried them I had the same response: with a little salt, they could be great. Eventually I noticed sea salt on the list of ingredients, and so I tried again—ahh, magical salt.

Javier Salmon grew up in Peru, where his family made traditional cheeses similar to those he and Patti make today, *crema,* a cream cheese; *casero,* a breakfast cheese similar to ricotta; *requeson,* an unsalted mascarpone-style cheese; *queso fresco,* an unbrined feta; and *cabrero,* a Spanish-style grating cheese like Manchego. The cheeses are available at local independent markets, health-food stores, and at the Santa Rosa Original farmers' market, as well as at the Gourmet Goat, the Salmons' tiny retail store in the town of Bodega.

Flesh

Wild King Salmon ❋ *Dungeness Crab* ❋ *Green Eggs* ❋ *Organic Chicken* ❋ *Liberty Duck* ❋ *Foie Gras* ❋ *Ostrich Meat* ❋ *C.K. Lamb* ❋ *Sausages* ❋ *Wild Boar* ❋ *Beeswax Candles* ❋ *Blackberry Honey*

The Fisherman of Bodega Bay

"Everyone seems to have the impression that we are catching the last one," said Chuck Wise, the president of the Fisherman's Marketing Association of Bodega Bay.

Chuck has been fishing since 1969, catching wild king salmon in the summer, Dungeness crab in the winter, and watching the fluctuations of fish and fortune. Today, California has the best salmon runs of the three contiguous western states, he explains, and credits the efforts of the Fish and Game Department and the fishermen themselves for the health of an industry that not so long ago was nearly dead.

Bodega Bay is a small port but it has the largest membership organization on the West Coast, though not all of the more than two hundred fishermen are working at any one time. Salmon and crab are the main catches, but some fish for albacore tuna, others for herring, and a few for rock cod for the specialty market. Much of the catch is sold in Bodega Bay, and virtually all is sold fresh.

Because supermarkets these days sell primarily farmed fish, it is worth a drive to Bodega Bay to buy wild fish off the boat or from one of the retail outlets such as Lucas Wharf or Paisano Brothers (see Resources, page 295). If you want to be positive where a fish is from, ask.

When the fishermen couldn't get a decent price for their salmon in 1998, a few began selling their catch at the Sebastopol Farmers' Market, a successful venture that has continued. Stan Carpenter sells whole salmon, salmon fillets and steaks, and some of the best smoked salmon I've tasted. The long strips with their intensely smoky flavor and lusciously oily texture are terrific. Paul Thornton also sells outstanding salmon, mostly smoked, at several local farmers' markets. In Bodega Bay, you'll find a variety of smoked fish at the colorful Crab Pot; be sure to bring along a camera—the bright pumpkin-colored smokehouse itself is quite photogenic.

The Oysters of Tomales Bay

There are no shellfish farms in Sonoma County, but the waters of Tomales Bay, immediately to the south, are home to millions of oysters, clams, and mussels. For more than a decade, the husband-and-wife team of Lisa Jang and Jorge Rebagliati operated Bay Bottom Beds, where they raised a single species of oyster, the Pacific *miyagi*, which they christened Preston Point after a tip of land near the farm. In 1999, they sold their lease—shellfish farmers lease acreage in the bay from the state—to Hog Island Shellfish Company.

Hog Island is the most accessible of the bay's farms; it is the only one with an actual destination for visitors, open five days a week for sales. There are picnic tables and Weber grills; they'll lend you oyster knives and gloves, and they'll teach you how to shuck. With the grounds flush against the bay, the sand dunes in the distance, and succulent oysters at your fingertips, it is a glorious place to spend a leisurely afternoon, especially in the fall and spring when oysters are their finest and the air is crisp and pure. Hog Island sells only shellfish, so bring everything else, including the cold bottle of sauvignon blanc you'll want.

The Egg Capital of the World

When gold fever spread across the world like a winter virus, the population of California expanded at breakneck speed. Between 1846 and 1860, for example, San Francisco swelled from fewer than five hundred residents to more than sixty thousand. Supplies did not keep pace; there was a fortune to be made if you had something to sell.

As late as the 1870s, the potatoes, eggs, chickens, and other agricultural products shipped by way of the Petaluma River to the city were not enough to meet the demand. According to Adair Heig, writing in *History of Petaluma*, many of San Francisco's eggs arrived from the East Coast, shipped in barrels held at room temperature for the entire journey. "The bartender who broke an egg for a drink had to do so under the counter," Haig writes, "because there was about one chance in twelve of getting a chicken."

In 1879 Lyman Byce, a Canadian who came to Sonoma County to recuperate from a long illness, developed an incubator that could keep eggs at a steady 103°F for three weeks, the conditions necessary to raise chicks effectively without a brooding hen. At first local farmers were skeptical and continued to farm as they had, growing asparagus, potatoes, beets, and other crops, but by about 1900 the egg and chicken boom was on. The demand for eggs had remained high, the price held, and those few farmers who had embraced the new incubator were expanding their operations, hiring employees, and buying automobiles. It seems that everyone in Petaluma joined in; a government report in 1904 estimated that 90 percent of the population was raising chickens. By 1920, there were more than sixty-two hundred egg farmers in the Petaluma area, and they were shipping about 16 million eggs a year to San Francisco, other rapidly growing Bay Area communities, and Southern California. The industry peaked in 1945 with 51 million dozen eggs shipped.

In 1918, the Petaluma Chamber of Commerce hired Herbert William Kerrigan, known for his public relations savvy, as its new manager. It was Kerrigan who put Petaluma on the map as the World's Egg Basket. In 1918 he founded the Egg Day Parade with its Egg Queen, advertised it throughout the country, and erected poultry kitsch such as giant chickens and huge egg baskets all over the city to greet visitors, some of which remain today.

The boom continued until after World War II, when several factors contributed to its near total demise. Many of the farmers who raised chickens had been Japanese; internment during the war was a bitter experience, and they wanted to move on to other pursuits rather than return to their prewar lives. Shipping on the Petaluma River declined, large co-ops such as Nu-Laid bought up small chicken ranches, production shifted to large farms in the Central Valley where land was cheaper, the price of eggs dropped, and diseases increased as flocks grew larger. Wire cages were transforming the industry as radically as the incubator had done decades earlier. The last parade was held in 1926. By the early 1960s, there were fewer than three hundred chicken ranches. The epithet Egg Capital of the World was quietly dropped. In 1982, Linda Buffo and Alice Forsythe resurrected the festival, rechristening it the Egg and Butter Parade and holding it on the last Saturday in April.

Today, there are just seven egg farmers in Sonoma County. Most sell their eggs to Nu-Laid, though one has bucked the trend. Steve Mahrt founded Petaluma Farms in 1984 with his Rock Island label for fertile brown eggs laid by little red hens that run free in coops, as they did before the introduction of wire cages. The eggs are distributed throughout Northern California. In 1996, Mahrt introduced a second brand, Judy's Family Farm eggs, the first organic eggs in California. A third brand, Gold Circle Farms, was introduced in 1999; these eggs are higher in DHA omega-3 fatty acids. The chickens are fed a vegetarian diet supplemented with cold water algae.

For the very best eggs, with orange-colored yolks and pure backyard flavor, buy them at the farmers' market where many small farmers sell eggs from chickens raised the old-fashioned way, without incubators, without wire cages, without anything at all but happy hens, good food, and a cocky rooster or two.

Rocky and His Siblings

In the mid-1980s, Bart Ehman, a rancher in western Sonoma County, was selling Sonoma Baby Lamb (a trademarked name) to such chefs as Wolfgang Puck and Bradley Ogden. After numerous requests from these chefs, Bart joined forces with Allen Shainsky, whose family had been in the poultry business in Sonoma County since the early 1900s, to develop a range chicken similar to the superior tasting chickens in France. After several months of trial and error, Rocky the Range Chicken and his little brother, Rocky Junior, were born. For a time, they went only to the chefs who were buying Bart's lamb, but retail interest grew as more and more people tried the chicken in restaurants. Now, Rocky and Rocky Junior are in independent markets all over the Bay Area. In the spring of 1999, a sister, Rosie, became the first certified organic chicken in the United States; she's available west of the Rockies and plans are underway to take her nationwide.

Rocky is identified as much by his graphics as by his superior taste. Labels and posters show a plump chicken wearing dark glasses, cowboy hat, and spurs, and holding a smoking gun. Rocky Junior looks like a mall dude, with athletic shoes and a cap on backwards. Rosie vamps across the printed page in a wide-brimmed hat, pearls, and red shoes (sometimes pink ones) with high heels, of course.

The term *range chicken* may be a bit misleading because it conjures images of flocks raised entirely outside, as cattle or sheep are. The reality is different. Shainsky's range and organic chickens live in spacious coops where they are free to run around, establish their pecking orders, and socialize as chickens do. They are allowed outside, though most chickens prefer to be indoors, especially during the heat of the day. Most commercially raised chickens are cramped into one-foot-square cubicles that are kept lit around the clock to encourage the birds to eat more than they do in a more pleasant, natural environment.

> ## Chicken Lady Wanted
>
> Must dress up like a hen, cluck greeting to Petaluma newcomers. No experience needed, but prefer woman who will put civic interest ahead of personal life.
>
> —Advertisement, *San Francisco Chronicle*
> *November 13, 1971*

Diet is a key factor in the taste of a chicken. These specialty chickens are fed a vegetarian diet, primarily corn and soy, and are given neither antibiotics nor hormones. Commercially produced chickens are fed animal byproducts, including large quantities of animal fat that encourage them to grow quickly, though much of the weight is in fat that is ultimately discarded. Rocky, Rocky Junior, and Rosie all have less fat than other commercial chickens do. Even though the superiority of range

Saving the Earth with Green Eggs

Although many experts will tell you there's no difference between white-shelled eggs and eggs with colored shells, they are wrong. Buying brown or green eggs, even supermarket brown eggs, is an effective gesture toward maintaining biodiversity. In his charming and useful book, *Rainforest in Your Kitchen,* Martin Teitel, who lived in Freestone for many years before moving to Texas in 1997, explains that white eggs are a genetic disaster waiting to happen. More than 90 percent of the 3 billion eggs sold each year in this country are white shelled and laid by a single species of chicken, the White Leghorn. If a heretofore unknown disease were to come along for which Leghorns have no immunity, the breed could be wiped out. This may not be a likely possibility, but relying on a single breed always presents such a risk and is not good agriculture. Brown eggs, laid primarily by Rhode Island Reds, increase the genetic pool to two; add the greenish blue eggs that come from Aracauna chickens, and you have three species of chickens working for you. It's easy to find brown eggs in your local supermarket; for the green ones, check your local farmers' market.

chicken is by now well documented, it represents less than one-half of 1 percent of the 140 million chickens that go to market each week in the United States.

Liberty Duck

For a cooking demonstration he'll give in front of my class "A Cook's Tour of Sonoma," Jim Reichardt unpacks an electric tire pump and a blow-dryer. He sets a kettle of water over a high flame and plunks a duck down on a cutting board next to the pump. After he inserts the pump's nozzle under the duck's skin near the tip of the neck, he turns on the electricity and slowly the skin balloons outward away from the body of the duck. Jim cuts the electricity before it actually blows up. As he tells how he did this at his local gas station before he purchased his own pump—at this point, students are weak with laughter—he plunges the duck into the boiling water, sets it back on the cutting board, and reaches for the hair dryer, with which he proceeds to dry the skin. He quickly cuts an orange into wedges and inserts it, along with a whole onion, into the cavity of the duck, which he then puts into a hot oven. Less than an hour later, the duck emerges from the oven beautifully browned, its succulent flesh encased in a cloak of perfectly crisp skin.

Jim's family has raised ducks commercially since 1901, when his great-grandfather,

Otto Reichardt, founded the business in South San Francisco. In 1958, the family moved north to western Petaluma where the Reichardt Duck Farm has flourished ever since. Today, the farm is operated by Don Reichardt, his son John, and his daughter Kathy; most of the ducks go to San Francisco's Chinatown, as they did in Otto's day. Only Jim, Don's oldest son, has flown the family coop.

Just as Ig Vella watched his father make cheese from the time he was a toddler, Jim witnessed the life of a duck farmer at his father's side. After graduating from college, he traveled and studied photography, knowing all the while that it was just a matter of time before he settled into a farmer's life. In 1992, after working on the family farm for four years, he and his wife Allison established the Sonoma Poultry Company, just a few miles away.

Jim's move was a response to the new generation of chefs who appeared in the wake of the gourmet revolution of the 1970s. Increasingly, America wanted the plump, succulent ducks—both leaner and meatier—available in France. Encouraged by several of the Bay Area's top chefs, Jim developed a lean duck that is slaughtered when it is about nine weeks old; most commercial ducks in America go to market at six to seven weeks. Today, Liberty ducks are considered among the best in the country. In the fall of 1999, Jim was completing plans for a processing plant. Currently, there is no place for specialty producers such as Jim to process their ducks; instead, they must be driven to Stockton.

In the town of Sonoma, Philip Payne, who raises squab, faces the same difficulty, as does Sylvia Mavalwalla, who raises geese and turkeys on her S & B Ranch, near Old Adobe Road in Petaluma. Sylvia does all the processing by hand and is growing weary of plucking several dozen geese the day before Christmas. Jim hopes not only to process his own ducks, raise other birds such as quail, and help producers such as Philip and Sylvia, but also to inspire a resurgence of the family poultry farm in the ideal climate of Sonoma County.

Sonoma Foie Gras

Enormous white ducks, too fat to waddle, sit snuggled together on straw in a humid barn cooled by huge fans. Overhead, plastic funnels with long, curved tubes hang like so many space-age jungle vines.

"The ducks, they love it," Junny Gonzales says as she moves her hands in a gesture that mimics the massaging of a duck's throat as the long tube is inserted. "They are happy," she continues, her pronounced South American accent contributing to the exotic air of the place, "because it is done with love." Although people who have observed this process confirm that the birds seem to enjoy it, animal rights activists rail against the procedure known as *gauvage*, a technique of force feeding first developed by the ancient Egyptians and later perfected by the French.

More than 5,000 years ago, Egyptians discovered the delicious livers of geese and ducks that were caught as they made their long migration. In expectation of a lengthy flight, the birds overfeed themselves. When caught early in their journey, their livers will be enlarged; the original and entirely natural foie gras. *Gauvage* mimics the process; after the tube is inserted through the duck's mouth, down its slender throat, and into its stomach, the funnel is filled with cooked corn. After the bird's stomach is full, the tube is gently pulled out. *Gauvage* begins with nearly mature ducklings, and the birds are fed twice a day for about three weeks.

Today, two companies in the United States produce foie gras, one in New York's Hudson River Valley, the other, Sonoma Foie Gras, was founded in Sonoma before moving inland near Stockton in 1996.

Piotrkowski Smoked Poultry

Among the increasing array of smoked foods produced in Sonoma County, Piotrkowski Smoked Poultry is among the best. Unfortunately, Fran and Joe Piotrkowski have cut the number of products they make. They no longer offer their exquisite smoked duck; nor do they make smoked pheasant or goose. They do, however, produce smoked chicken and smoked boneless turkey breasts, with whole smoked turkeys available during the winter holidays. You must place your order at least two weeks in advance (see Resources, page 295). It's worth the forethought; the rich, smoky flavor of their poultry is unsurpassed. And not only is the meat itself good, but also the carcasses make some of the best stock imaginable.

Willie Bird Turkeys & Smoked Poultry

If you're driving from Santa Rosa to Sebastopol on Highway 12 some evening in late November, don't be surprised if you have to swerve or slam on your brakes. This narrow stretch of highway is the gateway to the West County, bastion of all things politically correct. Every year about this time—usually on Thanksgiving eve—protesters gather up their picket signs and head to Willie Bird Turkeys, one of Sonoma County's best-known family farms. Their point? Free the turkeys, of course.

The Benedetti family has been in the poultry business here since 1924 and the turkey trade since 1948. By 1963, they had developed the bird, a turkey with a greater proportion of breast meat, that would become their claim to enduring fame. Willie Bird turkeys are range birds, raised in the hills of northeast Santa Rosa and sold throughout the country in catalogues such as Williams-Sonoma and in many independent markets.

Turkeys are the signature product of the farm, but smoked poultry—quail, game hens, ducks, chicken, and turkeys—is a major part of the business. The farm does not raise the birds the company smokes; rather, the locally raised turkeys are sold fresh, and poultry for smoking is purchased on the commodity market. Among the fans of Willie Bird Smoked Poultry, the company's web site boasts, is the Queen of England, who was served its smoked duck when the *Britannia* docked in San Francisco Bay.

The Campbell Kids' Experiment

In 1959, Susie, Linda, and Bruce Campbell each entered a lamb in the Healdsburg Future Farmers of America Fair. "We didn't do very well," Bruce recalls, "but we were quick learners." Unfazed when their lambs were sold at auction—they already understood cash flow, Bruce says—they used the money to buy breeding stock. By 1961, the Campbell kids had Champion Lamb. Over the next ten years, Campbell lambs took top prizes at the Sonoma County Fair, the Junior Grand National in San Francisco, and the California State Fair. In 1968, Bruce received California's Star Livestock Farmer Award.

Bruce left Sonoma County for Colorado State College, where he received a bachelor's degree in animal science and a master's degree in reproductive physiology. After graduation, he managed a ten-thousand-acre sheep ranch in Cloverdale, at a time when there were one hundred fifty thousand sheep in the county. He launched C. K. Lamb in the mid-1980s, raising young lamb first for restaurants in the Bay Area and soon for the retail market, too. Today, he supplies all of Wolfgang Puck's restaurants, and his lamb is available as far away as Rice Epicurean Markets in Houston, Texas. The lambs go to market when they are between 75 and 110 pounds, small enough that they have not yet developed the gamy flavors that some people find objectionable in older lamb.

Sheep farming is no longer what it once was in Sonoma County. There are now only about twenty thousand head of sheep, a number Bruce expects will drop further before it stabilizes. For the decline he blames a capricious market, influenced by profiteering in the Midwest, and substantial losses from coyotes. Only about a third of the nearly ten thousand head of sheep that go to the market each year under the name of C. K. Lamb now come from Sonoma County. Bruce contracts with ranchers in Mendocino County, Oregon, Nevada, and several other locations to raise lamb according to his specifications, that is, without antibiotics or hormones.

A Century of Sausage Making

Sausages aren't what they used to be. Modern refrigeration and the increase of the middle class have transformed them. Once made of meat scraps, fat, pork skin, and sometimes blood—valuable sources of nutrition for peasant populations during the lean winter months—today, sausages are made with premium cuts of meat, poultry, and seafood, cheese, fresh greens, chiles, herbs, dried tomatoes, exotic spices, and fruit, both fresh and dried. We eat sausages because we like them, not because they are all we have.

The sausage renaissance began in the early 1980s with the tremendous success of Aidells Sausage Company, founded by the well-known chef and writer Bruce Aidells. By the late 1980s, there were outstanding sausages everywhere.

Gerhard Twele of Gerhard's Sausage in Napa Valley captured the health-conscious market with his low-fat and low-cholesterol chicken sausages. He was so successful that virtually every sausage maker now feels obligated to offer chicken sausages even though it is a concept that would have utterly stymied early sausage makers, who understood that sausages need fat for flavor and texture. Independent markets such as Fiesta Market in Sebastopol, Pacific Market in Santa Rosa, and Oliver's Market in Cotati and Santa Rosa make their own sausages. Martindale's, a full-service meat market founded in northern Santa Rosa in 1990 by Ron Martindale, a native of Sonoma County, makes seventy different varieties, though it is a single one, the Hawaiian Portuguese sausage, that has countless fans.

Willowside Meats

Walking into the small, ramshackle building is like stepping through a time warp into old Sonoma. There's a butcher case in the center of the cramped retail area and a long, low freezer filled with about two dozen varieties of sausages. An old gray steel filing cabinet sits near the front door, and on the wall hangs a poster for the International Big Game Studio of Taxidermy, one corner curling outward, a tack missing. Don Alberigi has been making sausages and operating the custom-processing business of Willowside Meats since 1986. He learned his craft at the side of Costante Panizzerra, the patriarch of sausages, whose grandson carries on the family tradition at Panizzerra Meat Company in Occidental with seventeen types of sausages (only a few of which the traditionalist Costante would have approved), where Don once worked.

Begin a conversation with Don and it won't be long before he's telling stories of making sausage in the basement with Costante, Ben Gonnella, and the other old-timers, that generation of Italians who gave the town of Occidental both its character and its signature restaurants, Negri's and the Union Hotel.

Today Don makes about two dozen types of sausages. Among the selections are a spicy Cajun sausage, Louisiana-style hot links, *linguiça*, kielbasa, Polish sausage, British bangers, and smoked garlic sausage. His chorizo is one of the best I've tasted, and a Swedish-style potato sausage is wonderful. Much of Alberigi's business is custom preparation: he smokes fish and makes bacon, sausages, ham, and other products from the wild boar, deer, and bear brought to him by local hunters (it is illegal to sell these products to the public).

The Caggiano Company

Richard Caggiano began making sausages at home in the late 1980s as a labor of love, giving away all he made each week. Today, he uses the Piotrkowski Smoked Poultry facility, and the sausages are available at independent markets throughout the North Bay. The company's best-seller is a sausage Richard feels pressured to make, the popular chicken-apple sausage. "It has never been and never will be my favorite," he says. "You shouldn't make sausage with chicken." Caggiano is much more enthusiastic when he talks about pork. Using fresh (rather than frozen) pork butt from Iowa that he bones himself, he makes both traditional and contemporary varieties. You can recognize Caggiano sausages by their appearance; these hand-filled links are plump and moist.

Big Birds, Beef & Wild Boar

Early one morning Lou Preston was baking bread in his outdoor *forno*, a hand-built wood-burning oven that sits in the middle of his winery's bountiful garden, when he found himself eye to eye with an emu. The giant bird stared at him briefly and then wandered back from whence it came, mostly likely a neighbor's garden. The poor emu, a huge flightless bird native to Australia, was for a time the darling of American ranchers throughout the Southwest and in California. It never caught on as a low-fat meat, and now thousands of emus have been abandoned, which some people may think is a better fate than the slaughterhouse, but the creatures are lost here, as are their arboreal cousins the eucalyptus trees, both strangers in a strange land.

I often spot emus here and there—two or three grazing in the front yard of a compassionate farmer—as I drive along our back roads, but I don't know of any emu farms in Sonoma County, although its cousin the ostrich is being raised for its meat, eggs, and feathers. Bob and Eleanor Franceschi's ostrich farm, Sonoma Knolls Ranch, is in Sonoma Valley, and they sell their homemade jerky, fresh meat, eggs, eggshells (plain and painted; they're huge and beautiful), and feathers at the Santa Rosa and Sonoma farmers' markets. Although ostrich meat is usually compared to beef, its unmarbled flesh more closely resembles duck breast and benefits from similar handling. Cooked rare, it's flavorful and tender; overcooked, it's tough as shoe leather and about as tasty. Ostrich has less fat per ounce than virtually any other meat, fewer calories, and plenty of iron; it is also lower in protein, though not substantially.

What about Sonoma County beef, and the wild boar you hear about now and then? There are a few cattle ranches left, but there are no feed lots, where almost all the cattle sold on the commercial market spend their last weeks. You can buy beef directly from a few farms, but so far no one has introduced a "Sonoma Grown" beef. If you're looking for premium, environmentally sensitive meat raised humanely and without hormones, I recommend that of Niman Ranch (see Resources, page 295). For wild boar, you need, as they say, to know somebody—it is not sold commercially.

Tiny Livestock

You don't exactly herd them and you certainly can't milk them but, in fact, bees are classified by the United States Department of Agriculture as livestock. As you drive about the countryside, watch for clusters of rectangular wooden boxes here and there, in a field or an orchard, or on a hillside. Sometimes stacked two or three high and occasionally brightly painted—purple, pink, multicolored—the structures are commercial beehives, each one housing a colony of honeybees moved by their keeper from place to place in search of plentiful pollen and nectar.

Bees work year round, drinking nectar from a constantly changing selection of flowers and transforming their harvest into honey. As a bee sips, the nectar goes directly into a pouch known as a honey sac, where it mixes with enzymes. When the bee returns to the hive, it regurgitates the mixture into one of the thousands of wax cells that make up a honeycomb. This new honey is mostly water; one of the chores of the worker bees is evaporating the moisture, a feat they accomplish by beating their wings. When the honey is about 16 to 18 percent moisture, the bees seal over the cell with their impermeable wax, and there it stays until it is needed by the bees, or removed by a keeper, or, perhaps, a hungry bear. Sealed in this way, honey is almost indestructible. It has been found in perfectly edible form in ancient Egyptian tombs.

The primary endeavor of commercial beekeepers is not honey; rather, managed hives are used to pollinate crops such as almonds and apples that are nearly or entirely dependent upon bees. Beekeepers move their colonies to orchard, field, or farm and leave them for the duration of the bloom; the bees fly from flower to flower, their little bodies coated in pollen, which they inevitably deposit at each stop. Because it is impossible for a healthy colony of bees not to produce it, honey is an inevitable secondary endeavor for beekeepers. The honey must be managed because the bees don't know when to stop. They'll keep producing whether or not they have enough honey to sustain their colony.

The source of nectar is the definitive element in the color and flavor of honey. Clover, orange blossom, star thistle, certain spring wildflowers, and eucalyptus all yield a light, delicate honey. Blackberry, wild thyme, and cranberry flowers produce a darker, more robustly flavored honey. The famous honey of Provence, one of the most widely praised honeys in the world, is made with nectar from lavender flowers.

In Sonoma County, there are several dozen beekeepers, a few professionals with three hundred hives or more, a number of part-time professionals with fewer than three hundred colonies, and a lot of hobbyists, with fewer than twenty-five hives. (These are standard categories and do not imply that someone with, say, only two hives is not serious about harvesting a high-quality honey.) Several purveyors of local honey, including Stonecroft Farms and Orchard Farms' Archie Honey, sell their wares at farmers' markets in Sonoma County.

Hector Alvarez, who sells his honey under the name Hector's Bees, is a third-generation beekeeper. His grandfather kept bees in Mexico, providing honey for family and friends. His father is a commercial beekeeper in Mexico, as is Alvarez in Sonoma County. At the 1999 Sonoma County Harvest Fair, Hector's Bees honey received half a dozen medals as well as Best of Show, awarded to its eucalyptus honey. Most commercial honey is a blend from various sources, but Alvarez keeps his harvests separate, offering blackberry, star thistle, wildflower, eucalyptus, and several other types. In order to do this, he must harvest the honey right after bloom, before the bees go on to the next variety to blossom.

Hector also makes candles from the wax his bees produce; beeswax candles burn more slowly than do paraffin candles, have a better scent, and a natural beauty (and they are better for the environment). Carol Cole, a food stylist who lives in Sebastopol, also makes outstanding candles using beeswax; her candles burn longer and more evenly than any candle I've used. They are available at Putto & Gargoyle (see Resources, page 295).

Note: When it comes to honey, a word of caution is in order. Honey contains spores of the bacterium *Clostridium botulinum*, which can cause fatal food poisoning in infants and very young children. Older children and adults have acquired the ability to combat the spores.

Vegetable Love

Arctic Gem White Peaches ❉ Green Zebra Tomatoes ❉ Haricots Verts ❉ Rose de Lautrec Garlic ❉ Northern Lights Tomatoes ❉ Tahitian Melon Squash ❉ Chipotle Powder ❉ Dried Tomatoes ❉ Raspberry Vinegar ❉ Hot Horse Hot Sauce

Waving the Lacy Green Flag

Say *mesclun* today and no one bats an eyelash. The mix of tender young greens has become nearly as common as salt and pepper. But as recently as the late 1980s, it was still a revelation, considered fussy and unusual by many people. Now, we grow it on our porches, carefully harvesting pert little leaves just before serving them. We can buy it at almost every supermarket, where it may be called spring mix, fall mix, or salad mix, even though many old-timers refer to it as rabbit food.

Mesclun, both the word and the concept, has its roots in the south of France; it's one of many agricultural similarities Sonoma County shares with its sister region, Provence. In the Niçois dialect of French, the word *mescla* means "to mix" and refers to a toss of cultivated and wild leaves, the first of which appear in the spring. The specific greens vary with the seasons, of course. In addition to familiar lettuces such as oak leaf, red leaf, romaine, and red romaine, mesclun might include arugula, a variety of cresses, young mustard greens, spinach, herbs, edible flower petals, mâche, radicchio, copper fennel tips, and, if you're lucky, miner's lettuce and peppery nasturtium leaves.

Mesclun played a crucial role in the revival of small farms in Sonoma County. A few local growers—notably Jeff Dawson of Grandview Farms, Leonard Diggs of The Farmery, and Scott Mathieson of Laguna Farms—began to grow it in the 1980s in response to chefs' requests for better produce. It wasn't long before restaurants in the Bay Area featured these greens, and soon chefs as far away as Boston, New York, Honolulu, and Miami were serving mesclun from Sonoma County. Customers began to request it from their local markets, produce managers began carrying it, and growers were pleased with the price. Initially it could be as high as $12 a pound and more. Now there are dozens of wholesale producers and the price has plummeted. Of the three pioneers, only Scott remains. Leonard teaches farming at Santa Rosa Junior College, and Jeff has moved to Half Moon Bay and works as the personal gardener for Steve Jobs of Apple Computers.

Not all mescluns are the same, and with its popularity has come a plethora of new producers, not all of whom pay the same attention to quality as the first farmers did. The mergers that occur in national and international business are mirrored in the world of organic farming; small farms are being taken over by medium ones that in turn are swallowed by large farms. Quality is inevitably compromised. Today, many of the salad mixes you find in supermarkets have been harvested a week or more before you get them, they are often waterlogged, and they may be less than carefully grown. You can taste the difference. The sooner after harvest you eat the greens, the brighter, fresher, and better they taste. I recommend avoiding *all* prepackaged brands.

Scott sells about five hundred pounds of mesclun a week, much of it to his more than two hundred subscription customers. Although salad mix is the core of his business, Scott grows dozens of crops on about thirty acres that border the Laguna de Santa Rosa in southwestern Sebastopol, land that has been in his family since the 1960s, when his grandfather raised cows and horses. Now, Sebastopol's first new hotel in decades, the Holiday Inn, is less than a half mile away.

At the Santa Rosa Original farmers' market on both Wednesday and Saturday, Rafter Ranch offers some of the best, most interesting salad greens around, displaying each variety in a separate bag for customers to mix as they like. Rafter Ranch's

Shipments of Produce from Cloverdale, 1876

Robert Thompson, then the editor of the *Sonoma Democrat,* offers a particularly colorful portrait of Cloverdale, Sonoma County's northernmost town, around 1876. "Far up the valley, where the hills draw together," he wrote in 1877, "with [the] Russian river flowing between, is snugly nestled the town of Cloverdale . . . the hills produce an abundant grass crop, upon which thousands of sheep are kept. . . . Here is combined that geniality of soil and climate essential for the production of a light and highly-flavored wine." One of his more remarkable observations is that Mrs. Markle, apparently the first woman to settle in Cloverdale, "is said, by those who knew her, to have been remarkably pretty—a peculiarity for which her successors of the fairer sex in Cloverdale are still noted." He also offered, without explanation, the following accounting of "produce shipments" from town.

Dry hides, 1,437	Green hides, 874	Wool, 4,218 bales
Wool, 1,200 half bales	Hops, 1,630 bales	Quicksilver, 101,536 pounds
Tallow, 353 packages	Poultry, 3,920 dozen	Eggs, 47,000 dozen

—*Historical and Descriptive Sketch of Sonoma County, California,* 1877

mesclun is sold at the market and distributed to restaurants by Sonoma Organics.

For several years I taught a semester course at Santa Rosa Junior College that focused on Sonoma County foods. After field trips to farms and farmers' markets, the students developed their own recipes and menus. One student, a delightful woman full of tremendous enthusiasm, frequently wrote stories about the new foods she was offering her husband. Things were going pretty well, she said, until the mesclun. "Everything's great," he commented, "except that this salad looks like lace curtains." Weave it into a flag, I thought then, and wave it high.

The Aroma of Peppers

As I walked through the San Francisco farmers' market early one morning, the aroma of roasting peppers captured my attention. I followed my nose until I found the source, a huge round metal basket with a handle being turned by a vaguely familiar man. It was Larry Tiller of Warm Spring Farms, an eight-acre enclave tucked way off Westside Road in Healdsburg. Larry's peppers, roasted by a propane flame as they are continuously tumbled in the basket, are famous at every market he attends. During their season, from late summer through fall, he sells hundreds of pounds a week.

Larry owned a health-food store in Los Angeles when, he claims, a song on the radio made him long for the country life. He sold the store, headed north, and has been farming here since 1976, first in Windsor and now on Foreman Lane in Healdsburg. He has a magical piece of land near the river, with black topsoil that extends to a depth of sixty-five feet. It's a peaceful place that attracts hundreds of hummingbirds, drawn to the bountiful gardens but admittedly encouraged by the feeders of sugar water on the patio of Larry's house.

In addition to his celebrated peppers, Larry grows half a dozen varieties of tomatoes—including the best Sungolds, an orange cherry tomato, I've ever tasted—eggplant, herbs, sunflowers, shallots, and onions. As Scott Mathieson does, Larry relies upon farming for his livelihood, which gives him a somewhat different perspective from that of dozens of backyard gardeners who have turned to farming as a second career after retiring comfortably from a first. One of the reasons Larry does not attend local farmers' markets—he sells his produce at markets in St. Helena, Napa, San Rafael, and San Francisco—is that he finds it difficult to compete with the low prices asked by backyard gardeners who do not need to make a living off their harvest. Those other markets offer a large customer base of people used to paying higher prices than we do in Sonoma County.

Tierra Vegetables

You never know what a farmers' market might inspire.
Lee James was selling the dried chiles and fresh pro-
duce she and her brother Wayne have grown on Chalk
Hill Road east of Healdsburg since 1980 when a customer asked for "chipotles." When
Lee discovered that a chipotle was a smoked jalapeño, and not, as she had assumed,
an unfamiliar variety, she set out to make some with the chiles they grew.

Lee turned her grandmother's discarded refrigerator into a smoker by setting a
hibachi inside it and cutting a hole through the bottom to allow air to flow in. A
second hole cut in the back made a chimney. Using cuttings from grapevines, Lee
built a fire and then set the chiles on stainless steel racks. The new smoker worked
beautifully until the fire melted the plastic in the door of the fridge. After a few
alterations, the makeshift smoker produced a great batch of chipotles, which Lee
took to the market. When an article appeared in a Bay Area newspaper, sales skyrocketed in a single day. They have never slowed down. Eventually they retired
Grammy's fridge in favor of a new cinder-block smoker that holds three hundred
rather than thirty pounds of chiles. The chiles are smoked with dried grapevines,
prune, apple, and pear wood, and fresh basil and rosemary.

Tierra Vegetables' chipotles are packaged individually by variety: habanero,
jalapeño, Santa Fe, TAM jalapeño (milder, but with an enchanting flavor), serrano,
Hungarian wax, and New Mexico Mirasol, which means "looking at the sun," a reference to the fact that the pepper grows upside down, its tip pointing upward.

As good as these chiles are, the chipotle powder, a mixture of all the varieties,
is even better; it is one of the finest new products I have ever come across. Tierra
Vegetables' products are available by mail order, in selected stores, and, along with
their organic produce, at several farmers' markets in the Bay Area.

A Good Hoe and an IRA

One of the wonderful things about our farmers' markets is the opportunity they
give to small, and I mean *tiny*, farmers. By state or national standards, Scott Mathieson and Larry Tiller are small farmers, their annual incomes barely a blip on the
screen; compared with such market gardens as Singing Frogs Farm in Sebastopol
and La Bonne Terre in Healdsburg, they are huge.

Countless farmers offer their harvests at the area's markets, some for a few weeks
when a single crop comes into season—apples from an old grove, wild blackberries from the back forty, honey from a single hive—others during the summer and
fall, a few year round. The biggest and best of this tier of farmers, most notably

Green Man Farms and Middleton Farm, both in Healdsburg, have limited whole-sale distribution.

It is impossible to tell the story of each one; my most difficult task is to select from among so many gardeners and farmers whom I see weekly at the markets where I shop. Nancy Skall of Middleton Farm grows exquisite *haricots verts*, tiny green beans harvested when they aren't much bigger than pencil lead; it is just one of dozens of crops that Nancy's husband Malcolm brought to the market. Malcolm was a delightful addition to every market he attended; he chatted and joked with customers, all the while pitching his wife's produce with the suave skill of a pro-fessional marketer. As the 1999 harvest was in full swing, Malcolm was taken ill. He began chemotherapy and radiation therapy but never returned to the markets he so loved. He died in the fall, and now Nancy's face is the one we see smiling above her carefully tended crops.

With his black beret and sassy salesman style, Jack McCarley of Green Man Farms cuts such a dashing figure at the Healdsburg farmers' market. Over the years, Jack has introduced me to both sorrel and the most delicate wild watercress I've tasted anywhere. His display is one of the most beautiful at the market, and he handles his produce with a nearly heartbreaking tenderness. His strawberries are sensational.

Cliff Silva of Ma & Pa's Garden in Sebastopol is a year-round presence at the Santa Rosa and Sebastopol markets. In the spring, Cliff sells heirloom tomato vines

Larry's Bohemian Hot Sauce

When Larry Watson found himself married to a wine salesperson, my friend Susan Watson of Windsor Vineyards, he soon came up with a light-hearted way to deal with the pretensions of so-called wine connoisseurs, who quickly become tiresome if you don't share their penchant for endless analysis of what they're drinking. Inspired by time he spent in Mexico, Larry began making a hot sauce, aging it in oak barrels, and describing it in terms that poked fun at those wine aficionados. He intended to give the sauce, which he called Bustelo's, to friends, but it became so popular that he began bottling and selling it. In 1999, he changed the name to Larry's Bohemian Hot Sauce and now makes several hundred cases a year.

Others in Sonoma County have been inspired to make oak-aged hot sauces, including Iron Horse Vineyards. Hot Horse, a mild but extremely flavorful sauce made with estate-grown chiles, is sold at the winery's tasting room in Forestville.

Timber Crest Farms

Ruth Waltenspiel, who owns Timber Crest Farms with her husband, Ronald Walten-spiel, is an extraordinary woman. Singlehandedly she created the dried tomato industry in this country when she realized she could dry Roma tomatoes with the same equipment she used for her organic dried apricots and other dried fruits, which she has been selling to the natural foods market since 1957. If you're in Healdsburg, drop by the farm for a tour (no appointment is necessary). Ruthie is one of the most entertaining guides you will ever meet; ask her to tell the story of her first two truckloads of tomatoes (I borrowed it for the book *The Good Cook's Book of Tomatoes*). You'll find Timber Crest Farms Sonoma brand dried tomato products throughout the United States.

in 4-inch pots and some of the longest-lasting roses I've ever had; his potatoes and summer squash are among the best, and his celery root is unsurpassed. Cliff and Joy are both farmers, though it is Joy who nurtures the seedlings before they go into the ground. She's also the one who can tell you everything you need to know about planting in harmony with the moon's cycles.

Grandpa Garlic

For obvious reasons, you can't call Chester Aaron of Occidental a garlic maven or the West County Garlic Queen, but he definitely deserves some sort of title. He's done as much as anyone in recent years to make great garlic both visible and available, and he's done it with considerable flair. Perhaps Grandpa Garlic would be a suitable moniker for this elf of alliums. A retired teacher and writer of novels for young adults, Chester has turned his attention to the savory bulb with tremendous national and international success. After the publication of his books *Garlic Is Life*, a fictionalized memoir with recipes, and *The Great Garlic Book*, he began receiving seed garlic

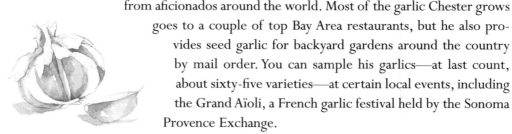

from aficionados around the world. Most of the garlic Chester grows goes to a couple of top Bay Area restaurants, but he also provides seed garlic for backyard gardens around the country by mail order. You can sample his garlics—at last count, about sixty-five varieties—at certain local events, including the Grand Aïoli, a French garlic festival held by the Sonoma Provence Exchange.

Egmont Tripp of Sunshine Farms in Cloverdale presides over

the north county's garlic kingdom. He launched both the Garlic-a-Month Club and the short-lived Cloverdale farmers' market, and is a tireless organic farmer in a part of the county few people ever see. With its pomegranate trees and sweltering summer heat, rural Cloverdale is evocative of the Sicilian countryside, quite a contrast to the lush forests and vineyards of the West County where Chester grows his garlic.

Fine Peaches

"I grow peaches because they were here when we bought the land," explains Steve Monroe, who was a dentist in Santa Rosa before he turned to farming. Dry Creek Peach & Produce in Dry Creek Valley has about seven hundred trees, twenty varieties of yellow peaches and ten varieties of white peaches. The first ripen in the spring, the last in October. Initially, Steve and his wife Johanna grew row crops, too, but as the Monroes discovered the remarkable quality of their peaches, they added trees and cut back other crops. The farm is now about 90 percent orchard, though you'll find their Ambrosia and Cren-shaw melons, Celebrity tomatoes, Walla Walla onions, and Sweet Hungarian peppers alongside their peaches at local farmers' markets.

The peaches, especially the Arctic Gem white peach, are exquisite, juicy, and sweet, with a wonderfully silky texture. When you ask Steve why his peaches are so good, he echoes sentiments expressed by virtually every farmer in western Sonoma County, regardless of the crop. "The cooler nights intensify the flavors . . . when nights are hot, sugar spikes too fast, before flavors develop . . . Dry Creek Valley peaches are more intensely flavorful than those grown in the Central Valley." You can say the same thing about apples, melons, pears, plums, and, of course, grapes. Our mild climate, the foggy mornings and cool nights, the pleasantly warm days, counts for a lot.

The Beloved Gravenstein and Other Apples

Although the local apple industry has been in decline for years, 1999 was the year the conflict over orchards and vineyards flared and nerves reached the flash point. "Stop the conversion!" became both a rallying cry and shorthand for a multitude of concerns over land use; historical perspective was often lacking. As the twentieth century drew to a close, apple orchards were making way for new vineyards. Yet in the *Illustrated Atlas of Sonoma County* published in 1897, there is no mention of apples even though planting had been underway since 1869. By 1915, there were apples all over the West County, displacing grapevines at a rapid rate. Apple prices were high, grape prices were plummeting, and farmers were struggling, then as now, to make a living. Crops, like fortunes, fluctuate in cycles that cannot necessarily be understood by taking a short view.

To understand the changes taking place in the apple industry, you need a cursory knowledge of the economics of apples. Apples are a commodity traded on the world market, sold as concentrate in 55-gallon drums. Domestic farmers neither set nor influence the price. "In 1998," Perry Kozlowski of Kozlowski Farms explains, "Argentina, Chile, and especially China . . . were dumping concentrate on the American market. We're getting the same price for our apples as we did twenty years ago." Those who sell both fresh and dried apples have a hard time, too. At the peak of the industry, there were eighteen major apple packers in the West County; today, there is one. In 1999, Vacu-Dry closed. Now farmers must send their apples to a plant in Washington to be dried. Perry Kozlowski's family began farming in Forestville in the 1940s, and apples have been a primary crop for decades. But even Perry has planted grapes.

Sebastopol's beloved Gravenstein apple is celebrated at the annual Gravenstein Apple Fair; Gravenstein Highway and nearly a dozen businesses bear its name. It's not going to vanish; this is one of the only places in the world where it thrives and there will always be a market for it. It is sought after by distributors in the summer, when it is the first of the year's apples to ripen. Major apple processors in Watsonville recognize its superior taste and add it to sauce and juice made from other apples to improve the flavor.

There are dozens of other varieties of apples grown in Sonoma County; the best places to find them are at farm stands and farmers markets (see For Apple Lovers Only, page 72). Apples are no longer a major cash crop in Sonoma County, but there will always be specialty growers.

The Moon and Stars

On 2½ acres in the flatlands of Penngrove, Larry Fields grows some of the best melons I've tasted anywhere, including my favorite, the Sunshine melon, an intensely sweet yellow watermelon. You usually find Larry, his son by his side, at local markets by early July, except when there's a cool spring or late rains; then he may not appear until late August. Although weather poses the biggest obstacle to a farmer such as Larry, once the tender melons begin to ripen he can also lose up to a dozen a night to hungry raccoons.

Until I met Larry, I assumed Sonoma County was not a great place for melons, that the weather was wrong. There just weren't that many; the crane melon, a good melon to be sure but not a watermelon, was about it. But the issue is land use not weather, Larry explains; melons could thrive in the rich soil and hot, dry days of inland Sonoma County. "We could be one of the major melon producing regions in the world," Larry says, "but we have to compete with vineyards for flatland acreage." He considered the possibility of farming melons in Costa Rica, but gave up when he discovered that poisonous snakes curl themselves under the melons and lie in wait for the rats that like to eat the sweet fruit. Here, he's found only gopher snakes near his melons.

Larry's melons are available only locally, and if you find yourself here at the right time, you should try them. Several other farmers have excellent melons, too, including David Gonzales, who grows two varieties, Israeli, similar to Sharlyn, and Savor, a French cantaloupe, and Joan Woodhull of Singing Frogs Farm, who grows several varieties.

For the most glorious melon you'll ever see, look for the Moon and Stars, a yellow watermelon grown at Middleton Farm. Its rich green skin is speckled with small bright yellow spots and there is a single larger sphere of yellow near one end. It is dazzling, full of intense flavors, and worth its high price tag at least once.

Kozlowski Farms

When Julia Child stopped by Kozlowski Farms to film a segment of *Good Morning America,* the jams, jellies, juices, mustards, and vinegars of this family farm were catapulted onto the national stage. A photograph of Julia and the matriarch Carmen Kozlowski, who developed many of the recipes for the family brand, hangs on the wall of the retail store where thousands of visitors come each year. The fruit vinegars of Kozlowski Farms have been among my favorite local products since I discovered them in the mid-1980s. Because they are low (4.5 percent) in acetic acid, the ingredient that makes vinegar sour, the fruit flavors shine through, making them perfect for such recipes as raspberry mayonnaise and raspberry hollandaise. Kozlowski Farms products currently are distributed in twenty-four states.

Dark Harvest

Trumpet Royale ❊ Shiitakes ❊ Portobello ❊ Hedgehog ❊ Chanterelles ❊ Shaggy Mane ❊ Morels ❊ Boletes ❊ Trumpet of Death ❊ Cauliflower ❊ Crimini ❊ Oyster Log ❊ Pom Pom Blanc ❊ Morel Cup ❊ Matsutake

AS I WAS WRITING THE LAST FEW PARAGRAPHS OF THIS BOOK, there was a knock at the front door. My friend Frédèrique stood there smiling, her cupped hands holding a small bounty of shaggy manes, an ephemeral mushroom that begins to digest itself shortly after its elfin cap pokes up into the light. I'd eaten them just once years earlier and had told Frédèrique, an expert mushroom hunter, that I remembered them as one of the best things I had ever tasted. I sautéed these immediately and a single bite confirmed the accuracy of my memory; there is no better mushroom than this elusive treasure.

Mushrooms of all sorts, gathered in the wild, purchased at farmers' markets, or grown at home on your kitchen counter, have never been more popular. Much has changed since the 1970s when the ubiquitous white button mushroom—*Agaricus bisporus*—dominated the retail market. Specialty mushrooms were available in ethnic markets, if at all, and were usually dried. Mushroom farmers, considered a rare breed, toiled in the dark, coaxing their fragile crops from murky mediums far from the sun's light. Hunting for wild mushrooms was a cult pursuit.

Now, we want our mushrooms to be flavorful again. Exotic mushrooms are everywhere, grown by hundreds of mushroom farmers around the country. Depending on the season, you can find chanterelles, hedgehogs, black trumpets, boletes, and dozens of other varieties in most supermarkets. Criminis and portobellos, which are the same species as the white button, are everywhere. No matter where you live, specialty mushrooms are never far away.

Gourmet Mushrooms, Inc.

"[Growing mushrooms] is not just hard science; there is an intuitive connection," Malcolm Clark of Gourmet Mushrooms, Inc., in Sebastopol likes to say. Encouraging the sensitive fungi to fruit is the difficult part, involving art and magic as well as knowledge. It's easy to think of Malcolm as a sorcerer, the Luther Burbank of 'shrooms, coaxing the best from spores he has gathered all over the world.

Gourmet Mushrooms was launched in the late 1970s when Clark, a Canadian biologist, and his business partner, David Law, were searching for a suitable climate in which to grow shiitakes using a technique Malcolm had perfected. Sebastopol, where the Gravenstein was introduced in the nineteenth century, is ideal—the

Gravenstein apple and the shiitake flourish in similar climates—and not only because of the weather. It was also close to the Pacific Northwest, a rich source of the wild mushrooms that play an important role in the company. Today, several species of fungi are cultivated at the West County facility, and professional foragers gather mushrooms throughout the northwest. For years most of the wild mushrooms were shipped to European markets, but now with increasing domestic demand, fewer mushrooms leave the country.

The small company grows over two dozen species of fungi, including six it has developed. The first signature mushroom was Pom Pom Blanc, a round, white fungus about the size of a tennis ball with a shaggy outer layer that resembles a sheepdog's mane. Next came the Cinnamon Cap, the Blue Oyster, the Golden Oyster, and the Clam Shell, all strikingly beautiful as well as delicious. Newest is the ghostly Trumpet Royale, with a white stem and tan cap that resembles the prized porcini (known in France as cèpes) in flavor. The company offers a retail basket that includes all of its signature mushrooms, along with one or two wild mushrooms that vary with the season. The two-pound basket may be shipped anywhere in the world by overnight express for $48. The company also makes inoculated mushroom pots for growing morels, shiitakes, three types of oyster mushrooms (blue, brown, and golden), and Pom Pom Blanc (see Resources, page 295).

Point Arena Mushrooms

The urge to grow one's own food is powerful, eclipsed but not erased by demanding schedules and the small plots of land so common today. Yet even if you live in an apartment there are ways to grow a bit of produce: a wine barrel of potatoes; a single vine of cherry tomatoes snaking across a front porch; a windowbox of herbs; flowerpots of baby lettuces. There are few activities as viscerally satisfying as cooking something you've just harvested. The small circle of self-sufficiency remains deeply rewarding, regardless of how removed from the land our lives may seem.

I first discovered the mushroom logs of Point Arena Mushrooms when I was wandering through the farm market one wet December morning looking for a holiday present for my daughter who was attending Brown University and longing for California produce. The log doesn't look like much, but the big brown lump of dirt wrapped in clear plastic shimmers with promise if you know what to expect. I shipped one east immediately. It sat on a shelf in Nicolle's kitchen for several weeks until one morning when she awoke to a miniature forest of mushrooms, much as you might spot near an oak tree after a fall rain. Five times the log fruited, yielding close to 3 pounds of mushrooms. She made omelets, risotto, pasta, and strudel.

She became the talk of the graduate English department.

John Richardson has been cultivating mushrooms in Point Arena, just north of Sonoma County in southern Mendocino County, since the early 1990s. He sells oyster logs year round because they'll fruit in any weather and shiitake logs, which need warm weather and humidity to fruit, in the summer and fall. John sells the logs, along with shiitakes, oysters, king oysters, and various other mushrooms, at the Santa Rosa Original farmers' market on Saturdays.

Wild About Mushrooms

As a kid, Charmoon Richardson had an innate fascination with food. For nearly three decades, his lusty appetite has focused on the wild mushrooms of Northern California. For much of the time, foraging for mushrooms was an avocation while he earned his living in other ways and slowly acquired the knowledge and expertise that comes only with experience. In 1997, he launched Wild About Mushrooms, a full-time endeavor. He conducts mushroom identification classes, tours, workshops, and seminars, leads mushroom forays, and hosts mushroom camps, some of which last several days and are rumored to be indulgent extravaganzas. He is also on the staff of the California School of Herbal Studies in Forestville and has recently embarked on a cultivation project that focuses on medicinal mushrooms.

Every few years, several people die of mushroom poisoning, usually a group of friends who gather and eat mushrooms together. In 1997 Sonoma County lost a favorite son when Sam Sebastiani Jr., one of the founders of Wine Brats, succumbed to poisonous fungi that were misidentified.

Charmoon explains that inexperienced foragers are often overconfident about their abilities to identify mushrooms. As you become more experienced, you realize that things are not always as clear cut as they seem and that such terms as *large gills*, a feature commonly used to identify species, are relative. A novice forager may not have seen enough species to assess variable and subtle characteristics accurately. Charmoon's best advice: Don't be overconfident, and don't forage when you've been drinking. And, of course, if you have even the slightest doubt about a mushroom, either don't eat it or consult an expert before you do.

Petaluma Mushroom Farm

As popular as specialty cultivated mushrooms and rare wild mushrooms are these days, it is still the common white mushroom and its cousins that take up most of the shelf space in America's supermarkets. The Petaluma Mushroom Farm has been cultivating *Agaricus bisporus* since the mid-1970s and sells its mushrooms at several farmers' markets in Sonoma County, distributes them throughout the Bay Area and Sacramento, and sells directly to consumers at the farm (see Resources, page 295).

The white mushrooms dominate commercial production primarily because they yield more mushrooms per foot of growing space than other edible fungi do. The crimini, which has more flavor, a longer shelf life, and is more resistant to disease, began to appear alongside its white cousin in the late 1980s.

The big, meaty portobello has grown enormously popular, too. It is relatively inexpensive, full flavored, and substantial enough that both vegetarians and carnivores can pretend they're indulging in a steak. Because the portobello is allowed to grow for a longer time than its paler cousins, it develops fiber and loses water. White button mushrooms are about 96 percent water, a portobello just 76 percent.

Straw into Gold

Artisan Breads ❊ *Della Fattoria* ❊ *Lou's Forno* ❊ *Alvarado Street Bakery* ❊ *Village Bakers* ❊ *Downtown Bakery & Creamery* ❊ *Basque Boulangerie* ❊ *Brother Juniper's Bakery* ❊ *Costeaux French Bakery* ❊ *Wild Flour Breads*

BY THE EARLY 1980s, the artisan bread revival had begun in earnest in America with Steve Sullivan's Acme Bakery, located in an upscale brick building shared with Kermit Lynch Wine Merchant and Alice Waters's Café Fanny in Berkeley. There was a nearly instantaneous demand for Acme's limited amount of European-style hearth breads, yet even after a major expansion in the late 1980s, very little made it to Sonoma County. As late as 1991, I drove to the East Bay whenever I craved the real thing.

The World Cup of Baking

Then Artisan Bakers came along in the summer of 1992. You could almost hear the crackle as people all over Sonoma County tore into the lusty, crusty, deeply flavored loaves crafted by Craig Ponsford. It wasn't long before others followed; suddenly great bread was everywhere. "We started Artisan Bakers because the type of bread we liked to eat just wasn't available here," Sharon Ponsford, Craig's mother and one of the bakery's founders, explains. "We had no idea what we were doing when we opened the bakery. We were used to the breads of Acme and Grace. We just kind of stumbled into this."

"Perhaps even, we will remember how to make good bread again," reads a small letterpress print that hangs at the bakery's retail outlet. The words are from M. F. K. Fisher's *How to Cook a Wolf*. Fisher herself died in nearby Glen Ellen only a month before Artisan sold its first loaves, but I suspect she would have approved of the handcrafted breads Craig produced at the rate of about 150 a day during the bakery's first months, a time when the only advertising was by word of mouth. If you wanted Artisan bread back then, you had to go to the tiny retail store, but the Ponsfords soon began limited distribution. The bakery has expanded three times since those early days; it now bakes about eight thousand pounds of bread a day and distributes it throughout the Bay Area.

The success of Artisan Bakery is international. In 1996, Craig was invited to join the three-person United States team at what is casually known as the Olympics of Baking in Paris. To almost everyone's astonishment, Craig's breads were awarded the Coupe de Monde de Boulangerie, or World Cup of Baking, the top prize. In

1999, he coached a new U.S. team, which again took the Coupe de Monde (regulations have changed since Craig first won; now teams rather than individuals win).

Increased production and the limelight have not changed Artisan's breads; these rustic loaves are as good as ever. The main difference is that there are more of them, not just of Artisan but of good bread in general. Sebastopol's Village Bakery opened in 1994, Della Fattoria followed in 1995, and by 1997, Lou Preston, who has an abiding passion for baking, had built a new wood-fueled oven that allowed him to bake four dozen loaves at a time, all of which are sold at his winery.

It wasn't long before the area's supermarkets got into the game. Today, most locally owned markets and several chains bake their own bread. In the spring of 1999, Wild Flour Bakery opened in Freestone, providing the West County with handcrafted hearth loaves from a wood-fired oven. No matter where you go in Sonoma County, you're never far from *really* good bread.

Della Fattoria

Ed Weber was born in a small farmhouse in western Petaluma where he lives today with his wife Kathleen. In 1995, the Webers sold their first breads, baked in a wood-fired oven built behind the house. Word spread rapidly and soon the breads of Della Fattoria were considered among the best in the county and were served at some of the area's best-known restaurants, such as the French Laundry in Napa Valley. Today they are sold at markets such as Oakville Grocery, Pearson & Co., Petaluma Market, Sonoma Market, and Dean & DeLuca in St. Helena, where the beautiful golden loaves command as much as six dollars each. In 1998, the Webers added two new brick ovens and can now bake about twenty-two hundred loaves a week, along with the line of rustic cookies and pastries that their daughter-in-law, Linda, bakes each day. Because the Webers have limited their bakery's expansion, Della Fattoria remains small and rustic, a family operation in the truest sense.

A Few Pioneers

To imply that there was no good bread at all before Artisan's would not be accurate, and it would insult many great bakers. Kathleen Stewart opened the Downtown Bakery and Creamery on the square in Healdsburg in 1987, in partnership with Lindsey Shere, the original pastry chef at Chez Panisse, and her daughter, Therese Shere. From the beginning, the bakery offered European-style breads, inspired by Steve Sullivan, a friend from their days at Chez Panisse. That bakery was the true precursor of the local bread revolution, and word spread quickly about the savory loaves in Healdsburg. But production was limited, and an afternoon drive north often yielded nothing more than the day's last piece of focaccia. Today, bread is about 25 percent of the bakery's business, with about four hundred loaves produced daily.

Other bakeries have played key roles in providing the county's daily bread. Brother Juniper's Bakery cleared a significant hurdle for everyone by charging more than double the usual price and thus proving there was an eager market for bread with character. Alvarado Street Bakery, founded in Sonoma County in 1978, is the largest organic bakery in the United States, with distribution throughout the United States and Canada. These dense, chewy breads are made entirely without flour; the loaves begin as whole berries that are soaked in filtered water until they sprout, drained, and then ground into something closer in appearance to hamburger than dough.

Brothers, Uncles & Grandfathers

The current industry has earlier mentors, too, several generations of bakers who were producing good bread long before anyone had used the term "gourmet revolution." The Franco-American Bakery can be traced to the turn of the century, when a saloon in Santa Rosa was transformed into a bakery. In 1938, Frank and Mario Bastoni bought the bakery, which has been owned by the family since that time. In the early 1940s sourdough was gaining in popularity; Franco-American concentrated on the style, for which it remains known today. The boutique bakery revolution has affected Franco-American much less than has the increase of in-store supermarket bakeries, which cut into sales in their traditional outlets.

Lombardi's was started by Bruno Lombardi in 1951 and soon expanded as demand for its San Francisco–style sourdough increased. Lombardi sold the bakery in the 1980s to a group of partners who use the original recipe; the bread is distributed throughout Sonoma County. The Sonoma French Bakery also opened in the 1950s, but its sale in the early 1990s resulted in a noticeable decline in quality.

Costeaux French Bakery is more of an uncle than a grandfather, arriving on the scene in 1973, when a temperamental Frenchman named John Costeaux purchased a facility in Healdsburg that had been a bakery since 1923. Costeaux went through fifty bakers in seven years as he developed his crusty loaves and pull-aparts. The breads are not European hearth breads, but rather echo the sourdoughs made famous by San Francisco. Nancy and Carl Seppi purchased the bakery in the early 1980s; Costeaux stayed on a few months, helping Seppi hone the skills he began developing as an employee. Costeaux has since returned to France.

The Breads of Sonoma County

The average quality of bread in bakeries and restaurants in Sonoma County is higher than at any place I've been, higher than anywhere in France or Italy.

—Edward Behr, who also is writing an in-depth book on the subject, *The Best Bread*, in "The Art of Eating," Winter 1999

Alvarado Street Bakery, ROHNERT PARK. Organic sprouted grain (not flour) breads, rolls, and tortillas from the country's largest organic bakery. On-site retail; national distribution.

Artisan Bakers, SONOMA. European hearth breads, including sourdough, sour country, sour country walnut, sour rye, multigrain, pugliese, Italian country, Italian country walnut, potato rosemary, pain français. On-site retail; Bay Area distribution.

Basque Boulangerie, SONOMA. Country-style French breads from the founders of the Sonoma French Bakery. About thirty varieties; known for their light, crackly, crisp crusts and flat pull-apart loaves. On-site retail; local distribution.

Bennett Valley Bread & Pastry, SANTA ROSA. European-style hearth breads, including pugliese; flavored breads, such as roasted garlic and jack; potato, onion, and chives; roasted onion and Asiago; Gorgonzola and walnut.

Brother Juniper's Bakery, SANTA ROSA. Struan, a coarse-textured sandwich bread; flavored specialty breads including Cajun Pepper, Wild Rice & Onion, and Three-Seed. On-site retail; Bay Area distribution.

Costeaux French Bakery, HEALDSBURG. Classic San Francisco–style sourdough in various sizes, shapes, and forms, including the popular pull-apart loaf. On-site retail, with café.

Della Fattoria, PETALUMA. Sour-leavened breads from wood-fired ovens, including campagne, levain, rye, and several flavored loaves. Limited Bay Area distribution to restaurants and specialty markets.

Downtown Bakery & Creamery, HEALDSBURG. European hearth breads, including sour French, sweet French, sour rye, Como, and potato. On-site retail.

Franco–American Bakery, SANTA ROSA. Classic San Francisco–style sourdough loaves and baguettes. Local distribution.

Lombardi's, PETALUMA. Classic San Francisco–style sourdough loaves and baguettes. On-site retail; North Bay distribution.

Lotus Bakery, SANTA ROSA. Dense, organic breads from spelt flour and other grains; no wheat. On-site retail; Bay Area distribution.

Lou's Forno, HEALDSBURG. European-style hearth breads with Preston's famous Dry Creek Valley starter made from the natural yeast of grapes from one-hundred-year-old zinfandel vines. On-site sales; bread hot line (see Preston of Dry Creek, Wineries, page 303).

Santa Rosa Bread Co., SANTA ROSA. Handcrafted breads made with organic ingredients. On-site retail; wholesale distribution.

Village Bakery, SEBASTOPOL. European hearth breads including organic country peasant, Sebastopol sourdough, and seeded sourdough; cakes and pastries, too. On-site retail; local distribution.

Wild Flour Bakery, FREESTONE. Pricey European hearth breads handmade by Jad Wallach, a nephew of the film critic Pauline Kael; beautiful wood-fired brick oven. Selections change daily. On-site sales only.

Second Harvest

Rincon Heights Pure Olive Oil ❀ *B.R. Cohn Estate* ❀ *DaVero Extra Virgin* ❀ *Sonoma Moment* ❀ *O* ❀ *McEvoy Ranch* ❀ *Spectrum Naturals* ❀ *Remazzano* ❀ *The Olive Press* ❀ *V. G. Buck* ❀ *York Creek*

MY SECOND BOOK, *The Good Cook's Book of Oil & Vinegar*, was published in the early fall of 1992, precisely two months before the renaissance of California olive oil was heralded by the release of the inaugural estate olive oil from B. R. Cohn Winery in Glen Ellen. It was a study in bad timing. So much changed with the success of Cohn's oil that the substantial portion of the book that dealt with olive oil was almost instantly out of date, whatever prescience I might have shown was eclipsed by an entire new industry. The rebirth of olive oil production in California changed everything.

The history of growing olives for the table and for cooking in California begins at the first mission, San Diego de Alcalá, where Spanish padres planted a variety we now call Mission. By the turn of the century, there were groves throughout the state—not just the Mission variety, but Italian, French, and other Spanish varieties brought by new immigrants—including here in Sonoma County. In 1900, a California olive oil took first prize at the World's Fair in Paris.

By this time, a frenzy of planting had been underway for years in Sonoma County. Prunes and apples were enjoying what one newspaper editor called a "fruit boom"; Luther Burbank was developing orchards in Sebastopol; walnuts were an increasingly lucrative crop. Olives were doing well, too. In her book *Santa Rosa, A Nineteenth-Century Town*, Gaye LeBaron writes that "Guy Grosse, a Swiss-born real estate salesman and promoter extraordinaire, was convincing people by the 1880s that Santa Rosa could become the olive oil capital of the United States."

Inspired by the success of olive growers in nearby Sonoma Valley, Grosse planted thousands of trees on his land above Rincon Valley, east of town. At the peak of his success, he supplied all of Santa Rosa's grocery stores with his Rincon Heights olive oil, yet just a few months after his best season in 1896, he sold his land for housing development. Perhaps he knew what was coming. Within a few years, the California olive oil industry fell on hard times when producers could not compete with the lower-priced oils from Italy. Many of the orchards vanished—lone trees linger here and there today, including one a few yards from my bedroom window—and others were abandoned.

The industry languished for decades, until several factors converged to ignite a fury of interest in olive oil. By the 1970s an increasing number of people were introduced to boldly flavored olive oils when they traveled to Europe, interest in nutrition focused attention on the oil's apparent health benefits, and the gourmet revolution sparked a fascination with handcrafted products of every sort. It was just a matter of time.

I met Ridgely Evers on a hot summer afternoon in 1993 when his first trees were barely three years old. Not yet convinced that California could produce an oil as wonderful as those I'd tasted in the heart of Tuscany, I was leery. But Ridgely dissolved my suspicions when he offered me a taste of his benchmark oil. If this was what he was aiming for, I was all for it.

During a vacation in Tuscany, Ridgely became inspired to plant olive trees on his Dry Creek Valley estate southwest of Healdsburg. At the time, Italian trees had not yet recovered from a devastating freeze and Italian olive oil was very expensive. Perhaps California could compete, he thought, and he began searching for an oil to serve as a model. "When I started tasting olive oils," Ridgely explained to me, "I

Sonoma County Olive Oils

Da Vero Extra Virgin: A premium, condiment-quality oil, full-flavored, peppery yet suave. After each new harvest, DaVero releases a limited amount of the just-pressed oil, called Olio Nuevo, or new oil. It is extraordinarily flavorful, but has a shorter shelf life than oils that rest in bulk for several weeks.

The Olive Press: A blend from California's only cooperative olive oil mill.

B. R. Cohn Estate: A golden oil made of picholine olives, smooth and buttery, a classic Provençal-style oil.

Luigi's Oil: A bold, complex oil from the estate olives of Preston of Dry Creek.

McEvoy Ranch: Technically, an olive oil in Marin County, but only by a couple of miles; well-made, delicate, condiment-quality.

Remezzano: Fruity, buttery oils from Spanish varieties.

Sonoma Moment: Spanish varietals (Mission, *manzanilla*, *sevillano*) transplanted from Napa Valley to Alexander Valley.

Asti: A typical California oil, with forward fruitiness and an oily texture.

V. G. Buck: Widely available, these oils are bottled but neither grown nor pressed in Sonoma County.

Chalk Hill Clematis Nursery Olive Oil: A blended olive oil from one of the largest clematis nurseries in the world. Sold only via the nursery's web site.

chose the oils of Tuscany in part because I preferred them but also because I felt the climate was most similar to here. As I learned more, it became clear that the Luccese climate is even more like Sonoma County than the Chianti climate. It's a little cooler and has more maritime influence." (The Luccese area embraces the lands west of Florence to Pisa, surrounding the town of Lucca, and is exposed to air coming in from the sea. Chianti stretches south from Florence to Siena; its warmer climate more closely resembles the Napa Valley's.)

Ridgely eventually discovered Fattoria Mansi Bernardini, whose oil he describes as magical. Marcello Salom's family has owned the *fattoria* for centuries; he allowed Ridgely to harvest cuttings from the estate's four varieties of olive trees—*leccino*, *frantoio*, *maurino*, and *pendolino*—and a nursery nearby in Pescia grew them until they were ready for the journey to Healdsburg. The first thousand trees went into the ground in 1991 and have been followed by subsequent plantings of thousands, some Italian cuttings, some cuttings from the new trees.

Ridgely was the first person to import olive trees from Italy in the twentieth century, and when he entered his 1997 DaVero Extra Virgin Olive Oil in a European tasting, he made history again. The oil not only took first place, it also became the first American oil to be certified as extra virgin, a designation that requires superior quality, by the European Olive Oil Council.

The early success of DaVero and B. R. Cohn oils and the growing interest in olive oil in general have launched a plethora of new businesses that will influence the industry for decades. Just beyond the southern border of Sonoma County on what was once a cattle ranch, Nan McEvoy has planted eleven thousand trees from the same nursery in Pescia that Ridgely used, and has installed a large olive oil mill. In 1999, McEvoy Ranch received its organic certification.

At last count, there were about two dozen olive orchards in Sonoma County and about a dozen producers, some using estate fruit and others making oil with fruit purchased from growers in Sonoma County and elsewhere. Still others buy oil in bulk and bottle it under their own label. It is a sexy, if not necessarily lucrative, endeavor. The economic realities of olive oil production are harsh, in large part because land and labor are expensive in Northern California. Greg Reisinger, a founder of B. R. Cohn's American Classics, says that it is virtually impossible to make money using olives solely from local trees. His company has expanded with a vast orchard in Mexico and produces oils, including an organic olive oil, at a fraction of the cost of oil made here.

In 1992, olive growers and oil producers in California organized as the California Olive Oil Council (COOC), which has created a tasting panel trained by the European Olive Oil Council and developed a voluntary certification program. Oils that are awarded certification can use the council's Extra Virgin Certification Seal.

With so many growers, producers, and bottlers, the picking of olives has become an important second harvest in Northern California. In most years, olives ripen after wine grapes have been picked. Just as activity in the vineyards is winding down, it begins again in our olive orchards. At certain locations, such as B. R. Cohn Winery, where an eight-acre olive orchard was planted in the 1870s, you can watch workers picking and gathering the olives as you taste both the wine and the oil from last year's harvest.

CHAPTER 2

Bacchus

The Appellations of
Sonoma County

*Alexander Valley ❋ Chalk Hill ❋ Dry Creek Valley ❋ Russian River Valley ❋ Green
Valley ❋ Knight's Valley ❋ Sonoma Valley ❋ Sonoma Mountain ❋ Los Carneros ❋
Sonoma Coast ❋ Northern Sonoma*

SONOMA MAY HANG LIKE A JUICY GRAPE CLUSTER ABOVE——that is, northwest——of Napa, but it lived in Napa's shadow for much of the twentieth century.
Napa is geographically compact, its sense of self as focused and as well defined as
its landscape. Napa grows grapes and makes wine. A single artery, Highway 29, runs
through the long, narrow Napa Valley, with the Silverado Trail forming an alternate,
parallel route. Most of its wineries are accessible from one of these two roads. With
the exception of Los Carneros, Napa is a hot inland valley surrounded by mountains. For decades, Napa has had an articulate patriarch and spokesperson, the affa-
ble Robert Mondavi.

Sonoma County, by comparison, is chaotic and geographically cumbersome, a
region of tremendous diversity. There are many Sonomas, layered one upon the
other, entwined, intermingled, and, in many cases, hidden. There are many voices,
but no single spokesperson. Wine grapes are currently the most important cash
crop, but dozens of farm products contribute to the more than one-half billion dollars that agriculture supplies annually to the local economy.

That Sonoma County is the birthplace of modern winemaking in America is probably the best known aspect of our story. By now the names and places are so familiar. There's Padre José Altimi, founder of the last of the California missions, planting
those first grapevines in 1823. There's the entrepreneurial genius of the nobleman
General Mariano Guadalupe Vallejo, reigning over the land and, in a moment of

stunning largess, deeding away what became Napa County. And there's Count Agoston Haraszthy, that flamboyant Hungarian rogue who gave Vallejo a run for his money by importing grapevines from Europe. Even though that prescient maneuver resulted in Haraszthy's being known today as the father of modern California viticulture, the rivalry between the two men remained friendly as they competed against each other in statewide and international wine competitions. Marriage—two of Vallejo's daughters to two of Haraszthy's sons—made them even closer, though Haraszthy wasn't one to settle down and play with grandchildren. Off the count went to meet his fate in a Nicaraguan river, where an alligator is said to have had the final say.

If it's our history you want, you'll find it all over Sonoma Valley, easy to explore in a single day. If it's our wine, take your time. There's too much to comprehend thoroughly unless you get paid for it. If you want to get your arms around Sonoma County wine, I recommended one of three approaches, or a combination of them all. It's how I've done it.

An easy way is to let someone else do the work. *California Wine Winners*, published annually by Varietal Fair in Sebastopol, fits neatly into glove box, purse, or pocket, and lists the results of major national wine competitions. Wines are organized by variety, and awards are tallied by both winery and region. Sonoma County surpasses Napa by a substantial margin in twenty-two of the twenty-four varietal categories;

Wine X

Not long after Jason Priestley, the actor, director, producer, race-car driver, and star of *Beverly Hills 90210*, was interviewed by *Wine X Magazine,* he became a partner in the venture founded in Santa Rosa by Darryl Roberts, who started the magazine on-line before launching it in glorious full-color print. "[It] totally reflects my attitude about wine," Priestley said about the magazine, whose target audience is between twenty-one and thirty-five years old. (His company is also developing a wine-related television show.) *Wine X* is long on both graphics and attitude yet it's not just a pretty, sassy face. The articles have substance, the wine reviews are unconventional ("Deux Amis 1996 Zinfandel: This wine is like Chevy Chase digging his own grave—dense and earthy, but fun"; "Clos du Bois 1998 Sauvignon Blanc: Doin' it with the hunk next door in an open field on a sunny August day—lots of sweet fruit, dry grass and heat") and practical (wines are fifteen dollars or less), and there are useful music and film reviews, too. And who can resist the mag's yapping at the heels of the big boys of wine publishing?

Napa leads only with dry riesling and sangiovese. When it comes to overall awards, Sonoma County has nearly twice as many total points as *any* other region. The weakness in this approach is that competitions are flawed. Entry into competition is voluntary; many outstanding wines, especially those of smaller vintners, are never submitted, and in the end, taste is highly subjective. Although every judge can (or *should*) recognize a flawed wine, a distinctive wine may dazzle some and leave others unmoved. Winners are often compromises.

A better approach is to find a good retailer, one who either shares or understands your taste. It's frustrating when your neighborhood merchant keeps directing you toward, say, blockbuster syrahs when you fancy a suave pinot noir. You want a dealer who understands your penchant for pretty wines and can lead you to unfamiliar wines you will enjoy. When I'm stumped, I often rely upon Paul Root of The Wine Shop in Healdsburg (see Resources, page 295); much of his business is mail order, so I'm not sharing a secret you can't use. I also call upon the wisdom of Bill Traverso (see Traverso's Gourmet Foods and Wines, Resources, page 295), whose palate and knowledge I admire and whose market I couldn't live without.

A third approach, if you've fallen in love with Sonoma County and want to examine each nook and cranny, if you're searching for every last plot of century-old zinfandel vines, is to explore our eleven viticultural areas. Find those areas that flatter the varietals you prefer and taste your way through them, when you visit, by ordering through a winery's web site, or by asking your local merchant about wines from the area.

The United States founded its system of American Viticultural Areas, or AVAs, in the late 1970s. AVAs, also called "appellations," are in theory defined by natural features, distinct physical characteristics such as mountain ranges, rivers, soil types, and weather patterns, that distinguish an area, findings that must be supported by geological survey maps. This system is based on the concept of the expression of place, what the French call *terroir*, the idea that agricultural products in general and grapes specifically are a product not only of their genes but also of their environment, of the soil and climate in which they grow.

Within any viticultural area, any variety of grape may be grown using any trellising technique to yield any amount of grapes. The French system of *appellation d'origine contrôlée*, codified in the early twentieth century primarily to protect the integrity of wines that were being compromised by the fraud and adulteration that had become commonplace in the French wine industry, is much more detailed, with laws specific to each area. Everything from variety of grape and maximum yield to winemaking technique and length of aging is governed by the French regulations. (The designation is also applied to certain regional foods.) The American system is much less specific, but it is young and inevitably will be refined. Until it is, designations are at best broad, directing you toward varietals and general styles well suited to specific areas.

Once a viticultural area has been established, the designation can be used on a wine label if at least 85 percent of the wine in the bottle is from the AVA. Additional information can further describe a wine within a region by identifying a specific vineyard or adding the designation Estate Bottled, which indicates that both the winery and the vineyard are within a single viticultural area, and that the winery either owns or controls the vineyard.

Alexander Valley

Rustic Alexander Valley stretches from southeast of Healdsburg northward for over twenty miles, encompassing Asti, Cloverdale, the old town of Preston, and part of the Russian River and its surrounding watershed. Bordered on the east by the Mayacamas Mountains and Knight's Valley, its southern boundary defines the northern edge of Chalk Hill. Over the decades, pears, apples, pomegranates, citrus, prunes, sheep, dairy cattle, and market produce in addition to grapes have thrived here. Today, grapes dominate. There are close to 30 wineries and 260 vineyards within the seventy-five thousand acres that make up the Alexander Valley AVA, officially recognized in 1984.

The region is warm. The fertile soils encourage vigorous, sometimes troublingly so, vine growth; we want a vine to put its energy into fruit, not foliage. Nearly every varietal grows with a measure of success—"the curse of versatility" the wine authority Jancis Robinson calls it—though chardonnay and cabernet sauvignon dominate in acreage and acclaim. Rodney Strong's Alexander's Crown Cabernet Sauvignon was probably the first to distinguish itself here, and wineries such as Clos du Bois Vineyards, Chateau Souverain, Geyser Peak Winery, and Jordan Vineyard have helped make the region well known nationwide.

The modern history of Alexander Valley begins with Cyrus Alexander, one of the region's original settlers who planted the valley's first vineyard in 1846. By the end of the nineteenth century, there were about three hundred acres planted to grapes and several established wineries, including Simi Winery and Geyser Peak. Falling grape prices, an epidemic of phylloxera louse that destroyed thousands of vines, Prohibition, and the Great Depression devastated viticulture in Alexander Valley, just as these forces did throughout most of California. Only Seghesio Winery, built in 1902 by Eduardo Seghesio and first planted in 1895, continued winemaking during these years, for decades selling bulk wines to other producers. In 1983, the well-known family established the Seghesio label, which thrives today in neighboring Dry Creek Valley.

Chalk Hill

In the hilly terrain due east of Windsor, nestled in the far corner of Russian River Valley, is the small viticultural area of Chalk Hill, with its rolling hillside vineyards, unusual white soil made not of chalk but of ancient volcanic ash, and its single estate winery. What distinguishes Chalk Hill from the surrounding regions is this distinctive soil and a mild climate (the jut of land known as Chalk Hill is on private property in Alexander Valley). Hills form a barrier that block coastal fog; temperatures are higher here than they are in the rest of Russian River Valley, of which it is a part. The orientation of Mount Saint Helena to the Pacific Ocean creates a chimney effect above Chalk Hill; a nearly constant breeze washes over the land, providing a slightly cooler climate than nearby Alexander and Knight's Valleys.

There are no open tasting rooms in Chalk Hill (with the exception of the areas that overlap with Russian River Valley), no European-style chateaus, few public events. There is a wildness to the terrain and little traffic. Chalk Hill, which is bordered on the south by Mark West Springs Road and on the west by Old Redwood Highway, seems much farther away from civilization than it actually is.

Rodney Strong was the first to use the Chalk Hill designation. It appeared on his 1977 Chalk Hill Vineyard Chardonnay five years before the appellation was formally established in 1983. In 1972, Fred Furth, an attorney in San Francisco and founder of Chalk Hill Winery, began planting his vineyards. In 1999, the twelve-hundred-acre estate included three hundred acres of vineyards, several lakes, a wedding park, stables, an organic vegetable garden, and the largest indoor equestrian arena in North America.

Dry Creek Valley

Dry Creek Valley stretches northwest, a long elegant finger of land, for about thirteen and a half miles from southern Healdsburg to Warm Springs Dam. At its widest, it is just three miles across; most of the valley is narrower. The AVA encompasses eighty thousand acres, or 125 square miles (including the valley's 23 square miles), embracing nearly all of Lake Sonoma and much of the wilderness surrounding it. There are nearly three dozen wineries, more than 250 vineyards, several orchards, a fish hatchery, and a handful of lush market gardens.

At 13½ miles long and about 2¼ miles wide, the island of Manhattan could fit nearly exactly into Dry Creek Valley. And there are more similarities than mere size and shape between these two remarkable pieces of land. Both Dry Creek Valley and Manhattan are defined by natural features rather than by geopolitical boundaries, both enjoy rich histories and seemingly boundless possibilities, and for both, their official borders—of the AVA and of New York City, respectively—reach far beyond their discrete geographic boundaries. Perhaps the most appealing quality of New York is that no matter how much time or money or effort you give, it will not yield all of its secrets, ever. Dry Creek Valley is similar, a place you could spend a lifetime studying and still not fully comprehend its intricate tapestry of influences. There are scores of microclimates, dozens of soils, and the fingerprints of countless individuals who have shaped the valley's character.

The first pioneers came to Dry Creek as farmers, not winemakers. They planted grapevines on the hillside benches so that they could make wine for their own tables but reserved their best plots of land for cash crops, wheat, hay, beans, apricots, prunes, peaches, strawberries, apples, pears, Asian pears, olives, herbs, and vegetables. Those early vineyards produced great wine, and zinfandel began to emerge as the sweetheart of the valley more than a century ago. Today, it remains the grape that struts and preens in this environment, with bright raspberry flavors and a delicacy other regions envy. Although Dry Creek is a warm inland valley, marine influences that enter from the southern portion where Dry Creek empties into the Russian River keep nights cool. Rich Thomas, a viticultural instructor at Santa Rosa Junior College, tells his students that God made one place on earth for zinfandel, Dry Creek Valley.

The modern boom began in the early 1970s. Zinfandel did not receive much attention initially, but it wasn't long before those old vines captured the imaginations of a new generation of vintners. Today cabernet sauvignon and chardonnay threaten to overtake zinfandel in acreage, and substantial plantings of merlot, sauvignon blanc, and several Rhône varietals thrive. Yet the most prized remains zinfandel. Old-vine zinfandel was honored recently as one of Slow Food's Ark Products, an international program that recognizes handcrafted products of limited production, regional distinction, and superior quality.

Dry Creek Valley is accessible. Most of the wineries are open at least some of the time, though if you want to savor the true nature of the valley, search out wines made from the valley's own grapes, such as the zinfandels of A. Rafanelli Winery, Nalle Winery, Preston Vineyards, Teldeschi Winery, Seghesio, and Quivira Vineyards.

Russian River Valley

The Russian River Valley AVA, established on November 21, 1983, resembles a roughly drawn square nearly exactly in the center of Sonoma County. The region surrounds about a third of the 120-mile-long river and its floodplains, sweeping from Monte Rio to western Santa Rosa and from Sebastopol to northern Healdsburg. Within the boundaries of the AVA are ninety-six thousand acres or 150 square miles, close to fifty wineries, and over ten thousand acres planted to grapes. Although there are tasting rooms, restaurants, and inns, much of the valley is sparsely populated, with quiet country roads shaded by bay, manzanita, and gnarled oaks garlanded with delicate Spanish moss. The region is defined by almost nightly fog that influences viticulture, agriculture, and quality of life. When inland valleys are sweltering, this natural air conditioning keeps nights pleasant.

Although acclaim came late to this fertile land, the history of grape farming extends back to the Russian period. Grapes were planted here as early as 1836, when Yehor Chernykh, a Russian immigrant, planted two thousand vines over a three-year period at Chernykh Ranch, which old maps indicate was located near where Green Hill and Graton Roads intersect today. According to the historian

William Heintz of Sonoma, this was the third planting of vineyards by the Russians. The first was in 1817, in what is today the Sonoma Coast AVA, five years before Padre José Altimi planted his grapes. Although the padre is generally credited with planting our first vines, the Russians apparently beat him to it, but their efforts don't seem to have influenced viticulture. The door of history won't open any wider on these early vineyards; we can see the vines through a small crack, but we don't know a thing about the wine, or even if any was made.

Today, grapes outstrip every other enterprise in acreage and in reputation. As the twentieth century drew to a close, old apple orchards were making way for new vineyards. A myriad varietals thrive in the fertile alluvial soils of Russian River Valley, and because of the moderate climate, they develop their flavors slowly, just as the peaches of Dry Creek and the grapes of the western slopes of Sonoma Mountain do. Foggy nights strengthen the acid necessary for properly balanced wine.

Chardonnay, both for still and sparkling wine, is highly successful. The sauvignon blanc made by J. Rochioli Vineyards is one of the best examples of the varietal in the state. There are scattered vineyards of old-vine zinfandel, syrah, cabernet sauvignon, valdiguié (also known as Napa gamay), and more than a dozen other varietals. Yet a single grape is responsible for the frenzy of attention that Russian River Valley is enjoying.

Everyone wants pinot noir from this valley. Joseph Swan Vineyards, founded in 1968, enjoyed early acclaim for its zinfandels, but was also one of the first successful producers of the seductive pinot noir grape. As knowledge of its wily ways has increased and as viticultural techniques have improved—pinot noir, arguably more than any other single grape, is made in the vineyard rather than the winery—Russian River Valley pinot noir has taken center stage. Dehlinger Winery, one of the region's most consistently excellent, appeared in 1975, and has been joined by Kistler Vineyards, Lynmar Winery, Paul Hobbs Cellars, and J Wine Company.

To understand the evolution of pinot noir here, we must look to Joe Rochioli, who was growing luscious fruit on Westside Road long before pinot noir became the county's most sought-after grape. The Rochioli family settled here in 1938, when most of the valley floor was planted to hops. Joe is full of colorful tales of this time, including stories of catching robins in the creek beds and eating them stewed with polenta, a story repeated by Italian immigrants throughout Sonoma County.

Rochioli planted his first vineyards in 1959 and sold his grapes for about two hundred dollars a ton. When Joe talks about this time, his eyes twinkle with mischief. Everyone was bragging about the high yields—ten tons, fifteen tons, they boasted—of their gamay vines. He refused to plant gamay. Instead he bought premium pinot noir buds from Wente Brothers and thinned his crop before it was fashionable. Was it vision or stubbornness that motivated him? I can't tell. The superiority of Joe's fruit remained a secret when the beautiful clusters were dumped in with a melange of inferior grapes that became an inexpensive bulk wine known as California burgundy. It's as if he could see the future, as if he knew what would come if he held his ground.

In 1971, Davis Bynum built the first winery on Westside Road. The labels of the winery's inaugural vintage, 1973, included the notation "From the vineyard of Joseph Rochioli, Jr. on Westside Road in the Russian River Valley," the first local label to give credit to a grower. By the early 1980s, Gary Farrell, who had come to Davis Bynum for summer work and stayed on first as a cellar worker and soon as winemaker, was attracting increasing attention with his finely crafted wines. In 1982, Farrell made Bynum's wine, wines for the newly established J. Rochioli label, and for his own label. By 1986, Joe Rochioli, joined by his son Tom, had built a winery and Tom had taken over as winemaker. Today the vineyard-designated wines of J. Rochioli are among the best in the country.

Davis Bynum's early recognition of growers, Joe's instincts and talents as a farmer, and Gary's inspired winemaking focused attention on this particular area of Russian River Valley. Williams & Selyem Winery, founded quietly by Burt Williams and Ed Selyem in a garage in nearby Fulton, eventually made an enormous impact with their hard-to-get wines that somehow garnered more exuberant praise from mainstream critics than the others did. From a small winery built near the famous Allen Vineyard, farmed but not owned by Joe Rochioli, Williams & Selyem helped position Russian River Valley pinot noir as among the best in the world. When the winery was sold in the late 1990s, its influence began to wane.

Although Gary Farrell has never sought the limelight, his influence on the area's winemaking cannot be overestimated. Whenever I try to write about his wines, I'm faced with a professional dilemma. Do I admit to having a favorite, or do I objectify my personal inclinations and declare that I have found the best? Either way, I have never had better wines than his. Gary's style, characterized by remarkably silky textures (think satin on velvet), generous but elegant fruit, and stunning delicacy and complexity, suits me.

Gary has been a leader in the development of vineyard designations, though his efforts on behalf of grape growers have worked against his best interests to some degree. "My philosophy has always been to credit the grower whenever possible with vineyard designations, but I've seen it go straight to their heads and then the price goes through the roof," Gary told me during the 1999 harvest when he was paying three thousand dollars a ton for zinfandel and thirty-five hundred dollars a ton for pinot noir.

In the fall of 1999 construction began on his new winery, located on Westside Road just south of Wohler Bridge. Although this is somewhat of an expansion—he will continue as consulting winemaker for Davis Bynum—Gary will remain the hands-on winemaker he's always been, using open-top fermenters, punching down by hand, focusing on fruit from single vineyards, and developing his own vineyards.

The future promises changes in Russian River Valley, including an adjustment of its boundaries. In late 1999, an application was submitted to the Bureau of Alcohol, Tobacco and Firearms (BATF) to redraw the lines in order to exclude those areas that do not share the region's definitive characteristics and to eliminate overlaps with the boundaries of adjacent AVAs. The application also identifies five sub-appellations (a category the BATF does not yet recognize), Green Valley, Los Molinos, Santa Rosa Plain, the Middle Reach, and Sebastopol Hills.

Green Valley

Nestled in the southeast corner of Russian River Valley, Green Valley AVA is defined by sandy Goldridge loam, almost daily fog, and cold nights. The pinot noir grape and the Gravenstein apple are its acknowledged stars. This is where the spring apple blossoms drape the hillsides like unfurled bolts of lace, and where the late summer light bathes the hillside orchards and vineyards in gold. Country roads curve through flower farms and market gardens, and wind up hills towards spectacular views of Mount Saint Helena. From the highest points, you can see the Pacific Ocean and watch the fog creep inland.

Forestville, Graton, and northern Sebastopol are within Green Valley's border, which was established in 1983 largely through the efforts of Barry Sterling of Iron Horse Vineyards. There are a total of thirty-two thousand acres, with over a thousand acres of grapes and more than six hundred acres of apples. There are nine wineries and dozens of vineyards. Before Prohibition, three wineries thrived in Green Valley, but during the dry years, most vineyards were converted to apples.

"Green Valley pinot noir has a distinct style. It is much more fruit driven, with bright fruit flavors, lush textures, and crisp acidity," according to Forrest Tancer, who has been the winemaker at Iron Horse Vineyards for three decades. "It is distinctly California . . . one of the really cool things about Green Valley," Tancer says, "is that it allows us to stop looking over our shoulders at Burgundy."

Chardonnay thrives here, too, of course; the signature white grape of Burgundy prefers the same climate as pinot noir. Dutton Ranch produces some of the area's most sought-after chardonnay; ten wineries currently produce vineyard-designated wines with Dutton grapes.

In spite of the enormous diversity of agriculture in Green Valley, its reputation has been secured by the region's ultrapremium wines such as Iron Horse and Marimar Torres Estate, in part because wines travel farther than other farm products and in part because it is wine that can bear a name on a label.

Knight's Valley

Knight's Valley, the most remote of our AVAs, is tucked between Alexander Valley, Chalk Hill, and Napa County, up against Mount Saint Helena. High above the floor of the valley, a peregrine falcon circles and glides on currents of warm air. Neat rows of chardonnay grapevines hug the ground and descend toward a wide bowl-shaped valley of flourishing red grapes, the Les Pavots Vineyard of Peter Michael Winery. Soils here are alluvial—literally, washed in water—and rocky; huge boulders here are often home to the rattlesnakes that thrive in dry heat. Rising above it all like a grand sentinel is Mount Saint Helena, the area's most influential feature, whose stark rocky summit seems close enough to touch. The still afternoon is interrupted only by the occasional melodic song or startling squawk of a lone bird.

Knight's Valley can be hard to find; even addresses encourage confusion—the nearest post office is in Calistoga. This obscure region feels like an extension of Napa Valley, yet it is one of Sonoma's richest historical treasures. Its history is agricultural. Shortly after Thomas Knight made the journey from his native Maine in 1845, an explosion destroyed his possessions, leaving him stranded in what was then known as Mallacomes Valley. Knight turned to farming and was so successful that he purchased Rancho Mallacomes, the northern portion of the valley, in 1853 from José de los Santos Berryessa, who had received the land in a grant from the Mexican governor. By the 1880s, Knight's Valley had several dozen acres of vineyards and three wineries, but by the early 1900s the industry all but vanished, and a succession of fires destroyed what remained of the once-bustling resort town of Kellogg.

Beringer Wine Estates in the Napa Valley is the principal landowner here with nearly six hundred acres of the valley floor under vines, the first planted in the 1960s. The enormously successful winery grows cabernet sauvignon, cabernet franc, merlot, sauvignon blanc, sémillon, and sangiovese here; Beringer's Knight's Valley Cabernet Sauvignon is one of the winery's most prized wines.

Although Peter Michael Winery, the AVA's only winery, is on the valley floor near the intersection of Ida Clayton Road and Highway 128, it is the winery's mountain vineyards that express the region's character. Elevation protects the vines from the valley's heat, and the rocky soils produce grapes with intense, concentrated flavors. Among the most obscure of all of Sonoma County's wines, they are also among the finest.

Sonoma Mountain

Four million years ago, an east-facing slope of Sonoma Mountain blew open, sending molten rock and hot ash raining out over the upper valley. Remnants of the eruption are everywhere: large obsidian boulders, veins of ash, extensive marine deposits, all characteristics of the ancient violence that shaped this hauntingly beautiful area. Sonoma Mountain itself rises to a peak of 2,463 feet, and the sleeping volcanic range, the western rim of Sonoma Valley, stretches from southern Santa Rosa southeastward more than fifteen miles to the Carneros wetlands. It is one of the county's most distinguishing features.

Although the mountain and much of the countryside that surrounds it are entirely within the large AVA of Sonoma Valley, a portion of this rustic region was declared an AVA in its own right in 1985, primarily through the efforts of Patrick Campbell of Laurel Glen Vineyard and David Steiner, who planted his first vineyards here in 1973. The three wineries and couple of dozen vineyards here are entitled to use either designation.

There are two distinct growing regions, the east-facing or Glen Ellen side, and the Santa Rosa–Petaluma side, with its west and northwest orientation. The eastern side, sheltered as it is from afternoon breezes rushing through the Petaluma Gap, is hot, ideal for the cabernet sauvignon that is considered the jewel of the mountain. Grapes on the eastern slopes receive sunlight earlier in the day, an orientation that also protects them from searing afternoon sun. This translates into slow, even ripening of the grapes, which reach maturity before sugars become too high, which in turn results in complex, suave wines with softer tannins and full fruit flavors.

"Sonoma Mountain cabernet is not like any other cab," Rod Berglund of Joseph

Swan Vineyards explains. "There is an unusual richness on the palate, the tannins are round and soft at the same time . . . these grapes truly are about the expression of a place, of *terroir*." This Russian River Valley winery has made Sonoma Mountain-designated wines for years, since the late Joe Swan fell in love with its chardonnay decades ago.

"Clearly, this is cabernet country," says Patrick Campbell, who saw the region's first vineyards while living at the Sonoma Mountain Zen Center. Campbell purchased his mountain property in the late 1970s and for several years sold his grapes to other wineries before launching his own label. The reputation of the mountain is largely based on the wines from Laurel Glen Vineyard, Campbell's signature label, known for its graceful cabernets that age elegantly. Only the winery's best estate cabernet sauvignon goes to market bearing that label. Counterpoint, a second label, is reserved for those lots of wine that don't meet the Laurel Glen standard. (For three other labels, Quintana, Terra Rosa, and REDS, Campbell uses grapes from Sonoma, Napa, the Central Valley, and Chile.)

David Steiner planted cabernet sauvignon on the Santa Rosa side of the mountain in 1973, but in the late 1990s turned his attention toward the Burgundy temptress. "There is a lot of coastal influence on the west side, particularly from the wind," David explains. "There is full sun all year, but it's not hot so you have light intensity without heat." Steiner's vineyards are about 1,000 feet above the valley floor; there is a temperature inversion as you ascend and it is fueling expectations about pinot noir.

The Benzigers have made Sonoma Mountain accessible to visitors. In the summer, hundreds make the short drive up the mountain to the vast, whimsical grounds of Benziger Family Winery, where the Acropolis, built by an eccentric doctor who previously owned the property, overlooks a small valley. Eighty-five acres of terraced vineyards sit above the valley floor in a natural bowl-shaped valley with both east and west exposure. Grapes from these vines produce the winery's two estate wines, Tribute Red and Tribute White, blends named to honor Bruno Benziger, the family patriarch who died in 1989. Other Benziger Family wines and those of its second label, Benziger Imagery, are made from grapes grown throughout California. The partly motorized tour of the winery includes budding, grafting, and pruning demonstrations, a visual history of the region's earthquakes, and a display of the process of cooperage or barrelmaking. The winery's art gallery houses original paintings commissioned to appear on the Benziger Imagery label series.

Tony Coturri has been quietly making organic wines at Coturri Winery on Sonoma Mountain since 1979, but because of traffic considerations and zoning restrictions, the county will not allow him to put in a tasting room. For now, Benziger is the only show, except, of course, for the imposing mountain itself.

Sonoma Valley

On a sunny spring day, Sonoma Valley is spectacular, bathed in a sea of vibrant, relentless green, nearly surreal in its intensity. This fertile arm of land that arcs between the Mayacamas Mountains and the Sonoma Mountains from San Pablo Bay north for twenty-five miles was declared an AVA in 1981; its history and geography made the declaration inevitable. It is the best known of the county's appellations.

Dozens of varieties of grapes thrive in microclimates throughout the valley. There are market gardens and farms, olive orchards, an olive oil mill, cheese factories, dairy cattle, and an ostrich farm in addition to more than 6,000 acres of grapes—total acreage is 103,200—many high above the valley floor on the western flank of the Mayacamas range, the eastern boundary of the appellation. In this rugged terrain, vineyards thrive in elevations higher than many on Sonoma Mountain. Here, Carmenet Vineyard is known for its bold Bordeaux-style reds with their stalwart tannins, wines reined in by military-style discipline you could say, soldiers of the vine. Not far from Carmenet is Louis Martini Winery's Monte Rosso Vineyard, which in some years delivers a truly memorable cabernet sauvignon. (Martini is a Napa winery; it is common for large wineries to maintain vineyards in several areas.)

Wine Brats

It was probably inevitable that a group such as the Wine Brats, founded in Sonoma in 1993, would emerge. In the late 1980s, with the neo-Prohibitionist movement in full swing and wine pretensions at an all-time high, the sons of several of the valley's oldest winemaking families went off to college. Their peers, they soon discovered, drank beer or tequila; wine was viewed as an affectation. Not so, insisted the young men who grew up with wine on the table (and probably in their own glasses) daily. After graduation, Jeff Bundschu, Jon Sebastiani, and Mike Sangiacomo compared notes, and it wasn't long before they began speaking publicly as a team. One thing led to another and Wine Brats, its title taken from the affectionate nickname used by their parents and townsfolk, was launched. Like *Wine X Magazine*, Wine Brats, which now has close to fifty chapters nationwide, has been tremendously successful with its exuberant, sassy approach to wine. Chapters host WineRaves ("wine tastings at hip venues featuring contemporary music, performance art, interactive fashion, new media and tasty food," one invitation reads) and pursue special projects, such as *The Wine Brats' Guide to Living, with Wine*, published in 1999 by St. Martin's Griffin.

On the valley floor, many of the best-known wineries can be reached by the heavily traveled Highway 12, the region's major artery. Several are within a stone's throw of one another. Only Matanzas Creek Winery is tucked away by itself on Bennett Valley Road, on the northern edge of Sonoma Mountain. It is worth the drive; the winery with its spectacular fields of lavender and inspired landscaping is one of the most beautiful estates in the county.

No single varietal has distinguished itself as the star performer here, but the old-vine zinfandels of Ravenswood, B. R. Cohn Olive Hill Cabernet Sauvignon, Gundlach-Bundschu Zinfandel, and the pinot noir and zinfandels of Kenwood Vineyards are among the valley's finest offerings.

On the Kunde estate near the northern end of the valley are the remnants of the Dunfillan Winery, built in 1880 by James Drummond and the site of the first cabernet sauvignon production in America. All that remains of the original structure are four brick and stone walls. In early spring, the walls are green with a thick layer of moss; oak branches hang overhead where the roof once stood. It is an enchanting location for a wedding, and many are held here. This two-thousand-acre estate is one of the largest of the valley. Seven lakes, a duck preserve with fifty species, and thousands of square feet of caves carved into the mountain are poised amidst seven hundred acres of new and old vineyards, some of which were planted in the 1870s by early Italian immigrants. For years, most of the grapes were sold to Sebastiani Vineyards, but the Kunde family launched its own label, Kunde Estate Winery, in 1989.

Sonoma Valley is a delightful place to visit; many of its wineries now offer special food and wine pairings on weekends, summer barbecues, concerts, art shows, golf tournaments, and Shakespeare festivals.

Los Carneros

It's a visual cliché: the blanket of morning fog that stretches itself over the vineyards; the mid-morning breezes that break it up; the tall grasses rippling in the winds that by noon have gathered strength and will blow until sunset. This is Los Carneros, the only AVA that defies geopolitical boundaries and in a grand gesture of geographic equality spans the southern borders of both Sonoma and Napa Counties.

The AVA became official on September 19, 1983, through the efforts of vintners from both counties. Unlike larger appellations that vary widely in terrain and temperature, Los Carneros is homogeneous, with a cool climate, minimal rainfall, infertile soils, and physical barriers: a bay, a river, a creek, and two mountain ranges. There are about twenty-two wineries and dozens of vineyards. Several wineries outside the AVA maintain vineyards here.

Among the wetlands of southern Carneros, along the edge of San Pablo Bay, are acres of salt marshes, returned to Napa County years ago by Cargill Salt; rumor has it that a keen observer might see pink flamingos feeding on tiny brine shrimp that tint the marshes pale pink, nearly the color of the exotic birds' feathers. A major stop along the Pacific Flyway, this land is home to dozens of species of waterfowl and shorebirds that spend at least part of the year nesting in the vast system of marshes, sloughs, and natural, restored, and manmade wetlands that form the northern rim of the bay.

Carneros is the land of tragic head-on collisions and the Sears Point Raceway, of the Cherry Tree and other roadside stands offering juice—alas, most of it from out of state—to thirsty tourists. It is the truest gateway to the wine country, the first appellation visitors from the south enter, a diminutive flower of a region that opens toward Napa Valley to the northeast and Sonoma Valley to the northwest. Standing near a century-old bridge over Huichica Creek, you can see the two valleys as they unfold northward, the Mayacamas rising between them. The view from this vantage point is singularly moving and reveals a spectacular grandeur that motorists, zooming by not far from this isolated enclave, never suspect. If ever there were an argument for turning onto that back road we pass daily, this is it.

Today, grapes dominate in Carneros, but its agricultural history includes pears, apples, truck farms, and, of course, the sheep for which the region is named. Of the 36,900 acres within Carneros, about 8,000 are planted to grapes. Some sheep still graze here, but there are more goats. Laura Chenel tends her growing herd and makes her cheese at the old Stornetta Dairy in the heart of the AVA.

As you would expect given the cool climate and long growing season of Carneros, chardonnay and pinot noir are the star varietals. But it is more than just the temperature that shapes the performance of these grapes. Virtually everyone involved in viticulture in Carneros talks about the distinctive qualities of these wines, claims that have been documented by independent tests and studies (the results of which are available at the wine libraries in Napa and Sonoma). High acid levels, a component that enhances a wine's ability to age, is a unifying element in most Carneros wines. Chardonnays are often leaner than they are elsewhere, with elements of citrus and cloves. You'll find clove in Carneros pinot noir, too, along with bright fruit flavors, most notably cherry, and a subtle complexity that makes some people think of mushrooms, tobacco, and leather.

"I would choose Carneros [for growing grapes] over anywhere in the world," says Mike Crumly, the vineyard manager at Gloria Ferrer. A growing season that stretches from early March to mid-October—several weeks longer than in other regions—allows the grapes to mature slowly, developing complexity and depth. Because of the minimal rainfall and limited ground water, flavors are concentrated. Soils here are at best moderately fertile and tend to reduce a vine's vigor, which is to say that the vine struggles to produce greenery; more of its energy goes into the fruit, a grapevine's investment in its future. Crumly sees his job as that of a shepherd, of making gentle alterations to a vine so that its seasonal rhythm can unfold naturally. Some clones, for example, have a tendency to produce abundant leaves, so he plants them on the rocky hillsides, where the infertile soil challenges the grapevine. Weaker clones are planted on the valley floor, where moderate fertility encourages growth. If he can grow a balanced vine, Crumly explains, the vine itself will do the rest. The famous winds of Carneros also have a tremendous influence on the character of its fruit. With winds blowing daily, often fiercely, grapes develop thicker skins in an attempt to stave off evaporation; this in turn results in the spiciness of the fruit.

Today there are celebrated sparkling wine estates here, including Domaine Carneros, Artesa (formerly Codorniu Napa), and Gloria Ferrer Champagne Caves. Schug Carneros Estate, best known for its elegant still pinot noirs and chardonnays, makes an exuberant sparkler. Domaine Chandon has seven hundred acres of vineyards here (the winery is in Napa Valley); the main Buena Vista Winery (the historic estate is in Sonoma Valley) is near the southern edge of Carneros. Viansa Winery and Marketplace, established by Sam and Vicki Sebastiani in 1988, includes a ninety-acre wetlands preserve ringed with a system of trails, boardwalks, and photography blinds; a staff naturalist leads early morning birdwatching tours in the spring, summer, and fall. If you know you'll be here, pack binoculars and pick up a copy of the *Field Guide to Carneros*, available at many of the region's wineries. Nearby, Cline Cellars defies current viticultural wisdom by focusing successfully on Rhône varietals such as roussanne, marsanne, syrah, and viognier as its estate wines. Roche Winery, the first estate one encounters when coming from the south, produces a delicate, almost ephemeral pinot noir.

It is not possible to speak of Carneros, especially its pinot noir, without acknowledging Saintsbury, founded in 1981 by David Graves and Richard Ward. The wines are consistently excellent and have done much to focus attention on Carneros. Yet there are many outstanding wineries and growers here, Tony Soter, with his Etude wines, Acacia Winery, MacRostie Winery, and Richardson Vineyards and Beckstoffer, DeSoto, Hudson, and Sangiacomo vineyards among them.

Northern Sonoma

Within Bordeaux, one of the best-known regions of France, are thirty-seven smaller appellations, nearly two hundred fifty thousand acres of grapes, and thirteen thousand vintners. It is helpful to keep this in mind when trying to understand Northern Sonoma as an AVA. The area is as vast and amorphous as its name, encompassing Chalk Hill, Knight's Valley, Alexander Valley, Dry Creek Valley, Russian River Valley, and most of Green Valley within its embrace. There are more than a hundred wineries, over 150 soil types, hundreds of vineyards, and tremendous variations in climate. From the point of view of *terroir*, Northern Sonoma makes little sense.

The original application for the appellation identifies three unifying elements; a climate cooled by the Pacific instead of by San Pablo Bay; sedimentary rather than volcanic soils (a claim that ignores the ancient lava beds of Chalk Hill); and a history shaped primarily by Italian immigrants. Gallo of Sonoma was the primary force behind the designation, made official on September 10, 1990, and is the only winery regularly using the description Northern Sonoma on its labels. It is reserved for Gallo of Sonoma's estate program, which consists of two wines, chardonnay and cabernet sauvignon. The winery is in Dry Creek, but its vineyards are located in several viticultural areas. Without an umbrella designation such as Northern Sonoma, these ultrapremium wines—the chardonnay sells for forty-five dollars; the cabernet for sixty-five dollars—could not be labeled Estate Bottled. Gallo owns six thousand acres here, three thousand of which are planted to grapes. In the 1940s, Julio Gallo made a commitment to preserve an acre of natural habitat for each acre planted with grapevines, a pledge the company honors today. With most large appellations, it is difficult to provide a succinct summary of the area's wines. With Northern Sonoma, it is impossible. Yet with Gallo's focus on just two varietals, the rest of the country may come to identify Northern Sonoma with ultrapremium chardonnay and cabernet sauvignon, a perception that can't hurt Sonoma County's reputation.

Sonoma Coast

"Welcome to the fog bank," a friend said as I stood on the deck of my new home and gazed at the frothy white soup on the horizon. As its name implies, marine influences are said to define this AVA, an area that encompasses all or portions of six other appellations and more than sixty wineries. Three wineries—Annapolis, Flowers Vineyard and Winery, and Wild Hog Vineyard—exist only in Sonoma Coast, which stretches from the border between Sonoma and Marin Counties north to the Mendocino County line. The AVA overlaps Carneros, intersects Sonoma Valley and

Sonoma Mountain, sweeps through Green Valley and Russian River Valley, and follows the coastal range to Mendocino County.

In reality, Sonoma Coast is illusive, its borders illogical. If it is ever to make sense as a unified region defined by fog and cool temperatures, the eastern boundaries need to be redrawn closer to the coast, where several vineyards of pinot noir have distinguished themselves. It was originally established through the efforts of Sonoma-Cutter Vineyards so that the company could use the description Estate Bottled on its wines that are made from grapes grown in the Russian River and Sonoma Valleys.

A frenzy of vineyard planting has been underway here. As the twentieth century drew to a close, battles raged between large companies intent on clear-cutting forests of tan oak and redwoods and environmentalists determined to limit viticulture. In the end, it may prove largely self-regulating, as history continues to teach us. In 1999, grape prices were high and yields were down. When grape prices plummet, as they surely will with the next bumper crop, recession, or shift in public interest, won't farmers rip out vines in favor of the next lucrative endeavor? Wouldn't you?

CHAPTER 3

Indulgence

Visiting Sonoma County

DRIVING FROM WINERY TO FARM TO NURSERY AND ON TO ANOTHER WINERY was not so long ago a leisurely way to spend a day in Sonoma County. It was something I did frequently. Sometimes my two young daughters and I would dress in pretty skirts, lacy tops, and big floppy hats, I'd pack a lavish lunch, and we'd pretend we were living in another time and place, Zola's France, say, or Hardy's England. The illusion was easy to sustain; we were often one of the only cars on the road.

Such an adventure is still a delight, but it is no longer so leisurely. So many layers have been superimposed upon this landscape that it is no longer simple to zip about the county, covering dozens of miles in an afternoon. In good conscience I cannot invite you here without offering a few cautionary words, and encouraging you to plan ahead. It is enormously helpful to study a map and identify alternative routes in case the main roads are jammed. You should not try to see the entire county in a day; this has always been impossible because Sonoma County is a big place, covering 1,560 square miles. These days it is best to concentrate on a single geographic area. You should be prepared for unpredictable traffic and plan a few adventures that don't require a car. Some of the most enchanting views can be seen from a canoe, a hot air balloon, a hiking trail, or on horseback. There is an increasing number of good bike trails, too. Come during the off-season (November through April), and visit on weekdays rather than weekends if you can. Traffic might still be a problem—the roads are crowded because of the county's population, not because of visitors—but it won't be as congested as it is at the height of the summer.

Most of the tours in this section do not focus specifically on wine or food, though both are included. Instead, I introduce you to aspects of the county that for the most part I do not discuss elsewhere in this book. If wine is your primary interest, you can easily devise your own tours by reading about Sonoma County's eleven viticultural areas and then referring to the winery listings on pages 303–315, organized by area. In the Resources section, farms and other food businesses that welcome visitors are noted.

As I did in *A Cook's Tour of Sonoma*, I have kept a few secrets. With the eyes of the world turning increasingly to this remarkably abundant, beautiful land, preserving what we all love is crucial. In these tours I lead you off the main trail, but every now and then I let a gate into a secret garden slip by unnoticed or leave a favorite country lane unexplored. Perhaps you will discover them yourself. I have tried to reveal the heart of Sonoma County yet honor the privacy we all cherish. And who knows? You might stumble upon a treasure I've yet to find. These few tours represent only a small glimpse of the grand diversity of the place I call home, a land that continues to delight and surprise me. *Welcome to Sonoma.*

A Gardener's Tour of Sonoma

GARDEN VALLEY RANCH, 10:00 A.M.
PETITE PLAISANCE, 11:15 A.M.
THE GOURMET GOAT, 12:15 P.M.
WILD FLOUR BREAD, 12:45 P.M.
WISHING WELL NURSERY, 1:00 P.M.
WESTERN HILLS RARE PLANTS, 2:15 P.M.
MINIATURE PLANT KINGDOM, 3:00 P.M.
CALIFORNIA CARNIVORES, 3:30 P.M.
BREAK, 4:00 P.M.
ENCHANTED GARDENS, 5:30 P.M.
FARMHOUSE INN, 7:00 P.M.

Sonoma County's reputation as a destination for outstanding wine, food, and geographic splendor is widespread. Still a well-kept secret is that we also have some of the finest nurseries and nursery gardens in the country, at last count, more than seventy, which is no surprise when you consider the work our most famous gardener, Luther Burbank, did here. People come from all over the Bay Area, some of them in rented vans, to purchase seedlings and other plants in the spring and fall. Others come simply to visit their favorite nurseries, which are much more than plant stores. They are tiny worlds of exquisite gardens, enchanting sculptures, radiant ponds and waterfalls, and endless imagination. You don't need to be a gardener to appreciate this lesser known aspect of the county. You just need to be willing to be dazzled.

If you *are* a gardener, get a copy of *The Guide to Sonoma County Nurseries* by Rita and Michael Ter Sarkissoff before you set out. Design a tour to focus on your specific interests—there are nurseries that specialize in cacti and succulents, bamboo,

How to Be a Good & Effective Visitor

· Consult a map for exact directions to all destinations listed here.

· Call for appointments and reservations, and confirm hours.

· If you plan a picnic, bring supplies, a sharp knife, a corkscrew, a small cutting board, a blanket, a tablecloth and napkins, glasses, plates, and silverware. (Traverso's Market in Santa Rosa sells a handy backpack with everything but the blanket.)

· Carry an ice chest (with ice) in the trunk of the car to keep cheese and other foods at the proper temperature.

· Spend your money locally, that is, at independent restaurants, markets, wine shops, record stores, book stores, video stores, clothing stores, movie theaters, and inns rather than at national chains in strip malls, discount malls, and shopping malls. If you aren't certain what's local and what isn't, ask. See Resources (page 295) for recommendations.

· Try new things, even if you're not certain how to pronounce them. (Hop Kiln Winery's Valdiguié, for example, is a worthy red wine; the tasting-room host will be happy to tell you how to pronounce it.)

· If you need to consult you map while driving, pull off the road safely rather than try to read and drive at the same time.

· Check your rearview mirror now and then and, if you're holding up traffic, pull over and let people pass.

· If you are running late, call and alert any restaurant or other location where you have a reservation.

· If your plans change, remember to cancel reservations.

· Call ahead to all wineries (and other locations) that say "by appointment only."

· Recycle, even though you're not at home. Tuck a trash bag into your picnic basket.

· Tip appropriately.

· Memorize: *Sonoma is not in Napa. Zinfandel is a red grape.*

orchids, carnivorous plants, herbs, water lilies, rhododendrons, heirloom vegetables, antique fruit trees, medicinal herbs, bonsai grapevines, Japanese maples, native grasses and trees, iris, daylilies, water plants, roses of every shade and size, and even nurseries that specialize in plants that attract butterflies and hummingbirds.

My tour skirts the edges of development, traveling back roads through dairy country, redwood groves, and too many points of interest to list. If something catches your eye, stop.

Your first destination is **Garden Valley Ranch and Nursery**, the spectacular estate of the writer Rayford Reddell. The main garden is home to thousands of roses, distributed all over the country, including to Caroline Kennedy's wedding in the mid-1980s. Roses from this garden are in a painting of M. F. K. Fisher, by the artist Ginny Stanford of Sebastopol, that now hangs in the National Portrait Gallery in Washington D.C.; Rayford knew Fisher well and for years took bouquets to her every week. A one-acre fragrance garden is tucked away behind the belvedere, where weddings and other events are held. There is a $4.00 charge ($2.00 for children) for self-guided tours of the gardens. Roses are available year round in containers; you can buy bareroot roses in January and February.

After leaving Garden Valley Ranch, head west through Two Rock, once known as Big Valley. There are no nurseries, wineries, or open markets in this pastoral region, just dairy farms, rolling green hills, and a couple of colorful ramshackle restaurants. Vestiges of the community of Bloomfield remain at the intersection of Bodega Highway and Bloomfield Road, where you can enjoy cocktails and a prime rib dinner at **Stormy's Tavern**.

In Valley Ford, you'll stop at **Petite Plaisance**, which grows rare and unusual orchids. Allow time to stroll through the small town before you continue on to the town of Bodega (not Bodega Bay); if you look closely you'll see the steeple of St. Theresa's Chapel, familiar to anyone who has seen Alfred Hitchcock's film *The Birds*. On the corner of Salmon Creek Road, you'll find the diminutive **Gourmet Goat**, the retail outlet for Bodega Goat Cheese, where you can gather a few things for a picnic lunch. (Don't worry about bread; you'll get that shortly.) Drive back through town, pass the Valley Ford-Freestone Road, and watch for Bohemian Highway, where you will turn left. (Look to your left, for the enormous sculpture of an ant on the side of a nearby house.)

This is Freestone, once a stagecoach stop known as Analy. **Wishing Well Nursery** will be on your left, with parking available in front and on the side. Park, and then walk back to **Wild Flour** for bread. On the far side of the parking lot next to Wishing Well is a manmade lake with a replica of the Statue of Liberty, built for the Bicentennial. There's a deck with tables, a good place to eat and relax. After lunch, take a leisurely stroll through the exuberantly eccentric nursery with its glorious sculpture, including the majestic Garland Ladies, who made their debut at the 1915 Pan Pacific International Exposition at San Francisco's Palace of Fine Arts, part of the celebration of the opening of the Panama Canal.

After Wishing Well, continue on Bohemian Highway not quite four miles into Occidental; turn left onto Coleman Valley Road and watch for **Western Hills Rare Plants**, about a mile and a half on your right. Before selecting plants, enjoy the

For Apple Lovers Only

Although the Sebastopol apple industry is no longer a major endeavor, you'll find some of the finest tasting apples in the country here from July, when Gravensteins ripen, through November, when there are still plenty of varieties to take home. For the best sources, pick up a FarmTrails map, visit the **Healdsburg Farmers' Market**, where Joel and Renee Kiff sell dozens of varieties from an experimental apple orchard planted on their farm by the UC Davis Cooperative Extension, and don't miss Sebastopol's **Ace in the Hole Cider** for tasty hard cider, some of it made with local apples. You'll also want a catalog from the **Sonoma County Antique Apple Nursery**, which sells dozens of varieties of apple trees by mail. If you're here in April, the two-day **Apple Blossom Festival** in Sebastopol, with its Saturday parade, is a wonderful, old-fashioned celebration. In August, the **Gravenstein Apple Fair** takes place in Ragle Ranch Park in Sebastopol. The **Harvest Fair**, held the first weekend in October at the **Sonoma County Fairgrounds** in Santa Rosa, includes an enormous display of apples, an apple tasting, and a pie competition.

spectacular three-acre garden with its bridges, ponds, paths, and enchanting varieties of plants collected from around the world.

Your next stop, the *Miniature Plant Kingdom,* is just three or four miles from Occidental, but there are several turns and it's best to get a detailed view before you set out. The Kingdom includes thousands of varieties of plants, including dwarf calla lilies and miniature fuchsias. After your visit, continue on Harrison Grade Road, turn right on Green Valley Road, and left when you get to Highway 116.

If you've had enough of gardens, there are plenty of nearby destinations, including the apple cider pub *Ace in the Hole*, *Kozlowski Farms*, *Iron Horse Vineyards*, *Green Valley Blueberry Farms*, and *Topolos Winery at Russian River Vineyards*. Consult a map and have a great time.

Otherwise, turn left onto Highway 116; in about two miles, you'll come to *California Carnivores* with its intriguing collection of voracious plants on your left. If you've never seen carnivorous plants before, you will be fascinated. But they're not just curiosities; these plants, collected from around the world, are beautiful.

If you need a break, you can get an espresso at nearby Kozlowski Farms, enjoy an apple or pear cider at Ace in the Hole, and take a walk through the *Forestville cemetery*, not far from California Carnivores. Gravestones are nearly as good as a library when it comes to local history.

You have one more stop before dinner, *Enchanted Gardens* on Mirabel Road in Forestville. Dale Greer, the owner of Sonoma County's largest collection of water plants, offers advice about water gardens, along with several dozen varieties of water flowers, including lotus, and bog plants. The displays here include thousands of waterlilies and the dazzling Angel's Trumpet that blooms only at night. Enchanted Gardens is open until dark, so enjoy the changing light before you head on to the *Farmhouse Inn*, on River Road not far from the gardens.

This tour does not reflect the only must-see nurseries in Sonoma County. If you are a serious gardener you'll want to visit the *Nursery at Emerisa's Gardens*, the statuary store *Absolute*, *Luther Burbank's Home and Garden*, and so many other locations; I have barely scratched the surface.

Seasonal tips: If you are in town during Memorial Day weekend, Labor Day weekend, or Artrails weekends in October, you should visit *Maile Arnold's* gardens in Sebastopol. She's one of the county's best landscapers and her themed gardens are accented with sculpture by her husband Warren Arnold, whose studio is here, too. On Sundays during the summer, do not miss *Mom's Head Gardens* in southwest Santa Rosa. Named for a beloved black cat named Mom (and also as a send-up of such English names as Brideshead and Boar's Head), there is no more whimsical, mischievous place in the county. Officially, Mom's Head specializes in herbs but that's not the half of it. There's the Buffalo Gals' Saloon, an old railroad caboose where herbs are dried, Mom's pyramid gravestone, and an infusion of the spirit of the owners, Vivien Hillgrove and Karen Brocco, both film editors, that will warm even the coldest hearts.

Celebration of the Russian River and Its Watershed

In 1998 a group of good souls, led by the energetic Kaye McCabe of Occidental, hosted a celebration of one of Sonoma County's most distinguishing features and essential resources, the 120-mile Russian River. In 1999, the event expanded and seems to be on its way to becoming an established tradition. The two-week celebration begins with a ceremony at the headwaters and ends nine days later when water drawn from the river during the opening ceremony completes its nine-day ritual relay to the mouth of the river and is blessed. The blessed water is taken by boat and poured into the ocean. As the water makes its 120-mile journey by foot, bicycle, canoe, and kayak, daily activities feature classes and workshops, creek restoration, river walks, storytelling, a river cleanup, dances, and art shows.

A Wild Sonoma Weekend

OAKVILLE GROCERY, 1:30 P.M.

TASTING ON THE PLAZA, 2:00 P.M.

ISIS OASIS, 3:00 P.M.

CHATEAU SOUVERAIN, 7:00 P.M.

HOT AIR BALLOON RIDE, 6:00 A.M.

SAFARI WEST, 10:30 A.M.

ARMSTRONG WOODS PACK STATION, 2:00 P.M.

DINNER AT TAVERNA SANTI, 8:00 P.M.

CALIFORNIA RIVERS OR TROWBRIDGE CANOE TRIPS, 8:00 A.M.

FORT ROSS, 10:00 A.M.

SALT POINT STATE PARK, 12:00 P.M.

PEPPERWOOD, OPTIONAL, DUSK

There's nothing like seeing a place from a vantage point other than out of a car window. On this tour, you'll rise above vineyards and farmland in a hot air balloon, meander along the Russian River in a canoe or kayak, ride horses through ancient redwood trees, and visit two wild animal preserves. I suggest making a long weekend of it.

To begin, you'll drive to Geyserville, stopping on the way in Healdsburg, at **Oakville Grocery** for picnic fare and **Tasting on the Plaza** or **The Wine Shop** for wine.

Isis Oasis in Geyserville is a ten-acre refuge of New Age sensibilities, a sanctuary not only for the body and the spirit, but also for endangered animals, including ocelots, bobcats, servals, and one hundred species of rare birds. In this parklike setting with its meadows, fountains, and hidden waterfalls, expect surprises—it is not a typical resort, bed and breakfast, or spa. It is a singular wonder, presided over by the formidable Loreon Vigne. Rooms include teepees, yurts, treehouses, a cottage, and a little bedroom built inside a wine barrel; some have private baths, others are shared. You can arrange for a massage or a tarot reading, attend past-life seminars, enjoy the occasional play at the small theater, or simply soak up the atmosphere. Whatever you choose, arrive early enough to relax and wander the grounds. Dinner is at nearby **Chateau Souverain**, where the chef Martin Coleman creates consistently pleasing meals at reasonable prices. If *langues des chats* are on the dessert menu (they will be an accompaniment), do not miss them; this is, after all, a wild weekend. Martin makes the most adorable *langues des chats* I've had.

You'll have to get up early to arrive at Rodney Strong Vineyards, where Bob Altieri of **Aerostat Adventures** may drive you to an alternate launch location, depending on the weather. The feeling of rising above the land is remarkable and totally unlike flying. There is no sense of acceleration, no struggle to overcome gravity. Rather,

A Scenic Place

When Alfred Hitchcock was making *The Birds,* each morning his limo would wind along D Street in Petaluma on its way to Bloomfield, Valley Ford, Bodega, Bodega Bay, and Bodega Head, where the film was being shot. Hitchcock rode with the window down, friends recall, and often waved to kids walking to school as he passed by. Most people know that *The Birds* and George Lucas's *American Graffiti* were filmed in Sonoma County, but dozens of other movies have been shot here. For a century, filmmakers have sought the open spaces, wild coastline, and classic Victorian buildings of the county. Among the best known:

True Crime (1998), *Scream* (1996), *Lolita* (1996), *Basic Instinct* (1991), *Tucker: The Man and His Dream* (1987), *Smooth Talk* (1986), *Shoot the Moon* (1982), *American Graffiti* (1973), *The Candidate* (1972), *Planet of the Apes* (1968), *The Birds* (1962), *It's a Mad, Mad, Mad, Mad World* (1962), *Shadow of a Doubt* (1942), *Valley of the Moon* (1913)

you feel released, effortlessly unbound. It is one of the most exhilarating feelings in the world. As I've drifted over the dairy country of northern Petaluma and hovered high above Highway 101, I have been amazed to see the ocean appear so close, the coastline a frothy shore of crashing waves. You'll be in the air about an hour, maybe a little more, but it seems like much less.

After you've landed and the balloon has been packed into the van, you'll head back to Rodney Strong Vineyards, where Bob will fix breakfast. By 10:00, you'll be ready for a guided tour of **Safari West,** the four-hundred-acre wildlife sanctuary established in 1978 by Peter Lang. This is neither zoo nor theme park, and visitors are allowed by appointment only. Your tour guide will meet you at the office, where you will likely join a small group. Your first stop will probably be to see Bubba, a beautiful serval—the only wild cat with both stripes and spots—who was orphaned as a youngster. You'll see dozens of species, several of which are extinct in the wild, including white-naped cranes, an Indian hornbill, small herds of addax, scimitar-horned oryx, Arabian oryx, zebra, wildebeest, eland, gazelle, and Watusi cattle with their enormous horns. Allow three hours for the tour. (Safari West also has accommodations, including a cottage, a lodge, and fifteen cushy safari tents, complete with queen-size beds, bathrooms, and fabulous views. This tour includes overnights at Isis Oasis because you're on the road so much and Isis is both less expensive and worth a visit. If you stay overnight at Safari West, don't go anywhere else.)

There are picnic tables near the entrance of Safari West; you can either enjoy lunch here or wait until you get to your next stop, **Armstrong Woods** and the **Armstrong**

Gaye LeBaron Remembers Louie Traverso

When, as a bride, I began my own personal cook's tour of Sonoma County, one of the first things I learned was that Italian counts for a lot.

My husband, who grew up in the southwestern corner of the county surrounded by first- and second-generation Italians and Swiss Italians, had plenty of contacts to get me started. One of our first shopping trips took us to Fred Barella's tiny grocery store and sausage factory at Sixth and Wilson Streets, where Fred's twin daughters watched the front counter and Fred himself, a short, bald, and cheerful man who had once owned a butcher shop in Valley Ford, spent his days in the big, airy back room, making ravioli and two kinds of sausage, breakfast and boiling.

A Saturday morning visit to Barella's always involved a ceremonial glass of Alfonso Rege red, which Fred poured into Kraft cheese-spread glasses from a gallon he kept hidden behind an on-end apple crate. Never mind that it was at least seven hours too early, according to my upbringing. Fred asked John, "How's you mama? How's you papa?," said, "Salute," and we drank. Then we bought our sausage, redolent of fennel, and went on our way.

I was fortunate enough to get in on the last of the Barella era, which ended about 1960. And I have been even more fortunate to have been a customer of Traverso's market for all these forty years and more.

The Traverso family, four generations now, has been teaching me the finer points of *cucina italiana* since the middle of the 1950s. I have thought often, since Louis Traverso died in June of 1997 at the age of eighty-eight, of all the things I know that I wouldn't have known if it hadn't been for Louie, his brother, Enrico, and their years of patient tutelage.

Would I know the difference between Parmigiano and Romano, the relative merits of coppa and Toscano salami, how best to bring dried fungi to full flavor? Not likely. Not without their commitment to teach Santa Rosans about Italian food. This was Louie's stated mission—to make sure that people like me, who didn't grow up with a mama like his in the kitchen—got the best that life had to offer. He did it with dedication, and love.

"Our customers are our friends," Louie told me fifteen years ago, when I sat down with him to talk about changes in California, in Sonoma County, and the progression of the market from "ethnic" to "gourmet."

"We taught them by sharing. We invite you home, eat ravioli with us. You learn."

We learned. We learned always to go hungry to the market, the better to appreciate the slices of prosciutto and fontina, of salami and provolone, that were handed over the counter to whomever happened to be passing the slicer. We learned that the best wine vinegar came from the back room of the old store at Second and A Streets, where 'Mama Lilla' Traverso was in charge of the barrels. We learned that there cannot be a Christmas or Easter feast without panettone. We learned the proper rice for risotto. We learned which canned pasta sauce was best when we were in a hurry. When Louie talked, we paid attention.

The "new" store (1973) is wonderful, but the very mention of the old store, a block over, a block down at Second and A Streets, is enough to bring tears to the eyes of long-time customers. I remember, more than anything else, the smell of that store—the warm bread and hint of vinegar, the smell of garlic and oregano and fennel and allspice, all mingle with our memories of Louie.

At Louie's funeral, the priest talked about the suspended sausages, cheeses, gnarled dried mushrooms. "The sense of smell," he said, "is one of the five windows to the soul, and Louie knew that his market had to reach the whole person."

Our children remember him—their first slice of salami, super thin, the chunk of chocolate from the barrel that widened a youngster's eyes. He taught all of us respect and love for the Italian people. And he reached us, as so many cultures reach us, through food.

He was proud of his role as a teacher. "I've always thought," he told me once, "that the Italian government should give us some recognition. We taught people about Italian food. Did they know what ricotta was? Or mozzarella? Or what to do with olive oil? Not until we showed them!"

—Gaye LeBaron, a columnist for the *Santa Rosa Press Democrat*

Woods Pack Station in Guerneville. You'll have gotten directions when you made your reservations for either a half-day or 1½-hour horseback ride. West Sonoma County was once covered with giant sequoias, the majestic redwoods of which so few remain; now is a good time to remember that this land was the Redwood Empire long before it became the wine country. Your trip will begin with a talk about the ways and wiles of horses, a favorite topic of the owner and tour guide Jonathan Ayers. Depending on the length of the ride, you'll pass through redwood forests, bay forests, and forests of several varieties of oak as you head toward McCray Ridge, an extinct volcano that is now a huge meadow, affectionately called Horse Heaven.

You'll be tired after a day of such adventure, so head back to Isis Oasis and enjoy the hot tubs. You might want to plan ahead and arrange for a massage. For dinner, you'll head to *Taverna Santi* in Geyserville, where Thomas Odin and Francis Dunn, who both worked as chefs at Jordan Winery, offer rustic Italian fare.

On Sunday, you'll have three choices. Do you want to go canoeing on the Russian River, go on a guided kayak tour, or tour the countryside, visiting the Russian settlement of *Fort Ross*, *Salt Point State Park*, and *Kruse Rhododendron Preserve*? (If you've had enough wild adventure, you can always relax in town and visit the area's wineries. *Chateau Souverain*, *Clos du Bois*, *deLorimier Winery*, *Trentadue Winery*, and *Canyon Road Winery* are all nearby, and both *Alexander Valley* and *Dry Creek Valley* are about fifteen minutes away. It won't be as wild as the day I've planned for you, but you'll have a great time.)

Seasonal options: Depending on the time of year, you can arrange a mushroom foray with *Wild About Mushrooms*. Another option is a night at *Pepperwood*, a 3,100-acre estate adjacent to Safari West owned by the *California Academy of Sciences*. This educational and research institution includes the *Hume Observatory*. The academy offers classes here several times a year, and other organizations can arrange private visits for groups up to twenty. Pepperwood is one of Sonoma County's best-kept secrets, yet a night of observing our spectacular sky, with a naturalist on hand to bring the heavens into focus, is one of the best ways to appreciate this area.

Wild Sonoma Picnic Menu

FROM OAKVILLE GROCERY

Della Fattoria bread
Local cheeses: Redwood Hill, Bellwether, St. George, Laura Chenel
Salametti (small hard salami)
Mixed olives
Roasted peppers
Tabbouleh
Sparkling water

FROM TASTING ON THE PLAZA

Gary Farrell Pinot Noir
Gary Farrell Zinfandel
and fruits and vegetables from the farmers' market

Note: You'll need to buy extra food if you plan a night at Pepperwood.

Historic Sonoma

If you really want a sense of the history of any area, visit old cemeteries. The names, dates, and ages of death on gravestones offer many clues to earlier times. There are old cemeteries all over the county, just south of the town of Bodega, on Sullivan Road in Graton, nearby on Green Valley Road, tucked above Highway 116 just before you come into Forestville from the south, and north of Geyserville near the old town of Preston, to name a few of the more rustic ones. A cemetery tour has a special appeal, and so this excursion features more traditional destinations.

Begin at **Buena Vista Winery**, where you *must* see the caves that once housed the tasting room. Today the area is a small museum, but as late as the 1970s it was a charming tasting room. Buena Vista, founded by Count Agoston Haraszthy, is credited as the birthplace of modern California viticulture.

Downtown Sonoma is just five minutes away by car, and you'll find Vella Cheese Factory about a block north of the plaza, on the east side. After your tour, buy some cheese and butter, both for home and for a picnic at your next stop. Although it is not an historical destination, stop at **Artisan Bakers** for bread. If you'd rather not picnic, have lunch late at **Water Street Bistro** in the old downtown section of Petaluma; it offers some of the finest food in Sonoma County in a thoroughly charming, hand-spun room with a small patio for outside dining. If you forego the picnic, take time to see **General Vallejo's Home** on Spain Street.

At **Bartholomew Park Winery**, allow time to walk the grounds and visit the museum, which documents the history of the valley's viticulture with detailed charm. Bartholomew Park Winery includes 450 acres near the eastern edge of Sonoma Valley. For decades, it belonged to Frank and Antonia Bartholomew, who leased the winery and vineyards to Hacienda Winery, which sold the label and closed its doors in 1993. Antonia built a reproduction of Count Haraszthy's mansion, an imposing structure that stands like a manifest ghost in the center of the park, as a memorial to Frank, who died in 1985. When Antonia died in 1990 at the age of ninety, the estate was placed in perpetual trust. The Bundschu family leases the winery and vineyards, and the museum shares space with the tasting room. The building

The Spirit of Lakeville

Several years ago a friend called to tell me that a restaurant was for sale and that it was perfect and I should think seriously about making a bid on it. I knew the place, the old Gilardi's Lakeville Marina; for nearly a decade I had lived not far away in the sprawling, quiet dairy country east of Petaluma. My friend Patrick, who was then a chef I worked with often, and I headed toward Lakeville one afternoon. The rusty old Gilardi's sign was still there, but alongside another one proclaimed "Cold Beer and Weird Food." Inside, Phyllis, the wizened owner, stood behind the bar, smoking and drinking with a couple of friends. After giving us a tour of the ramshackle kitchen, she told us to make ourselves comfy. And then she vanished. Patrick and I waited at the counter and soon were joined by hungry customers eager for burgers. Phyllis was nowhere to be found. Eventually, Patrick and I went behind the counter and fixed up a nice meal for the customers and for ourselves.

Phyllis ran a colorful, wild place with jazz on the weekends and a menu featuring eclectic home cooking, pretty much whatever she felt like making. Among her better-known bartenders was Anne Lamott, who worked here during her drinking days before she became a nationally known writer. Discouraged more by the bad plumbing and limited water supply than anything else, I decided not to follow in Phyllis's admittedly intriguing footsteps.

The history of the marina stretches back to 1852, when it was known as Lakeville Landing and was the point of entry for visitors when there were no highways and few roads. The river—really more of a broad creek and tule marsh—was shallow and steamboat captains were reluctant to traverse its length. Instead, passengers had to board stagecoaches and goods had to be transferred to oxcarts to complete the bumpy journey to town.

For years now, the place has been a Greek restaurant called Papa's Taverna, and it continues to live up to its colorful past. Upstairs in the sedate cafe, customers linger over early dinners, watching the placid river and the occasional boats that dock here, completely unaware that, downstairs, there's a Greek band playing and dancing lessons are underway while customers down ouzo and cheap red wine amidst some of the kitschiest decor in the county. Phyllis's spirit lives on. And here's a tip: This is one of the best places in the county to watch the rising of the full moon.

itself is rich with historical significance; it has been a women's prison, a home for epileptic boys, and a receiving hospital.

The next stop is **Petaluma Adobe State Historic Park**, where General Vallejo presided over his sixty-six-thousand-acre ranchero. Recently restored, the Adobe offers a glimpse of early California architecture and daily life, with displays, demonstrations, and historical reenactments. There are costumed docents and hands-on activities, so forego the next destination if you can't tear yourself away.

But if it's time to get out into the sun, head to town for a **walking tour of Petaluma**. Take your time, and stop by the **Twisted Vine** for a glass of wine, if you'd like. On the edge of downtown is **Volpi's**, your last stop before dinner. Check out the plaque on the side of the building; Volpi's is said to have operated continuously during the dry years and was the first local establishment to be issued a license to serve alcohol after Repeal. The market is no longer the jumble of enticing Italian ingredients it once was—too much competition, the owners say—but the Speakeasy in the back is unchanged, and old-timers still gather here after a day of farming. Sometimes there's an accordionist, and the place is utterly without modern conceits. I usually feel as if I'm intruding on a private party, but folks are friendly and will welcome you if you relax. If you get really comfy, you could step next door to Volpi's Restaurant for a family-style Italian meal. But I suggest you head out to **Papa's Taverna** (see The Spirit of Lakeville, opposite), not because the food is better—it isn't—but because it's a one-of-a-kind place, with an interesting history.

Seasonal options: Both **Petaluma Adobe** and **Fort Ross**, about an hour and a half drive to the north, recreate early community life through **Living History Days**. Contact the specific park for details.

Sonoma Provence Tour

SONOMA VALLEY FARMERS' MARKET, 9:30 A.M.

B. R. COHN WINERY, 11:00 A.M.

THE OLIVE PRESS, 11:30 A.M.

MATANZAS CREEK WINERY, 1:00 P.M.

DE LOACH VINEYARDS, 2:00 P.M.,
    OR IRON HORSE VINEYARDS, 2:30 P.M.

PRESTON OF DRY CREEK, 3:30 P.M.

HEALDSBURG TOWN SQUARE, 4:30 P.M.

HEALDSBURG CHARCUTERIE, 7:30 P.M.

As one enters Provence from the north, there is a place that never fails to have a magical effect on my spirits . . . the road passes through a gorge that pinches right up to the shoulder of the autoroute, then opens out upon a vast, vine-covered plain. The effect is emotionally exhilarating, like the untying of a mental knot, a release and a shock of open

space within that mirrors the widening landscape without. . . . Shortly afterward, a large
road sign announces: *Vous êtes en Provence.*

—Kermit Lynch, *Adventures on the Wine Route* (Farrar, Straus and Giroux, 1988)

Although Kermit Lynch, a well-known wine merchant in Berkeley, wrote this passage about the south of France, it expresses the feeling I have each time I drive north through the Novato Narrows, the stretch of Highway 101 that connects northern Marin County to southern Sonoma. There is a moment when I relax in spite of myself, when diary farms and rolling hills suddenly appear, when the sky widens and a sudden physical knowledge that I am home swells in me, emanating it seems from the very marrow of my bones.

The similarities between these two agricultural regions are so striking that in 1995 they were joined together in an official sisterhood, out of which grew the Sonoma Provence Exchange (which, in the spirit of full disclosure, I should tell you that I founded). Visitors who come here from all over to bask in our glorious, expansive landscape and idyllic climate make the connection. Even Parisians notice. They take a look at our huge blue sky and rolling golden hills and say to their hosts, "Ah, c'est la Provence ici." It is not just the open, agricultural areas of Sonoma, nor the nearby Pacific Ocean; there is something about the size of the sky, the way the sun hits the far hills at dusk, the luminous light of fall, that stirs a physical remembrance in people. They try to give it voice and, more often than not, it comes out as "Provence."

There are other moments when the similarities between Sonoma County and Provence resonate with particularly clarity, the view of the sea from Coleman Valley Road, for example, or the narrow part of Riebli Road as it passes through the remnants of a working farm. M. F. K. Fisher, who spent the last twenty or so years of her life in Glen Ellen, wrote of the dry, parched hills of Provence as resembling the folds of the tawny brown coat of a resting lion, an image she surely saw around her in the dry, parched land along Highway 12.

These similarities are based on much more than the inevitable resemblance of any one wine-growing region to another—the undulating hills, the grazing sheep, cattle, and goats, the olive orchards, the ubiquitous vineyards are all interchangeable. Lavender grows lavishly in both Sonoma and Provence; both regions produce outstanding honey. This tour takes you to the most tangible locations, but wherever you are in Sonoma County, open your eyes to the sky overhead, the horizon, the light streaming through a window. You'll notice, too.

Begin at the *Sonoma Valley Farmers' Market*, where in the summer you'll find sunflowers, the year's first figs, and local honey, all important crops in Provence, too. On your way to the town of Glen Ellen, you'll stop at *B. R. Cohn Winery* to

The Valley of the Hunter's Moon

There is no more beautiful sight than October's Hunter's Moon, an enormous red orange sphere that rises above the vineyards and hillsides of the place Jack London christened Valley of the Moon. Lovely any time, in October the valley is breathtaking. Try to plan your Sonoma Provence tour at this time, and make adjustments in the itinerary so that you stay on the eastern side of the mountain. After Matanzas Creek, head back to **Jack London State Park**. London was dazzled by Glen Ellen, and eventually purchased fourteen hundred acres overlooking the grand valley. If you're energetic, take the trail to Mount Sonoma (a little over three miles). Otherwise, walk the mile to the foundation of Wolf House, an extraordinary structure that had four levels and twenty-six rooms, which Jack built at the height of his success. Sadly, he and his wife Charmian never lived in it. Shortly before it was completed, a fire—the source of which was never discovered—destroyed it; only the foundation remains. At Jack's grave nearby, you can soak up the peaceful beauty he so loved. Before you leave, visit the House of Happy Walls, where Charmian lived after Jack's death. To see the moon rise, you will need a vantage point on Sonoma Mountain, facing eastward and unobscured by trees or buildings. There are plenty of back roads but I must refer you to a map and your own instincts, as I do not want to focus undue attention on this road or that. When the moon rises, it will illuminate the landscape so completely that if your car is safely parked, you should enjoy a stroll and a moon bath. For dinner, I suggest **La Salette**, a charming Portuguese café.

see the vineyards and eight-acre orchard of picholine olive trees and taste the oils and the wines. In Glen Ellen, you'll visit **The Olive Press**, the cooperative mill and store inspired by similar boutique factories all over the south of France.

Next you'll wind over the northern flank of Sonoma Mountain to **Matanzas Creek Winery,** with its spectacular 2½-acre field of lavender. Inside the tasting room, there's not just good wine but also a panorama of lavender-inspired products.

De Loach Vineyards on Olivet Lane in Santa Rosa has been an enthusiastic supporter of the Sonoma Provence Exchange from the start, but you won't have time to visit both De Loach and **Iron Horse Vineyards**, where the founder Barry Sterling is articulate on the similarities between the two regions. If you feel like sparkling wine, head to Iron Horse; otherwise, visit De Loach and be sure to see the beautiful gardens.

Next you'll drive along Westside Road to West Dry Creek Road, winding through vineyards, market gardens, and olive orchards on your way to **Preston of Dry Creek** at the northern end of Dry Creek Valley. The Rhône region of France borders Provence on the north, and here in Dry Creek Valley Preston specializes in Rhône-style blends (as well as old-vine zinfandel).

In **downtown Healdsburg**, you'll have three hours before dinner. You can relax on the square, browse through the shops, or visit the wine library at the Healdsburg branch of the county library, about three blocks north of the square.

Dinner is at the lively **Healdsburg Charcuterie**, where Patrick Martin, who's family is from Provence, offers a robust French-inspired cuisine and his wife Robin presides with good humor in the dining room.

Seasonal options: In August, the **Sonoma Provence Exchange** hosts the **Grand Aïoli**, a Provençal-style celebration of garlic. In December, the **Healdsburg Charcuterie** presents a special holiday dinner, **Provençal Christmas**, which features the traditional thirteen desserts. In June, the Charcuterie has a bouillabaisse dinner, with the traditional fish stew of Provence accompanied by Provençal and Sonoma County wines. In May, the **California Olive Oil Festival** welcomes the public for a day of tasting.

Antiquing in Sebastopol

SEBASTOPOL FARMERS' MARKET, 10:00 A.M.
SEBASTOPOL FINE WINE COMPANY, 11:30 A.M.
THE QUICKSILVER MINE, 11:00 A.M.
PUTTO & GARGOYLE, 11:30 A.M.
SEBASTOPOL'S ANTIQUE SHOPS, NOON TO 5:00 P.M.
LUNCH AT TEA & TAROT ENGLISH TEA ROOM
MARIPOSA, 8:00 P.M.

Sebastopol has a sweet little farmers' market, with tarot card readers, a masseuse, political information tables, and a preponderance of organic farmers, some of whom attend this market and no other. The market runs from June through the end of November, with a constantly evolving selection of fruits and vegetables. When wild king salmon is in season, you'll find it here. Paul Thornton of **Paul's Pacific Fresh** usually sells it smoked; **Stan Carpenter** sells it fresh and smoked, and sometimes has fresh tuna, too. You'll find Susan Parker offering her lotions and creams under the **Solum & Herbe** label. I'm never without the Rose & Silk moisturizing cream. Most of the produce here is organic, whether or not it's certified. You'll find Cliff Silva of **Ma & Pa's Garden** offering his wonderful potatoes, zucchini, celery root, tomatoes, and roses; Ken Orchard of **Orchard Farm** with a bountiful year-round harvest; Nancy Skall of **Middleton Farm** with flawless zucchini blossoms, minuscule haricots verts, and yummy red shallots; and Joan of **Singing Frog Farms** with her extraordinary selection of garlic. But don't limit yourself; talk to all the farmers and try new things before heading to your next destination. **Lucy's Bakery and Restaurant** sells its breads at the market; the pecan sticky buns are positively addictive.

Across the parking lot from the market is the **Sebastopol Fine Wine Company**, where the owner Tony Marti features a diverse collection of wines from around the world, several of which are available by the glass. If you will not be visiting wineries during your visit, this is a great place to pick up some of the county's best selections.

Next, you'll walk a block to Main Street and the **Quicksilver Gallery.** The front of the store offers locally made pottery, knives, and scarves, books by local authors, and a limited but worthy selection of wines and prepared food products from the county's artisan producers. In the back of the store is one of the best galleries in the West County.

You can either walk or drive to your next destination, the diminutive **Putto & Gargoyle**, just one block west of Main Street across from the library on the corner of Bodega Highway and High Street. Putto & Gargoyle can only be described as adorable; its collection of handcrafted candle holders, shelves, vases, cups, bowls, plates, tiles, gargoyles, and other whimsical treasures are thoroughly enchanting. Gerry and Peter Lu are both artists; their work reveals a thoughtful and exuberant spirit. Be prepared to do some holiday and birthday shopping; if you've left your car near the market, you may want to leave your purchases here while you go get it.

You'll next spend the rest of the afternoon visiting antique stores. There are over two hundred antique dealers in Sebastopol, and they attract an enormous number of visitors each year. Stop by any antique shop along Gravenstein Highway South to pick up a map, or get one from the **Sebastopol Chamber of Commerce** across the street from the post office. For lunch , you'll visit Myra Bates Portwood's **Tea & Tarot** which is located inside the Sebastopol Antique Mall. Tea & Tarot is an English tea room, but with several twists. In England, tea is a late afternoon meal, traditionally served at 4:00. Here, tea—both the beverage and the meal—is served all day. Salads are offered along with the more classic selections of finger sandwiches, scones, clotted cream, lemon curd, and scrumptious pastries (a lemon roulade is one of the best things I've ever tasted). As the name implies, there is another dimension, too, one that might make tourists raise their eyebrows and sigh, "only in California." As your tea brews, you will be invited to select a Tarot card (there's a deck on each table); your server will interpret it and encourage you to use it as a source of wisdom and inspiration. For dinner, you'll head to downtown Windsor, where Raymond Tang offers some of the finest cuisine in the North Bay at the diminutive and charming *Mariposa* that he operates with his wife Shawn Kearney-Tang; the wine list always includes some of the finest selections from small Russian River Valley vintners.

Saturday option: If you find yourself in town on Saturday instead of Sunday, you should head to the **Powerhouse Brewing Company**, where rhythm & blues legend Johnny Otis ("Hand Jive," and hundreds of other recordings) hosts a three-hour radio show, broadcast live throughout northern and central California on KPFA-FM from 9 A.M. to noon. As I write this book, Johnny—who has an organic farm just south of town—is in his early eighties and still going strong. And if you have a clothing jones, don't miss *Punch*, with its wild collection of velvet and animal prints, and *Dressers*, one of the best locally owned women's clothing stores in the North Bay. In Cotati, about eight miles southeast of town, is *Threadbare Kid*, Dressers' sister location.

Hispanic Sonoma

In many ways, the Hispanic community of Sonoma County forms a separate but parallel universe, a substantial society that is sadly separate from the dominant culture. Hispanic immigrants may work in the vineyards, farms, and orchards of Sonoma County for years, but usually do not become part of the larger community until they move on to jobs other than farm labor. It's too bad; the separation impoverishes everyone and creates tremendous misunderstandings.

This is not really a tour, because I do not want to create the impression that this valuable community exists for anyone's entertainment. Rather, I want to let you know of this remarkable resource and rich culture. The best tortillas are available in Latino markets, such as *Lepe's Tienda* in Sebastopol and *Lolita's Market* in Petaluma. They are usually delivered in the early afternoon, and they're always still warm and tender. At each of these markets you'll find whatever you need—nopales, *queso cotija*, chorizo, epazote, corn husks, chipotles, annatto seeds, achiote, *lengua*— to make authentic Mexican food.

If it's a meal you want, you must stay out of chains such as Chevy's and the Cantina, which serve Mexican-American food, and look for places with Mexican customers. (If you are offered the choice of a soft or crispy tortilla, it's a clue that you should go elsewhere.) Across from Santa Rosa Junior College, *Taqueria Santa Rosa* serves authentic tacos and burritos. On Todd Road in southwest Santa Rosa,

How Sebastopol Got Its Name

People logically assume the town's name came from the Russians who settled nearby, but Robert Thompson, writing in 1877, credits a fist fight between Jeff Stevens and a man we know today only as Hibbs. Hibbs made a fast retreat to Ben Dougherty's store, with Stevens in pursuit. Dougherty stopped Stevens and refused him entry. The local boys, always keen to see a fight, Thompson says, were displeased that someone was interfering with their fun. The Crimean War was the big news of the day, a constant topic of conversation. The Russians were holding onto Sebastopol on the Crimean Coast, frustrating the French and British troops who were attempting to take it. The boys, eager to fuel the fight, shouted that the store was Stevens's Sebastopol, and the name stuck. It had previously been known as Pine Grove and in 1876 had a population of 250, with a livery stable, a hotel, a butcher shop, blacksmith shop, two doctors, a literary society, a temperance society, and a Grange of the Patrons of Husbandry.

—*Historical and Descriptive Sketch of Sonoma County, California,* 1877

there's **Carniceria Contreras**, an out-of-the-way retail meat shop with an almost exclusively Mexican clientele. If you're looking for *cabrito* (goat), this is the place. On the weekends, you can sometimes find *carnitas* and *chicharron* here, too.

One of my favorite locations for lunch or dinner is **Lolita's Market and Taqueria**, an enormous store with an old-fashioned counter. There's *lengua* (tongue), *birria* (stewed goat), *cabeza* (beef cheeks), *carnitas*, *chile verde*, and a dozen or so other traditional dishes of Mexico. It's not fancy, it's not dining, but it's great traditional food.

In Sonoma, look for **Milagros** on the east side of the town plaza, a great source for Mexican folk art. The charmingly funky **Juanita Juanita** on Arnold Drive is the neighborhood taqueria.

For more information about the Hispanic community of Sonoma County, contact the **Hispanic Chamber of Commerce**. For winery tours in Spanish, call Suzanne Reda of **A Vine Line Tour** (see Resources, page 295).

Seasonal options: Each year, several events—art shows and installations, poetry readings, musical performances—commemorate **Día de Los Muertos**, or Day of the Dead, the Mexican holiday that follows Halloween on November 1 and 2. The **Sonoma County Museum** often sponsors a show, and there are others, too. Check local listings because shows vary year to year. *Día de Los Muertos* is a colorful holiday, with complex myths, traditional foods, and gorgeous decorations. It is also how

Dalliances for Kids

I don't recommend keeping children separate from adults, of taking the kids to McDonald's before real dinner begins, or of dropping them off at the mall. Everyone is enriched when all ages enjoy things together, whether it's a fancy dinner or a hike. We pass on essential cultural knowledge in this way, from the pleasures of the table and the art of conversation to respect for the land and how to deal with a crisis. How can we do this if we don't let our kids eat with us? But I have a hard time seeing the point of schlepping kids from winery to winery; a few have play areas and grape juice tastings, but for the most part, it's a big bore to tag along if you can't see over the counter. If you've come to the wine country with your family, add destinations that will delight youngsters. Here are a few favorites:

SONOMA: Train Town

SANTA ROSA: Howarth Park, Safari West

PETALUMA, PENNGROVE, & COTATI: The Corn Maze, Grossi Farms, Peters Pumpkin Patch, Anderson's Organic Vegetable Patch

WEST COUNTY: Pet-A-Lama Ranch, Westside Farms

I became known as a widow. In 1989, I suggested a story about the holiday to the *Press Democrat*, for which I now write, and offered to prepare some traditional foods and create an elaborate altar (which I often do anyway). At the time, there was no celebration in Sonoma County, and I wanted to lift the profile of the holiday, largely for selfish reasons: I wanted to participate, I wanted altars I could visit. Everything went fine—the altar was my most beautiful ever—until the photographer left my house. Five minutes later, at 5:06 P.M. on October 17, the Loma Prieta earthquake struck. With the San Francisco Marina in flames, the Bay Bridge closed, and more than one major freeway collapsed, there was a good deal of chaos over the next several days. The photographer never returned for the food shots, and when the story ran a week late, the painting above my altar—by the artist Ginny Stanford of her husband, the poet Frank Stanford, who died in 1978—was incorrectly identified as of *my* deceased husband. It never occurred to me to request a printed correction, and so the myth of my widowhood lives on.

CHAPTER 4

Salvation

Saving Paradise

AGRICULTURAL LAND AND OPEN SPACE ARE SO VERY FRAGILE. In a blink of an eye, today's orchard becomes tomorrow's business park, mini-mall, housing development, or starter castle. People who have lived in Sonoma County all their lives feel that the transition from rural land to crowded suburb is already a done deal.

Certainly there has been a sea change, but we're not yet San Jose, a sprawling metropolis south of San Francisco that was as late as the 1960s productive farmland. In fact, agriculture in Sonoma County is enjoying a remarkable vitality. The county's increased population supports better restaurants that in turn support local farms and wineries. Responding to increased consumer awareness, independent grocery stores offer an expanding selection of local foods, many organically grown. The national and international attention given our wines not only allows grapegrowers and winemakers to thrive but also presents lucrative opportunities for specialty food producers who benefit from the value attached to anything with "Sonoma" on its label. Even General Motors warrants a nod of thanks for naming a truck "Sonoma," and thus making the name familiar to thousands of people who never heard of us before.

Countless dedicated, visionary individuals deserve credit for Sonoma County's current status and prosperity; the pioneers who nurtured our singular bounty when it was a well-kept secret have been joined by uniquely talented individuals who bring enthusiasm and innovation to the arena of agriculture and its preservation. Certainly everyone in this book has made an essential contribution to the land's health and the county's prosperity. In this chapter, I take a look at individuals, organizations, and ideas that I believe have either created the foundation or envisioned a future that will allow Sonoma County's rural character to flourish.

Farm Trails

Farm Trails was founded in 1973 by John Smith, then the agricultural commissioner, with the hope that a consortium of small growers, farmers, and producers could gain more public attention than a single farmer could and would be able to encourage people to buy direct from the farm. The map that the group published has been updated every year since (see Sonoma County Farm Tracts, Resources, page 295).

Farm Trails was a novel idea at a time when food shopping had become centralized in supermarkets. All these years later there are people throughout the country with wrinkled Farm Trails maps in the glove boxes of their cars; it has become a model for others like it around the country.

Farm Trails members offer everything from dye plants (Pyr Creek Farms) and medicinal herbs (Jonathan's Palette) to plants that attract hummingbirds and butterflies (Hallberg Butterfly Gardens). There are sources for wine barrels to use in your garden (Born Again Barrels) and Sonoma County's oldest farm stand, Imwalle Gardens, founded in 1886 and presided over today by the charming Joe Imwalle (get him to tell you about the sauerkraut they used to make, and the enormous cabbages they grew for it).

The *Farm Trails Guide* is an indispensable source for Halloween pumpkins and cut-your-own Christmas trees. Many of the tree farms offer wreaths and garlands, holiday crafts, cookies and hot apple cider, farm animals, and music in addition to trees. Pumpkin farms might feature ghoulish decorations, crafts, hay bale labyrinths, displays with live baby farm animals, and the occasional hunter's moon bonfire.

Through Farm Trails, you will discover many of Sonoma County's hidden treasures, only some of which I have been able to highlight here. However, not every member represents an authentic family farm (this is particularly true of the wineries), though these members offer valuable support to the organization.

Farmers' Markets

"If you want to understand the seasons," I tell my students and readers, "just go to the farmers' market and open your eyes." A farmers' market mirrors the earth's rhythms, shrinking to a few vendors in winter, expanding as spring harvests get underway, sizzling in summer heat, and overflowing with fall's bounty. At the peak of the season there are more than a dozen farmers' markets in Sonoma County (see Resources, page 295) and around three hundred statewide; they have become an essential part of many people's lives, including mine. I rarely buy produce elsewhere.

Modern farmers' markets are fairly new. Before 1977, farmers could not sell directly to consumers without using size and packaging guidelines set by the

California Department of Food and Agriculture. Those in conventional farming—the term, however ironic, applied to agricultural techniques in place only since World War II—opposed any relaxation of the guidelines because they feared that farmers would sell inferior produce at lower prices, thus depreciating its value. Retail grocers saw farmers' markets as unfair competition.

Eventually state regulations were adopted that allowed exemptions to standardization laws specifically for direct sales from farmers to consumers. Certified farmers' markets are considered an extension of the farm, a concept and requirement that governs who works at the market; it must be the farmer or the farmer's employee. Each farmer must file and post an application that lists everything offered for sale; market managers make annual visits to each farm to guarantee that every item listed on the application is actually grown on the farm. A farmer caught selling anything purchased elsewhere can be fined and expelled.

The effect of farmers' markets has been exactly the opposite of what opponents feared. Produce at farmers' markets is almost always better than supermarket produce, and consumers have been willing to pay a premium for it. Farmers markets' have increased the value of produce everywhere, and their success has launched a general improvement in produce everywhere.

It's easy to feel small and insignificant when faced with such enormous realities as the building of another shopping mall. Shopping at farmers' markets is an effortless and infinitely pleasurable way to help ensure the vitality of small farms.

Select Sonoma County

In the late 1980s, a group of local farmers, growers, and food producers worked with the Board of Supervisors, the Sonoma County Economic Board, and the UC Davis Cooperative Extension to develop a program to promote local agricultural products to the public. SCAMP (Sonoma County Agricultural Marketing Program) was the first such effort in the country. In 1999, the organization, which by then had changed its name to Select Sonoma County (SSC), celebrated its tenth anniversary. Among SSC's many local, regional, and national campaigns and projects is a certification program that insures that when a product bears the trademarks Sonoma Grown or Sonoma Made, it is what it claims to be: either grown or processed locally.

SSC publishes a guide listing members by category, and like the map published by Farm Trails, SSC's guide has changed format over the years. Today, it's in magazine format, published in association with *Sonoma Business Magazine*. The organization also publishes a quarterly newsletter for members, which include consumers as well as producers. For $35 anyone anywhere can join, receive the newsletter and member guide, and enjoy the satisfaction of supporting family farms and local agriculture (see Resources, page 295).

Synergy

In the summer of 1999, four local agricultural support groups—Select Sonoma County, Sonoma County Grape Growers Association, Sonoma County Wineries Association, and the Sonoma Valley Vintners & Growers Alliance (see Resources, page 295, for these addresses)—came together under one roof, in a complex shared with the California Visitors Center, just off Highway 101 in northern Rohnert Park. It's a great place for visitors to get their bearings and pick up maps, guides, and other tourist information. There's a retail area selling Sonoma County products, and wine is available for tasting and purchase. The Sonoma Provence Exchange, a program of Select Sonoma County, has a display of members' products and information for visitors in both English and French (see Resources, page 295).

Sonoma Land Trust

As distressing as the disappearance of even a single farm is, the transition is a matter of degree, the ebbing of a tide rather than the crashing of a wave. Land will be saved a farm, a dairy, a redwood forest at a time, by organizations such as the Sonoma Land Trust, founded in 1976 by the late Otto Teller of Oak Hill Farm, a self-described curmudgeon with an exuberant commitment to the environment. The Red Barn, where Otto's wife Ann Teller operates a glorious farm stand from April through December, bears a sign proclaiming that the land is protected by a conservation easement. Oak Hill Farm is just one of the properties that the land trust either owns outright or holds a conservation easement on that allows the trust to monitor the use of the land; as of 1999, ten thousand acres were protected by the trust.

Each year, the Sonoma Land Trust sponsors a series of hikes on land that is otherwise rarely accessible to the public. Other events offer visits to farms and gardens such as the Laufenberger Ranch and Steve and Nancy Oliver's sheep ranch, with its renowned but private sculpture gardens, in Geyserville. The trust is a membership organization, but you don't need to live in Sonoma County to join (see Resources, page 295). You just have to care. The newsletter alone is worth a basic membership.

The Rose Room

Michael Presley's home rests in a hollow in the midst of a well-managed farm that, at first, seems wild and overgrown, about as far as you can get from the orderly farms of California's Central Valley, where perfectly manicured rows of single crops stretch as far as the eye can see. Here, you must be still while your mind stops its efforts to impose familiar order. Just wait; the thoughtful beauty of Taylor Maid Farms begins to come into focus with each breath.

As we walk through the garden, we pass rabbit hutches, earthworm hatcheries, small chicken coops, a hearth carved in the earth and surrounded by natural "couches" of silvery santolina. Suddenly, a vibrant green fever of entwined vines appears. "Come see the rose room," Michael says enthusiastically.

Rose vines—from canes of roadside bramble roses that Michael gathered in the winter, when they are dormant—climb up a circular frame made from a picket fence and weave between arches of fir branches that rise for about ten feet. When the dead wood of fence and fir finally rots away, there will be living rose wood in its place. There's a small archway leading inside, where a patch of periwinkle blue sky glistens overhead through the circle of vines, in the center of which is an iron-framed double bed covered with leaves and a few fading rose petals.

Michael built the rose room for his daughter, and when she sleeps here at the height of the bloom, she awakens in the morning covered in petals. The image— this bed, the exuberant vines, the tender vision that created this place—evokes in me a primal longing, an inarticulate, visceral yearning that engulfs me. We continue our meandering stroll through the gardens, but I keep looking back toward this delicate miracle.

Organic farming is just a beginning here, as Michael seeks to mirror the natural landscape of a healthy forest *and* run a productive commercial farm. The guiding philosophy in this magical enclave is a deep sense of place, of indigenous harmony, an idea that permeates Michael's conversation, his very breath, it seems at times. His practices are informed by the principles of permaculture, biodynamics, organic farming, and native California agriculture as well as by the subtle tracks of the creatures that once roamed here.

"Large mammals were the original gardeners of this land," he says, "and even though they've been gone for 150 years, I can see their trails. I want to create a farm that will run as efficiently as their garden did." Roosevelt elk once roamed these coastal hills, compacting the soil and carving narrow pathways, fertilizing nearby plants with their excrement and paving the way for the bear and other animals that followed in their wake, feasting on berries and other wild fruits. Today, Michael uses goats and a weed whacker to make pathways through the forests that mimic the elks' ancient trails. He encourages native trees and shrubs that improve the soil, attract good insects, and discourage other ones.

Taylor Maid Farms was founded by Chris Martin, a Sebastopol native with a profound commitment to restoring and preserving the land. The company is best

M. F. K. Fisher

I first encountered M. F .K. Fisher one New Year's Day morning while visiting a friend in Santa Barbara. When I awoke early, I browsed the bookshelves of the bedroom where I slept and spotted *Map of Another Town,* one of Fisher's two books about Provence. I pulled it off the shelf and returned to bed. Here was a woman who had done exactly what I longed to do, I marveled as I read, and with two daughters depending on her, too. I knew nothing of her other writing and was unaware that she lived near me in eastern Sonoma County. I didn't even register her name, but in that early morning moment in an unfamiliar bedroom when I was so full of optimism, she became my muse, a touchstone of hope and courage. If one single mother had gone to France with her children, why couldn't another, I reasoned.

Eventually, an opportunity to write about food presented itself, and I embraced it. Before too long I rediscovered the woman who had given me such hope, and again she became a steadying influence and source of inspiration. Yet I never made an attempt to meet her, and in retrospect I wish I had. One winter morning in 1989 my friend and editor John Harris, who had encouraged me to write *A Cook's Tour of Sonoma*, took me to her home in Glen Ellen. We became friends quickly, and I regret the years when I was too shy to consider even writing to this woman who lived just a few miles from me and wrote so tenderly about two places I so loved, Sonoma and Provence. There was a sweet resonance between Mary Frances and me, and she represents an essential element in my Sonoma. She is as vital to my sense of this place as Luther Burbank and Kate Wolf.

known for the organic coffees and teas it imports from India, China, and Japan. Yet it is the garden itself, and the classes held in its midst (see Resources, page 295), that offer such hope. I can imagine a verdant future filled with gardeners and farmers that have been inspired by this place and the man who tends it.

The Mother Garden

Tucked away down a long driveway in western Occidental is a extraordinary place known as the Mother Garden, an exuberant sanctuary that has been nurtured by the same man, Doug Gosling, since it was founded as part of the Farallones Institute in 1974; he has managed the garden since 1984.

Today it is part of the Occidental Arts & Ecology Center, an educational facility that offers classes, seminars, and residential workshops in permaculture; biodiversity and seed saving; whole-systems ecology; sustainable communities; social, economic, and environmental justice; and fine arts to thousands of students a year. The classes are open to everyone, from backyard gardeners to professional landscapers and chefs. Some students come for a day; others stay for months. One of OAEC's programs, inspired by the Edible Schoolyard Project, provides training, technical assistance, and support for vegetable gardens at public elementary schools. Each year, OAEC selects twelve schools to be part of the project.

Among OAEC's many endeavors, the seed-saving program created by Doug Gosling—think of him as a modern-day Luther Burbank with a passion to preserve, rather than create, diversity—may offer the most hope for the future of agriculture. As the number of species declines at an alarming rate—consider that worldwide we rely on just *twenty* plants to produce 90 percent of our food—the Mother Garden has a collection of more than a thousand edible, medicinal, and ornamental perennials and more than thirty-five hundred varieties of annual plants. It is a steward of biodiversity, a repository of the world's germ plasm, a teaching garden, a source of inspiration to thousands of visitors and students who come here; see Resources, page 295, for the address.

PEA Sprouts

Driving into town one fall day, I spotted a small sign stuck into a lawn. PEA, it said, and that was all. Over the next several weeks I saw more and more of the elegantly lettered signs. Friends began mentioning that they had seen the signs, too, and soon word spread that a group of young people was planting gardens all over Sebastopol. For weeks no one seemed to know who they were or how to contact them. But by spring, everyone had heard of the group of West County friends, most of whom were in their late teens or early twenties, who founded Planting Earth Activation, or PEA, and new chapters had formed in Healdsburg, Santa Rosa, Sonoma, San Francisco, and other communities.

Members of PEA plant organic gardens in urban and suburban areas, providing all of the seeds and plants, all of the labor, and even returning regularly to water a garden, if necessary. They find locations by knocking on the doors of homes that look as if they might have room, and they ask only that they be allowed to return to harvest a quarter of the crop in order to collect the seeds for use in the following year's gardens. In 1999, PEA planted fifty gardens in Sebastopol; in the spring of 2000, sixty new gardens had been planned.

Toward a Diverse Future

With prices for premium grapes and wine at a record high, is monoculture inevitable? Environmental experts predict a collapse of agriculture if land continues to be degraded by the large wineries that strip the soil of every living thing, fumigate with methyl bromide, alter water patterns, and use herbicides, pesticides, and chemical fertilizers to force vines to produce high yields.

Yet in the midst of the furor over the conversion of orchards, pastures, and forests to vineyards, pockets of diversity are emerging in surprising arenas. The viticulture program at Santa Rosa Junior College offers courses in organic farming; increasingly wineries are reducing or eliminating pesticides and other farming chemicals. Davis Bynum Winery has established a polyculture forest, a two-and-a-half-acre noncontiguous area with dozens of species and varieties that fit the natural contours of the land and incorporate native species among the oranges, pomegranates, avocados, guavas, figs, lavender, caperberries, hazelnuts, olives, and old-clone zinfandel that will eventually offer a year-round harvest rather than a single fall frenzy.

I can see you sitting there
Beneath the trumpet vine
The sunlight through the window
In the kitchen in my mind
You came when you were needed, I could not ask for more
Than to turn and find you walking through the kitchen door.

—Kate Wolf, "The Trumpet Vine," 1977

PART II

A Sonoma Cookbook

ABOUT THE BEVERAGE RECOMMENDATIONS: Many of the recipes here include recommendations for wine or other beverages particularly well suited to a dish. The recommendations are just that, *suggestions*, not rules, not absolutes; they are inspired by the luxury of living in a region that makes an enormous variety of extremely high-quality wines. Some specific recommendations may be impossible to find in certain areas, but we've tried not to be overly esoteric. If you want to keep the spirit of a suggestion when you can't locate a wine, ask your wine merchant to recommend something similar. Other recommendations are generic and we leave it to you to fill in the details. (Recommendations other than my own are initialed: B. T. is Bill Traverso of Traverso's Market in Santa Rosa; D. R. is Darryl Roberts, the publisher of *Wine X Magazine;* P. R. is Paul Root of The Wine Shop in Healdsburg; and R. T. is Rick Theis, who was the executive director of the Sonoma County Grape Growers Association for fourteen years.)

CHAPTER I

Appetizers

THINK OF AN APPETIZER AS A MEAL'S MUSE, a call to the appetite to pay attention, there are yummy things to come. Appetizers are enticements, their purpose
to pique our interest, not sate our hunger. A few olives, a garlicky purée such as
Finger-Lickin' Skordalia (page 101), and a few juicy dolmas are often enough. When
appetizers are a prelude to a meal, they must leave us longing for more. Too abundant, and the natural arc of a meal will be lost.

Appetizers also can be the meal itself, a common occurrence at gatherings where
guests stand rather than sit. You see this frequently in Sonoma County, where events
might feature a dozen wines or more for tasting, each paired with an appetizer or
two. For such a fete, appetizers should be substantial, and you should consider how
each will interact with both the wines and the other dishes: If there are spicy dishes,
there should be cool ones, too; if there are creamy dishes or cheese, there should
be crunchy, refreshing elements as well. The recipes here range from lean to voluptuous, and each includes beverage recommendations.

An appetizer can also be the first course of a special dinner, especially when you
plan to linger at the table—then, you'll want to begin slowly rather than jump right
to a main course. Queso Fundido (page 109), Crescenza with Sautéed Mushrooms
(page 110), and Bruschetta (opposite) are ideal served in this way.

Bruschetta

Serves 3 to 4

For two reasons, bruschetta is one of the most commonly served appetizers in Sonoma County, in both homes and restaurants. The widespread appeal of Mediterranean cuisine is one reason, but it's really the remarkable quality of Sonoma County breads that accounts for its local popularity. In the late 1980s, the bread renaissance was just getting underway. Brother Juniper's Bakery and the Downtown Bakery and Creamery had begun making excellent specialty breads, and there were the great sourdough pull-aparts from Costeaux Bakery in Healdsburg, but it was still necessary to drive to Berkeley's Acme Bakery to get the very best hearth breads. And then in the early 1990s, along came the renowned Artisan Bakers in Sonoma and the Village Bakery in Sebastopol. Now, there's great bread—the single most important ingredient in bruschetta—everywhere. Most bruschetta I'm served is more elaborate than the classic version; I've had it topped with everything from minced tomatoes and puréed white beans to grilled rock shrimp and mango salsa. At the end of the main recipe, you'll find several seasonal variations.

> *1 loaf of good, crusty country bread, cut in ¾-inch-thick slices*
> *6 to 8 large garlic cloves, cut in half but not peeled*
> *½ cup best-quality extra virgin olive oil, such as DaVero*
> *Kosher salt or sel gris*
> *Black pepper in a mill*

Prepare a charcoal fire in an outdoor grill, heat a stove-top grill, or preheat an oven broiler. Grill or toast the bread until it is golden brown on both sides. Transfer to a platter, rub each piece of bread on one side with cut garlic, and drizzle with olive oil. Sprinkle with a little salt and black pepper and served immediately.

To drink: Sparkling wine—D. R.; J. Rochioli Sauvignon Blanc—B. T.; Matanzas Creek 1998 Sauvignon Blanc—P. R.

SEASONAL VARIATIONS

Winter: Fresh ricotta with new olive oil (see page 46). Season 8 ounces of fresh ricotta with black pepper and serve it with the bruschetta. Guests spread the ricotta on the bread after rubbing it with garlic, then drizzle olive oil over the cheese, and season it with salt and more black pepper.

Spring: Fava beans. Blanch 1½ cups fresh peeled fava beans in boiling salted water for 1 minute and shock in ice water. Drain the beans, peel them, add a tablespoon or so of good olive oil and a teaspoon of balsamic vinegar, season with salt and pepper, and serve alongside the bruschetta, with a chunk of Bellwether Pepato for grating on top.

Summer: Cherry tomatoes. Slice 2 cups ripe cherry tomatoes into quarters and toss with 2 minced garlic cloves and a tablespoon of olive oil. Season with salt and pepper, and spoon onto bruschetta after it has been rubbed with garlic.

Fall: Mozzarella fresca. After the bread is toasted on one side, remove it from the grill, rub the toasted side with garlic, and top with a thin slice of fresh mozzarella. Return to the grill and toast the other side of the bread, transfer to a plate, top with a leaf of fresh basil and a slice of tomato, drizzle with olive oil, season with salt and pepper, and serve immediately.

Chips and Salsa

The popularity of salsa has skyrocketed since I wrote the first edition of *A Cook's Tour of Sonoma*. It has surpassed ketchup as the most popular condiment in America; dozens of fresh salsas are now available in markets all over the country. Several are made locally, beginning with the Sonoma Salsa from Edible Ecstasies, a company in Petaluma founded by Carol Newman Hernandez in 1983.

Traditionalist that I am, I must offer a warning. As an increasing number of salsas appear in the market, companies resort to nontraditional flavor combinations to entice new customers and compete with their rivals. But no new concoction comes close to the classic versions made with either tomatoes or tomatillos, onions, garlic, fresh chiles, a bit of lemon or lime, and, sometimes, avocado. There are dozens of variations on this theme, and they all work better with chips than do the mango, papaya, black bean, couscous, and multitude of other inventive salsas we see these days. Save those to use as condiments with grilled seafood, poultry, and meat, or as salads. And keep in mind, too, that it's very hard to put salsa in a bottle—it usually ends up tasting like spaghetti or ranchero sauce. That said, chips and salsa make a great appetizer, especially on a hot evening. And this is one time a great Sonoma wine may not be the beverage choice; instead, an agua fresca, apple cider, or cold ale is much more refreshing. (For an early summer salsa recipe, see page 266.)

Smoked Salmon Spread

Serves 6 to 8

In the summer, the fishermen of Bodega
Bay head out to the open ocean to fish for king
salmon, a species that deserves its name. Of the salmon of the northeast Pacific—
sockeye, chum, coho, silver, and king—the king is the most prized and the most
praised, and for good reason. It's the best, a large salmon with dense, sweet flesh.
Sockeye is also a large, dense salmon with striking red flesh, but much of that catch
is exported to Japan. You can make this spread with any smoked salmon, but I've
liked it best made with sockeye—by the Barker family of Olga Bay, Kodiak,
Alaska—and with king, in my own kitchen. If you find yourself in Bodega Bay, stop
by the Crab Pot (see Resources, page 295), take a look at the rustic old smoker,
and then step inside to buy some great smoked fish.

> *8 ounces old-fashioned cream cheese, at room temperature*
> *1 small red onion, minced*
> *1 to 2 teaspoons Worcestershire sauce*
> *Juice of 1 lemon*
> *5 to 6 ounces dry-smoked salmon, broken into chunks*
> *Carr's crackers or other thin cracker*

Put the cream cheese into a medium bowl, add the red onion, Worcestershire
sauce, and lemon juice, and mix with a fork until it is fairly smooth. Fold in the
salmon but do not overmix; it should remain rather chunky.

Transfer to a serving bowl, cover, and chill for 30 minutes. Serve with the crackers
on the side.

To drink: Pinot noir—D. R.; Gloria Ferrer Blanc de Noir—B. T.

Finger-Lickin' Skordalia

Serves 6 to 8

My second book, *Oil & Vinegar*, was published shortly before virtually everything
about olive oil changed, especially in California. In November of 1992, B. R. Cohn
Olive Oil Company released its inaugural pressing of estate olive oil, made with
the fruit from eight acres of picholine olive trees planted in Glen Ellen in the 1880s.

During the next several years, the California olive oil industry was transformed, with much of its success right here in Sonoma County. When I first made skordalia, a purée of potatoes, garlic, and olive oil based on an old Greek recipe that originally called for almonds and bread crumbs (potatoes were eventually substituted for pricy almonds), I used a full-bodied Tuscan olive oil. A Tuscan oil will produce a luscious skordalia, certainly, but more often than not these days, I use DaVero (see Toscano-Sonoma, Resources, page 295), a Luccese-style oil from Sonoma County and one of my favorites. Skordalia is so good that it should not share the spotlight with a lot of other foods. I once served it as one of several appetizers; now, I make a double batch and serve it with plenty of Carr's crackers seasoned with black pepper, which provide the ideal contrast in texture and don't compete with the taste. The name of this version refers to the many fingers (you know who you are) that are plunged into the skordalia from the minute I finish making it until the last lick has vanished.

> 2 or 3 (about 1¼ pounds total) russet potatoes
> 8 to 10 garlic cloves
> 1 teaspoon kosher salt, plus more to taste
> 2 egg yolks
> ¾ to 1 cup extra virgin olive oil, such as DaVero
> Juice of 1 lemon
> White pepper in a mill

Preheat the oven to 400°F. Use a fork to pierce the potatoes in several places and bake them until they are tender, about 40 to 60 minutes, depending on their size. Let the potatoes cool slightly, but not completely. Meanwhile, crush the garlic and salt in a mortar or suribachi and grind it until it is nearly liquefied; mix in the egg yolks.

Break each potato in half, put one half at a time in a potato ricer, and press it through into a medium bowl. Remove the skin from the ricer, discard it, and continue until all of the potatoes have been riced. Use a rubber spatula to fold the garlic mixture into the riced potatoes. Mix in the olive oil, a tablespoon or two at a time, until the skordalia is thick and dense and will not absorb any more oil. Taste, season with a little more salt if necessary, and add a little of the lemon juice. Taste again, and continue to add lemon juice until the flavors all come together and no one flavor dominates. Season with several turns of pepper. Transfer the skordalia to a serving bowl, cover, and refrigerate for at least 1 hour before serving with crackers or toasted slices of baguette.

To drink: Alsace pinot blanc—D. R.; Seghesio 1998 Arneis—P. R.

Baked Three-Pepper Chèvre with Croutons

Serves 6 to 8

A powerful wallop of both chipotles and fresh chiles combined with the rich tangi-ness of chèvre will delight anyone who favors bold, searing flavors. If you prefer a more restrained amount of heat, omit the puréed chipotles and use Larry's Bohemian Chipotle Sauce (see Bohemian Foods, Resources, page 295) instead, which is fairly subtle heatwise but very good.

5 ounce fresh chèvre, such as chabis

9½ ounces (1 piece) Taupinière

3 tablespoons puréed chipotles in adobo sauce

Black pepper in a mill

3 garlic cloves, minced

1 serrano or jalapeño chile, minced

2 eggs, beaten

1 tablespoon minced fresh cilantro or oregano

3 dozen croutons, made from a baguette (see below)

Croutons Two Ways

To make the little toasts called croutons, preheat the oven to 250°F. Cut a 1-pound baguette into thin (¼-inch) diagonal slices and set the slices in a single layer on a baking sheet. Brush each slice with a little olive oil, and sprinkle with salt and pepper. Bake the croutons until they are dry and have turned golden brown, about 15 to 20 minutes. Serve the baguettes hot, or cool them to room temperature and store them in an airtight container. One baguette will make about 25 croutons.

To make square croutons for use in salads and certain pasta dishes, cut country-style bread into 1-inch cubes. For most recipes, you'll want about 1½ to 2 cups. Pour about ¼ cup extra virgin olive oil into a quart jar, add the bread cubes, season with salt and pepper, and shake vigorously until the bread has absorbed all the oil. Spread the bread cubes on a baking sheet and bake, turning once or twice, in a 250°F oven until the croutons are dry and lightly toasted. Use them immediately, or let them cool to room temperature and store them in an airtight container.

In a medium bowl, use a wooden spoon to cream together the cheeses, 1 teaspoon of the chipotle purée, and a generous amount of black pepper. Add the garlic, chile, and eggs and mix until smooth. Spoon into individual porcelain ramekins, or a single 8-inch porcelain baking dish, and use the back of a spoon or a rubber spatula to smooth the surface of the cheese mixture.

Preheat the oven to 400°F. Brush the top of the cheese with the remaining chipotle purée. When the oven is hot, bake until the cheese is hot and bubbly, about 15 minutes for individual ramekins, 20 to 25 minutes for a large dish. Sprinkle the minced cilantro or oregano over the top and serve immediately, with the croutons in a basket alongside.

To drink: Hard apple cider; Mexican beer; agua fresca

Thai Dolmas with Yogurt-Mint Sauce

Serves 6 to 8

My friend Steve Garner, the host of the longest-running food and wine radio show in California (*The Good Food Hour*, KSRO-AM), insisted that this recipe be included in the new edition. So here it is, Steve, just for you.

> ½ cup olive oil
> 6 scallions, trimmed and thinly sliced
> 2 serrano chiles, minced
> 1 cup Arborio rice
> ¼ cup minced fresh mint
> ¼ cup minced fresh cilantro
> 1 tablespoon minced fresh dill
> 2 tablespoons minced fresh Italian parsley

½ cup dried currants
Kosher salt
Black pepper in a mill
Juice of 1 lime
⅓ cup coconut milk
⅔ cup boiling water
30 to 40 grape leaves, fresh blanched (see page 108) or preserved
Yogurt-Mint Sauce (page 265)

Heat the olive oil in a medium sauté pan set over low heat, add the scallions and serranos, and sauté until soft, about 5 minutes. Add the rice, sauté, stirring continuously, for 2 minutes, add the mint, cilantro, dill, parsley, and currants, stir, and cook 2 minutes more. Season with salt and pepper, add the lime juice, coconut milk, and boiling water, and cook, continuing to stir, until the liquid is absorbed, about 10 minutes. The rice will still be hard in the center. Remove from the heat and let cool to room temperature.

To fill the grape leaves, set a leaf, dull-side up and tip pointed away from you, on your work surface and set a generous teaspoon of filling in the center. Fold the bottom of the leaf up and over the filling, fold the two sides in, overlapping them, and then roll the bundle loosely toward the tip of the leaf. Set it aside, seam-side down. Continue until all of the filling has been used.

Line a large pot with any extra grape leaves and arrange the dolmas in the pot, making a second and third layer as needed. Add just enough water to cover the dolmas and set the pot over medium heat. When the water boils, set a heavy plate on top of the dolmas, reduce the heat to low, cover the pot, and simmer for 45 minutes. Cool slightly, and use tongs to transfer the dolmas to a serving plate. Serve hot, or chilled, with the Yogurt-Mint Sauce on the side.

To drink: Alder Fels Gewürztraminer—B. T.; Nalle 1998 Dry Riesling—P. R.

Merguez Dolmas with Harissa and Yogurt

Serves 6 to 8

For several years, I cooked at Preston of Dry Creek during Passport to Dry Creek Valley, a two-day spring celebration in which many of the valley's wineries participate. The popular event now sells out months in advance. In 1999, Lou Preston wanted a Moroccan theme. Among the dishes was a wonderful merguez sausage that Willowside Meats made for us. I had a few pounds left over, and used some to make these tangy dolmas, which have become my favorite version. Merguez, a spicy lamb sausage, is very popular in France, where it is often served grilled and sliced as an appetizer. If your local butcher shop doesn't have any, it's not difficult to make your own.

> 1½ pounds merguez sausage (see Note below), casings removed
> 6 garlic cloves, minced
> ⅓ cup long-grain rice, rinsed
> Kosher salt
> Black pepper in a mill
> ¼ teaspoon ground cayenne pepper
> Pinch of cinnamon
> Juice of 1 lemon
> 30 to 40 grape leaves, fresh blanched (see page 108) or preserved
> Harissa (recipe follows)
> 1½ cups beef or chicken stock
> 2 tablespoons minced cilantro leaves
> 2 tablespoons minced Italian parsley leaves
> ¾ cup plain (unflavored) yogurt

Fry the merguez in a medium sauté pan set over medium heat, stirring continuously with a fork to break up the meat. When most of the fat has been released, drain and discard it. Return the pan to the heat, add the garlic and rice to the meat, cook for 2 minutes, season with salt and pepper, add the cayenne and cinnamon, and remove from the heat. Stir in the lemon juice and set aside to cool to room temperature.

To fill the grape leaves, set a leaf, dull-side up and tip pointed away from you, on your work surface and set a generous teaspoon of filling in the center. Fold the bottom of the leaf up and over the filling, fold the two sides in, overlapping them, and then roll the bundle loosely toward the tip of the leaf. Set it aside, seam-side down. Continue until all of the filling has been used.

Line a Pyrex baking dish with leftover grape leaves and arrange the dolmas in a single layer. Cover with a tea towel and set aside. Preheat the oven to 325°F, and make the harissa.

Preheat the oven to 325°F. Stir the stock into the harissa and pour the mixture over the dolmas; add enough water so that the grape leaves are completely submerged in liquid. Seal the dish tightly with aluminum foil and bake for 40 minutes. Let cool for 5 minutes; use tongs to transfer the dolmas to a serving plate. Stir the cilantro and parsley into the yogurt, season with a little salt and pepper, and put it in a small serving bowl. Serve the dolmas immediately, with the yogurt alongside.

HARISSA

½ ounce (about ¾ cup, loosely packed) dried hot chiles

3 garlic cloves, crushed

2 teaspoons cumin seeds, toasted

2 teaspoons coriander seeds

1 teaspoon caraway seed

1 teaspoon kosher salt

Black pepper in a mill

¼ cup olive oil

¼ cup lemon juice

In a mortar and pestle or suribachi, grind the chiles, garlic, cumin seed, coriander seed, caraway seed, salt, and several turns of black pepper together to make a thick paste. Stir in olive oil and lemon juice, taste, and correct seasoning.

To drink: Preston Zinfandel—R. T.; Martinelli 1999 Gewürztraminer—P. R.

Note: To make your own merguez, mix together 1½ pounds ground lamb (that is about 30 percent fat), 6 minced garlic cloves, 2 tablespoons minced fresh cilantro, and 2 tablespoons minced fresh Italian parsley. In a small bowl, combine 1 tablespoon paprika, 1 teaspoon ground cumin, 1 teaspoon ground coriander, 1 teaspoon kosher salt, ½ teaspoon ground cinnamon, ½ teaspoon ground cayenne pepper, and several turns of black pepper. Add the mixture to the meat and use your hands to mix it together thoroughly. (The merguez can be shaped into patties, stuffed into lamb casings, or shaped into sausages around a metal skewer; they will keep, properly refrigerated, for 3 or 4 days.)

Grapevines and Their Leaves

In the early summer, I like to drive through a certain stretch of the Russian River Valley where the road looks down on acre after acre of vineyards. The vines then are in full leaf, and as they stretch off toward the horizon, I always think of the nearby river itself, which the vines mirror in their nearly continuous flow west. There is, of course, more to the story than the visual beauty of grapevines and their inherent promise of the good wine to come. In the past decade, hundreds of new acres of grapevines have been planted, many in areas of the county that have never grown anything other than grasses and grains, or even redwood trees. Many local residents are concerned about the long-term effects of this rapidly increasing monoculture. A thousand grapevines are always better than a strip mall or a generic housing tract, but there are less visible issues that must be considered. How will the change in water use required by vineyards affect existing native plants and wildlife? If grape prices fall—they've been artificially high, some feel—what will happen to the vineyards planted by speculators, by people without generations of farming to tie them to the land? Will they sell the land to the developers who are always lurking in the shadows of Sonoma County, cash in hand, ready to exploit the landscape? As we delight in the remarkable current success of our wine industry, we all need to keep a watchful eye, too.

Back to the grape leaf. Here in the midst of millions of them, most people (myself included) still buy bottled grape leaves. But if you live near grapevines, it's worth it to spend a couple of hours putting up a year's supply. Of course, I don't recommend that you steal them; if they're not yours, you must ask. But if you have a grapevine or two of your own, or if your neighbor has some, here's how to preserve the leaves. Gather them in the early summer, when they are young and tender, about 4 to 5 inches across. Carry a basket and a handful of rubber bands with you. Pick a dozen or so, choosing carefully and not stripping an area (leaves provide shade for growing grapes), stack them dull-side up and all pointed in the same direction, roll them loosely, secure them with a rubber band, and drop them in the basket. Continue until you have harvested as many leaves as you think you will use in a year, but do not take more than the vines can tolerate losing.

Bring a large pot of water to a boil and add 2 tablespoons of kosher salt for each quart of water. Fill a large bowl with ice water and set it nearby. Remove the rubber bands, open the leaves, and using metal tongs, submerge them, a stack at a time, into the boiling water for 30 seconds. Shock the leaves in the ice water for 1 minute, then drain them in a strainer or colander.

You can use the leaves immediately. To freeze them, roll them back into bundles, wrap each bundle in freezer wrap or aluminum foil, label with the date, and store in the freezer. To preserve them, you will need 1 cup of lemon juice for each quart of leaves. Roll the leaves into bundles and fit several bundles lengthwise into quart canning jars. Add 1 cup of lemon juice to each jar, and then fill the jar with the cooking liquid. Add the lids and rings, and process the filled jars for 15 minutes in a boiling-water bath. Check the seals on the jars, label, and store in a cool, dark cupboard. To use them, remove the grape leaves from the jar and soak in fresh water for 5 minutes. Drain and dry on tea towels.

Queso Fundido

Serves 6 to 8

A traditional Mexican dish, Queso Fundido is an irresistible appetizer perfectly suited to the multitude of wonderful cheeses produced in Northern California. But be warned: This dish is so good that you might want to encourage your guests not to overindulge so they'll still have room for the rest of the meal. Sometimes I use a single type of cheese, most often Sonoma Jack. If I have no queso cotija, I'll use feta in its place.

> 1 pound Sonoma Jack cheese, grated
> ½ pound St. George cheese (or medium cheddar), grated
> ½ pound queso cotija, crumbled
> 6 garlic cloves, minced
> 2 serrano chiles, minced
> 1 teaspoon chipotle powder
> 2 poblano chiles, roasted, seeded, and cut into strips
> 3 tablespoons minced fresh cilantro or 4 scallions, trimmed and thinly sliced
> 2 to 3 dozen small corn tortillas, hot

Preheat the oven to 475°F. In a large bowl, toss together the cheeses, garlic, serranos, and chipotle powder. Place in an ovenproof earthenware dish and bake until the cheese is completely melted and bubbly, about 15 minutes. Add the poblano strips and bake 5 minutes more. Sprinkle cilantro leaves or scallions over the top and serve immediately, with hot tortillas alongside. Each guest takes 2 tortillas (one on top of the other), smears a generous portion of the queso on top, and rolls it up.

To drink: Cold Mexican beer, such as Bohemia or Negro Modelo; iced hibiscus tea; agua fresca

VARIATIONS

Spring: Grill 2 or 3 spring onions until they are tender, slice them, and scatter them over the top of the cheese in place of the poblanos. Peel and dice 1 Hass avocado, toss with the juice of a lime, 1 teaspoon kosher salt, and the minced cilantro, and spoon it over the cheese just before serving.

Summer and Fall: Peel, seed, and dice 2 tomatoes, and toss with 1 diced Haas avocado, 1 teaspoon kosher salt, and the juice of 1 lime. Spoon over the top of the cheese before adding the cilantro.

Winter: Cook 1 pound of Mexican-style chorizo removed from its casing, drain off the fat, toss with 1 cup minced cucumber and 1 minced serrano chile, and spoon over the cheese before adding the cilantro.

Crescenza with Sautéed Mushrooms

Serves 4 to 6

Bellwether Farms Crescenza is a young cheese made of milk from Jersey cows that graze near the Callahan's ranch in Two Rock, west of Petaluma. It is buttery, mildly tart, and shaped in a traditional Italian square form. Because it is such a young cheese, it does not have a long shelf life. I developed this recipe specifically for Crescenza, though you can serve these sautéed mushrooms with other creamy cheeses, such as Teleme, ripe Camembert, or Brie. There are seasonal variations following the main recipe.

> *1 pound Crescenza, cut into 4 to 6 equal squares*
>
> *2 tablespoons brown butter (see Note, below)*
>
> *8 ounces mushrooms, such as Trumpet Royale, Blue Oyster, golden chanterelle, or black chanterelle, cleaned and broken into medium pieces (see Note, below)*
>
> *¼ cup dry white wine*
>
> *Kosher salt*
>
> *Black pepper in a mill*

2 tablespoons shelled hazelnuts, toasted and peeled

1 tablespoon snipped fresh chives

12 to 16 baguette slices, toasted

Set a square of Crescenza on each of 4 to 6 individual plates and set them aside. Heat the browned butter in a medium sauté pan set over medium heat, add the mushrooms and the wine, cover the pan, and simmer until the mushrooms are wilted, about 5 minutes. Uncover and simmer until the liquid is reduced and the mushrooms are completely cooked, about 7 to 8 minutes or longer, depending on the variety. Season with salt and pepper and spoon over the cheese. Scatter some of the hazelnuts and some of the chives over each serving, garnish with the baguette slices, and serve immediately.

To drink: Dehlinger Chardonnay; Korbel Blanc de Blanc

VARIATIONS

Spring: Prepare Roasted Asparagus (page 221) and, when it is cooked, cut each stalk in half lengthwise and crosswise. While the asparagus cooks, sauté 1 minced shallot and 1 minced garlic clove in a little olive oil until they are tender, add 2 tablespoons white wine and 2 teaspoons minced chives, and season with salt and pepper. When the mixture is hot, add 4 tablespoons olive oil and remove from the heat. Taste, correct the seasoning, toss with the asparagus, spoon over the cheese, garnish with baguette slices, and serve immediately.

Summer: Make Cherry Tomato Vinaigrette (page 225), spoon it over the cheese, garnish with baguette slices, and serve immediately.

Notes: Brown butter, or *beurre noisette* as it is called in France, begins with clarified butter. To make it, melt ¼ pound (1 stick) unsalted butter in a small saucepan set over very low heat. Do not let the butter simmer. Skim off any foam or other solids from the surface of the butter and then carefully pour the melted butter into a clean saucepan, leaving behind the whey that settles on the bottom of the pan. (Clarified butter can be stored, tightly covered, in the refrigerator for several days.) To make brown butter, set the clarified butter over low heat until it turns golden brown and develops a nutty aroma. Remove from the heat and let cool slightly before using.

Trumpet Royale and Blue Oyster mushrooms are produced only by Gourmet Mushrooms, Inc., of Sebastopol (see page 295).

Sonoma Crudités

Platters of fresh, seasonal vegetables served with a dip or sauce alongside are a popular appetizer. The ultimate expression of this concept is a traditional Provençale meal celebrated each year in Sonoma County when the Sonoma Provence Exchange hosts its Grand Aïoli, or *aïoli monstre*. It is a glorious affair, with tasty tomatoes of every size from nearby farms, crisp wedges of lemon cucumbers, crunchy French Breakfast radishes with their pert leaves still attached, delicate blanched haricots verts, marinated zucchini, silky oven-roasted peppers, three varieties of beets roasted and seasoned with fragrant black pepper, and just-harvested potatoes roasted with good organic butter until tender. Our Grand Aïoli also includes poached salt cod, Sonoma lamb studded with garlic and roasted in Lou Preston's *forno,* and of course, the aioli itself, made with hand-pounded garlic grown at Sunshine Farms in Cloverdale and local olive oil from DaVero and B. R. Cohn. The eggs—both for the aioli and to serve hard-cooked with the vegetables—are from the free-range chickens of Triple T Ranch & Farm in Santa Rosa. Crudités are never better than when served in this way, but it is possible only in the summer months. The rest of the year, you must turn to those vegetables that are in season and you must prepare them properly. Few things are more dismal than out-of-season vegetables, raw when they should be cooked, and utterly lacking in flavor. An actual recipe for crudités isn't really necessary. Just follow this seasonal guide and the cooking recommendations for each vegetable, and you'll be able to offer guests a feast any time of year. Always offer good bread, cut into chunks, alongside. Recommendations for sauces follow each seasonal listing. (Note: Vegetables are listed in the season when they are at their peak.)

SPRING

Asparagus, roasted (see page 221) in a hot (475°F) oven and seasoned with salt and pepper

Belgian endive

Sugar snap peas

English peas, shelled

Fava beans, shelled and peeled

Young lettuce leaves

Cardoons, peeled, boiled until tender, shocked in ice water, and drained

Artichokes, boiled and chilled

French Breakfast radishes (late spring)

Spring onions, grilled or roasted

Sauces: Garlic and anchovy butter; romesco sauce

SUMMER AND EARLY FALL

New potatoes, oven-roasted

Fingerling potatoes, oven-roasted

French Breakfast radishes (only in cool years)

Tomatoes, cut in wedges

Cherry tomatoes, cut in half

Currant tomatoes, whole

Multicolored sweet bell peppers, oven-roasted (see page 227), peeled, and cut in wedges

Beets, oven-roasted, peeled, and quartered

Lemon cucumbers, in wedges

Armenian cucumbers, in ⅛-inch rounds

Fennel, sliced

Japanese eggplant, cut in half lengthwise and grilled

Sauce: Aioli (page 264)

WINTER

Broccoli florets, blanched and shocked in ice water

Cauliflower florets, blanched and shocked in ice water

Potatoes, cut in wedges and roasted in the oven

Crimini mushrooms, marinated in olive oil and lemon juice

Young lettuce leaves

Carrots, cut in wedges if large; trimmed if small

Sauces: Extra virgin olive oil seasoned with good vinegar, salt, and pepper; Smoked Salmon Spread (page 101)

Wild Mushroom Triangles

Makes about 60 triangles

Gourmet Mushrooms, Inc., of Sebastopol is one of the world's leading producers of specialty mushrooms, and I first made these yummy triangles using some black chanterelles and shiitakes that the founder, Malcolm Clark, gave me. Use whatever mushrooms you have, except for the standard commercial white mushrooms, which contain too much water.

> *1 cup butter*
>
> *3 shallots, minced*
>
> *1½ pounds mushrooms: shiitake, chanterelle, or portobello, or a mixture*
>
> *3 tablespoons Madeira*
>
> *1 teaspoon fresh thyme leaves*
>
> *1 tablespoon minced fresh Italian parsley*
>
> *6 ounces Laura Chenel Taupinière (see Laura Chenel Chèvre, Resources, page 295), or other chèvre*
>
> *Kosher salt*
>
> *Black pepper in a mill*
>
> *1 package phyllo pastry*
>
> *2 tablespoons sesame seeds, toasted*
>
> *2 bunches Italian parsley*
>
> *Chèvre Sauce (page 267), optional*

In a heavy saucepan, melt ½ cup butter, add the shallots, and sauté until limp and fragrant, about 10 minutes. Clean the mushrooms, removing and discarding any woody stems. Chop them coarsely, add to the shallots, and sauté until limp, about 15 minutes. Add the Madeira, thyme, and minced parsley, stir in the Taupinière, and remove from the heat. Taste and season with salt and pepper.

In a small, heavy saucepan, melt the remaining butter. Prepare the phyllo pastry by cutting a 2-inch piece off the roll of dough. Cover the remainder with a towel. Remove 2 sheets of the cut phyllo at a time, keeping the rest covered. Spread them out on a cutting board. Brush a thin swipe of melted butter on one sheet, cover it with the second sheet, and brush the entire top layer with melted butter. Place about 1 heaping teaspoon of the mushroom mixture in the lower right corner and begin to wrap the phyllo strip into a triangle by folding it end over end, as you fold a flag. Place the finished triangle on a buttered baking sheet, cut another 2-inch piece off the roll of dough, and repeat the process until done. Brush the tops of the triangles with butter and sprinkle with a few sesame seeds. Bake at 400°F for 20 minutes, until the triangles are lightly browned. Remove from the oven, arrange the Italian parsley on a large platter, and set the triangles on top of the parsley. Serve hot, with the Chèvre Sauce alongside for dipping.

To drink: Korbel Rouge Pellegrini 1997 Carignane—P. R.

Nopales Tamales

Serves 4 to 6

These tasty nuggets, excellent served with chips, salsa, and a pitcher of cold margaritas, must be made with fresh nopales; the pickled ones are too soft and too tart.

> *1 pound trimmed and diced nopales (see Note, below)*
> *1 small white onion, diced*
> *3 scallions, trimmed and thinly sliced*
> *Kosher salt*
> *Black pepper in a mill*
> *1 teaspoon minced fresh epazote*
> *1 teaspoon minced fresh oregano*
> *16 dried corn husks, soaked in hot water for 1 hour*
> *4 ounces Sonoma Jack cheese, grated*

Start a charcoal fire in an outdoor grill. Fry the nopales in a dry skillet set over medium heat, stirring now and then, until all of their liquid has evaporated. Toss with the onion and scallions, season with salt and pepper, add the epazote and oregano, and toss again. Put a generous spoonful in the center of each corn husk, top with some of the cheese, fold the corn husk over the vegetable mixture, and tie it closed. Repeat until all of the filling has been used. Grill the tamales directly over the hot coals, or on a rack set close to the coals, until they are steaming hot, about 5 minutes. Serve immediately.

To drink: Mexican beer

Note: You'll find nopales—flat cactus paddles—at farmers' markets throughout California. They are also available fresh, frozen, and pickled in Mexican grocery stores. If you buy the paddles, you should wear gloves as you clean them because they have almost invisible spines that will lodge in your fingers if you are not careful. Use a sharp knife to pare away the tiny spines and trim around the edges of the paddle. Cut the nopales into ½-inch-wide strips and then cut the strips into ½-inch cubes. Some markets, Lepe's Tienda in Sebastopol, for example, and the Santa Rosa Farmer's Market, sell nopales that have already been cleaned and diced.

CHAPTER 2

Soups

"OF SOUP AND LOVE," wrote Thomas Fuller in *Gnomologia* in 1732, "the first is the best." A romantic at heart, I can't agree, though in my experience soup is without doubt more reliable, and entirely possible without the cooperation of anyone other than yourself. In times without love, soup, both the making and the eating of it, is a welcome balm. In times of abundant love, soup is a perfect restorative. "To feel safe and warm on a cold wet night," Laurie Colwin writes in *Home Cooking* (Knopf, 1988), "all you really need is soup." I embrace Laurie's wisdom without reservation.

Making great soups is a cinch, and I've never understood why so many home cooks are afraid to try it. If you begin with homemade stock and good ingredients, it's almost impossible to fail. Because stocks require several hours, it is easiest if you have them on hand. Twice a year, I make several batches of stock—chicken, duck, or beef, and sometimes turkey—and freeze them in 2-cup portions. An afternoon of cooking pays off in months of flavorful soups that are ready in less than an hour. In a pinch, you can used canned broth, which will add flavor but not the depth of texture contributed by stock (broth is made from flesh only; stock contains natural gelatin from bones). And one other word of advice: Don't forget to season with salt as you cook; without doing so, you risk bland soups that don't ever quite come together. If you love to make soup, you might want to keep Demi-Glace Gold, Glace de Poulet Gold, and the other concentrated stocks made by More Than Gourmet on hand for emergencies (see Resources, page 295). These highly concentrated stocks do not require refrigeration and are made without chemicals or preservatives.

My daughter Gina loves to make soup, and her passion has inspired me. She has become my soup muse, the one for whom I am always cooking, whether she is here or not. Born with a subtle and honest palate, she is my best critic. As I complete this book—hurry up, mama, she urges, I need your help—Gina is planning a special soup café, a movable tureen, you could say. She is on her way, her friends tease her, to becoming the Soup Queen of the Sierras, where she lives.

Spicy Apple Chowder

Serves 4

When I found myself with a bounty of newly harvested Gravenstein apples, I was thrilled to discover stock in the freezer that I had made the previous winter from a flavorful Virginia ham bone. The smoky elements—the chipotle, the stock, and the cheese—with their interplay and depth, blend beautifully with the rich sweetness of the apples for a sensational late-summer soup.

> 2 tablespoons butter
> 4 sweet-tart apples, such as Gravensteins, peeled, cored, and diced
> 2 russet potatoes, peeled and diced
> Kosher salt
> Black pepper in a mill
> ½ teaspoon chipotle powder
> 4 cups smoked ham, smoked chicken, or smoked duck stock
> 3 tablespoons sour cream
> 3 tablespoons half-and-half
> 4 ounces smoked goat cheddar, other naturally smoked cheese, or Italian fontina
> 2 tablespoons snipped chives

Melt the butter in a large soup pot set over medium heat, add the apples and potatoes, and sauté 3 or 4 minutes, until they just begin to soften and take on a bit of color. Season with salt, pepper, and the chipotle powder. Add the stock, bring to a boil, reduce the heat to low, and simmer until the apples and potatoes are completely tender, about 15 to 20 minutes. In a small bowl, mix together the sour cream and half-and-half and set aside. Purée the soup using an immersion blender, add the cheese, and stir until it is melted. If the soup seems too thick, thin with a little stock or water. Season with salt and a generous amount of black pepper, taste, and correct the seasoning. Ladle the soup into warmed soup bowls, drizzle some of the sour cream mixture over each serving, scatter with chives, and serve immediately.

To drink: Ace in the Hole Gravenstein Cider; Chardonnay—D. R.; Geyser Peak Riesling, not overly chilled—B. T.

Gazpacho

Serves 4 to 6

This simple version of the classic Andalusian soup would hardly have been possible a decade ago. The availability of heirloom varieties of tomatoes, grown for flavor instead of for efficiency of transport, has increased tremendously. Even though the county is not hot enough or dry enough to be a major producer of tomatoes, Sonoma County farmers have been among the most innovative growers of specialty varieties. Beginning in July, our farmers' markets offer dozens of colorful tomatoes; the season lasts until the first frost, which can come as early as mid-September, as late as November, or in some years, not at all. You must use superior tasting tomatoes in this soup; otherwise it will be bland and flat.

2 pounds ripe red tomatoes
½ red onion, very finely minced
2 tablespoons freshly minced Italian parsley leaves
2 tablespoons freshly minced basil leaves
2 tablespoons freshly snipped chives
1 tablespoon red wine vinegar
1 ½ teaspoons kosher salt
Black pepper in a mill
2 pounds ripe yellow or orange tomatoes
1 tablespoon white wine vinegar
White pepper in a mill
2 tablespoons olive oil
1 cup fresh bread crumbs
3 tablespoons extra virgin olive oil, such as DaVero

To prepare the red tomatoes, peel them by spearing them, one at a time, on the tines of a dinner fork and holding them over an open flame or hot electric burner. Rotate the fork quickly as the tomato skins blister. Set the tomatoes aside to cool and, when you can handle them, peel off the skins with your fingers. Holding each tomato over a large strainer set over a bowl, remove the stem core, cut the tomato in half through the equator, and squeeze out the seeds and juice. Mince the tomatoes to a fine pulp, working in batches so that the juice does not run off the work surface. Transfer the pulp and juice to a bowl and add the juice reserved from the seeding process. Add two-thirds of the finely minced red onion, half the herbs, and the red wine vinegar. Season with salt and, generously, with black pepper.

To prepare the yellow tomatoes, peel and seed them as described for red tomatoes, straining the juice from the seeds into a separate bowl. Mince the tomatoes finely, and add the minced tomato pulp to the bowl. Add the remaining one-third of the minced onion, the remaining half of the herbs, and the white vinegar. Season with salt and, generously, with white pepper.

Cover and chill the two bowls of prepared tomatoes for at least 1 hour or overnight.

Heat the olive oil in a heavy sauté pan set over medium heat, add the bread crumbs, and sauté, stirring continuously, until toasted golden brown. Remove from the heat and set aside to cool.

To serve, place the red tomato pulp and the yellow tomato pulp in separate pitchers and pour simultaneously from opposite sides of individual soup plates so that the purées merge in the center of the bowl but do not mix. Drizzle extra virgin olive oil over each serving, scatter bread crumbs over the top, and serve immediately.

To drink: Sherry; sparkling wine

VARIATIONS

Omit the bread crumbs. Cut 1 firm-ripe avocado into small dice, toss it with ½ teaspoon salt and 2 teaspoons lime juice, and scatter on top of the gazpacho in place of the bread crumbs.

Omit the herbs. Remove the stems and seeds of 2 serrano chiles, mince them, and stir them into the tomato pulp (half in the red, half in the yellow). Mince 4 tablespoons of fresh cilantro, stir 1 tablespoon into the red pulp, 1 tablespoon into the yellow pulp, and scatter the remaining 2 tablespoons over the soup just before serving.

Top each serving of gazpacho with a generous spoonful of Aioli (page 264) before serving.

If ripe green tomatoes are available—farmer's markets often have several varieties—prepare them in the same way as the yellow and pour a three-tone soup instead of a two-tone soup. (It will serve 6 to 8.)

Corn Chowder

Serves 4

For ten years, Betsy Timm of Santa Rosa headed Select Sonoma County, an agricultural marketing association (see page 295), as its executive director, guiding the organization along a wise path and being a tireless cheerleader for local agriculture. She resigned as I was working on this book. When her departure was mentioned in Fiesta Market's weekly Chef-in-the-Hood ad, she contributed this recipe, calling it one of her favorites. In fact, it's how we met—she introduced herself to me years ago when we were both shopping at Fiesta, coincidentally for the ingredients for this soup.

6 ears corn
¼ pound bacon
1 small red onion, thinly sliced
5 small new red potatoes, cut into quarters
1 red bell pepper, seeded and diced
2 poblano chiles, seeded and diced
3 cups chicken stock
1 cup heavy cream
Kosher salt
Black pepper in a mill
Pinch of cayenne
3 tablespoons cilantro leaves

Using a sharp knife, cut the kernels from the ears of corn and set them aside. In a large heavy pot, cook the bacon until it is crisp, transfer to absorbent paper, and pour all but 2 tablespoons of the bacon fat out of the pan. Sauté the onion in the bacon fat until it is soft and fragrant, about 10 minutes. Add the potatoes, pepper, and chiles and sauté for 5 minutes more. Add the chicken stock, bring to a boil, reduce the heat to low, and simmer until the potatoes are tender, about 15 minutes. Add the corn, simmer for 2 minutes, add the cream and season with salt, black pepper, and the cayenne. Crumble the bacon and stir it into the chowder. Ladle into warmed soup bowls, garnish each portion with cilantro leaves, and serve immediately.

To drink: Sémillon—D. R.; Quivira Sauvignon Blanc

Sorrel Soup

Serves 3 to 4

Gen Barnhardt, a sculptor who lives in west Sebastopol, gave me this recipe the first time she offered me sorrel from her garden. I like it so much that now I grow my own and harvest it year round. Nothing could be simpler, and when the sorrel is freshly picked, it's a bit like eating soup made of sunlight.

> *2 tablespoons olive oil*
> *1 onion, diced*
> *3 garlic cloves*
> *4 cups shredded sorrel (about 1 pound, trimmed)*
> *1½ cups chicken stock or broth*
> *1½ cups water*
> *Zest of 1 lemon*
> *Kosher salt*
> *Black pepper in a mill*

Heat the olive oil in a large soup pot set over medium-low heat, add the onion, and sauté until very tender and fragrant, about 15 minutes. Add the garlic and cook for 2 minutes more. Stir in the sorrel, sauté until limp, add the chicken stock and water, and bring to a boil over medium heat. Reduce the heat to low and simmer for 8 to 10 minutes. Stir in the lemon zest, season with salt and pepper, and serve immediately.

To drink: Toad Hollow 1999 Chardonnay—P. R.; Taft Street Sauvignon Blanc

Sorrel & Potato Soup

Serves 4

Using a base of sautéed onions and potatoes, you can make a variety of excellent seasonal soups, such as this one with fresh sorrel. In cool weather, serve it hot, topped with sour cream; when the weather turns hot, chill the soup and top each portion with a thin slice of fresh lemon.

> *3 tablespoons olive oil*
>
> *1 onion*
>
> *1 ½ pounds Yukon Gold potatoes, scrubbed and sliced about ¼ inch thick*
>
> *1 ½ cups chicken stock or broth*
>
> *1 ½ cups water*
>
> *3 garlic cloves, minced*
>
> *4 cups shredded sorrel (about 1 pound, trimmed)*
>
> *Zest of 1 lemon*
>
> *Kosher salt*
>
> *Black pepper in a mill*
>
> *2 tablespoons sour cream thinned with 1 tablespoon half-and-half,*
> *   or 3 tablespoons crème fraîche*

Heat two tablespoons of the olive oil in a large soup pot, add the onion, set over medium-low heat and sauté until the onion is very tender and fragrant, about 15 minutes. Add the potatoes, sauté for 2 minutes, add the chicken stock and water, and bring to a boil over medium heat. Reduce the heat and simmer, partially covered, until the potatoes are tender, about 12 to 15 minutes.

Heat the remaining tablespoon of olive oil in a sauté pan, add the garlic, and sauté for 30 seconds. Add the sorrel and sauté, stirring constantly, until it is limp, about 2 to 3 minutes. Add the sorrel to the potatoes and stir in the lemon zest. Using an immersion blender, purée the soup until it is almost but not completely smooth. Taste and season with salt and pepper. Ladle into warm soup bowls, top each portion with a tablespoon of sour cream or crème fraîche, and serve immediately.

To drink: Jordan 1997 Chardonnay—P. R.

Blue Potato Soup

Serves 4

If you don't have blue potatoes, you can use almost any other potato except large russets for making this soup, though it won't be as striking and rich looking. The little nuggets of minced orange carrot shimmer in the deep purple soup like stars in a night sky, so I think it's worth the effort to get the blue potatoes. As far as the chipotle powder goes, there are now several brands on the market, though the best comes from Healdsburg's Tierra Vegetables (see Resources, page 295).

> *3 tablespoons olive oil*
> *1 yellow onion, minced*
> *2 carrots, minced*
> *Kosher salt*
> *Black pepper in a mill*
> *½ to 1 teaspoon chipotle powder*
> *1 pound peeled and sliced celery root (from 1 large root)*
> *2 pounds Oregon Blue potatoes, scrubbed and sliced*
> *4 cups chicken stock or broth*
> *2 cups water*
> *2 tablespoons fresh minced Italian parsley or snipped chives*

Heat the olive oil in a medium soup pot set over medium-low heat and sauté the onion and carrots until soft and fragrant, about 10 minutes. Season with salt, pepper, and chipotle powder, using the larger quantity of powder for a bolder, hotter taste. Add the celery root and potatoes, stir, and sauté for 2 minutes. Add the chicken stock and water. Increase the heat to high and bring the mixture to a boil. Reduce the heat and simmer until the potatoes and celery root are tender, about 20 to 25 minutes.

Use an immersion blender to purée the soup, taste, and season with more salt and pepper as necessary. If the soup is too thick, add water, stir, and heat through. Ladle into soup bowls, garnish with parsley or chives, and serve immediately.

To drink: Iron Horse Rosato

Poblano Soup with Roasted Onion Rajas

Serves 6 to 8

Here's another example of potatoes providing a canvas for bright and spicy flavors. This soup, updated from the original *Cook's Tour*, is hot; to tame it a bit, omit the serranos or jalapeños. You can make this soup using varieties of potatoes other than the one I recommend here, but you'll need to make allowances for differences in texture by adding more water if the soup seems too thick.

> *1 large onion, peeled and quartered*
> *10 poblano chiles, stemmed, seeded, and cut in half*
> *2 serrano or jalapeño chiles*
> *5 tablespoons olive oil, plus more as necessary*
> *4 garlic cloves, minced*
> *2½ pounds Yellow Finn potatoes, sliced*
> *Kosher salt*
> *Black pepper in a mill*
> *2 cups chicken stock*
> *4 cups water*
> *Juice of 1 lime*
> *2 tablespoons minced fresh cilantro*

Preheat the oven to 375°F. Place the onion, poblanos, and serranos or jalapeños on a baking sheet and brush lightly with olive oil. Roast until the chile skins are blistered and the onion is just turning golden brown; turn the onion pieces once during roasting. Let cool to room temperature, peel the poblanos, and peel and seed the serranos or jalapeños.

To prepare the rajas, cut 4 (8 halves) of the poblanos into ¼-inch strips and put the strips in a medium bowl. Cut 1 serrano or jalapeño into very thin julienne, and add to the poblano strips. Cut 2 of the onion quarters into thin strips and put them in a separate small bowl. Set these vegetables aside.

Mince the remaining poblanos and serrano or jalapeño, and dice the remaining half onion. Heat 3 tablespoons of the remaining olive oil in a large soup pot set over medium heat, add the diced onion, and sauté until soft and fragrant, about 5 minutes. Add the garlic and sauté for 2 minutes more. Add the potatoes, sauté for 2 or

3 minutes, add the poblanos and serrano, and season with salt and pepper. Add the chicken stock and water, increase the heat to high and, when the liquid boils, reduce the heat to low and simmer until the potatoes are tender, about 15 to 20 minutes. Purée the soup with an immersion blender, taste, and correct the seasoning.

Meanwhile, heat 2 tablespoons of the remaining olive oil in a sauté pan, add the sliced roasted onion, and sauté, stirring frequently, about 5 minutes. Add the poblano and serrano strips, heat through, add the lime juice, season with salt and pepper, remove from the heat, and add the cilantro. Set aside.

To serve, ladle the soup into warmed soup bowls, top with a generous spoonful of the rajas, and serve immediately, with the remaining rajas on the side.

To drink: Negro Modelo

Sonoma Soupe au Pistou

Serves 6 to 8

Pistou is the Provençal equivalent of Italian pesto; the soup of the same name is a sort of French minestrone. It is best made in the late summer and early fall, when there are fresh shell beans, fresh basil, and plenty of good vegetables at the farmers' market. The addition of duck is my own contribution, but you can omit it if you would like a vegetarian version of this soup, in which case you'll want to begin with a good vegetable stock. You cannot, however, omit the pistou. Without it, the soup is unremarkable; the pistou transforms it into one of the best fall soups around.

> *6 duck legs, or 3 duck leg and thigh pieces, skinned*
> *8 cups water*
> *Pistou (recipe follows)*
> *3 tablespoons olive oil or duck fat*
> *2 yellow onions, minced*
> *1 carrot, minced*
> *1 celery stalk, minced*
> *8 garlic cloves, minced*
> *Kosher salt*
> *Black pepper in a mill*
> *3 pounds fresh shell beans (a mix of cranberry, white, red, or pinto), shelled*
> *1 pound winter squash (such as Tahitian Melon), cubed*

1 pound Roma tomatoes, peeled, seeded, and diced

1 pound small new potatoes, quartered

½ pound zucchini, halved and sliced

1 cup (3 ounces) ditalini, pennette, or other small dried pasta

Dry Jack or Parmigiano-Reggiano, in one piece

Place the duck in a large pot, add 8 cups of water, bring to a boil over high heat, reduce the heat to low, and simmer until the meat falls off the bone, about 1½ to 2 hours. Skim off and discard any foam that forms.

While the duck simmers, make the pistou. Cover it with plastic wrap, pressing the wrap directly onto the surface of the sauce. Set it aside.

When the duck is completely tender, use tongs to remove it from the cooking liquid and let it cool to room temperature. Reserve the cooking liquid, remove the meat from the bones, discard the bones, wrap the meat, and refrigerate it until ready to use.

Heat the olive oil in a large clean pot set over medium-low heat, add the onions, carrot, and celery, and sauté until soft, about 15 minutes. Add the garlic and sauté for 2 minutes more. Season with salt and pepper, increase the heat, and add the reserved duck stock and 4 cups of water. Add the shell beans, bring to a boil, reduce the heat to medium-low, and simmer until the beans are nearly completely tender, about 1 hour. Add the winter squash, tomatoes, and potatoes, simmer for 10 minutes more, add the reserved duck meat, zucchini, and pasta, and simmer until the pasta is tender, about 12 minutes. Taste and correct the seasoning.

Ladle the soup into warmed soup bowls, stir a spoonful of the pistou into each serving, grate some cheese over each portion, and serve immediately, with the remaining pistou, cheese, and a grater alongside.

PISTOU

4 large garlic cloves

Kosher salt

Black pepper in a mill

4 ounces (about 2 cups, packed) fresh basil leaves, torn into pieces

1 Roma tomato, peeled, seeded, and diced

¼ cup olive oil

3 ounces Dry Jack cheese, grated

In a heavy mortar or in the bowl of a suribachi, use a pestle to crush each clove of garlic. Add several generous pinches of salt and several turns of pepper, and pound the garlic until it is nearly liquid. Add the basil, a small handful at a time, and continue to pound until the basil is incorporated into the mixture. Add the tomato and continue to pound the mixture. Stir in the olive oil and the cheese, taste the pistou, and correct the seasoning. Cover and set aside or refrigerate until ready to use.

To drink: Joseph Swan Côte du Rosa; Preston Faux; dry rosé

Caldo Verde

Serves 6 to 8

In 1998, Manuel Azevedo opened La Salette, a small Portuguese restaurant on the northern edge of the town of Sonoma. As a young boy, Manuel and his family came to Northern California from São Jorge, an island in the Azores off the coast of Portugal. There are many people from the region in Sonoma County, and they have brought their food preferences and cooking traditions with them, of course. Manuel learned to garden and cook at his mother's side, and his restaurant is named for her. His version of Portugal's national dish, *caldo verde,* is served at the restaurant, and is easy to make at home. Note that the bones take about 1½ hours to smoke.

> *1 tablespoon olive oil*
> *2 carrots, cut into ¼-inch dice*
> *1 celery stalk, cut into ¼-inch dice*
> *1 onion, cut into ¼-inch dice*
> *Kosher salt*
> *3 pounds beef bones, smoked (see Note, below)*
> *2 garlic cloves, peeled*
> *¾ pound linguiça*
> *3 quarts water*
> *3 cups collard greens*
> *2 large russet potatoes, peeled, diced, and cooked until tender*
> *1 to 2 teaspoons freshly ground white pepper*

Heat the olive oil in a large soup pot set over medium-low heat, add the carrots, celery, and onion, and sauté for 3 to 4 minutes, stirring constantly, until the mixture begins to soften but does not brown. Season with salt, add the bones, garlic, linguiça (whole), and the water, increase the heat to high, bring to a boil, reduce the heat to low, and simmer, partially covered, for 2 hours. Skim off any foam that forms on top.

Bring a medium pot of salted water to a boil, add the collard greens, stir for 2 minutes, drain, and shock in an ice-water bath. Drain thoroughly.

Strain the stock, use tongs to pick out and reserve the linguiça, and discard the bones and vegetables. Return the stock to the heat, bring to a boil, add the potatoes, and when the stock returns to the boil, add the collard greens, and simmer for 10 minutes, until the greens are tender. Slice the linguiça and heat the slices in a small pan. Purée the soup with an immersion blender, add the white pepper, season with salt, and ladle into warm soup bowls. Garnish with the linguiça slices and serve immediately.

Note: To smoke beef bones, prepare a fire in a commercial smoker according to the manufacturer's instructions, or start a small wood fire in an outdoor grill. Add flavorful wood chips such as hickory, place the bones on a fireproof pan, set the pan in the smoker or grill, cover, and smoke for 1½ hours.

To drink: Laurel Glen Terra Rosa Cabernet Sauvignon—D. R.

Marrowfats Soup with Chipotle Oil

Serves 6 to 8

If you have fresh shell beans in your garden or at your local farmers' market, use them to make this soup. If you don't have fresh beans, use dried ones but soak them overnight before cooking them. My favorite bean for this soup is the plump white marrowfat, but many other delicious heirloom beans, such as the two-tone calypso, the black Valentine, and the White Aztec, will give good results. (see Resources, page 295, for sources.)

The slow sweating and simmering of diced winter squash creates a rich sweet clear broth that is wonderful with pumpkin ravioli, though they are admittedly time-consuming to make.

> *1 winter squash, such as Tahitian Melon, banana, or acorn, about 6 pounds*
> *4 tablespoons olive oil*
> *1 leek, white part only, trimmed and thinly sliced*
> *½ teaspoon cumin seed*
> *1 teaspoon whole black peppercorns*

1 chipotle chile

3 quarts water

2 pounds fresh marrowfats, or other shell beans, shelled (about 2 cups)

¾ cup (about 2½ ounces) dried pennette

Kosher salt

2 tablespoons Chipotle Oil (page 262)

2 tablespoons cilantro leaves

Cut the squash in half, scoop out the seeds and fibers, and cut it into manageable pieces. Use a sharp paring knife or vegetable peeler to peel each piece of squash; cut it into medium dice.

Pour the olive oil into a large pot set over medium low heat, add the leek, and sauté until it is limp, about 4 to 5 minutes. Decrease the heat to low, add the squash, and sweat it slowly, partially covered, until it softens, about 30 to 40 minutes. Add the cumin seed, black pepper, and whole chipotle.

Pour 3 quarts of water into the pot, increase the heat to high, and when the water boils, reduce the heat and simmer, partially covered, for 1½ hours. Strain the broth through a fine sieve, clean the pot, and return the broth to the pot. Set it over medium heat and reduce it by about half; there should be 6 cups.

Meanwhile, cook the marrowfats in boiling water until they are very tender, about 1 hour. Cook the pasta in boiling salted water according to package directions. Taste the broth and season it with salt if it seems a little flat. Add the beans and pasta, and ladle the soup in wide soup bowls. Drizzle each serving with a little chipotle oil, scatter a few cilantro leaves on top, and serve immediately.

To drink: Hanna 1998 Sauvignon Blanc—P. R.

Butternut Chipotle Soup with Walnut Gremolata

Serves 6 to 8

Winter squash makes outstanding soup. You can add
puréed roasted garlic, minced hot chiles, rosemary,
nutmeg, or a variety of other seasonings and aromatics.
This version, from Tierra Vegetables, has a whisper of curry
spices and a healthy wallop of the smoky chipotle peppers for
which the Healdsburg farm is best known. I find the use of walnut gremolata in this
context both unique and inspired, a perfect combination of fall flavors.

> *3 tablespoons olive oil*
>
> *2 yellow onions, diced*
>
> *2 garlic cloves, peeled*
>
> *1 teaspoon curry powder (see Note, page 215)*
>
> *1 teaspoon ground cumin*
>
> *Kosher salt*
>
> *1 medium butternut squash, about 3 pounds, peeled and cut into
> 1½-inch cubes*
>
> *2 whole chipotle chiles, preferably from Tierra Vegetables*
>
> *6 cups chicken stock or broth*
>
> *Juice of 1 lemon*
>
> *1 cup half-and-half*
>
> *Black pepper in a mill*

Heat the olive oil in a large soup pot set over medium-low heat. Add the onions
and sauté until limp and fragrant, about 8 to 10 minutes. Add the garlic, curry powder, and cumin, sauté for 2 minutes more, and season with salt. Add the squash,
chipotles, chicken stock, and enough water to cover the squash completely. Increase
the heat to high, bring to a boil, reduce the heat to low, and simmer until the squash
is tender, about 30 to 35 minutes.

Meanwhile, make the gremolata.

Remove the whole chipotles from the soup and discard them, or for more heat,
remove their stems, mince the chiles, and then purée them, with a ladleful of the
soup, in a food processor or blender, before returning them to the pot. Purée the
soup using an immersion blender or a food mill. Return to medium-low heat, add

the lemon juice, stir, and add the half-and-half. Taste and season with salt, if necessary, and several generous turns of black pepper. Heat through but do not let boil. Ladle into warm soup bowls, top each portion with a spoonful of gremolata, and serve immediately.

WALNUT GREMOLATA

Zest of 1 lemon, minced
½ cup shelled walnuts, toasted and minced
½ cup Italian parsley leaves, minced
4 garlic cloves, minced
¼ teaspoon chipotle powder
Kosher salt

Combine the lemon zest, walnuts, parsley, minced garlic, and chipotle powder in a small bowl. Season with salt and set aside.

To drink: Chardonnay—D. R.; Alder Fels Gewürztraminer—B. T.; Alexander Valley Vineyards New Gewürz

Chestnut Soup

Serves 6 to 8

Several years ago, Greg Dabel, a writer and consultant who lives in the West County, bought some land on Green Valley Road that included an orchard of 110-year-old Gravenstein apple trees. In the early 1990s, he added six acres of chestnuts, which today are thriving. He sells most of the chestnuts through the Internet (see Resources, page 295), though every fall a few customers call and stop by to purchase them directly at the farm. Frédèrique Lavoipierre, who for a decade operated Shoestring Nursery in Sebastopol and later became the producer of my radio show, *Mouthful*, made this soup one Thanksgiving, as part of a Sonoma County menu.

½ cup (1 stick) unsalted butter
4 cups whole chestnuts, roasted and peeled
1 carrot, minced
1 parsnip, minced
1 cup minced celery root
Kosher salt
Black pepper in a mill

½ cup Madeira
8 cups chicken stock
4 Italian parsley sprigs
Whole nutmeg
½ cup crème fraîche
2 tablespoons fresh minced Italian parsley
Scant ⅛ teaspoon chipotle powder or ground cayenne pepper

Melt half of the butter in a medium sauté pan set over low heat, add the chestnuts, and sauté for 5 minutes, stirring frequently, until heated through. Set them aside.

In a large soup pot, melt the remaining butter, add the carrot, parsnip, and celery root, and sauté until soft, about 8 to 10 minutes. Season with salt and pepper, add the Madeira, increase the heat, and stir in the stock. When it boils, add the chestnuts, parsley sprigs, and several gratings of nutmeg. Reduce the heat to medium-low and simmer, partially covered, until the chestnuts are tender. Remove and discard the parsley sprigs and, using an immersion blender, purée the soup until it is quite smooth. Taste the soup and season with salt and pepper. Ladle into warm soup plates, top each serving with a dollop of crème fraîche and a sprinkling of parsley and chipotle powder or cayenne, and serve immediately.

To drink: Vintage Champagne—D. R.; Toad Hollow Eye of the Toad

CHAPTER 3

Toast, Breads, Sandwiches, Eggs, Tarts, Pizzas & Calzone

I DO NOT KNOW ANYONE WHO CAN RESIST THE SEDUCTIVE AROMA OF FER-MENTING DOUGH, bread as it bakes, or toast as it turns, grain by grain, an invit-ing golden brown. In this chapter, I offer a disparate selection of recipes, unified by a common need of dough of some sort, a crust, a loaf, a slice, a shell either to make or complete them. The recipes are for the most part simple and lend themselves to your innovation and interpretation. If you've never made pizza dough or pie crust before but rather have relied on frozen varieties, do be brave and give it a try. It doesn't take long to get the hang of it, and both the process and the results are pal-pably rewarding.

Cheese and Scallion Toasts

Makes about 2 to 2½ dozen small toasts

For a casual lunch, afternoon tea, or appetizers before a barbecue, you can't beat these crunchy, tangy toasts. If you don't have walnuts, you can omit them or you can substitute pine nuts or pecans.

1 ½ cups minced scallions (white and green part), from about 2 bunches

⅓ cup minced Italian parsley

8 ounces (about 2 cups) Bellwether Carmody, St. George, or medium-sharp cheddar cheese, grated

½ cup walnut pieces, toasted and minced

½ cup mayonnaise

2 teaspoons Worcestershire sauce

½ teaspoon Larry's Bohemian Chipotle Sauce (see Bohemian Foods, Resources, page 295) or Tabasco sauce, plus more to taste

Black pepper in a mill

1 baguette, thinly sliced and toasted

In a medium bowl, mix together the scallions, parsley, cheese, walnuts, mayonnaise, Worcestershire sauce, chipotle or Tabasco sauce, and several turns of black pepper. To make the mixture in a food processor, put all of the ingredients in the work bowl and pulse until thoroughly mixed.

Preheat an oven broiler. Spread some of the scallion mixture over the surface of each slice of toasted baguette and broil until the cheese is bubbling and golden brown, about 2 to 3 minutes. Remove from the oven and serve immediately.

To drink: Taylor Maid Farms Genmaicha Tea

Mexican Cheese Bread

Serves 4

When I operated a small pub café in Cotati, we sold dozens of cheese breads a day. As soon as I added this colorful spicy version to the menu, it became a favorite among customers and was universally reviled by the staff, who hated making it. It's really not difficult at all, especially if you're making four instead of forty.

4 sourdough French rolls, unsliced

¼ cup extra virgin olive oil

8 garlic cloves, minced

3 red bell peppers, roasted, peeled, seeded, and sliced

2 serrano chiles, roasted, peeled, and minced

6 ounces (about 1 ½ cups) Sonoma Jack cheese, grated

1 firm-ripe Hass avocado, peeled and sliced lengthwise

Preheat the oven to 400°F. Use a sharp bread knife to make four crosswise cuts in each French roll, being careful not to cut all the way through the bread. Mix together the olive oil and garlic and use a pastry brush to slather some of the mixture onto each cut in the bread. Toss the red bell pepper with the roasted serranos and stuff a little of the mixture into each cut of bread, followed by some of the cheese. Set the rolls on a sheet pan and bake until the cheese is hot and bubbly, about 12 to 15 minutes. Remove from the oven, set a slice of avocado in each cut, pressing it into the melted cheese, and serve immediately.

To drink: Iced tea; Mexican beer

VARIATIONS

To make plain cheese bread, use butter instead of olive oil, and omit the peppers, serranos, avocado, and lime. Toss 4 ounces grated Carmody or mozzarella with the jack and, after stuffing the cheese into the bread, top it with minced fresh herbs.

To make cheese bread on a grill, wrap each assembled roll in aluminum foil and set it on the grill, away from the source of heat. Turn once; it will take about 12 minutes for the bread to heat through and the cheese to melt, though the time will vary depending on the intensity of the heat.

Radish & Chive Sandwiches

Serves 4 to 6

These simple sandwiches are entirely dependent on the quality of the ingredients. You must have the best-tasting radishes or these sandwiches will be rather dull. Likewise, you should begin with a good, chewy baguette, not one of those dry, crumbling things that go stale in a couple of hours.

> *5 ounces Laura Chenel chabis*
> *3 tablespoons fresh minced chives*
> *1 fresh baguette, cut in half lengthwise*
> *2 bunches French Breakfast radishes, trimmed and sliced lengthwise*
> *Kosher salt*
> *Black pepper in a mill*
> *1 ounce radish sprouts (optional)*

Use a fork to mix together the chabis and the chives. Spread the mixture over the bottom half of the baguette. Top the cheese with the radishes, season with salt and pepper, and set the sprouts, if using, on top. Press the top half of the baguette on top, and cut the sandwich into several diagonal slices. Serve immediately, or wrap tightly in plastic wrap until ready to serve.

To drink: de Lormier Sauvignon Blanc; Clos du Bois Sauvignon Blanc

Farm Market Panino with Seasonal Variations

Serves 4

The first version of this sandwich sprung to life in the late 1980s, early one morning at the Santa Rosa farmers' market while I was giving a cooking demonstration with some great locally grown garlic. Bob Cannard, a farmer in Sonoma Valley who grows produce for Chez Panisse and other high-end restaurants but no longer sells at local markets, came to my table, scooped up some of the sauce I had just made, drizzled it over a sandwich, and handed it to me. Made on a whole wheat hot dog bun from Alvarado Street Bakery, it had strips of cucumber, sweet golden tomatoes, and thin slices of baby torpedo onions. It was unforgettable, and I've used the sauce as a condiment on sandwiches ever since. Traditionally, the sauce itself is the centerpiece of the Italian meal called *bagna cauda,* in which seasonal vegetables and chunks of good bread are served alongside for dipping. You can think of this sandwich as a hand-held version. The anchovies are an essential ingredient in the sauce, but vegetarians can omit them and still have a great sandwich.

> *6 garlic cloves, minced*
> *1 cucumber, peeled and seeded*
> *2 carrots, peeled*
> *Kosher salt*

¼ cup dry white wine

3 tablespoons extra virgin olive oil

3 tablespoons butter

2 anchovy fillets, minced (optional)

4 country-style round sourdough rolls

10 radishes, thinly sliced

1 red onion, sliced into thin rings

Black pepper in a mill

3 cups fresh greens, such as arugula, mizuna, or watercress

Set aside a generous pinch of garlic. Use a vegetable peeler to shave the cucumber and the carrots into thin strips. In a medium bowl, toss them together with the pinch of garlic, a generous pinch of salt, and the white wine. Set them aside.

In a small saucepan, combine the olive oil, the butter, the remaining garlic, and the anchovies, if using, set over medium-low heat, and simmer for 3 or 4 minutes. Set aside to cool slightly. Cut the rolls in half, toast them lightly in the oven, and use a pastry brush to coat both sides of the bread with the olive oil mixture. Cover the bottom piece of each roll with a layer of cucumbers and carrots, followed by layers of radishes and onion. Season with salt and pepper, spoon a little of the remaining sauce over each sandwich, add the greens and the top part of the roll, and either serve immediately or wrap in wax paper or plastic wrap until ready to serve.

To drink: Meyer lemonade or other fresh-squeezed lemonade

SEASONAL VARIATIONS

Summer and early fall: At the peak of tomato season, omit the carrots and the wine, and cut the cucumbers into thin, crosswise slices. Cut 3 or 4 medium heirloom tomatoes into ¼-inch-thick rounds, cover the bottom piece of each roll with them, and top them with 2 or 3 fresh basil leaves before adding the sliced cucumbers. Continue to build the sandwiches as directed in the main recipe.

Late fall and early spring: Trim 1 medium fennel bulb and cut it into very thin, crosswise slices. Begin to build the sandwiches with the fennel, setting the cucumber and carrots on top of it.

Winter: Slice 2 or 3 waxy-fleshed potatoes and cook them in boiling salted water until they are just tender, about 4 or 5 minutes. Drain them thoroughly and begin to build the sandwiches with them. Omit the cucumbers and use shredded cabbage in place of the greens.

Toasted Teleme Sandwiches with Tapenade & Soppressata

Makes 2 sandwiches

Certainly, soppressata is not made in Sonoma County, but it is one of the classic Italian preserved meats I first tasted at Traverso's. It's similar to salami, only a thousand times better. Teleme is a true California cheese and is made by just two producers, one of which is the Sonoma Cheese Factory.

> 2 country-style sourdough rolls, split
> 8 to 10 slices (about 3 ounces) soppressata
> 4 ounces Teleme cheese
> ¼ cup Easy Olive Tapenade (page 269)

Toast the rolls lightly. Cover the bottom half of each roll with slices of soppressata and top with tapenade. Spread Teleme cheese over the surface of the top half of each roll, set the cheese down on the tapenade, and press the two halves together firmly. Cut each sandwich in half and serve immediately or wrap in a cloth napkin until ready to serve.

To drink: Seghesio Zinfandel—R. T.

Salmon & Tapenade Sandwiches

Serves 4

If you cook whole salmon, as I sometimes do in the summer when wild king salmon is abundant, you need recipes for leftovers. This is one of my favorites, and I often don't even wait until I have some left from a previous meal.

> ½ cup Easy Olive Tapenade (page 269)
> ½ cup mayonnaise
> 8 slices of French or Italian bread (such as Village Bakery's Sebastopol Sourdough)

1 ½ pounds salmon fillet, left over from a whole salmon, grilled or pan-roasted
Kosher salt
Black pepper in a mill
12 medium fresh basil leaves

In a small bowl, mix together the tapenade and mayonnaise. Set it aside. Lightly toast or grill the bread on both sides; spread some of the tapenade mayonnaise on each slice. Top 4 of the slices of bread with a portion of salmon, season with salt and pepper, and place 3 basil leaves on top of each piece of salmon. Top each salmon with a piece of bread. Serve immediately or wrap in wax paper and refrigerate until ready to serve.

To drink: Moshin Pinot Noir—R. T.; Gary Farrell Allen Vineyard Pinot Noir; Frick Cinsaut Rosé—P. R.

Sonoma Pan Bagnat

Serves 4 to 6

Shortly after the official sisterhood between Sonoma County and Provence, France, was established in early 1995, I found myself in northern Provence in the town of Nyons, where I visited the cookbook author and cooking teacher Lydie Marshall. Before we drove on, my friends and I stopped at the local farmers' market for sandwiches to eat in the car. The classic pan bagnat, a drippy affair, with olive oil oozing out the sides with each bite, was the best sandwich I have ever eaten, though my raging hunger likely influenced my perception. Still, it's a great sandwich and one that lends itself to life in Sonoma County. It's perfect picnic fare, so if you're heading to the beach or are on your way for a day of wine tasting, you might want to take a few sandwiches with you. Be sure to include plenty of napkins. If you don't have cooked salmon, you can use the traditional canned tuna (packed in olive oil).

1 can (2 ounces) flat anchovy fillets, drained
2 tablespoons red wine vinegar
1 large baguette
6 garlic cloves, minced
¼ cup best-quality extra virgin olive oil
1 ½ cups cooked salmon, broken into small pieces
2 tablespoons capers
3 tablespoons black olives, pitted and sliced
2 hard-cooked eggs, peeled and sliced
1 red onion, sliced into thin rounds
2 medium tomatoes, cored and sliced (through the equator, not the poles)
Kosher salt
Black pepper in a mill
¾ cup Garlic-Roasted Peppers (page 270)

About 30 minutes before making the sandwich, combine the anchovies and red wine vinegar in a small bowl and set aside.

Slice the baguette in half lengthwise. In a small bowl, combine the garlic and olive oil and use a pastry brush to brush both the top and bottom portions of the bread with the mixture, pressing firmly to push the garlic into the bread. Use all of the mixture.

Toss together the salmon, capers, and black olives, spoon the mixture over the bottom portion of the bread, spreading it evenly and pressing it into the bread. Set the eggs, slice by slice, on top of the salmon, followed by the onions and tomatoes. Season with salt and a generous amount of black pepper. Top with the anchovies, the roasted peppers, and the top portion of the bread. Cut the baguette into four sections, and wrap each tightly in plastic wrap. Refrigerate between two weights (such as two cutting boards) for several hours or overnight before serving.

To drink: Preston Vin Gris

Eggs on the Half Shell

Serves 4

I would love to serve this elegant but easy dish at midnight, after the symphony, perhaps, or at 6 A.M., following a night on the town. Nights on the town being what they are—more rare than a dinosaur's egg these days, especially in Sonoma County, which tends to be a somewhat sleepy place after dark—I'm much more likely to serve it at a dinner party, as a first course. And what begins the evening? Martinis, of course.

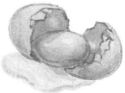

16 fresh oysters in their shells (medium-sized are best; see Note, below)
4 tablespoons butter
1 small shallot, minced
½ cup cream
8 eggs, backyard or farm market, if possible
Kosher salt
3 tablespoons snipped chives (see Note, below)
Black pepper in a mill
2 tablespoons salmon caviar or other caviar (optional)
8 baguette slices, toasted

Prepare a double boiler so that the water comes just below the bottom of the insert. Bring the water to a boil and reduce to a simmer.

Shuck the oysters over a medium bowl so that you catch their liquor. Remove the oysters from the shells and set on a plate. Reserve the lower halves of the shells (the cupped side); discard the flat halves of the shells. Strain the oyster liquor through a very fine sieve or through a strainer lined with cheesecloth. (In a pinch, you can strain it through a coffee filter, though this will take longer.)

In a small saucepan, melt ½ tablespoon of the butter over low heat, add the shallot, and sauté until very soft and fragrant, about 8 minutes. Add the cream and the oyster liquor, bring to a simmer, and reduce by half. Set aside.

Melt a small amount of butter in the top of the double boiler. Break the eggs, one at a time, into a small dish and then add them to a large bowl. Use a whisk to whip them together until they are relatively smooth. Break the remaining butter into small bits and add it to the eggs, along with 2 teaspoons of kosher salt, 2 tablespoons of the chives, and 5 or 6 turns of black pepper. Place the egg mixture in the top of the double boiler. Use a wooden spoon or rubber spatula to break up the curds and move them toward the center of the pan. Work slowly and gently; it will take about 12 to 15 minutes for the eggs to cook. When they are done, they should be moist and creamy.

Meanwhile, wash and dry the cupped oyster shells and divide them among 4 serving plates. Just before the eggs are done, return the cream mixture to medium-low heat and when it simmers add the oysters; poach for 30 seconds, and use a slotted spoon to transfer them to the eggs. Fold them in gently.

Fill the oyster shells with the scrambled egg mixture, making sure to distribute the oysters evenly. Taste the sauce, correct the seasoning, and spoon a little over each portion. Top each with a scattering of chives and a little dollop of caviar, if using, garnish with baguette slices, and serve immediately.

Notes: Although you can slice chives into thin rounds using a knife, it is easier if you snip them with scissors. Hold a small bunch in your hand and with your other hand snip the chives crosswise, as thin as possible.

Fresh oysters are often available in the meat and seafood department of good supermarkets, or at specialty fish markets. Sometimes the clerk will shuck the oysters for you, and if this is the case when you buy oysters for this recipe, ask that the liquor and shells be reserved. Strain the liquor through cheesecloth before using it.

To drink: Martinis; Gloria Ferrer Brut in magnums—D. R.

Apple & Bellwether Blue Omelette

Serves 2

Apples have been an important crop in Sonoma County since the Russians planted trees in the early 1800s. Although many farmers have been struggling for years and orchards have been replaced with vineyards, other growers are planting antique varieties. Beginning in July and continuing into October, you'll find such varieties as Pink

Lady, Empire, Almatta, Enterprise, Gala, Fuji, and, of course, the Gravenstein, at local farmers' markets. Here, you want an apple that will not fall apart when it is sautéed. Bellwether Blue is to my knowledge the first commercial blue cheese made in Sonoma County. Its lush yellow color comes from Jersey cow's milk; its creamy texture evokes Gorgonzola, though it is a milder cheese.

3 tablespoons unsalted butter

2 large apples, peeled, cored, and sliced

¾ teaspoon kosher salt, plus more to taste

¼ teaspoon freshly ground black pepper, plus more to taste

⅛ teaspoon cinnamon

6 eggs

3 ounces Bellwether Blue, Maytag Blue, or imported Gorgonzola, broken into pieces (see Resources, page 295)

Buttered toast

Gravenstein Apple Butter (page 274)

Melt 2 tablespoons of butter in a large sauté pan set over medium heat, and when it is foamy, add the apples and sauté them until they are golden brown on both sides. Add the salt, black pepper, and cinnamon and toss gently but thoroughly. Remove from the heat and set aside.

The omelettes are best made one at a time. Heat 2 teaspoons of the remaining butter in a 7-inch omelette pan set over medium heat. Break 3 of the eggs into a small bowl, season with salt and pepper, quickly beat with a fork or whisk, and when the butter is foamy, pour the eggs into the pan, swirling the pan to distribute the eggs evenly. Using a fork, move the cooked eggs toward the center of the pan and let the uncooked egg flow out toward the edges.

When the eggs are almost set, place half of the cooked apples over half of the omelette, top the apples with half of the cheese, fold the omelette in half, and cook for 30 seconds more. Carefully transfer the omelette to a warmed plate by tipping the pan over on top of the plate. Make the second omelette in the same manner. Serve immediately, with buttered toast and apple butter alongside.

To drink: Ace in the Hole honey cider

Burbank Tortilla

Serves 4 to 6

Tortilla español is the classic potato and egg dish, similar to an omelette or a frittata, and served in tapas bars all over Spain and the Basque region of France. It is usually accompanied by *allioli,* or aioli. I've added diced and sautéed nopales to my version because they grow all over Sonoma County and because I'm always looking for new ways to use them. These spineless cactus paddles owe their existence to the botanist Luther Burbank, who envisioned turning the desert into grazing land for cattle; he thought the cattle would love them and he was right. There was just one problem; the cattle liked them so much that they chewed them down to the quick so that they could not regenerate, a fact that must have distressed Burbank. He said many times that he was able to communicate directly with his plants, that his work involved more than just science and simple intuition. As he worked to develop a cactus without those long, sharp needles, he told the plants that they had nothing to fear, that they could give up their defensive spines without worry, that he would protect them. In the short run, he was wrong, and I've always wondered if he felt as if he'd broken a promise. Today, the cactus thrives all over Sonoma County and far beyond our borders. The one he planted at his Santa Rosa home is enormous; if you find yourself nearby, be sure to take a look.

> 8 ounces trimmed and diced nopales (see Note, page 116)
> ½ cup olive oil, plus more as needed
> 1 small yellow onion, diced
> 6 garlic cloves, minced
> 2 pounds potatoes, cooked, peeled, and thinly sliced
> Kosher salt
> Black pepper in a mill
> 8 large eggs

In a medium sauté pan set over medium-low heat, cook the nopales until all of the liquid they release has evaporated—about 10 to 15 minutes; stir them occasionally so they do not brown. Transfer the nopales to a small bowl. Return the pan to the heat.

Heat 3 tablespoons of the olive oil in the sauté pan, add the onion, and sauté slowly until it is very soft, fragrant, and beginning to color, about 25 minutes. Add the garlic cloves, sauté for 2 minutes more, and transfer the mixture to the bowl with the nopales. Add 3 more tablespoons of the olive oil to the sauté pan and fry the potatoes, tossing frequently, until they are golden brown, about 15 minutes. Season with salt and pepper and remove from the heat.

In a large bowl, beat the eggs with a whisk as you would for an omelette, fold in the nopales and onion mixture, and stir in the potatoes. Wipe the sauté pan clean, add the remaining 2 tablespoons of olive oil, and set the pan over medium-low heat. When the pan is hot but not too hot or smoking, pour in the egg mixture, reduce the heat to low, and cook without stirring until the bottom is golden brown, about 10 minutes. Loosen the edges of the tortilla with a rubber spatula. Set a plate that is slightly larger than the pan on top of the pan and turn both over together, so that the tortilla drops onto the plate. If the pan seems very dry or if egg has stuck to it anywhere, add another tablespoon of olive oil and heat it through before sliding the tortilla back, cooked-side up. Cook until the eggs are completely set and the bottom is golden brown, about 3 to 4 minutes more.

Transfer to a serving plate, let rest 5 minutes, cut into wedges, and serve warm.

To drink: Fino sherry; Geyser Peak 1999 Sauvignon Blanc—P. R.

Savory Italian Bread Pudding

Serves 4 to 6

Savory bread pudding makes an excellent accompaniment to grilled or roasted meats and poultry. It can also be served on its own, accompanied by soup and salad. You can vary it according to what you have in your pantry. Use walnuts in place of pine nuts, for example; add some diced dried tomatoes and minced olives; or replace the oregano with sage.

2 teaspoons olive oil

1 loaf (1 pound) of Italian country-style bread, cut into ¾-inch cubes

¾ cup pine nuts, toasted

4 ounces Bellwether Carmody, St. George, Sonoma Jack, or Italian fontina, grated

4 garlic cloves, minced

4 eggs, beaten

1 tablespoon minced fresh Italian parsley

2 teaspoons minced fresh oregano

3½ cups whole milk

Kosher salt

Black pepper in a mill

Preheat the oven to 350°F. Brush the inside of a 9- by 13-inch glass baking dish with the olive oil. In a large bowl, toss together the bread cubes, pine nuts, cheese, and garlic and put the mixture into the baking dish. Whisk together the eggs, parsley, oregano, and milk, season with salt and pepper, and pour over the bread. Place in the oven, lower the temperature to 300°F, and bake for 35 minutes. Increase the heat to 400°F and bake until the top is golden brown, about 10 to 15 minutes more.

Cool slightly, cut into squares, and serve immediately.

To drink: Iron Horse Sangiovese; Clos du Bois Temperanillo

Tomato Custard Tart in a Cornmeal Crust

Serves 4

The custard in this tart is soft and tender, providing a voluptuous contrast to the crunchy cornmeal crust. For the custard to be at its most delicious, the tart should be served warm. Be sure to read about peeling tomatoes on page 120.

> 3 medium or 2 large heirloom tomatoes, such as Brandywine or Northern
> Lights, peeled and sliced
> Kosher salt

CRUST
> ⅔ cup plus 2 tablespoons all-purpose flour, plus more for the work surface
> ⅓ cup coarse-ground cornmeal
> ¾ teaspoon kosher salt
> ½ teaspoon baking powder
> 4 tablespoons unsalted butter, chilled and cut into pieces
> 1 egg

> ⁂

> 3 strips bacon
> 1 ounce Bellwether Carmody cheese
> 1 to 2 teaspoons olive oil

CUSTARD

1 whole egg

1 egg yolk

½ cup cream

½ cup half-and-half

Kosher salt

Black pepper in a mill

Set the sliced tomatoes on a plate, sprinkle with a little salt, and set aside.

Make the pastry dough for the crust. Place the flour, cornmeal, salt, and baking powder in the work bowl of a food processor and pulse two or three times. Add the butter, pulse several times until the mixture is crumbly, add the egg, and pulse just until the dough comes together. Turn out onto a floured work surface, knead two or three times, and form into a ball. Pat the ball into a 9-inch circle, cover with plastic wrap, and refrigerate for at least 30 minutes.

While the dough is resting, fry the bacon until it is crisp, drain it on absorbent paper, crumble it, and set it aside. Grate the cheese and set it aside.

Preheat the oven to 350°F. Brush the olive oil onto the inside of an 8-inch tart pan that has a removable bottom. Press the chilled dough into the pan and scatter the bacon over the surface of the dough.

To make the custard, in a medium bowl, whisk together the whole egg and egg yolk until well blended; add the cream and half-and-half, season with salt and pepper, and whisk until smooth.

Drain any liquid from the tomatoes and dry each slice on a tea towel. Arrange in a single layer on top of the bacon, sprinkle with the grated cheese, and carefully pour in the custard. Place in the center of the oven's lowest rack and bake until the custard is just set, about 35 to 40 minutes. Set on a rack to cool for 5 minutes, remove the ring of the pan, cut the tart into wedges, and serve warm.

To drink: Toad Hollow Zinfandel—R. T.

Tomato Galette

Serves 4

The crust of this tart is light and flaky and is perfectly complemented by the crunchy crystals of coarse salt. Of course, the success of the tart depends entirely on the quality of tomatoes. Standard supermarket tomatoes will produce disappointing results; instead, use tomatoes from the farmers' market and choose a variety that has thick, dense flesh so that they aren't too watery. This tart should be made only in the late summer and early fall, when tomatoes are in season.

CRUST

1 cup all-purpose flour

¾ teaspoon kosher salt

1 teaspoon whole black peppercorns, ground in a mortar with a pestle

6 tablespoons butter, chilled and cut into cubes

¼ cup ice water

❋

4 to 5 medium-sized, dense-fleshed heirloom tomatoes, such as Brandywine or Northern Lights

Kosher salt

4 strips bacon or pancetta

3 ounces Italian fontina, thinly sliced

Black pepper in a mill

2 tablespoons fresh snipped chives or fresh minced Italian parsley

1 egg white, mixed with 1 tablespoon of water to make a wash

1 teaspoon coarse sea salt or Hawaiian alaea salt

First, make the galette dough. Combine the flour, salt, and ground black peppercorns in a small work bowl, and use your fingers or a pastry cutter to work in the butter so that the mixture resembles coarse-ground cornmeal. Add the ice water, gently press the dough together, and gather it up into a ball. Chill for 1 hour.

Meanwhile, remove the stem cores of each tomato and slice off each end. Cut each tomato into ⅜-inch-thick rounds, season with salt, cover the slices with a tea towel, and set them aside. Fry the pancetta or bacon until it is just barely crisp; transfer to absorbent paper and set aside. Drain the juices that have collected around the tomatoes, using your fingers to press out any large pockets of seeds and gel.

Preheat the oven to 400°F. Line a baking sheet with parchment paper and set it aside. Set the chilled dough on a floured work surface and use the palm of your hand to pat it flat. Roll it into a 14-inch circle about ⅛ inch thick and carefully transfer it to the parchment-lined baking sheet.

Arrange the cheese over the surface of the tart, leaving a 2-inch margin around the edges. If more juices have accumulated around the tomatoes, drain them again and place the tomatoes on top of the cheese in concentric circles that overlap slightly. Season the tomatoes lightly with kosher salt and generously with black pepper from the mill. Scatter the chives over the top of the tomatoes, arrange the bacon strips on top, and then gently fold the edges of the tart up and over the tomatoes, pleating the edges as you fold them. Using a pastry brush, brush the edge of the tart lightly with the egg wash and sprinkle it with the coarse or Hawaiian salt. Bake until the pastry is golden brown and the tomatoes soft and fragrant, about 35 to 40 minutes. Transfer to a rack to cool, cut into wedges, and serve warm.

To drink: Nalle 1998 Zinfandel—P. R.

Wild Mushroom Pizza

Serves 3 to 4

Once you discard the idea that pizza needs tomato sauce, the possibilities expand enormously. Without tomato sauce, the flavors of other ingredients stand on their own and complement one another in ways that are impossible when tomato sauce is the common denominator. Wild mushrooms are widely available these days, in supermarkets, at farmers' markets, and by mail order (see Gourmet Mushrooms, Inc., Resources, page 295). If you gather your own, you must either go with an expert guide or consult an expert if you are not 100 percent certain that your mushrooms are safe.

> *3 tablespoons olive oil, plus more as needed*
> *1 shallot*
> *4 garlic cloves, minced*
> *½ pound wild mushrooms, such as chanterelle, black chanterelle, hedgehog, boletes, or matsutake*
> *2 teaspoons grated fresh ginger*
> *¼ cup sherry*
> *Kosher salt*

Black pepper in a mill
All-purpose flour or fine-ground cornmeal
One 12-inch pizza shell (recipe follows)
4 ounces Italian fontina, thinly sliced
1 bunch scallions, trimmed and thinly sliced

Heat the olive oil in a large, heavy sauté pan set over medium-low heat and sauté the shallot until it is soft and fragrant, about 5 to 6 minutes. Add the garlic and sauté for 2 minutes more. Increase the heat to medium, add the mushrooms and ginger, toss thoroughly, add the sherry, cover the pan, and simmer until the mushrooms are completely wilted, about 5 to 12 minutes, depending on the variety. Remove the lid and simmer until the liquid is evaporated. Season with salt and pepper and let cool to room temperature.

Preheat the oven to 450°F and place a pizza stone or baking tile in the center of the middle rack of the oven. Brush the surface of the dough lightly with olive oil, cover it with the cheese, and spread the mushrooms on top in an even layer. Sprinkle the scallions on top.

Carefully transfer the pizza to the baking stone. Bake for 12 to 15 minutes, until the edges of the crust are golden brown. Remove from the oven, cut into wedges, and serve immediately.

PIZZA DOUGH
1 teaspoon active dry yeast
½ cup warm water
1¾ cups all-purpose flour, plus more as needed
¾ teaspoon kosher salt
¾ teaspoon fresh ground black pepper
1 tablespoon extra virgin olive oil, plus more for the dough
Cornmeal

Combine the yeast and water in a large mixing bowl, and set the bowl aside for 10 minutes. Stir in ½ cup of the flour, followed by the salt, pepper, and olive oil. Stir in the remaining flour, ½ cup at a time.

Sprinkle your work surface generously with flour, turn out the dough, and knead it until it is velvety, about 7 or 8 minutes, working in more flour as you knead. Coat the inside of a large mixing bowl with olive oil, set the dough inside, cover it with a damp towel, and set it aside in a moderately warm but not overly hot place. Let the dough rise for between 2 and 3 hours, until it has doubled in size. Gently turn the dough out onto a lightly floured surface and let it rest for 5 minutes. Pat it into a flat circle and then use a rolling pin to roll it into a 10- to 12-inch circle. Sprinkle a layer of cornmeal over a pizza paddle, set the pizza dough on top, and let it rise for 1 hour before adding toppings and baking it.

To drink: Chardonnay—R. T.; Unti 1998 Syrah—P. R.

Winter Squash & Feta Calzone

Serves 3 to 4

Mary Karlin, an enthusiastic supporter of Sonoma County food, wine, and agriculture, has a wonderful outdoor kitchen, small, rustic, beautiful, and warmed by a wood-burning oven and fireplace. When Mary invited me over to experiment with her oven—I hadn't cooked in one at that time—I made this calzone, which puffed up and browned perfectly in the hot dry heat. The crust was superb, the inside fragrant and hot.

> *6 cups cubed winter squash (see Note, below)*
> *1 large or 2 small yellow onions, cut in chunks*
> *2 tablespoons extra virgin olive oil, plus more for the dough*
> *Kosher salt*
> *Black pepper in a mill*
> *½ to 1 teaspoon chipotle powder*
> *2 poblano chiles, roasted, seeded, and cut in chunks*
> *6 garlic cloves, minced*
> *6 ounces feta cheese, cut in ½-inch dice*
> *1 recipe pizza dough (page 151)*
> *Coarse sea salt, such as sel gris*
> *Cornmeal or polenta*

Preheat the oven to 350°F. Place the squash and onions in a shallow, ovenproof baking dish, drizzle with the 2 tablespoons of olive oil, season with salt, pepper, and ½ teaspoon of the chipotle powder. Stir to coat all of the squash and onions evenly with the olive oil and seasonings and bake until the squash is just tender, about 20 to 40 minutes, depending on the variety. Stir two or three times as the vegetables cook. Let cool, stir in the poblanos, garlic, and feta cheese, taste, and correct the seasoning with more salt, more pepper, and the remaining chipotle powder if necessary.

Increase the oven heat to 500°F, and if you have a pizza stone, place it in the oven. Drizzle a little olive oil over the pizza dough and set the filling on one half of the dough, spreading it so it covers the surface with a ¾-inch edge left free. Fold the dough across the filling and match up the edges; crimp them closed with a fork. Brush the top of the dough with a little more olive oil and sprinkle the coarse salt on top. Let rest for 15 minutes.

Sprinkle cornmeal or polenta over the surface on which you will cook the calzone and carefully transfer the calzone onto it. Bake until the dough is puffed up and golden brown, about 12 to 16 minutes, depending on the oven. Let rest on a cutting board for 3 to 4 minutes before cutting into wedges and serving.

Note: A firm-fleshed squash such as Tahitian Melon is ideal here because it becomes tender without disintegrating; butternut, buttercup, kuri, and kabocha are good, too; avoid the common jack-o-lantern pumpkin, which is too stringy and watery for most recipes.

To drink: Laurel Glen 1996 Counterpoint Cabernet Sauvignon—P. R.

Shell Bean & Chard Calzone

Serves 3 to 4

Calzone, a large savory turnover of sorts, is best when it's more than just a typical American pizza with the filling on the inside. In this recipe creamy shell beans combined with Swiss chard makes a luscious but not heavy dish. Variations following the main recipe feature some of my favorite versions, but you should feel free to experiment with your own combinations, too.

> *4 ounces dried beans, such as marrowfats, soaked for several hours and drained*
> *1 bay leaf*
> *1 small yellow onion, quartered*

1 celery stalk

2 tablespoons olive oil

8 garlic cloves, minced

1 large bunch (1 ¼ pounds) Swiss chard, large stems trimmed and discarded, cut in 1-inch-wide crosswise strips

Kosher salt

Black pepper in a mill

Zest of 1 lemon

½ teaspoon red pepper flakes or chipotle flakes

2 tablespoons minced Italian parsley

4 ounces Dry Jack, grated on a large blade

1 recipe pizza dough (page 151)

Cornmeal or polenta

Chipotle Oil (page 262) or more olive oil

White wine or champagne vinegar

Place the beans in a medium saucepan, add the bay leaf, onion, celery, and enough water to come 1 inch over the beans. Bring to a boil over high heat, reduce the heat to medium-low, and simmer until the beans are tender, about 40 to 60 minutes, depending on the age and variety of bean. Discard the bay leaf, onion, and celery, drain the beans, and place them in a mixing bowl.

Heat the olive oil in a medium sauté pan set over medium-low heat, add the garlic, and sauté for 30 seconds. Do not let the garlic burn. Add the chard, toss with the garlic, season with salt and pepper, cover the pan, and cook until the chard is wilted, about 6 or 7 minutes. Toss the cooked chard with the beans, add the lemon zest, pepper flakes, parsley, and Dry Jack, and toss together thoroughly. Taste and correct the seasoning.

Preheat the oven to 500°F, and if you have a pizza stone, place it in the oven. Drizzle a little olive oil over the pizza dough and set the filling on one half of the dough, spreading it so it covers the surface with a ¾-inch edge left free. Fold the dough across the filling and match up the edges; crimp them closed with a fork. Let rest for 15 minutes.

Sprinkle cornmeal or polenta over the surface on which you will cook the calzone and carefully transfer the calzone onto it. Bake until the dough is puffed up and golden brown, about 12 to 18 minutes, depending on the oven. Brush the top with chipotle oil and let rest on a cutting board for 3 to 4 minutes before cutting into wedges and serving, with the vinegar alongside.

To drink: Pedroncelli Sauvignon Blanc—B. T.

VARIATIONS

Fry 3 spicy Italian sausages until they are firm and evenly browned; cool slightly, cut in half lengthwise, and cut each half into ¼-inch-wide half moons. Toss with the beans and chard.

For a somewhat creamier calzone, use 4 ounces of mozzarella fresca, torn into small pieces, in place of the Dry Jack.

Use black beans, omit the chard and lemon zest, and use Garlic-Roasted Peppers (page 270) in their place. Fry two smoked andouille sausages, slice them, and scatter them on top of the filling before closing the calzone.

CHAPTER 4

Pasta, Rice
& Other Grains

IN THE 1950S, Americans called pasta "macaroni" and "noodles" and avoided it because it would make you fat. With the popularity of the Mediterranean diet in the early 1990s, pasta became a panacea; we could eat mounds of it without a worry because a carbohydrate-based diet would make us healthy, thin, and immune to heart disease. Drench the pasta in olive oil and add a glass of red wine alongside and we'd live forever, or nearly. The nutritional pendulum continues to swing, blessing foods as it passes over them, condemning them as it moves on. But by the time nutritionists questioned the value of indulging quite so heavily in grains—eaten with abandon, some warned, they actually *do* make you fat and might cause type II diabetes, to boot—pasta had become an indispensable element of our diet. We cook our linguine al dente, we tackle risottos without fear, make lump-free polenta with our eyes closed. As you cook these recipes—or simply use them for ideas and inspiration for your own dishes—keep in mind that grains should taste like themselves, pasta of wheat, polenta of corn, rice of rice. There is a tendency to cover everything up with an abundance of sauce, but we'll be better off if we think of the grain itself as the point, and the sauce as a condiment to highlight but not eclipse it.

Linguine with Mesclun

Serves 4

This is one of my favorite casual recipes, and I've been reluctant to put it in print because it's so simple and the ingredients really don't need to be measured. Recipes being what they are, I've given the traditional cues, but if you want to make it up for yourself, all you need to do is grab a couple of big handfuls of salad mix and toss it with the quantity of pasta you usually make for yourself. You can add other ingredients if you like—minced sun-dried tomatoes, minced olives, or toasted walnuts—or you can use any vinaigrette. The main thing is to use excellent greens; I like the winter salad mix from Paul's Produce in Sonoma because the little leaves are so hardy they don't wilt completely, but stay pleasantly crunchy. The variation in the amount of mesclun called for reflects the different styles of mix—lighter lettuces and greens will have more volume, hardier winter mixes, such as Paul's, will be heavier.

> *1 pound dry linguine*
> *¼ to ½ pound mesclun (salad mix)*
> *Kosher salt*
> *Olive oil*
> *2 lemons*
> *Black pepper in a mill*
> *Dry Jack or Parmigiano-Reggiano, in one piece*

Cook the linguine in boiling salted water according to package directions. When it is done, drain thoroughly and rinse briefly in warm water.

Place the greens in a large serving bowl, sprinkle them with salt, and toss quickly. Drizzle 3 or 4 tablespoons of olive oil over the greens and toss again. Add the pasta, toss, and add a little more olive oil if necessary to moisten the linguine. Squeeze lemon juice over the mixture, add several turns of black pepper, and toss again. Taste, correct the seasoning, grate a generous amount of cheese over the top, and serve immediately.

To drink: Sauvignon Blanc; Beaujolais; Beaujolais Nouveau

Pasta with Uncooked Tomato Ricotta Sauce

Serves 4 to 6

As tomatoes eventually come into season, you can incorporate them into a huge variety of uncooked pasta sauces. Here, they are paired with rich fresh ricotta for a very refreshing summer dish. Fresh ricotta is quite different from what we're used to finding in most American supermarkets. It is light, delicate, with large, tender, distinct curds; if you can't find it, ask a local Italian deli if they can locate some for you.

3 cups cherry tomatoes, halved (or quartered, if large)

4 or 5 garlic cloves, minced

4 tablespoons extra virgin olive oil

1 tablespoon red wine vinegar or fresh lemon juice

½ cup sliced pitted olives, any variety (optional)

A handful of fresh herbs (basil, thyme, oregano, Italian parsley),
    torn into small pieces

Kosher salt

Black pepper in a mill

Pasta with Herb Flowers & Dry Jack

Because of the long growing season and fertile soils in Sonoma County, it is easy to have a garden, even if it's just a small border of herbs. It also makes a lot of sense to do so. Fresh herbs taste different from dried herbs, and you rarely need as much of a single fresh herb as you have to buy at the market. In much of coastal California including Sonoma, you can grow most herbs year round—I almost always have rosemary, sage, a few varieties of thyme, marjoram, oregano, epazote, winter savory, and chives just outside my kitchen door. In late spring, there's cilantro, and in the summer there's plenty of basil, too. To keep plants producing, you should harvest the flowers before they turn to seed. Herb flowers picked on long stems make lovely, fragrant additions to bouquets. They contribute delicate flavors and aromas to green salads, and they can be minced and added to sauces and omelettes. To enjoy them on their own, pick a cup or so of herb flowers and add them to hot spaghettini tossed with good, organic butter. Grate a generous amount of Dry Jack cheese over the pasta, season with salt and pepper, and serve immediately. (Twelve ounces of dried pasta will serve 3 to 4 people.)

1 pound orecchiette or large pasta shells

6 ounces (¾ cup) fresh Bellwether ricotta or fromage blanc

1 tablespoon fresh snipped chives

In a large bowl, combine the tomatoes, garlic, olive oil, vinegar or lemon juice, olives (if using), and herbs. Season with salt and pepper, cover, and set aside at room temperature for 30 minutes.

Bring a large pot of salted water to a boil and cook the pasta according to package directions. Toss the ricotta with the tomatoes. Drain the pasta, do not rinse it, and immediately add it to the tomato and ricotta mixture. Toss thoroughly so that the cheese melts from the heat of the pasta. Taste, correct the seasoning, scatter the chives over the top, and serve immediately.

To drink: Seghesio Pinot Grigio—B. T.

Spaghetti Carbonara Sonoma

Serves 4

Although Niman Ranch is not in Sonoma County, its primary location is on Chileno Valley Road, just past the Sonoma County line in Marin County. After years of success raising beef in ways that are both humane and environmentally considerate, Bill Niman has expanded to pork and lamb, too, which is very good news when it comes to bacon. You can find bacon from Niman Ranch at Trader Joe's Markets.

Kosher salt

12 ounces dried spaghetti

1 tablespoon olive oil

4 garlic cloves, minced

¼ pound Niman Ranch bacon, diced

3 eggs, beaten

3 tablespoons minced fresh Italian parsley

2 teaspoons freshly crushed black pepper

4 ounces Dry Jack cheese, grated

Black pepper in a mill

Bring a large pot of water to a boil, add 1 tablespoon of salt, and cook the pasta according to package directions. Drain, but do not rinse, the pasta.

Meanwhile, heat the olive oil in a heavy skillet set over medium heat, add the garlic, and sauté for 30 seconds. Do not let it brown. Add the bacon and cook until it is just crisp. While the bacon cooks, combine the eggs, parsley, crushed black pepper, 1 teaspoon of kosher salt, and the cheese in a large bowl. Let the cooked bacon cool slightly and pour it into the egg mixture, mixing continuously. Add the cooked pasta and use two large forks to toss it quickly and continuously so that the mixture coats the pasta but the eggs do not set. Serve immediately.

To drink: Rabbit Ridge Sangiovese—B. T.

Pasta with Confetti Tomatoes & Basil Flowers

"You don't need to memorize what's in season," I tell people. "Just go to the farmers' market and open your eyes. If it's there, it's in season." Sadly, there *are* exceptions to this simple logic, but the abuses are smaller than the ones at the supermarket. You may see hydroponic tomatoes in March, but you won't see watermelons or apricots in January. Cherry tomatoes are almost always the first tomatoes of the season and, as the harvest continues, many farmers sell baskets of multicolored cherry tomatoes. I'm not sure who first called them confetti tomatoes, but the name has caught on. They are beautiful and delicious, and perfect for a quick summer pasta. Just slice up a couple of pint baskets of tomatoes, cutting the smallest ones in half and the larger ones in quarters. If you begin as soon as you put a big pot of water on the stove to boil, you'll be done by the time it's rolling. Add a tablespoon of salt and about 12 ounces of dried orecchiette (or other small but not tiny pasta shape) to the boiling water and cook according to package directions. Mince 2 or 3 garlic cloves and a handful of basil flowers, and toss them with the cherry tomatoes in a large pasta bowl. When the pasta is done, drain it and immediately toss it with the tomatoes, along with ⅓ cup of the most flavorful olive oil you have. Cut some fresh mozzarella into cubes, toss with the pasta, season it all with salt and pepper, and serve it immediately.

Vella's Pasta alla Campagna

Serves 4 to 6

Ig Vella offered me this exuberant recipe for the first edition of *A Cook's Tour of Sonoma*. I find the combination of flavors—the tangy mustard and vinegar, the sultry bacon, the sweetness of the pecans, the kiss of heat from the pepper flakes—utterly irresistible. If you can get California Gold Dry Jack—the same as Vella's other Dry Jacks, only aged longer—this is a great place to use it; its nuttiness and depth of flavor is perfect in this complex (but easy to make) dish.

1 pound bacon, diced
1 pound Swiss chard
1 tablespoon Dijon mustard
3 tablespoons red wine vinegar
1 tablespoon kosher salt, plus more to taste
12 ounces penne
3 tablespoons olive oil
3 cloves garlic, pressed
½ teaspoon red pepper flakes, or more to taste
Black pepper in a mill
8 ounces Vella Dry Jack, grated (2 cups)
1 cup shelled pecans, coarsely chopped and toasted

Cook the bacon in a large saucepan or sauté pan until it is just crisp, use a slotted spoon to transfer it to absorbent paper, and drain off and discard all but 3 tablespoons of the bacon fat. Set the pan aside. Wash the chard, dry it thoroughly, and remove the stems. Trim and discard the base of the stems, and cut the stems into thin slices. Cut the leaves into ½-inch-thick crosswise strips. Keep the leaves and stems separate and set both aside. In a small bowl, mix together the mustard and vinegar and set the mixture aside.

Bring a large pot of water to a boil, add the 1 tablespoon kosher salt, and cook the pasta according to package directions until it is just tender. Drain thoroughly but do not rinse.

While the pasta cooks, heat the bacon fat and the olive oil over medium-low heat and, when it is hot, add the chard stems, garlic, and pepper flakes. Sauté until the chard stems are tender. Add the chard leaves, cover the pan, and cook until the leaves are wilted, about 4 or 5 minutes. Season with salt and pepper and remove from the heat.

Place the hot pasta in a large bowl, pour the mustard mixture over it, and toss thoroughly. Add the chard mixture, the cheese, and three-quarters of the pecans and toss again. Top with the remaining pecans and serve immediately.

To drink: Geyser Peak Syrah—B. T.

Chicken Liver & Chorizo Spaghetti

Serves 4 to 6

Chicken livers come in and out of fashion; regardless of their general popularity at any particular time, there are those who love them and those who hate even the sight of them. If you love them, you'll want to try this recipe; after making it once, it will become a staple, I promise. It is important to buy the best livers you can find, and that means livers from free-range chickens that have been fed organically and have not been treated with antibiotics. Livers from such chickens taste better, and they are also healthier for everyone involved, from the chicken and the people who tend it and process it to you and the environment at large. Sonoma County has been a pioneer in poultry for decades; the first free-range chicken, Rocky, came from Sebastopol. His organic sister, Rosie, was developed in Petaluma and introduced to retail markets in eleven states in 1999.

> *1 tablespoon kosher salt, plus more to taste*
> *1 pound dried spaghetti*
> *3 tablespoons olive oil*
> *2 shallots, minced*

10 garlic cloves, minced

¾ pound Spanish chorizo or linguiça, thinly sliced

1½ pounds free-range chicken livers, cleaned, trimmed, and sliced

½ teaspoon ground allspice

1 teaspoon minced fresh sage

½ teaspoon thyme leaves

Juice of 1 lemon

Black pepper in a mill

3 tablespoons extra virgin olive oil

1 cup red Oven-Roasted Peppers, julienned (page 227)

Sage sprigs, for garnish

Thyme sprigs, for garnish

Fill a large pot with water, add the tablespoon of kosher salt, set it over high heat, and bring it to a boil. Cook the spaghetti according to the package directions.

Meanwhile, heat the olive oil in a large sauté pan set over medium heat, add the shallots, and sauté until soft and fragrant, about 7 to 8 minutes. Add the garlic and sauté for 2 minutes more. Add the chorizo or linguiça and sauté until cooked through and just beginning to brown. Add the chicken livers and sauté for 2 minutes, tossing or stirring continuously; do not overcook. Add the allspice, sage, thyme leaves, and lemon juice, and season with salt and pepper.

Drain the pasta but don't rinse it. Place it in a large pasta bowl and toss with the extra virgin olive oil. Add the chicken liver mixture and all but a small handful of the peppers and toss again, lightly. Scatter the remaining peppers on top, garnish with herb sprigs, and serve immediately.

To drink: Foppiano Petite Sirah—B. T.

Potato Gnocchi with Duck Ragout

Serves 4 to 6

The little potato dumplings known as gnocchi owe something to Sonoma County's most famous gardener, the botanist Luther Burbank, who sold his Burbank russet for enough money to fund his move from his native Massachusetts to Sonoma County. Gnocchi are never better than when they're made with a good Burbank potato. In the summer, dress gnocchi simply, with pesto, pistou, or butter and herbs. In the winter months when we want heartier fare, this duck ragout is perfect. For a beautiful and delicious fall version with beets, consult the variation at the end of the recipe.

> *Gnocchi (recipe follows)*
> *3 tablespoons olive oil*
> *1 yellow onion, minced*
> *4 garlic cloves, minced*
> *Kosher salt*
> *Black pepper in a mill*
> *Pinch of cinnamon*
> *Whole nutmeg*
> *2 cups duck stock*
> *2 cups duck leg or thigh meat, cooked and shredded*
> *1 can (28 ounces) diced tomatoes, preferably Muir Glen brand*
> *¼ cup minced fresh Italian parsley*
> *Dry Jack or Parmigiano-Reggiano, in one piece*

Make the gnocchi but do not cook them. Heat the olive oil in a medium sauté pan set over medium-low heat, add the onion, and cook until it is very soft, fragrant, and sweet, about 25 to 30 minutes. Add the garlic, cook for 2 minutes more, and season with salt and pepper; add the cinnamon and grate in a little nutmeg. Increase the heat to medium-high, add the duck stock, and simmer until the stock is reduced by two-thirds, about 10 minutes. Stir in the duck meat and the tomatoes, reduce the heat to medium low, and simmer for 20 minutes. Taste the sauce, correct the seasoning, and remove from the heat while you cook the gnocchi.

When the gnocchi are cooked, stir half of the Italian parsley into the sauce and, if necessary (it shouldn't be), reheat it. Pour the sauce over the gnocchi, toss gently, garnish with the remaining Italian parsley, and serve immediately. Pass the cheese and a grater alongside.

GNOCCHI

1½ pounds Burbank russet potatoes

1 teaspoon kosher salt

1 cup all-purpose flour

Preheat the oven to 375°F. Bake the potatoes until they are tender when pierced with a fork, about 1 hour. Let cool briefly and break each potato in half, crosswise. Press a potato half, torn-side down, through a potato ricer into a medium bowl; remove and discard the peel, and continue until all of the potatoes have been riced.

Add the salt and the flour, ¼ cup at a time, to the potatoes until the mixture will not take any more flour. After the second or third addition of flour, knead the dough between additions. The dough should be smooth, somewhat soft, and slightly sticky. Sprinkle flour over your work surface, dust your hands with flour, and break the dough into 4 pieces. Roll each piece into a long cord about ¾ inch in diameter; cut each cord into ¾-inch lengths.

Next, take a fork with long, thin prongs that are slightly rounded. In one hand, hold the fork sideways, with the prongs parallel to the cutting surface and the concave side facing towards you. With the other hand, place a potato dumpling on the inside curve of the fork just below the points of the prongs and press it against the prongs with the tip of the index finger pointing directly at and perpendicular to the fork. While pressing the dumpling with your finger, flip it away from the prong tips and toward the handle of the fork. Flip it; don't drag it. As it rolls to the base of the prongs, let it drop to the counter. The dumpling will be somewhat crescent shaped, with ridges on one side formed by the prongs and a deep depression on the other formed by your fingertip. Set the gnocchi on a sheet of wax paper and cover them with a tea towel.

To cook the gnocchi, fill a large pot two-thirds full with water, add 1 tablespoon of kosher salt, and bring the water to a boil over high heat. Carefully drop in about 20 gnocchi, and watch until they float to the surface. Cook them for 10 seconds more and use a small strainer or slotted spoon to remove them from the water. Shake them briefly, put them in a heated serving bowl, and cover with a tea towel. Continue until all of the gnocchi are cooked. Toss the gnocchi with their sauce and continue as directed in the main recipe.

To drink: Arrowood Merlot—B. T.; Gloria Ferrer Pinot Noir

Fall variation: Bake a medium-sized golden or red beet in the oven until fork tender. Cool, put through a ricer, and add to the potatoes. Increase the amount of flour by ½ to ¾ cup, adding it until the dough reaches the proper texture. Serve with Chèvre Sauce (page 267) and top with fresh snipped chives.

Bernadette's Creamy Polenta

Serves 4 to 6

Dempsey's Restaurant & Brewery in Petaluma is one of the best places in the county for a great meal. Bernadette Burrell is a talented and impassioned chef, her husband, Peter Burrell, a fine and subtle brewer of flavorful ales. She developed this polenta for him; he'd never liked the stuff, he said, until he tasted his wife's version. You can serve this voluptuous polenta neat, with a simple sauce, or as a filling for the zucchini blossoms (page 230) that are a signature specialty at the restaurant.

> *2 ears of corn, shucked*
> *2 tablespoons unsalted butter*
> *1 small yellow onion, minced*
> *6 garlic cloves, minced*
> *2 cups heavy cream*
> *2 cups water*
> *½ cup polenta or coarse-ground cornmeal*
> *1 cup semolina flour*
> *Whole nutmeg*
> *¼ cup (1 ounce) grated Dry Jack, Bellwether Carmody, or aged Asiago*
> *Kosher salt*
> *Black pepper in a mill*

Using the large blade of a hand grater set over a bowl, grate the corn off the cob. Set it aside.

Melt the butter in a medium saucepan with a heavy bottom set over medium-low heat, add the onion, and sauté until it is soft and fragrant, about 7 to 8 minutes. Add the garlic and sauté for 2 minutes more. Add the grated corn, cream, and 2 cups of water, increase the heat to medium, cover the pan, and bring to a boil.

Meanwhile, combine the polenta and semolina flour in a small bowl and add several generous gratings of nutmeg. Slowly add the dry mixture to the boiling liquid, stirring continuously in the same direction with a wooden spoon. Reduce the heat to low and simmer, stirring constantly, until the polenta is tender, about 10 to 15 minutes. Stir in the cheese, season with salt and pepper, taste, and remove from the heat. Let rest 5 minutes before serving, or let it firm up to use in another recipe.

To drink: Microbrewery pale ale

Stewed Quail with Polenta

Serves 3 to 6

Polenta with songbirds is a highly prized and praised dish in Bergamot, Italy, where polenta has long been a staple. It is also illegal; songbirds have been hunted to near extinction. Mention the local version—polenta with robins stewed in tomato sauce—and you're likely to hear interesting tales. I heard about them first from Joe Rochioli, who remembers them from his childhood on Westside Road outside of Healdsburg. Newton Dal Pogetto, an attorney in the town of Sonoma, remembers his aunt preparing the dish; Newton sent me a copy of the her handwritten cookbook—an historical treasure—but the recipe is not in it, likely because it was such a basic dish that everyone knew how to make. The dish was popular in many spheres, but it was a staple for poor families. In this modern version, I use quail and pancetta; it's not as humble a dish, but it is entirely legal as well as delicious.

> *6 quail, bone-in*
> *Kosher salt*
> *Black pepper in a mill*
> *½ pound pancetta, thinly sliced*
> *3 tablespoons olive oil*
> *1 yellow onion, diced*
> *6 garlic cloves, minced*
> *1½ cups chicken or duck stock*
> *2 tablespoons Glace de Poulet Gold (see More Than Gourmet, Resources, page 295)*
> *½ cup zinfandel or other medium-bodied dry red wine*
> *1 can (28 ounces) diced tomatoes, preferably Muir Glen brand*
> *2 teaspoons salt*
> *1½ cups coarse-ground polenta*

1 tablespoon butter

3 ounces Teleme cheese, cut into pieces

2 tablespoons minced Italian parsley

Rinse the quail under cool running water and dry them on a tea towel. Season them inside and out with salt and pepper. Wrap each quail in a strip of pancetta, beginning with the quail's legs, which you should push against the body and secure with the pancetta. Heat the olive oil in a large sauté pan set over medium-low heat, carefully set the quail in the pan, and sauté until golden brown, about 5 minutes. Turn the quail over and cook until browned on the other side, about 5 minutes more. Transfer the quail to a plate, add the onion to the pan, and sauté it until it is soft and fragrant, about 15 minutes. Dice the remaining pancetta, add it to the cooked onion, increase the heat to medium, cook for 7 minutes, add the garlic, and cook for 2 minutes more. Add the chicken stock, Glace de Poulet, and red wine, increase the heat to high, and boil until reduced by one-third, about 5 minutes. Stir in the tomatoes, reduce the heat to low, return the quail to the pan, cover, and simmer for 30 minutes.

Meanwhile, bring 4 cups of water and the 2 teaspoons of salt to a boil in a large, heavy pot. Pour another 4 cups of water into a second, smaller pot and bring that to a boil, too. Stir the water in the larger pot rapidly with a whisk, moving it in one circular direction to create a vortex. Pour the polenta into the vortex in a thin, steady stream, stirring continuously all the while to prevent the formation of lumps. Continue to stir after all the polenta has been added, and lower the heat so that the mixture simmers slowly rather than boils. When the polenta begins to thicken, replace the whisk with a long-handled wooden spoon. Add 1 cup of the remaining water and continue to stir. Should you find lumps, use the back of the spoon to press them against the sides of the pot until they break up. At this point, you can let the polenta cook on its own; just be sure to keep a close eye on it, stir it frequently so that it does not scorch, and add more water if it becomes too thick.

After 25 minutes, taste the polenta to be sure the grains are tender; if they are not, cook it a little longer. Stir in the butter, season with salt and pepper, add the Teleme, and stir until it is nearly but not entirely melted; you should see little pools of white cheese. Remove the polenta from the heat, let it rest for 4 or 5 minutes, and ladle into individual serving bowls. Set 1 or 2 quail on top of each serving of polenta, taste the sauce, correct the seasoning, and spoon a generous amount of sauce over each quail. Sprinkle each serving with parsley and serve immediately.

To drink: Limerick Lane Zinfandel—B. T.; Davis Bynum Old Vines Zinfandel

Little Chicken, Olive & Polenta Pies

Serves 4 to 6

One of the many endearing things about polenta is the way it holds the shape of whatever container which it was poured into while still hot and creamy. The grains of corn adhere to one another, making neat little pies and tarts and loaves. Usually, polenta is left to set up on its own, and is then fried, broiled, or grilled and topped with sauce or cheese. Here, the toppings are added before the polenta is poured in, for a sort of upside-down polenta pie. You can prepare these pies several hours or even the night before serving them, but do not use instant polenta; it lacks the texture of true polenta.

> *4 free-range chicken thighs*
> *Kosher salt*
> *Black pepper in a mill*
> *1 cup coarse-ground polenta, such as Guisto's organic polenta*
> *2 tablespoons olive oil, plus more as needed*
> *4 garlic cloves, minced*
> *½ cup cracked green olives, pitted and sliced*
> *1 tablespoon minced fresh Italian parsley*
> *2 teaspoons minced fresh oregano leaves*
> *1 teaspoon minced fresh thyme leaves*
> *1 teaspoon minced fresh sage leaves*
> *½ cup dry sherry*
> *2 tablespoons butter*
> *2 ounces Dry Jack cheese*
> *¼ cup cracked green olives, pitted and minced*
> *Herb sprigs, for garnish*

Preheat the oven to 375°F. Season the chicken thighs on both sides with salt and pepper, and bake them for 20 minutes, or until they are cooked through. Let them cool to room temperature. Remove the skin, cut the meat from the bone, and cut the meat into medium pieces.

In a large, heavy pot, bring 3 cups of water to a rolling boil. Pour another 3 cups of water into a second, small pot and bring that to a boil, too. Add 2 teaspoons of salt to the larger of the two pots of water and stir the water rapidly with a whisk, moving it in one circular direction to create a vortex. Pour the polenta into the vortex in a thin, steady stream, stirring continuously all the while to prevent the formation of lumps. Continue to stir after all the polenta has been added, and lower the heat so that the mixture simmers slowly rather than boils. When the polenta begins to thicken, replace the whisk with a long-handled wooden spoon. Add 1 cup of the remaining water and continue to stir. Should you find lumps, use the back of the spoon to press them against the sides of the pot until they break up. At this point, you can let the polenta cook on its own while you prepare the chicken; just be sure to keep a close eye on it, stir it frequently so that it does not scorch, and add more water if it becomes too thick.

Heat the 2 tablespoons of olive oil in a medium sauté pan set over medium-low heat, add the garlic, and sauté for 2 minutes; do not let it burn. Add the chicken meat, sliced olives, half of the parsley, half of the oregano, half of the thyme, and half of the sage, season with salt and pepper, and toss together thoroughly. Increase the heat to medium, add the sherry, cover the pan, and simmer until the sherry is evaporated, about 4 to 5 minutes. Remove from the heat.

Brush the insides of 12, preferably nonstick, muffin tins with a little olive oil and divide the chicken mixture among them. Cover with a tea towel and set aside.

Taste the polenta to be sure the grains are tender; if they are not, cook a little longer. Fold in the butter, cheese, minced olives, and remaining parsley, oregano, thyme, and sage and stir until the butter and cheese are melted and evenly incorporated into the polenta. Season with salt and pepper, taste, and adjust the seasoning. Ladle the polenta into each of the muffin tins, let them set up for 5 minutes, cover tightly with plastic wrap, and cool to room temperature.

To serve, preheat the oven to 375°F. Brush a baking sheet lightly with olive oil. Remove the plastic wrap from the polenta pies and use your fingers to loosen the edges of each one. Set the baking sheet, oiled-side down, on top of it, and invert the entire affair. Tap lightly on each of the containers and remove the tin, which should lift off easily at this point. Bake until the edges of the polenta are just beginning to color and the pies are steaming hot, about 20 minutes. Set on individual plates, garnish with herb sprigs, and serve immediately.

To drink: Sausal Century Vine Zinfandel—B. T.; Gary Farrell Russian River Valley Pinot Noir

Polenta Loaf with Walnuts and Teleme

Serves 4 to 6

The first edition of *A Cook's Tour of Sonoma* included a recipe for a polenta loaf with pesto and dried tomatoes, a combination that has become so overdone I can barely stand to use the words in the same sentence, let alone put the ingredients on the same plate. There is a seasonal incompatability, as well, that I have come to understand and appreciate more deeply than I did then. Although we can now find fresh basil in supermarkets nearly year round, it is in fact a summer herb. Pesto tastes best and nourishes us well when it is made and served in its own true season. Likewise dried tomatoes—they are best in their own season, that is, when good fresh tomatoes are not available. Originally, drying tomatoes in the hot sun was a technique used to preserve the last of the harvest. As it dries, a tomato's flavor is deepened and intensified, making it ideal in winter dishes that require lengthy cooking. All this is to say that I no longer think pesto and dried tomatoes belong in the same dish. I almost omitted this recipe entirely, but because so many people have requested it, I thought I'd offer a new version, ideal in the fall when local walnuts are harvested.

> 1¼ cups coarse-ground polenta, such as Guisto's organic polenta
>
> 2 teaspoons kosher salt, plus more to taste
>
> ¾ cup shelled walnuts, toasted and minced
>
> ¼ cup minced fresh Italian parsley
>
> 6 garlic cloves, minced
>
> 4 ounces Dry Jack cheese, grated
>
> Black pepper in a mill
>
> ⅓ cup extra virgin olive oil, plus more for the loaf pan
>
> 3 tablespoons butter
>
> 4 ounces Teleme cheese
>
> 1 tablespoon minced lemon zest
>
> ¼ cup walnut halves, for garnish
>
> Parsley sprigs, for garnish

In a large, heavy pot, bring 4 cups water to a rolling boil. In a different, smaller pot, bring an additional 4 cups of water to a boil over high heat, reduce the heat to low, and simmer. Add 2 teaspoons kosher salt to the water in the large pot and stir the water rapidly with a whisk, moving it in one circular direction to create a vortex. Pour the polenta into the vortex in a thin, steady stream, stirring continuously all the while to prevent the formation of lumps.

Continue to stir after all the polenta has been added, and lower the heat so that it simmers slowly rather than boils. When the polenta begins to thicken, replace the whisk with a long-handled wooden spoon. Stir 1 cup of the simmering water into the polenta and continue to stir, being sure to reach down to the bottom of the pot, until the polenta is thick and pulls away from the sides of the pot. Taste the polenta to be sure that the grains are tender; add more water as necessary. It will take about 25 to 35 minutes for most polenta to become tender.

Meanwhile, mix together the minced walnuts, parsley, half the garlic, and half the Dry Jack cheese, and season with salt and pepper. Stir in the olive oil and set the mixture aside.

During the last 5 minutes of cooking, add the remaining garlic, remaining Dry Jack cheese, butter, Teleme cheese, and lemon zest to the polenta and stir until the butter and cheeses are completely incorporated. Taste, adjust the seasoning, and remove the polenta from the heat.

Brush the inside of a 5-cup loaf pan with a little olive oil and pour half of the polenta into the pan; let rest for 3 or 4 minutes. Carefully spread the walnut mixture over the polenta, and then pour the remaining polenta on top. Cover with aluminum foil and let sit for at least 20 minutes. Unmold the loaf onto a serving platter, garnish with walnut halves and parsley leaves, and serve immediately.

To drink: Staley Grenache—B. T.

Overleaf Sweetwater Springs Road winds over Mt. Jackson, west of Healdsburg.

Above A worker turns a wheel of drying jack at Vella Cheese Factory.

Right/Top In the heart of Two Rock, Bellwether Farms ewes provide milk for the company's acclaimed sheep's-milk cheese.

Right/Bottom Bellwether's San Andreas adds a seductive flavor to creamy Golden Beet Risotto with Walnuts.

Below Momento (right), a prize Alpine, and her half-sister, Simone, gaze through the fence of Redwood Hill Farm on Occidental Road, in Green Valley.

Left/Bottom Bellwether Blue, made with milk from Jersey cows, ages.

Left/Top In Two Rock, dairy farms rather than vineyards define the landscape.

Right   Olives and cabernet sauvignon at B. R. Cohn Estate in Glen Ellen.

Far Right   In early spring, mustard blooms between the dormant grape vines.

Bottom   Old hop kilns, near Hop Kiln Winery.

Below   A head-pruned vine of carignane, planted in 1959, at J. Rochioli Vineyards.

Above Late apples at the Duryee ranch in Sebastopol, a few steps from the author's home.

Right Wohler Bridge, wide enough for a single car, crosses the Russian River not far from Del Rio.

Below A thin-crusted Spiced Apple Tart is brushed with hot pepper jam instead of the traditional currant jelly.

Left Unpicked apples near the Laguna de Santa Rosa wetlands, north of Sebastopol.

Above A windmill and lone horse near Valley Ford Road west of Petaluma.

Right Slow-cooked pork seasoned with chipotle powder from Tierra Vegetables.

Below A storm moves in above Westside Road, with the shadowed Mayacamas in the distance.

Left Quail wrapped in pancetta replaces the stewed robins that once topped creamy polenta in homes and restaurants throughout Sonoma County.

Above The Olive Press, inspired by similar ones in Provence, is California's first public cooperative olive mill.

Right New oil is labeled with the date it is crushed and is kept separate from other oils.

Below Green olives—that is, olives that are not fully ripe—contribute spicy, peppery flavors to an olive oil.

Left Ripe olives are dark purple, their oil buttery and opulent; for balance, most oils are made using a blend of unripe and ripe olives.

Right A rainbow of heirloom tomatoes, including Northern Lights (lower right) and Green Zebra (lower left).

Far Right Tomato Custard Tart in a Cornmeal Crust uses St. George cheese and just-harvested Black Prince tomatoes.

Below Tomato Galette pairs dense-fleshed golden and red heirloom tomatoes with pancetta.

Right / Top Puff Lane Organics of Santa Rosa offers a selection of locally grown citrus.

Right / Bottom Fresh honeycomb and handmade candles from Hector's Bees of Santa Rosa.

Below A sunflower umbrella, at the Healdsburg Farmers' Market.

Left Orchard Farms of Sebastopol sells its broccoli, Romanesco broccoli, and parsnips at the Santa Rosa Original Farmers' Market.

Overleaf / Top At Jenner, the Russian River ends its 120-mile journey to the Pacific Ocean.

Overleaf / Bottom The sun sets at Bodega Bay, with Bodega Head in the distance.

them in

ntil the butter
about 10 min-
of black pepper,
ns to turn milky
eat. Add the stock
is nearly absorbed.
18 to 20 minutes.

chives

Golden Beet Risotto with Walnuts

Serves 4 to 6

This scrumptious fall risotto—perfect in October, just after the walnuts are harvested—resembles the gorgeous hunter's moon, which rises huge and orange over
the Valley of the Moon. If you cannot find golden beets (be sure to check your local
farmers' market), you can use red beets, but be careful: their juices will stain everything from your fingertips to your cutting board.

> 4 small or 3 medium golden beets
>
> 3 tablespoons olive oil
>
> Kosher salt
>
> Black pepper in a mill
>
> 2 tablespoons unsalted butter
>
> 2 medium leeks, white and palest green parts only, trimmed, thoroughly cleaned
>   and cut into very thin rounds
>
> 1½ cups Arborio or Carnaroli rice
>
> 5 cups chicken broth, hot
>
> 2 ounces (½ cup) Laura Chenel's Tome, Bellwether San Andreas,
>   or aged Asiago, grated
>
> ¾ cup shelled walnuts, toasted and diced
>
> 2 tablespoons minced fresh Italian parsley

First, prepare the beets. Preheat the oven to 350°F. Wash the beets, place
a small, ovenproof pan or baking dish, toss with 1 tablespoon of the
olive oil, and season with salt and pepper. Bake until the
beets are tender when pierced with a fork, about 40
to 60 minutes, depending on their size. Remove from
the oven, cool to room temperature, cut into small
dice, and set aside or refrigerate until ready to use.

To make the risotto, heat the remaining 2 tablespoons of olive
oil and the butter together in a large sauté pan over medium heat
is melted. Add the leeks and sauté until they are completely wilted
utes. Season with a generous pinch or two of salt and several turns
add the rice, and stir with a wooden spoon until each grain beg
white, about 3 minutes. Keep the stock warm in a pot over low
half a cup at a time, stirring after each addition until the liquid
Continue to add stock and stir until the rice is tender, abou

Before the last addition of stock, stir in the beets and cheese, taste, correct the seasoning, and stir in the last of the liquid. Divide the risotto among individual soup plates, top each portion with some of the walnuts and some of the Italian parsley, grind black pepper over it all, and serve immediately.

To drink: Sonoma-Cutrer Russian River Ranch Chardonnay—B. T.; Clos du Bois Calcaire (Chardonnay)—B. T.; Gary Farrell Rochioli Vineyard Chardonnay

Turkey Risotto

Serves 3 to 4

Nearly all of us have leftover turkey in late November, an ideal time to prepare this risotto, which mirrors the flavors of the traditional holiday meal. Because risotto is rich, you'll want simple, refreshing accompaniments, such as an appetizer of peeled and sliced oranges seasoned with a little salt, pepper, and olive oil, and a simple green salad (page 233).

> 3 tablespoons olive oil
> 1 onion, diced
> 1½ cups Carnaroli or Arborio rice
> Kosher salt
> Black pepper in a mill
> 1 tablespoon minced fresh sage leaves
> ½ cup dried cranberries
> 5 to 6 cups turkey stock, hot
> 1½ cups cooked dark turkey meat, shredded
> 3 ounces smoked goat feta or Dry Jack cheese, grated
> Fresh sage leaves, for garnish

Heat the olive oil in a large, deep saucepan set over medium heat, add the onion, and sauté until it is soft and fragrant, about 8 minutes. Add the rice and sauté for 2 minutes, stirring continuously, until each grain begins to turn milky white. Season with salt and pepper, add the sage and cranberries, and stir. Begin to add the stock, half a cup at a time, stirring after each addition, until all of the liquid is absorbed. Continue adding stock and stirring until the rice is just tender but not at all mushy, about 18 to 20 minutes. Just before making the last addition of stock, stir in the turkey meat and the cheese, add the remaining stock, taste, and adjust the seasoning. Ladle into warmed soup plates, garnish with fresh sage leaves, and serve immediately.

To drink: Chateau St. Jean Merlot—B. T.; Gary Farrell 1998 Russian River Valley Pinot Noir—P. R.

Minted Rice with Lamb & Chickpeas

Serves 4

I've always thought lamb raised in Sonoma County is among the best in the world. I also appreciate the sight of sheep grazing on our hillsides because I know their presence safeguards the land and helps insure that it will remain undeveloped. This fragrant dish is inspired by this easy availability of good lamb, and by a Tunisian rice dish I had in a tiny restaurant in New York City. The dish should be fairly dry but intensely flavored.

> 2 tablespoons olive oil
> 1 small yellow onion, minced
> 4 garlic cloves, minced
> 1 pound lamb meat, cut in 1½-inch cubes
> Kosher salt
> Black pepper in a mill
> 2 cups meat stock, boiling hot
> 1½ cups long-grain white rice
> ½ teaspoon red pepper flakes
> 1 cup boiling water
> 1 cup cooked chickpeas
> ½ cup finely minced fresh mint leaves
> ¼ cup finely minced fresh Italian parsley leaves
> ¼ cup finely minced fresh cilantro leaves
> Zest of 1 lemon
> 1 lemon, cut in wedges

Heat the olive oil in a large, heavy sauté pan set over medium-low heat, add the onion, and sauté until soft and fragrant, about 15 minutes. Add the garlic and sauté for 2 minutes more. Transfer the onion mixture to a small bowl, increase the heat to medium, and brown the lamb evenly on all sides. Season with salt and pepper, add the meat stock, reduce the heat to low, and simmer the lamb very gently until it is tender, about 40 minutes. Stir in the cooked onions and garlic, the rice, the red pepper flakes, and the boiling water, cover the pan, and simmer until the rice is almost tender and nearly all of the liquid has been absorbed, about 10 minutes. Stir in the chickpeas, mint, parsley, and cilantro, cover the pan, and continue to cook until the liquid is completely absorbed and the rice is tender. Remove from the heat and let sit, covered and undisturbed, for 10 minutes. Fluff with a fork, taste, adjust the seasonings, sprinkle lemon zest on top, and serve immediately, with lemon wedges alongside.

To drink: B. R. Cohn Silver Label Cabernet Sauvignon—B. T.

Mexican Quinoa Pilaf

Serves 4

Luther Burbank offered quinoa in his catalog of plants as early as 1887, and by 1918 he called it "the new breakfast food, a forgotten cereal of the ancient Aztecs." It was not to catch on in Burbank's lifetime. It is only now coming into its own. Quinoa thrives in poor soil in dry, mountainous terrain. It has been cultivated in western South America for 5,000 years and is said to have sustained the Incas. Today, it is grown domestically on the high slopes of the Colorado Rockies, but much of what we find in stores is imported. Quinoa is related to Swiss chard and spinach and the greens are edible, though you rarely see them. It is the tiny, grainlike seeds that are harvested and sold commercially. The seed is nearly 20 percent high-quality protein and includes substantial quantities of iron (more than any grain), potassium, riboflavin, magnesium, niacin, zinc, copper, manganese, and folacin. There is a bitter coating on quinoa that acts as a natural pesticide, keeping birds and insects from eating it before harvest. Most of this substance, saponin, is removed before quinoa is sold, but all quinoa should be thoroughly rinsed to remove any residual amounts that could influence the taste of the cooked grain. Quinoa has a pleasantly crunchy texture that is provided by the germ, which in this case is on the outside; as quinoa cooks, the germ opens outward to form a tiny crescent-shaped tail on the pearly seed. You can use quinoa as you would rice, in salads, pilafs, and stuffings as well as in puddings, breads, and tarts; people who are allergic to wheat can find pasta made with quinoa flour. Just remember, however you enjoy it, that it's nothing new, but rather, is part of the legacy of agricultural Sonoma County, thanks to our most famous gardener.

1 tablespoon butter

1 small yellow onion or large shallot, minced

1 poblano chile, seeded and minced

½ teaspoon chipotle powder

1 ⅓ cups quinoa, thoroughly rinsed

2 cups vegetable stock, hot

1 ripe tomato, peeled, seeded, and diced, or 3 tablespoons tomato sauce

Kosher salt

Black pepper in a mill

2 limes

2 tablespoons cilantro leaves

In a medium sauté pan, melt the butter, add the onion or shallot and the chile, and sauté over medium heat until soft and fragrant, about 7 minutes. Add the chipotle powder and quinoa and sauté, stirring constantly, for 5 minutes. Add the stock and tomato or tomato sauce, season with salt and pepper, bring to a boil, reduce the heat, cover, and simmer until the liquid is absorbed, about 15 to 20 minutes. Remove from the heat and let stand 5 minutes. Fluff with a fork, taste, add the juice of 1 lime, correct the seasoning, and transfer to a serving platter. Cut the remaining lime into wedges, add to the platter, scatter the cilantro leaves over the quinoa, and serve immediately.

To drink: Hanna 1999 Sauvignon Blanc—P. R.

Variation: Stir in 1 cup of freshly shelled peas with the tomato.

CHAPTER 5

Flesh

ALTHOUGH MANY PEOPLE NO LONGER FEEL THAT EVERY MEAL, particularly every evening meal, must be organized around a large piece of animal protein, there are times when it sure hits the spot. In December, when the Dungeness crab season opens in Sonoma County, what could be better than a mound of it, surrounded with a few simple condiments? Most of the recipes in this chapter are festive dishes, things we might prepare for a holiday or when friends come to dinner. That doesn't mean they are difficult, not at all. It simply means that dinner on a school night or work night might be a simple pasta dish, a hearty soup, or a robust salad, while we reserve Sonoma's succulent lamb and plump tasty ducks for those evenings—and they are quite frequent—when we can linger around the table a bit longer.

Mussels with White Wine & Herbs

Serves 4

It is only fairly recent conventions of cookbook publishing that make a recipe seem cast in stone once it has been written. Until exact measurements and step-by-step instructions were developed as part of the domestic science movement of the late-nineteenth and early-twentieth centuries, recipes were passed along casually, almost as gossip.
The spirit of a recipe was conveyed in a few sentences, and it was understood that everyone—every woman, anyway—knew the necessary techniques not only for cooking but also for determining quantities. Recipes still evolve in this fashion, though you wouldn't know it by looking at most contemporary cookbooks. The differences between this recipe and the one that appeared in the original edition of the book illustrates how these evolutions take place. Bob Engel, the chef at the Restaurant at Russian River Vineyards in Forestville, prepares these mussels with chardonnay. Over the years, I've found that I prefer the lean character of sauvignon blanc, a more acidic wine. Eventually, I wanted even more acid so I added the juice of a lemon, which in turn made me think of different herbs from those in the original version. The recipe has evolved in other ways, too, and it should continue to do so in the kitchen of anyone who uses it.

> 4 dozen fresh blue mussels (not green-lipped)
> 2 tablespoons butter
> 2 tablespoons olive oil
> 1 large shallot, minced
> 6 garlic cloves, minced
> 1 tablespoon minced fresh Italian parsley
> 1 teaspoon minced fresh tarragon
> 1 teaspoon minced fresh oregano
> ½ teaspoon minced fresh thyme
> ½ cup sauvignon blanc or other dry white wine
> Juice of 1 lemon
> Hot country-style bread, sliced

Scrub the mussels, trim off the beards, if any, rinse them in cool water, and drain them in a colander. Melt the butter in a large, heavy saucepan set over medium-low heat, add the olive oil, and when it is hot, sauté the shallot until it is limp and fragrant, about 4 to 5 minutes. Add the garlic and herbs and sauté for 2 minutes more. Increase the heat to medium, add the mussels, toss thoroughly, and sauté for 2 minutes. Add the wine and lemon juice, cover the pan, and cook until the mussels have opened, about 5 to 7 minutes. Transfer the mussels to 4 individual soup plates or large bowls, pour some of the cooking liquid over each portion, and serve immediately, with the hot bread alongside.

To drink: Dry Creek Vineyards DCV 3 Sauvignon Blanc—B. T.; J. Rochioli Sauvignon Blanc

Cracked Dungeness Crab with Meyer Lemon Rémoulade

Serves 3 to 4

Although the official season for Dungeness crab stretches from mid-November through June, the best time to enjoy California's favorite crustacean is in December and January. That's when crab trapped off the coast of Bodega Bay is at its peak. By early February, the local harvest is usually over, and fresh crab is shipped in from the north. Nearly all crab is cooked shortly after it reaches the shore and is then sold chilled. It needs no further cooking and is certainly delicious, but it is not quite the same as crab you've cooked yourself. Aficionados can tell the difference. For the absolutely freshest possible Dungeness crab, you need to buy them live. Live crab is easy to prepare—simply drop the wriggling crustacean head first into a pot of boiling water and leave it until its brown shell turns red, 8 to 10 minutes. Use tongs to remove it from the water, cool slightly, clean it, and either serve it hot or plunge it into an ice water bath for about 30 minutes to chill it. The legs will need to be cracked, and I find the best way to do this is to provide everyone with a nutcracker.

MEYER LEMON RÉMOULADE

1 ½ cups mayonnaise

½ cup ketchup

¼ cup Dijon mustard

4 scallions, white and green part, thinly sliced

1 Meyer lemon, blanched, seeded, and minced (see Note, below)

2 tablespoons prepared horseradish

1 teaspoon Worcestershire sauce

½ to 1 teaspoon Tabasco sauce

✻

2 cooked, cleaned, and chilled Dungeness crab (about 3½ pounds total live weight)

2 lemons, cut in wedges

In a small bowl, mix together the mayonnaise, ketchup, mustard, scallions, Meyer lemon, horseradish, Worcestershire sauce, and ½ teaspoon Tabasco sauce. Taste the mixture, and add the remaining Tabasco sauce for more heat.

Break the legs away from the bodies of the crabs, then use your hands to break the bodies in half. Place the crab bodies and legs on a large platter, add the lemon wedges, and serve the sauce alongside.

Note: Meyer lemons are sweeter than other varieties, and their skin is thinner and more tender. To blanch a Meyer lemon, carefully drop it into a small saucepan of boiling salted water for 3 minutes; drain it and return it to the boiling water for 3 minutes more. Let it cool before mincing it. If you use a Eureka lemon, the most common commercial variety, you should discard the peel. You can also use 3 tablespoons minced preserved lemons in place of fresh lemon if you have any on hand.

To drink: Davis Bynum Shone Farm Fumé Blanc—B. T.; J Brut

Cayenne Snapper with Fresh Pasta & Corn Salsa

Serves 4

The tenderness of fresh pasta is important to the overall success of this recipe, but if you absolutely can't get it, use 10 to 12 ounces of dried fettuccine in its place. You can use salmon fillets or ahi tuna steaks in this recipe instead of snapper if you prefer.

Corn Salsa (recipe follows)
½ cup all-purpose flour
2 tablespoons cayenne pepper
Kosher salt
2 teaspoons freshly ground black pepper

4 snapper fillets (6 to 8 ounces each)
3 to 4 tablespoons unsalted butter
2 lemons, halved
1 pound fresh fettuccine
6 garlic cloves, minced
Black pepper in a mill
Cilantro sprigs, for garnish

First, make the corn salsa and set it aside.

Fill a large pot two-thirds full with water and bring it to a boil over high heat.

Meanwhile, combine the flour, cayenne pepper, 2 teaspoons kosher salt, and the 2 teaspoons black pepper in a wide, shallow bowl (such as a glass pie plate) and dredge the fillets in the mixture. Pat off excess flour and set the fillets on a piece of wax paper or a plate.

Melt half of the butter in a heavy skillet set over medium heat until it is foamy, add two of the fillets, and sauté for 3 to 4 minutes, until they are golden brown. Turn the fillets, squeeze the juice of half a lemon over them, and sauté until cooked through and golden brown on the second side, about 3 to 4 minutes more. Transfer to a platter, keep warm, and sauté the remaining two fillets, adding some of the remaining butter if necessary. When you turn the fillets, add a tablespoon of salt to the boiling water and cook the pasta until it is just done, about 2 to 3 minutes for most fresh pasta.

Drain the pasta thoroughly, place it in a large bowl, and toss it with all but ½ cup of the corn salsa. Divide it among warm individual plates. Top each portion of pasta with a snapper fillet. Quickly melt the remaining butter in the sauté pan, add the garlic, sauté for 30 seconds, squeeze in the juice of the remaining lemon, swirl the pan until the butter, garlic, and lemon juice come together, and spoon a little of the sauce over each piece of snapper. Top with a spoonful of the remaining corn salsa, season with several turns of black pepper, garnish with cilantro sprigs, and serve immediately.

CORN SALSA

3 large ears of fresh corn, shucked

1 red onion, quartered

2 ripe tomatoes, peeled, seeded, and minced

¾ cup (about 4 pieces) Oven-Roasted Peppers (page 227), diced

1 serrano chile, minced

⅓ cup minced fresh cilantro leaves

3 tablespoons fresh lemon juice (from 1 lemon), plus more to taste

Kosher salt

Black pepper in a mill

⅓ to ½ cup extra virgin olive oil

Heat a stove-top grill, and when it is hot, grill the corn and the onion, turning frequently, so that they color and cook evenly. Let cool to room temperature. Cut the kernels from the cobs and put them in a medium bowl; mince the onion and add it to the corn, along with the tomatoes, peppers, serrano, and cilantro. Stir in the lemon juice, season with salt and pepper, and stir again. Add the olive oil, taste, and correct the seasoning. Let rest for at least 15 minutes before serving at room temperature.

To drink: Quivira 1998 Zinfandel—P. R.

Grilled Salmon with Chipotle & Lime

Serves 4

When this recipe appeared in my column "Seasonal Pantry" in the summer of 1999, I received an e-mail note from Evie Truxaw, who sells the wonderful chipotles grown and smoked by her partner, Wayne James, and his sister, Lee James. Evie's the one who ships me emergency supplies of chipotle powder when I run out. She couldn't have imagined how so few ingredients could result in such a good dish, she wrote, even though she loves their chipotle powder and uses it all the time. There is no secret here; the success is entirely dependent on the quality of the ingredients; if you use good salmon and Tierra Vegetables chipotle powder, you can't go wrong.

1 tablespoon kosher salt

2 teaspoons chipotle powder

1 medium wild king salmon fillet (about 2 pounds), scaled and cut into 4 pieces
of equal weight

Black pepper in a mill

1 lime, cut in wedges

Prepare a charcoal fire in an outdoor grill or heat a stove-top grill to medium. Mix together the salt and chipotle powder and rub it over the cut surface of the fillet. Grill, cut-side down, for about 8 minutes, rotating it once to mark it. Turn the salmon, and grill until it is just cooked through, about 2 to 3 minutes for a 1-inch fillet, longer if the fish is thicker. Transfer to individual plates, season with black pepper, garnish with a lime wedge, and serve immediately.

To drink: Fritz Melon—B. T.

Variations: You can prepare tuna, snapper, butterfish, halibut, or shark in the same manner.

Mama's Paella

Serves 6

When Julia Martin Lorenzo came to the United States in 1919 from a small town in southern Spain, she brought this recipe with her. Carol Kozlowski Every, Julia's granddaughter, remembers enjoying her cooking and recalls that that was how she brought her family together. I've made a few small updates in the recipe, primarily to reflect the availability of certain ingredients. Julia included frozen artichoke hearts in her paella, but because they are readily available in the fall, I've suggested using fresh ones.

½ cup extra virgin olive oil

3 boneless chicken breasts, cut in half

3 boneless center-cut pork chops, cut in half

2 Spanish chorizo, cut in 1-inch diagonal pieces

1 large yellow onion, diced

1 small red bell pepper, stemmed, seeded, and diced

2 ripe tomatoes, peeled, seeded, and diced

Kosher salt

Black pepper in a mill

2 cups Arborio rice

1 cup dry white wine

1½ cups chicken stock or broth

2 cups water

1 cup fresh peas or 8 ounces frozen peas

4 fresh artichoke hearts, cooked and trimmed (see Note, below),
    and cut into quarters

½ pound bay scallops, rinsed and dried

½ pound calamari, cleaned, cut in 1-inch slices, rinsed, and dried

3 garlic cloves, crushed and mashed in a mortar

1 teaspoon Spanish saffron

1 pound fresh manila or cherrystone clams, scrubbed and rinsed

1 pound fresh mussels, scrubbed and rinsed

½ pound medium shrimp, unpeeled, rinsed, and dried

12 asparagus tips, roasted (see page 221), for garnish

½ cup Oven-Roasted Peppers (page 227), sliced, for garnish

Heat ¼ cup of the olive oil in a heavy Dutch oven or other large, ovenproof pot set over medium heat and, when it is hot, sauté the chicken until it is golden brown on both sides. Set it aside and keep it warm. Brown the pork and set it aside with the chicken. Brown the chorizo and transfer to absorbent paper.

Preheat the oven to 375°F. Heat the remaining ¼ cup olive oil in the pan, add the onion, and cook until very soft and fragrant, about 15 minutes. Add the bell pepper and tomatoes, season with salt and pepper, and cook for 5 minutes. Stir in the rice, wine, chicken stock, and 2 cups water, stir, cover, and cook on top of the stove for 20 minutes. Fold in the peas, artichoke hearts, scallops, calamari, garlic, and saffron. Cover the pan, put in the oven, and bake for 20 minutes.

Meanwhile, put the clams and mussels in a large, heavy pot, add 1 cup water, and bring to a boil over high heat. Cover and cook for 2 minutes. Add the shrimp, cover, and cook until the clams and mussels open, about 2 minutes more. Remove from the heat. If necessary, reheat the chicken, pork, and chorizo.

Remove the rice mixture from the oven and turn it into a large paella pan. Arrange the chicken, pork, chorizo, and shrimp on top, arrange the opened clams and mussels around the outer edge, and garnish with asparagus spears and strips of roasted peppers. Bake for 10 minutes, until the paella is heated through. Serve immediately.

Note: To prepare the artichoke hearts, cook the artichokes in boiling salted water until the heart is tender when pierced with a fork or a wooden skewer. Drain thoroughly and let cool to room temperature. Remove and discard the tough outer leaves, pull off the remaining tender leaves, and reserve them for another recipe. Using a paring knife to cut out the choke from each heart, trim the stem so that it's no more than ¼ inch long, and cut each heart into four pieces.

To drink: Sebastopol Vineyard Dutton Ranch Chardonnay; Geyser Peak Sparkling Shiraz—B. T.; Iron Horse Brut Rosé

Oven-Roasted Chicken with Fried White Peaches

Serves 4 to 6

"I only added about half the honey you called for," a friend said after testing this recipe for me. "It looked like enough." Sometimes what looks like enough actually is, but other times, as in this recipe, *slather* should be the operative concept. This is an exuberant dish, and for it to blossom into its full self it needs the full amount of honey (and all of the butter, too); otherwise, the toasted garlic will overpower all of the other flavors.

> 1 teaspoon cumin seeds, toasted and ground
> 1 teaspoon coriander seeds, ground
> ¼ teaspoon cardamom seeds, ground
> 3 tablespoons olive oil
> 4 free-range chicken leg-and-thigh pieces
> Kosher salt
> Black pepper in a mill
> ⅓ cup honey, warm
> 10 large garlic cloves, peeled and thinly sliced
> 6 ripe white peaches
> 4 tablespoons butter
> ¼ cup brown sugar
> Juice of 1 lemon

Preheat the oven to 425°F. In a small bowl, mix together the cumin seeds, coriander seeds, and cardamom seeds. Add the olive oil to make a thick paste. Season the chicken all over with salt and pepper and use your fingers to rub the spice paste into it. Set the chicken on a roasting rack in a roasting pan and roast until the skin is crisp and the chicken reaches an internal temperature of 160°F, about 40 minutes. Baste the chicken with honey during the last 15 minutes of cooking. Let it rest for 5 minutes.

Meanwhile, toast the sliced garlic in a dry sauté pan set over very low heat, tossing frequently, until the garlic is lightly browned and *just* crisp, about 15 to 20 minutes; do not let it burn. Set it aside.

Peel the peaches by carefully using your fingers to pull off the skins; if the peaches are ripe, they will come off easily. Cut each peach in half and remove its pit.

Melt the butter in a skillet large enough to hold the peaches in a single layer, and when the butter is melted, arrange the peaches cut-side down. Fry over medium heat for 3 to 4 minutes, until the peaches just begin to brown. Turn them cut-side up, add a spoonful of brown sugar to the center of each, scatter any remaining sugar over the tops, cover the pan, and cook until the peaches are tender, another 5 or 6 minutes.

Set the chicken on a large serving platter, scatter the toasted garlic over it, and surround the chicken with the cooked peaches. Add the lemon juice to the pan in which you cooked the peaches, swirl to pick up the pan juices, and pour them over the peaches. Serve immediately.

To drink: Alderbrook Viognier—B. T.; Clos du Bois Alexander Valley Reserve Chardonnay

Roasted Duck with Apple, Chestnut & Bacon Stuffing

Serves 3 to 4

When Laura and Allan Bernstein bought the former Sullivan Ranch in Graton, a place they call Iggy's Orchard, they discovered seven healthy chestnut trees among the 2½ acres of apples. Chestnuts are harvested in the fall and are a classic ingredient in poultry stuffing. My version is based on a recipe for roasted chicken that Laura shared with me. I couldn't resist adding my own touch, bacon, which provides a smoky, salty element that is an ideal counterpoint to the sweetness of the chestnuts and the apples. You can use this same stuffing with chicken, or you can double it and use it with turkey.

STUFFING

4 tablespoons butter

2 yellow onions, diced

3 celery stalks, with leaves, minced

2 apples, peeled, cored, and diced

1 tablespoon minced fresh sage

2 tablespoons minced Italian parsley

½ teaspoon paprika

Whole nutmeg

Kosher salt

Black pepper in a mill

8 ounces thick-cut bacon, cut into ½-inch-wide crosswise strips

1 loaf sourdough bread, torn into small pieces

*2½ cups whole roasted chestnuts (see Note, below), 2 cups diced, and ½ cup
reserved whole for garnish*

¾ to 1 cup homemade chicken or duck stock or canned chicken broth

½ cup kosher salt, plus more to taste

2 ducks (preferably Liberty Duck), 4 to 5 pounds each

Sage sprigs, for garnish

First, prepare the stuffing. Melt the butter in a large sauté pan, add the onions and
celery, and sauté until the vegetables are limp and fragrant, about 10 minutes. Add
the apples and sauté for 2 minutes more. Stir in the sage, parsley, paprika, and several gratings of nutmeg, and season with salt and pepper. Remove from the heat
and let cool slightly. Fry the bacon until it is almost but not quite crisp and drain it
on absorbent paper.

Place the bread in a large bowl, add the onion mixture, the bacon, and the chestnuts, and toss thoroughly. Add enough of the stock or broth to moisten the dressing lightly. Cover and set the mixture aside.

Fill a large stockpot with 4 quarts of water, add the ½ cup salt, and bring to a
boil over high heat. Rinse the ducks under cool, running water, and dry them with
clean tea towels so the skin will not be slippery. Use the tip of a sharp knife to pierce
the skin of the ducks in several places. Plunge one duck into the boiling water and
leave it until the water returns to a boil. Transfer the duck to a rack set over clean

tea towels; repeat the process with the second duck. Pat the ducks dry, and then use a blow dryer to dry the skins thoroughly. Season them inside and out with salt and pepper.

Preheat the oven to 450°F.

Fill the main cavity of the ducks with the dressing; do not pack it too tightly. Truss the ducks, and set them, breast-side up, on a rack set in a roasting pan. Roast for 30 minutes, reduce the heat to 350°F, and roast until the ducks are cooked through, about 20 to 30 minutes more. Use an instant-read meat thermometer inserted into the inner thigh and remove the birds from the oven when the temperature reaches 160°F.

Let the ducks rest for 10 to 20 minutes. Transfer the dressing to a serving platter, carve the ducks, and arrange the meat next to the dressing. Garnish with the whole chestnuts and sage sprigs and serve immediately.

Note: To roast chestnuts, preheat the oven to 425°F. Use a knife to score the skin of the chestnuts with an X on the tip, set the chestnuts on a baking sheet in a single layer, and roast until tender, about 20 minutes. Let cool until they are easy to handle and then peel. Or, if you prefer, you can cook the scored chestnuts in boiling water until they are tender; drain, cool, and peel them.

To drink: Gary Farrell Russian River Valley Pinot Noir—B. T.; Gary Farrell Rochioli Vineyard Pinot Noir; Landmark Grand Departure Pinot Noir

Smoked Duck Breast with Mary's Red Onion Marmalade

Serves 4

The flavor of smoke has, I think, an atavistic appeal; it is compelling on a nearly cellular level, evoking, perhaps, ancient memories of the first foods humans cooked. Another more contemporary pleasure is the dimension a delicate smoky flavor can add to wine. This simple recipe insists on pinot noir, though certain Rhône-style red wines will work in a pinch. For the best results, use a pinot noir when you make the marmalade, too. For accompaniments, I recommend Bernadette's Creamy Polenta (page 166) or Celery Root and Potato Purée (page 226), followed by Fall Greens with Grilled Figs & Bacon Vinaigrette (page 238).

Mary's Red Onion Marmalade (page 269)
4 half Liberty duck breasts, cold-smoked (see Note, below)
Kosher salt
Black pepper in a mill

Prepare the marmalade and set it aside.

Build a fire in a charcoal grill or heat a stove-top grill. Make several crisscross cuts in the duck skin, being sure not to cut through the meat. Season the duck breasts on both sides with salt and pepper, and when the grill is hot, set them, skin side down, on the grill. Cook for 3 minutes, rotate each breast 90 degrees to mark the skin, and cook for 4 to 5 minutes more, until the skin is golden brown and crisp and most of the fat underneath the skin has been rendered. (If you are using a stove-top grill, you may have to pour off some of the fat.) Turn the breasts over, cook for 3 minutes, rotate each breast 90 degrees to mark it, and cook 3 to 4 minutes more for rare meat. Transfer to a warm platter and let rest 3 to 4 minutes. Cut each breast into ⅛-inch-thick crosswise slices, arrange on individual plates, garnish with a generous spoonful of marmalade, season with salt and pepper, and serve immediately.

Note: The easiest way to smoke duck and other meats is to purchase a small commercial home smoker, available wherever grills are sold. Follow the manufacturer's instructions. It is an easy process that can be done the day before cooking the duck; allow about two hours from start to finish.

To drink: Gloria Ferrer Pinot Noir; J. Rochioli Pinot Noir; Clos du Bois Pinot Noir

Turkey Gumbo

Serves 6 to 8

I make gumbo in the days following Thanksgiving, when there's plenty of leftover turkey, which makes a fuller-flavored gumbo than the more commonly used chicken does. To make real gumbo, you must learn how to make a dark roux. The very best gumbos are made with black roux, which is the most difficult to make, and so in this recipe I use the dark brown version. If you have mastered the art, feel free to use black here. If not, relax, be prepared to throw it out and start over if it burns, and trust not only that you'll get the hang of it but also that the rich flavor it provides is worth the effort. I like to serve gumbo with a coleslaw, which I make with cranberry vinegar and minced fresh cranberries (see Raspberry Coleslaw with Black Raspberry Mayonnaise, page 237).

8 cups turkey stock

½ cup duck fat, peanut oil, or clarified butter

½ cup all-purpose flour

1 yellow onion, diced

2 green bell peppers, diced

4 large celery ribs, diced

2 tablespoons filé powder (gumbo filé, ground dried sassafras)

2 teaspoons kosher salt, plus more to taste

½ teaspoon garlic powder

½ teaspoon ground black pepper

¼ teaspoon ground white pepper

⅛ teaspoon cayenne pepper

1 pound smoked sausage such as andouille or kielbasa, cut into ¼-inch rounds

1 tablespoon minced fresh garlic

4 cups cooked turkey meat (preferably dark), cut into medium chunks

4 cups cooked white rice, hot

Fresh sage leaves and minced fresh sage, for garnish (optional)

Place the turkey stock in a large pot, set it over medium heat, bring it to a boil, and reduce it by one quarter. Set the stock aside.

To make the roux, place the fat, oil, or clarified butter in a large, heavy skillet or soup pot set over medium-high heat. When it smokes, use a long-handled wooden spoon or metal whisk to stir the flour, about 2 tablespoons at a time, into the hot oil. Whisk or stir constantly as the flour begins to color. (If black specks appear, the flour has burned; discard the mixture and begin again.) When the mixture is a very dark reddish brown, remove it from the heat and stir in the onion, green peppers, and celery. Continue to stir for 3 or 4 minutes as the roux cools and ceases to darken. Stir in the filé powder, 1 teaspoon of the salt, garlic powder, and black, white, and cayenne peppers.

Bring the stock to a boil and add the roux, a large spoonful at a time, whisking after each addition. Add the sausage and minced garlic, reduce the heat to low, and simmer for 45 minutes, stirring occasionally. Add the turkey, simmer for 15 minutes, taste, and correct the seasoning with salt and pepper.

Place a large scoop of rice in each soup plate, ladle the gumbo over the rice, garnish with sage leaves and minced sage, if using, and serve immediately.

To drink: J. Rochioli 1998 Pinot Noir—P. R.

Roasted Pork Tenderloin &
Apricots with Apricot Risotto

Serves 4 to 6

Although there are feral pigs and wild boar in Sonoma County
and a few farmers who raise pigs, there is no local pork industry. If you can get
Niman Ranch pork (see Resources, page 295), use it; otherwise, you'll have to make
do— I must—with whatever pork your local butcher has. Be sure not to overcook
it or it will be unpleasantly dry and tough.

> 4 tablespoons olive oil
> 2 pork tenderloins, about 1 pound each
> Kosher salt
> Black pepper in a mill
> ½ cup apricot conserve or apricot jam
> 6 ripe apricots, cut in half, pits removed
> 2 tablespoons butter
> 1 yellow onion, diced
> 3 garlic cloves, minced
> 1 ¼ cups Carnaroli or Arborio rice
> 1 cup medium-dry white wine
> 5 to 6 cups chicken stock or vegetable stock, hot
> ½ cup minced dried apricots
> 3 ounces Bellwether Pepato or Vella Dry Jack, grated
> 3 ounces pancetta, diced, cooked until crisp, and crumbled
> 1 tablespoon fresh snipped chives

Preheat the oven to 400°F. Heat 2 tablespoons of olive oil in a heavy skillet set over
medium heat, season the pork tenderloins with salt and pepper, and brown them
on all sides; it will take 3 to 4 minutes. Use tongs to set the loins on a roasting rack
over a roasting pan and brush them all over with apricot conserve. Roast the pork
until it reaches an internal temperature of 145°F, about 15 minutes. Brush the loins
with conserve two or three times, and during the last 10 minutes of cooking, set
the fresh apricot halves on the roasting rack, brush them with apricot conserve, and
roast with the pork. Cover the pork loosely with aluminum foil and let it rest for
5 to 10 minutes before carving into ¼-inch-thick slices.

Meanwhile, heat the butter in a large sauté pan over medium heat until the butter is completely melted. Add the onion and sauté until it is very soft, fragrant, and just beginning to turn golden brown, about 15 minutes. Add the garlic, sauté for 2 minutes more, and season with salt and pepper. Add the rice and stir with a wooden spoon until each grain begins to turn milky white, about 3 minutes. Add the wine to the stock and keep it hot in a pot set over low heat. Add the stock to the rice half a cup at a time, stirring after each addition until the liquid is nearly absorbed. After the third addition of stock, add the minced dried apricots and continue to add stock and stir until the rice is tender, about 18 to 22 minutes. Just before the final addition of stock, stir in the cheese and pancetta, taste, and correct the seasoning. Stir in the last of the liquid, ladle the risotto into warm soup plates, and sprinkle some chives over each portion. On each plate, arrange several slices of pork tenderloin on one side of the risotto and two apricot halves on the other. Season with black pepper and serve immediately.

To drink: Mill Creek Gewürztraminer—B. T.; Collier Falls 1998 Zinfandel—P. R.

Stuffed Pork Shoulder with Pepper Jam Glaze

Serves 6

Adamson's Happy Haven Ranch, formerly a strawberry farm in Sonoma's Valley of the Moon, makes the best hot pepper jam I've ever had. Neither the red nor the green variety is overly sweet, and the taste of the peppers is heightened by vinegar. It is probably easier to make this using a pork loin rather than shoulder, but I prefer the flavor and tenderness of a shoulder roast. Use pork loin if you prefer it, but be sure to remove it from the oven when it reaches an internal temperature of 145°F. As it sits, its temperature will rise to close to 155°F.

1 pork shoulder roast, about 3½ to 4 pounds

Kosher salt

Black pepper in a mill

1½ pounds Mexican chorizo, casings removed

2 shallots, minced

2 jalapeño chiles, stemmed, seeded, and minced

6 garlic cloves, minced

2 teaspoons achiote, crumbled

1 jar Adamson's Happy Haven Ranch Green Pepper Jam
    or other hot pepper jam or jelly

¼ cup sherry vinegar

1 tablespoon minced fresh cilantro

Sprigs of cilantro, for garnish

Set the pork roast on your work surface and use a sharp knife to make a 2-inch-wide cut through the center of the roast. Season the roast all over with salt and pepper and cover it with a tea towel.

Cook the chorizo in a heavy sauté pan set over medium heat, using a fork to break it up and crumble it as it cooks. When it has released most of its fat, drain off all but 1 tablespoon of the fat, add the shallots and jalapeños, reduce the heat to low, and sauté until the shallots are soft and fragrant, about 7 minutes. Stir in the garlic and achiote and sauté for 2 minutes more. Remove from the heat and let cool slightly. Taste and season with salt and pepper if necessary.

Preheat the oven to 400°F. Place the chorizo mixture in a pastry bag (without a metal tip), push the tip of the bag into the pocket cut in the pork, and squeeze the mixture into the pocket.

Set the pork on a roasting rack in a roasting pan, coat the entire surface with jam, and set in the oven. Reduce the heat to 325°F and cook until the pork reaches an internal temperature of about 150°F; brush the pork with more jam every 20 minutes or so. Remove the roast from the oven, set it on a cutting board, and let it rest for 20 minutes. Set the roasting pan over medium-high heat, deglaze it with the sherry vinegar and ½ cup water, and simmer until the liquid is reduced by half. Carve the roast, arrange it on a serving platter, drizzle with the sauce, sprinkle with the minced cilantro, garnish with the cilantro sprigs, and serve immediately.

To drink: Geyser Peak 1998 Sauvignon Blanc—P. R.

Slow-Roasted Chipotle Pork

Serves 4 to 6

When I first began making chipotle pork, one of the best flavor combinations in the world, there was no such thing as chipotle powder, not in this country anyway. Dried chipotle peppers were very hard to find, too, but a few local markets had chipotles canned in adobo sauce. The Chipotle Pork in the first edition of *A Cook's Tour* was developed using canned chipotles. Then Tierra Vegetables came along with a chipotle powder made using several varieties of their home-grown chiles slow-smoked at the farm in Chalk Hill east of the town of Healdsburg. In most recipes, I prefer the rich, complex flavor of the powder to that of the canned chiles. Do not use pork loin instead of the cut recommended here; pork loin does not have enough fat to be cooked successfully in this way.

> 3 tablespoons kosher salt
> 1 tablespoon chipotle powder
> 1 pork shoulder roast, about 3½ pounds
> 2 dozen small corn tortillas
> 2 limes, cut in wedges
> ¼ cup minced fresh cilantro

In a small bowl, mix together the salt and chipotle powder and rub it into the pork, being sure to cover the entire surface of the meat with the mixture. Put the pork in a clay roaster or other deep roasting pan with a lid, place the covered roaster in the oven, and turn the heat to 275°F. Cook until the pork falls apart when you press it with the back of a fork, about 3½ to 4 hours. Remove it from the oven and let rest, covered, for 15 minutes.

Heat the tortillas on a medium-hot griddle, turning them frequently, until they are warmed through and soft. Wrap them in a tea towel and place them in a basket. Transfer the pork to a large serving platter and use two forks to pull it into chunks. Add the lime wedges to the platter, place the cilantro in a small serving bowl, and serve immediately, with the tortillas on the side.

To fill the tortillas, set two, one on top of the other, on a plate, spoon some of the pork on top, squeeze a little lime juice over the pork, sprinkle some cilantro on top, and fold in half.

To drink: Ravenswood Cook Vineyard Zinfandel—R. T.; BC Cellars 1998 Zinfandel —P. R.

Pork Shoulder Stewed with Nopales, Hominy & Chiles

Serves 4 to 6

As are most of the dishes in this book, this recipe is flexible. If you can't get fresh or frozen nopales, you can make a good version of this robust and homey dish using the canned ones available in Latin markets. And feel free to use dried pozole instead of canned hominy. It requires lengthy cooking, but the results are wonderful. Do not, however, use pork loin or the dish will be too dry.

2 large yellow onions, cut in thick rounds

4 cups cleaned nopales, diced or cut in strips (see Note, page 116)

2 cans (28 ounces each) hominy

8 garlic cloves, cut in half lengthwise

4 poblano chiles, roasted, skinned, seeded, and cut in strips

3 jalapeño chiles, seeded, stemmed, and cut in thin julienne

2 serrano chiles, minced

2 tablespoons kosher salt

Pork shoulder roast, about 3½ to 4 pounds

¼ cup dry sherry or marsala

2 limes, cut in wedges

12 small corn tortillas, hot

Prepare a clay cooker according to the manufacturer's directions. Spread the onions over the bottom of the pot. In a medium bowl, toss together the nopales, hominy, garlic, and chiles and spread the mixture on top of the onions. Rub the salt into the surface of the pork and set it on top of the vegetable mixture. Add the sherry or marsala, cover the clay cooker with its lid, and place in a cold oven. Set the oven at 275°F and bake until the pork is fork tender, about 3½ to 4 hours. Test after 3 hours.

Remove from the oven and let rest, covered, for 15 minutes. Remove the lid, scatter cilantro over the top, and serve immediately, with the limes and tortillas on the side.

To drink: Mexican beer such as Negro Modelo; iced hibiscus tea

Lamb Kebabs with Lemon & Orzo

Serves 4

I confess to a sentimental attachment to this recipe, which has its genesis not in Sonoma County at all but in the kitchen of the White House during the Kennedy administration. The first cookbook I ever bought was *The White House Chef Cookbook* (Doubleday, 1967), written by René Verdon, who was hired by Jacqueline Kennedy in 1961.

Although I was attracted to the book because of my affinity for the Kennedy family, I taught myself a great deal as I cooked my way through it. Perhaps the single most valuable lesson is one that I now pass on to students at every opportunity. Read a recipe all the way through before you begin to cook. I am always amazed by how many students are surprised by such advice, though I shouldn't be, for I certainly learned the hard way. As I prepared Verdon's lamb kebabs for one of my college professors and his wife, I realized that I had no lemon juice, the second ingredient listed, and so scurried off to the store. I returned home and continued cooking, only to realize I had no olive oil; in fact, I had never purchased olive oil before. Off I went again. By the time I got to the rosemary and had to return to the store a third time, I had learned this essential rule and one that now seems so obvious that I am almost embarrassed to admit it. Like many cookbooks published before the gourmet renaissance of the 1980s, *The White House Chef Cookbook* does not include a headnote with every recipe, only chapter introductions for each course. Thus, we never learn the circumstances under which Verdon served these skewers of tangy lamb, nor do we know what he served alongside. For years, I served simple steamed rice tossed with butter, but these days I'm more likely to serve riso, orzo, or rosamarino, seed-shaped pastas similar in size to rice. And of course, I always begin with lamb raised in Sonoma County.

1 ½ pounds lamb shoulder, cut into 1-inch cubes
¾ cup fresh lemon juice
⅓ cup olive oil
1 bay leaf
1 garlic clove
1 teaspoon fresh thyme
1 teaspoon fresh rosemary
Kosher salt
Black pepper in a mill

12 (10-inch) bamboo skewers

6 small red onions, cut in half

12 crimini mushrooms, stems removed

6 ounces seme di melone, riso, orzo, or rosamarino
  (or other small seed-shaped pasta)

1 tablespoon butter

Zest of 1 lemon

Thyme sprigs, for garnish

Rosemary sprigs, for garnish

Arrange the lamb in a shallow glass baking dish. Put the lemon juice, olive oil, bay leaf, garlic, half of the thyme, and half of the rosemary in the work bowl of a blender or food processor, cover, and pulse until the mixture is smooth. Season with the salt and several turns of black pepper and pulse again, briefly. Pour the marinade over the lamb, cover it, and refrigerate, turning the lamb occasionally, for 24 hours.

Soak the bamboo skewers in water for at least 30 minutes. Fill a medium pot half full with water and bring to a boil over high heat. Preheat an oven broiler.

Remove the lamb from the marinade and thread it on skewers, alternating the lamb with onions and mushrooms. Set the kebabs on a rack over a roasting pan and broil, about 3 inches from the heat, until the lamb is cooked through, about 15 minutes. As they cook, turn the kebabs several times and brush them generously with the marinade.

Meanwhile, add 1 tablespoon of kosher salt to the boiling water and cook the pasta according to its package directions. Drain it, place it in a medium bowl, and toss it with the butter, lemon zest, and remaining ½ teaspoon each of thyme and rosemary. Season it with salt and pepper and divide it among individual serving plates. Top each portion of pasta with 2 or 3 kebabs, garnish with thyme and rosemary sprigs, and serve immediately.

To drink: Schug Rouge de Noir—B. T.; Iron Horse Brut Rosé

Butterflied Leg of Lamb with Garlic, Two Ways

Serves 6 to 8

In the past several years, wood-burning ovens have become very popular both in restaurants and in homes. Alan Scott of Tomales is largely responsible for this resurgence of popularity; he's built dozens of them all over the United States and a few in other countries. If you're the handy sort, you might try building one. I hear it's  not at all difficult (Scott sells plans; see Resources, page 295), and I can attest to the superior results that come from cooking in such ovens. They are a delight, and I can't wait until mine is completed. In the meantime, I cook in friends' ovens when I can. I first made this lamb in Lou Preston's original *forno,* the one he and his crew at the winery made using willow branches from Dry Creek, clay from his farm, and manure and hay from his cellarmaster's horse. My friend and colleague Rick Theis did the actual cooking—of about twenty-five of these butterflied legs for our annual Grand Aioli celebration at Preston Vineyards. Be sure not to overcook the lamb; the temperature will rise at least 10 degrees after you remove it from the oven.

> 2 garlic bulbs, cloves separated
> 1 leg of lamb, about 5 to 6 pounds, boned and butterflied
> Kosher salt
> Black pepper in a mill
> Several sprigs thyme
> ½ cup plus 2 tablespoons extra virgin olive oil
> ¾ cup meat stock or red wine
> 16 baguette slices, toasted

Peel 10 of the garlic cloves and cut them in half lengthwise. Set the lamb on your work surface, use the tip of a sharp knife to make a small slit in the meat, and insert a slice of garlic. Repeat, inserting garlic slices all over the lamb. Season the lamb all over with salt and pepper, set on a large plate or baking dish, tuck two or three thyme sprigs into the lamb, drizzle ½ cup of the olive oil over it, cover it loosely, and refrigerate for at least 2 hours or as long as overnight. Warm to room temperature before cooking.

Preheat the oven to 425°F. Place the remaining garlic cloves in a small saucepan with 2 sprigs of thyme, pour the meat stock or red wine over them, and set over medium heat. When the liquid boils, reduce the heat to low and simmer until the garlic is just barely tender, about 15 minutes. Remove from the heat and transfer the garlic in its sauce to a large roasting pan.

Set a rack in the roasting pan, set the lamb on the rack, and roast until the lamb reaches an internal temperature of 125° to 130°F, about 25 minutes; be sure to insert the thermometer into the thickest part of the meat. Remove the roasting pan from the oven, use a long spoon to pull the garlic from under the roasting rack and transfer it to a bowl, cover the lamb loosely with foil, and let it sit for 10 to 15 minutes.

Meanwhile, set the garlic on a clean work surface and press the pulp from each clove by setting a fork on it and slowly pressing the fork down with the heel of your hand. The pulp should easily ooze out of the root end of the garlic. Mash the garlic thoroughly with a fork, scoop it up into a bowl, mix in the remaining 2 tablespoons of olive oil, and season it with salt and pepper. Spread each slice of baguette with some of the mixture.

Carve the lamb into ¼-inch-thick slices, arrange them on a serving platter, surround the lamb with the garlic croutons, and garnish with thyme sprigs. Serve immediately.

Leftovers: Cut any leftover lamb into strips, sauté them in a little olive oil to heat through, and use in place of the *lengua* in Tacos Lengua (page 205).

To drink: Preston Faux—B. T.; Merry Edwards Olivet Lane Pinot Noir—R. T.

Greek Lamb Loaf

Serves 6 to 8

Kept properly chilled in a cooler and then reheated over a campfire, this Greek Lamb Loaf makes a great picnic food. Simply cook the loaf as directed, cool it to room temperature, and refrigerate it. Store it in a cooler until you are ready to cook it outside; it will take 15 to 25 minutes to heat the loaf through, depending on the intensity of the campfire.

1 long (not round) 1-pound loaf of San Francisco–style sourdough bread

2 tablespoons olive oil, plus more as needed

8 garlic cloves, minced

8 ounces baby spinach, rinsed

Kosher salt

Black pepper in a mill

2 pounds ground lamb

2 teaspoons fresh Greek oregano, minced

1 teaspoon fresh thyme leaves

½ teaspoon fresh rosemary, minced

¾ cup fresh bread crumbs

1 egg, beaten

6 ounces feta cheese, coarsely crumbled

SAUCE

¾ cup tomato sauce

½ cup chicken broth

Juice of 2 lemons

1 teaspoon fresh Greek oregano, minced

½ teaspoon fresh thyme leaves

¼ teaspoon fresh rosemary, minced

Kosher salt

Black pepper in a mill

Preheat the oven to 275°F. Use a sharp bread knife to cut the ends off the loaf of bread. With your fingers, pull out all of the soft insides of the bread, creating a shell of the crust. Spread the inside pieces of the bread on a baking sheet and toast them in the oven until they just begin to color, about 10 to 12 minutes. Remove from the oven, let cool, and put them in the work bowl of a food processor. Pulse briefly, to reduce the bread to coarse crumbs. Set them aside.

Heat the olive oil in a medium sauté pan set over medium-low heat, add the garlic, and sauté for 2 minutes. Do not let it burn. Add the spinach and cook, tossing frequently, until it is just wilted, about 2 or 3 minutes. Season with salt and pepper and transfer the mixture to a bowl to cool.

Return the pan to the heat and sauté the lamb, using a fork to crumble it, until it just begins to lose its color, about 5 to 7 minutes. Drain off and discard the excess fat, stir in the oregano, thyme, and rosemary, and let the lamb cool slightly. Toss the lamb with the spinach mixture, add the bread crumbs and toss thoroughly, fold in the egg, add the feta cheese, taste, and season with salt and a generous amount of black pepper. Let the mixture cool to room temperature.

Preheat the oven to 350°F. Fill the inside of the hollowed loaf of bread with the lamb mixture, adding half of the filling in one end and half in the other. Press the filling in, so that it is packed evenly throughout the loaf. Wrap the loaf in aluminum foil, closing the foil along the top of the loaf, and bake it for 20 minutes. Open the foil so that the top of the loaf is exposed; brush it with olive oil and bake for 10 minutes more. Let the loaf rest for 5 minutes.

Meanwhile, make the sauce. Combine the tomato sauce, chicken broth, and lemon juice in a small saucepan, set over medium-low heat, and stir in the oregano, thyme, and rosemary. Taste the sauce and season with salt and a generous amount of black pepper. Remove from the heat.

Cut the loaf into 1-inch-thick slices, set 2 slices on individual plates, and top with a little sauce. Serve immediately, with the remaining sauce on the side.

To drink: Frick Cinsaut—B. T.; Seghesio 1998 Barbera—P. R.

Lamb's Tongue in Vinaigrette

Serves 4 to 6

Here it is at last, one of my all-time favorite recipes and
one I wouldn't be able to make without the lambs' tongues that
Bruce Campbell of C. K. Lamb saves for me. This recipe has been deleted from several of my books by squeamish editors who apparently believe that it will drive people away. Given its popularity whenever I serve it, I'd say just the opposite is the case; it vanishes quickly and guests ask for more. Most are surprised when I tell them what it is. Americans are timid about meats such as tongue, or anything else that looks so clearly like what it is. Yet tongue is one of the most tender and flavorful parts of any animal, like the cheeks of larger fish and the head of beef, both acknowledged delicacies. In earlier times, including not so long ago in California and Sonoma County, it was essential to glean as much food as possible from whatever source was available. Now you find such fare as tongue served predominantly in ethnic communities, which have retained their culinary traditions.

> 1 small shallot, minced
>
> 1 garlic clove, minced
>
> 2 tablespoons Vinaigre de Banyuls or other high-quality white wine vinegar
>
> 2 teaspoons minced fresh Italian parsley
>
> 6 poached lambs' tongues (page 206)
>
> 18 small fingerling potatoes, cooked until tender, cooled, and sliced lengthwise
>
> 1 teaspoon kosher salt
>
> Black pepper in a mill
>
> 6 tablespoons extra virgin olive oil
>
> 2 or 3 handfuls of young fresh mâche or other young salad greens

In a small bowl, mix together the shallot, garlic, vinegar, and parsley and set aside for 20 minutes. Place the tongue and potatoes in a medium bowl. Season with a generous pinch of salt and several turns of black pepper. Add the remaining salt and several additional turns of black pepper to the shallot mixture, whisk in the olive oil, taste, and adjust the seasoning. Pour the dressing over the tongue and potato.

Place the salad greens on medium plates and spoon the tongue and potatoes over the greens. Serve immediately.

To drink: Peter Michael Mon Plaisir; Landmark Demaris Chardonnay—B. T.; Clos du Bois Flintwood Chardonnay

Tacos Lengua

Serves 4

One July afternoon, an enormous old truck painted sunshine yellow lumbered up the long driveway into my backyard and set up shop. An awning was opened from one side of the truck, providing shade for the two windows where you could place an order. Inside, two women were busily preparing food. On the side of the truck next to the window, a menu was written in blue ink in a scrawling cursive hand. There were burritos and agua fresca, but the tacos were the point of this party. In my opinion, a traditional taco is a thing of beauty and perfection. It should consist of two small corn tortillas, heated until soft and tender but not at all crisp, and set one on top of the other. Next comes the filling, which should be nothing more than a bit of chopped meat, some minced white onions, fresh chiles, cilantro, and a squeeze of lime juice. The meat might be *al pastor*, barbecued pork; *carne asada*, thinly sliced and grilled steak; *carnitas*, succulent pork fried in its own fat; *cabeza*, beef cheeks as tender as butter; *sesos*, fried beef brains that are definitely not for the timid; and my favorite, *lengua*, which is beef tongue. Many of the guests that day probably thought (and still think) I'm completely nuts, but I've long believed that some of the best Mexican food in California, including in Sonoma County, is available in these portable restaurants that you see parked here and there wherever there's an Hispanic population. Because I can't always get to a taco truck and because I learned one day when I had some leftover poached lamb's tongue that tacos lengua is never better than when it is made with lamb, I now make them for myself regularly.

> *6 poached lambs' tongues (page 206), peeled*
> *2 or 3 tablespoons poaching liquid*
> *1 or 2 minced serrano chiles*
> *2 tablespoons minced white onion*
> *2 tablespoons minced fresh cilantro*
> *Juice of 1 lime*
> *Kosher salt*
> *Black pepper in a mill*
> *16 small corn tortillas*
> *1 lime, cut in wedges*

Cut the lambs' tongues into ½-inch dice. Preheat a stove-top griddle. Put the poaching liquid in a medium sauté pan. Set it over low heat, add the lamb, and slowly heat through, tossing and stirring as it heats. In a small bowl, mix together the serranos, onion, cilantro, and lime juice and season with salt and pepper.

Heat the tortillas on a dry griddle, turning them frequently until they are soft and hot but not crisp or burned. Put 4 tortillas on each of 4 plates, setting 2 tortillas on top of each other. Top the double tortillas with a generous spoonful of lamb's tongue and add a spoonful of onion mixture. Garnish with a lime wedge and serve immediately.

To drink: Mexican beer, such as Bohemia or Negro Modelo

Poached Lamb's Tongue

Serves 4 to 6

If you live in an area where lamb is raised, you should easily be able to purchase lamb's tongue. Just ask your butcher. This recipe makes enough for both Tacos Lengua (page 205) and the Lamb's Tongue in Vinaigrette (page 204).

> 2 yellow onions, halved
> 2 shallots, halved
> 1 head of garlic, cloves separated
> 3 to 4 celery stalks, cut in half
> 1 carrot, cut in chunks
> 1 teaspoon black peppercorns
> 3 to 4 juniper berries
> 3 to 4 allspice berries
> A handful of Italian parsley sprigs
> 2 pounds (about 10 to 12) lambs' tongues

Pour 8 cups of water into a large stockpot and add the onions, shallots, garlic, celery, carrot, peppercorns, juniper berries, allspice berries, and parsley sprigs. Cover the pot, set over high heat, bring to a boil, reduce to a simmer, and add the tongues. Simmer, uncovered, for about 2 hours, or until the tongues are completely tender when pierced with a fork. Using tongs or a slotted spoon, remove the tongues from the pot, strain the poaching liquid, discard the vegetables, spices, and parsley, and return the liquid to the pot. Return the tongues to the liquid and allow them to cool until they are easy to handle. Use a sharp paring knife to peel the tongues. Slice or chop and serve immediately, or return to the poaching liquid, and chill until ready to use.

Grilled Steak with Gorgonzola Butter

Serves 4

Beef tenderloin with Gorgonzola butter was one of the most popular recipes in the first edition of *A Cook's Tour of Sonoma*. Here's a variation on the original; everyone loves to gild the lily now and then, which is just what this scrumptious butter does to broiled steaks. The butter is also yummy tossed with roasted potatoes or hot pasta. In Northern California, we're lucky to have Bill Niman and Niman Ranch, located near the border between Sonoma and Marin Counties on Chileno Valley Road southwest of Petaluma. Bill raises beef in a humane and environmentally friendly way, and does not use hormones or antibiotics. For many years, Niman Ranch beef was available almost exclusively in high-end restaurants. Now, it's sold in several markets in the Bay Area as well as through Webvan, an Internet super-market (see Resources, page 295).

> 1 small shallot, minced
> ¼ cup (2 ounces, ½ stick) unsalted butter, at room temperature
> 1½ ounces imported Gorgonzola, at room temperature
> 2 teaspoons fresh snipped chives or minced fresh Italian parsley
> 4 ribeye or market steaks, about 14 ounces each and about 1¼ inches thick
> Kosher salt
> Black pepper in a mill

In a small bowl, use a fork to mix together the shallot, butter, Gorgonzola, and chives until very smooth. (This can be done in a food processor, but then it is best to double the quantities and save half for another recipe.) Set a strip of plastic wrap on a work surface, use a rubber spatula to transfer the mixture to the plastic, and fold the wrap over the mixture but do not close the ends. Use your palms to roll the butter into a log about 1¼ inches in diameter. Wrap tightly and refrigerate for at least 30 minutes.

Build a fire in an outdoor grill or preheat a stove-top grill. Season the steaks generously on both sides with salt and pepper. Grill until well browned on one side,

rotating once, about 4 minutes, turn, and grill until done, about 3 minutes more for rare, a little longer for medium-rare.

Let rest for 5 minutes. Cut 8 coins of Gorgonzola butter about ¼ inch thick. Set the steaks on individual plates, and top each one with two slices of the butter. Serve immediately.

To drink: B. R. Cohn Olive Hill Cabernet Sauvignon; Laurel Glen Estate Cabernet Sauvignon—B. T.; Laurel Glen Counterpoint Cabernet Sauvignon—B. T.

Beef & Shiitake Kebabs

Serves 6

The secret to making good kebabs is to prepare each ingredient in advance so that when the skewers of meat and vegetables are grilled, everything is perfectly cooked. That means that certain foods, shiitake mushrooms for example, will need to be partially cooked in advance. It's not unlike making a successful stir-fry; you must consider how long each element takes to cook, or you'll end up with some things overcooked and others unpleasantly raw, or nearly so.

MARINADE
1 cup dry red wine
½ cup red wine vinegar
Juice of 2 lemons
½ cup olive oil, plus more as needed
5 cloves garlic, crushed
2 teaspoons fresh thyme
Kosher salt
Black pepper in a mill

𝕏

2 pounds beef, cut into 1½-inch cubes
24 medium shiitakes (about 1½ pounds), stems removed
1 large red bell pepper, cut into 1½-inch-wide strips
3 medium red onions, quartered, or 12 very small torpedo onions, halved

24 cherry tomatoes

1 dozen 12-inch wooden skewers, soaked in water for at least 1 hour

1 lemon, cut in wedges

3½ cups (from 1 cup raw) steamed jasmine rice, hot

Several hours before serving, combine the wine, vinegar, lemon juice, olive oil, garlic, and thyme and season the mixture with salt and pepper. Place the beef in a nonreactive bowl or crock, pour the marinade over it, cover, and refrigerate until 1 hour before cooking.

Drain 1 cup of the marinade into a medium saucepan, add the shiitakes, bring to a boil over medium heat, and simmer for 4 minutes to soften them slightly. Use a slotted spoon to transfer the shiitakes to absorbent paper. Cut the bell pepper strips in half, crosswise.

Prepare a hot fire in an outdoor grill, or heat a stove-top grill. Brush the onions lightly with olive oil and grill them, turning frequently, until they are lightly charred and almost tender. Set aside to cool. To assemble, thread each skewer with a cube of beef, a mushroom, a cube of beef, a cherry tomato, a cube of beef, a wedge of onion, a cube of beef, a slice of red pepper, etc. Pack the skewers tightly. Grill the kebabs for 3 to 4 minutes, rotate them, and grill for another 3 to 4 minutes for rare and longer for medium or well-done beef, basting now and then with the marinade. Arrange on a platter, garnish with lemon wedges, and serve immediately, with steamed rice alongside.

To drink: Ferrari-Carano Siena—B. T.

La Daube Provençale

Serves 8 to 10

A daube is a beef stew, a perfect cold-weather meal that gets better the longer it sits. If you can begin making it a full two days in advance, you should. This version is from Patrick Martin, the chef and co-owner, with his wife Robin, of the Healdsburg Charcuterie. Patrick, whose father is from Provence, and Robin are enthusiastic supporters of the Sonoma-Provence sisterhood and host several special meals each year at their restaurant, including a traditional bouillabaisse in June and Provençale Christmas in early December.

MARINADE

4 to 5 large carrots, peeled and cut into thick diagonal slices (3 cups)

2 to 3 yellow onions, peeled and thickly sliced (3 cups)

¼ cup fresh thyme leaves, minced

2 large strips dried orange peel

1 bay leaf

12 garlic cloves, peeled

1 bottle dry red wine, such as a Rhône-style, syrah, or zinfandel

❀

3 pounds boneless beef shank meat (from about 5 pounds beef shanks), cut into large (3-ounce) pieces

3 pounds beef chuck roast, cut into large (3-ounce) pieces

4 ounces bacon, in one piece, cut into thick julienne

Kosher salt

Black pepper in a mill

Pinch of sugar

Bouquet garni of 3 fresh thyme sprigs, 3 fresh Italian parsley sprigs, 1 bay leaf, and 2 strips dried orange peel

2 pounds potatoes, washed and cut into chunks

¼ cup niçoise olives, pitted

Assemble the marinade in a large bowl. Combine the carrots, onions, thyme, orange peel, bay leaf, garlic, and red wine. Place the beef and bacon into the mixture, cover, and refrigerate for 24 hours, stirring occasionally.

Prepare a clay pot roaster according to the manufacturer's instructions. Pour off the marinade, straining it into a clean bowl. Place the meat in the clay pot and season it all over with salt, pepper, and a small pinch of sugar, add the bouquet garni, and pour the marinade over it. Set the marinated vegetables aside. Set the clay pot in a cold oven, turn the temperature to 300°F, and bake for 3 hours. Add the reserved vegetables, bake for 45 minutes, add the potatoes and olives, and bake until the potatoes are tender, about 35 minutes more. Let rest at least 20 minutes before serving. For the best flavors, let the daube cool to room temperature and refrigerate it overnight. Bring the daube back to room temperature, set it in a cold oven, turn the heat to 300°F, and bake until heated through, about 45 minutes. Remove and discard the bouquet garni and serve.

To drink: Hamell Syrah—B. T.; Golden Creek Shiraz—B. T.

Potato Zucchini Stew with Andouille Sausage

Serves 4

For several years, the Opera House Café in Petaluma was one of the best restaurants in Sonoma County. Lea Bergen, the chef, made refined yet homey food that was sensational, and I've never forgotten a stew, similar to this one, that I had for lunch on my birthday one year. The café eventually closed, and Lea is now executive chef for Webvan, an Internet supermarket that provides home delivery.

> 2 smoked or fresh andouille sausages (see Note below), cut in ¼-inch
>   half moons
> 4 tablespoons olive oil
> 1 yellow onion, diced
> 1 pound small new potatoes, quartered, boiled until almost tender, and drained
> Kosher salt
> Black pepper in a mill
> 1 pound small zucchini, cut in ¼-inch half moons
> 1 teaspoon fresh summer savory
> 1 teaspoon fresh thyme
> ¼ cup crème fraîche

Fry the sausages in a medium skillet set over medium heat until they are just lightly browned on both sides. Transfer them to a bowl and cover them to keep them warm. Return the pan to medium-low heat, add 3 tablespoons of the olive oil, and sauté the onion until it is soft and fragrant, about 15 minutes. Increase the heat to medium, add the potatoes, and sauté until they are golden brown, about 10 to 15 minutes. Season with salt and pepper and add to the bowl with the sausages. Add the remaining 1 tablespoon of the olive oil to the pan, set over medium heat, add the zucchini, and sauté until just tender, 4 to 5 minutes. Add the summer savory and thyme, season with salt and pepper, return the sausages, onions, and potatoes to the pan, toss thoroughly, and transfer to a serving platter.

Stir the crème fraîche to loosen it, drizzle it over the stew, grind black pepper over everything, and serve immediately.

Note: If using fresh andouille sausages, parboil them first. Use a fork to prick their skins in several places, boil for 5 to 6 minutes, drain, and let cool before slicing.

To drink: Preston Marsanne—B. T.; Seghesio 1998 Sangiovese—P. R.

Hot Italian Sausage with Spinach & Spaghetti

Serves 4

Of the dozen or so varieties of Caggiano sausages I've tasted, my favorite is the classic hot Italian sausage. In this recipe, from Richard Caggiano, the sausages contribute a burst of spiciness to this colorful pasta dish. I do not recommend using a different type of sausage—the flavor of chicken sausages, for example, so popular because they are marketed as low-fat, will dominate this dish and be quite another thing from what is intended.

> 3 tablespoons olive oil
>
> 3 or 4 hot Italian sausages
>
> 1 small yellow onion, minced
>
> Several garlic cloves, minced
>
> Kosher salt
>
> 3 or 4 canned plum tomatoes (or fresh tomatoes, when in season)
>
> 1 pound dried spaghetti
>
> 12 ounces baby spinach leaves or 1 large bunch mature spinach, large stems removed
>
> 3 to 4 ounces Parmigiano-Reggiano cheese, in one piece
>
> Chipotle Oil (page 262), optional

Bring a large pot of water to a boil.

Heat the olive oil in a large frying pan, add the sausages, and sauté, turning occasionally, over medium-low heat until they are cooked through, about 12 minutes. Transfer the sausages to a plate and set them aside.

Add the onion to the pan and sauté until limp and fragrant, about 8 to 10 minutes. Add the garlic and sauté for 2 more minutes.

Add 1 tablespoon or so of salt to the boiling water and cook the spaghetti according to package directions. Cut the sausages into thin rounds and add them to the cooked onions. Use your fingers to crumble the tomatoes into the pan (if you are

using fresh tomatoes, cut them into small dice), add 3 or 4 tablespoons of the pasta cooking water to the pan, and simmer for about 5 minutes.

Drain the pasta and place it in a large bowl. Add the spinach to the sausage mixture, cook until it is just wilted, toss with the sausages, and pour the mixture over the pasta. If using the chipotle oil, drizzle a teaspoon over each portion. Add a generous grating of cheese, toss quickly, and serve immediately, with the cheese and a grater alongside.

To drink: De Loach Petite Sirah—B. T.; Pellegrini Barbera—P. R.

Sicilian Sausage & Lentil Stew

Serves 4

Caggiano Sicilian sausages include diced provolone cheese, which will ooze out when you cut into the cooked sausage. They are best braised whole, so that they are not sliced until on someone's plate where the tangy cheese may be enjoyed instantly. Certainly, you can use almost any type of sausage in this dish, but Richard Caggiano, who developed the recipe, uses his Sicilian sausage, as do I.

> *3 tablespoons olive oil*
> *1 yellow onion, in ¼-inch dice*
> *2 carrots, in ¼-inch dice*
> *3 celery stalks, in ¼-inch dice*
> *Half a red bell pepper, in ¼-inch dice*
> *Kosher salt*
> *1 pound brown lentils*
> *3 canned plum tomatoes, diced*
> *2 cups chicken stock*
> *4 Sicilian sausages*
> *3 cups water*
> *Black pepper in a mill*
> *¼ cup minced fresh Italian parsley*
> *Parmigiano-Reggiano cheese, in one piece*

Heat the olive oil in a soup pot, add the onion, carrots, celery, and bell pepper, and sauté over medium-low heat until soft, about 10 to 12 minutes. Season with salt. Add the lentils and sauté for 2 minutes, stirring constantly. Add the tomatoes, chicken stock, sausages, and 3 cups of water. Cover the pan and simmer over low heat until the lentils are tender, about 45 minutes. Check occasionally and add more water if necessary; the stew should be fairly thick, but not too thick. Season with several turns of black pepper and more salt to taste. Divide among four soup plates, garnish each serving with Italian parsley, and serve immediately, with the cheese and a grater alongside.

To drink: Marietta Old Vine Red—B. T.

Curried Onions with Sausage Stuffing

Serves 4

Sausages made with chicken and turkey became quite popular in the 1980s and 1990s because those meats have been perceived as being healthier than the pork, beef, and veal traditionally used to make sausage. I have almost always found them unsatisfying and often even cloying, especially when they include ingredients—mango, cranberries, pistachios, and sun-dried cherries, for example— that never strayed into the mix when sausage was a way to use every last bit of the fall harvest, a time when hogs were slaughtered because there was not enough food to keep them through the winter. The one consistent exception has been chicken-apple sausages flavored with curry spices; that combination works particularly well.

4 large, round sweet onions, such as Vidalia, Walla Walla, or Candy

3 teaspoons curry powder (see Note, below)

Kosher salt, plus more to taste

2 tablespoons olive oil, plus more as needed

3 garlic cloves, minced

1 teaspoon ground cumin

½ teaspoon ground turmeric

Black pepper in a mill

1 pound East Indian–style chicken-apple sausages, casings removed

½ cup golden raisins

½ cup fresh bread crumbs, toasted

1 egg, beaten

¾ cup fruity but dry white wine, such as viognier or Gewürztraminer

Ground cayenne
1 cup plain (unflavored) yogurt
Chutney of choice

Fill a medium-sized pot two-thirds full with water and bring it to a boil over high heat.

Meanwhile, use a sharp knife to slice off the root end of each onion so that it will stand upright. Cut a flat slice off the stem end of each onion and carefully peel off the skin. Cut a cone shape out from the middle of each onion and use a melon-ball cutter to hollow out the inside, leaving a ⅜-inch wall of flesh on the sides and bottom of the onion. Mince the onion corings and set them aside.

Add 1 teaspoon of the curry powder and 1 tablespoon of kosher salt to the boiling water and blanch the onion shells until they are somewhat tender but still hold their shape, about 6 minutes. Use tongs to transfer them to absorbent paper; set them upside down to drain and cool.

Heat the 2 tablespoons of olive oil in a medium sauté pan set over medium heat and sauté the minced onion until it is soft and fragrant, about 10 minutes. Add the garlic, the remaining 2 teaspoons of curry powder, the cumin, and the turmeric and sauté for 2 minutes more, stirring continuously. Season with salt and pepper, add the sausage, and sauté for 5 or 6 minutes, using a fork to break up the sausage as it cooks. Add the raisins and bread crumbs, toss together, and remove from the heat. Taste, correct the seasoning, and let cool to room temperature. Fold in the egg.

Preheat the oven to 375°F. Pour a little olive oil into the palm of your hand and rub the outside of each onion, using more olive oil as needed. Spoon sausage filling into each onion shell and place the filled onions in an ovenproof dish just large enough to hold them. Return the sauté pan to medium heat, add the wine, deglaze the pan, and simmer until the wine is reduced by half. Season with a generous pinch of cayenne pepper and a pinch of salt, and pour the liquid over the onions. Cover the dish with its lid or with aluminum foil and bake for 35 to 40 minutes, until the onions are completely tender. Transfer the onions to a serving plates, stir ½ cup of the yogurt into the pan juices, and pour the sauce over the onions. Top each onion with a spoonful of chutney and serve immediately, with the remaining yogurt and chutney on the side.

To drink: Alderbrook Gewürztraminer; Preston Viognier—P. R.

Note: The best curry powder is made by toasting and crushing spices shortly before using them, but Penzeys Spices (800-741-7787; www.penzeys.com) has excellent commercial mixtures.

CHAPTER 6

Vegetables

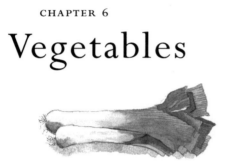

WHAT DEFINES A SEASON? The weather, of course, scents and aromas carried on the wind, our desire to sleep, to work or play, to flirt or lounge all afternoon on a hammock in the shade are all defined by the seasonal rhythms of the earth as it tilts on its axis, leaning into the sun's light or away from it. Not so long ago, we knew the seasons by the harvest, by what we gathered from our gardens or bought at the store. Today it's not so easy; everything, it seems, is available year round. To remember we turn to farmers' markets, where a panorama of vegetables evolves with the seasons, providing us with bright, refreshing, and perishable crops in the summer (a tomato picked when ripe lasts just three or four days, zucchini not much longer) and a hearty, bone-warming harvest that keeps for months in the winter.

We've come a long way since vegetables—often painfully overcooked—were merely side dishes, accompaniments that frequently remained on the plate and were considered of dubious nutritional value. Now we praise vegetables for themselves and are told they will make us live forever, or close. We often make a meal of them whether we are vegetarians or not.

Sometimes the best preparation is the simplest: broccoli rabe braised in a little stock and served over creamy polenta; wilted spinach with minced garlic and lemon; steamed broccoli tossed with olive oil and red pepper flakes; radicchio grilled and drizzled with vinegar; summer corn with salt and pepper; a fat baked potato drenched in butter. To enjoy vegetables prepared so simply, they must be of good quality, grown properly, picked at the right moment, and sold soon thereafter. These preparations need no recipes, just good ingredients and a bit of common sense. The recipes here are more complex, but only slightly; their purpose remains the same, to highlight the goodness of the vegetables themselves.

Artichokes Stuffed with Green Garlic & Potato Purée

Serves 4

A decade ago, you never saw green garlic in the market. Now, there are beautiful piles of it at farmers' markets every spring; some supermarkets carry it, too. Although it is unmistakably garlic, its flavor is more delicate than that of mature garlic. Green garlic and artichokes are spring vegetables. If you do not have green garlic but do have artichokes, refer to the variation at the end of the recipe.

> *12 to 18 stalks of green garlic*
> *4 to 6 medium Yukon Gold or Yellow Finn potatoes, about 3 inches long*
> *4 large artichokes, preferably Green Globe variety*
> *Extra virgin olive oil*
> *Kosher salt*
> *Black pepper in a mill*
> *2 or 3 ounces Parmigiano-Reggiano, grated*

Trim the green garlic, removing the roots and any dirt that may cling to them. Place them in a large saucepan (big enough to hold the artichokes and potatoes) and add about 4 cups of water; it should cover the garlic by about 2 inches. Set over medium heat, cover, and simmer until the garlic is very tender. Using tongs or a slotted spoon, transfer the garlic to a plate to cool.

Scrub the potatoes, removing any specks of dirt; do not peel them. Trim the artichokes, cutting the stem end to just ¼ inch or so. Place the artichokes in the saucepan with the poaching liquid from the garlic. Cut the potatoes in half lengthwise and tuck the pieces in between the artichokes. The liquid should come about halfway up the sides of the artichokes; if it doesn't, add a little more water. Drizzle a teaspoon or two of olive oil over each artichoke and season with a little salt and pepper. Bring to a boil over medium heat, reduce to a simmer, cover, and cook until the artichokes and potatoes are tender, about 25 to 40 minutes, depending on the size and age of the artichokes.

While the vegetables cook, prepare the green garlic purée. First, cut away and discard the dark green tips of the garlic, saving about 3 to 4 inches of the tender green stems. Chop these coarsely, place them in a food processor, and pulse until they are reduced to a pulp. Transfer to a small bowl.

Remove the artichokes and potatoes from the cooking water and let cool until they are easy to handle. Using a heavy, sharp knife, cut the artichokes in half lengthwise. In the center of each half, there will be small prickly leaves. Use your fingers to pull these out. Using a sharp paring knife, cut the choke (the fuzzy little fibers) away from the heart and discard it. Place the artichokes, cut sides up, in a baking dish.

Preheat the oven to 350°F. Place the potatoes in a medium bowl and use a fork to smash them (do not use a mixer or a food processor). Add the green garlic purée and enough of the cooking liquid to create a moderately moist (but not at all runny) purée. (Save the remainder of the cooking liquid to make soup.) Fold in the cheese, taste, and season with salt and pepper. Using a tablespoon, fill the cavity of each artichoke half with the potato and green garlic purée. Grind a little black pepper over each and bake until heated through, about 15 to 20 minutes. Remove from the oven and serve immediately.

To drink: Cline Cellars Roussanne—B. T.

VARIATIONS

Instead of making the purée, place the artichoke halves on a large platter, surround with the potatoes and the tender part of the green garlic. Spoon the cooking liquid over everything, season with salt and pepper, and serve with hot bread to sop up the delicious juices.

When you can't get green garlic, use leeks, trimming 4 to 5 and using just the white parts and tenderest pale greens. Cut the leeks in half lengthwise and cut each half into thin, crosswise strips. Sauté the sliced leeks in a little olive oil until they are completely wilted and tender; purée them in a food processor and continue as directed in the main recipe.

John Kramer's Stuffed Artichokes

Makes 6

Home cooking is, or should be anyway, an inexact art rather than a strict science. In that spirit, as John Kramer, a professor of political science at Sonoma State University, was describing this dish to me, he gestured to explain both quantities and techniques. You have to bond with the recipe, he says, though not exactly in those words, and make it taste really  good; that's when you know it's ready. John has taken to hiding this stuffing in a high cupboard so that his wife and kids don't eat it all before he has a chance to stuff the artichokes.

> 6 large artichokes
> 2 to 3 lemons
> ¼ cup olive oil
> ¼ pound (more or less, to taste) pancetta, prosciutto, or ham, minced
> 6 garlic cloves, minced
> 3 cups fresh bread crumbs (see Note, below)
> 1 cup minced Italian parsley
> 4 ounces (more or less, to taste) Parmigiano-Reggiano, grated
> Kosher salt
> Black pepper in a mill

First, trim the artichokes. Cut the stems down to 1 inch and use a vegetable peeler to peel them. Cut about an inch off the top and then use a large, heavy spoon to scoop out the smallest inner leaves and the choke. After cutting each artichoke, rub the cut surface with lemon to prevent browning.

In a large, heavy pot, heat a little of the olive oil, add the pancetta, and sauté for several minutes. Add the garlic and sauté for 1 minute more. Remove from the heat. Place the bread crumbs in a large bowl, add the garlic mixture, parsley, and cheese, and toss. Add enough of the remaining olive oil so that the stuffing sticks together, squeeze lemon juice over it, taste, season with salt and pepper, and add more lemon juice until it tastes really good.

To stuff the artichokes, hold each one over the bowl of stuffing and fill the center of the artichoke. Press the leaves toward the center so that the artichoke closes over the stuffing. Set a large, heavy pot over medium-low heat, and add the first stuffed artichoke, setting it on its side. As you fill each artichoke, add it to the pot, and turn the others, so that by the time all have been stuffed, they have been slightly browned, as well. Add about ¾ inch of water to the pot, bring to a boil, cover, and simmer for about 45 minutes, until the artichokes are tender.

Note: To make fresh bread crumbs, cut two- or three-day-old country-style bread into cubes (or tear it into pieces), place a large handful of cubes in the work bowl of a food processor, and pulse until the cubes are reduced to crumbs. If the bread is particularly fresh, the crumbs might be fluffier, in which case you'll need more than the amount given.

To drink: Iron Horse Blanc de Blancs

Asparagus Andalusia

Serves 4 to 6

It's a romantic story. She was the chef at a local restaurant, he was often a customer. He planted a lot of olive trees on his nearby ranch, she cooked with olive oil. Now, they're married. In celebration of their first olive harvest, which came shortly after they returned from their honeymoon in Italy, they invited their friends for a day of olive picking followed by a huge feast, an event that has become one of my favorite annual traditions. Colleen McGlynn no longer works as a restaurant chef, but she continues to cook, often in conjunction with the promotion of DaVero olive oil, made from the trees her husband Ridgely Evers planted before they met. She offered this recipe during a class about olive oil that she taught at Ramekins cooking school.

> 1½ pounds (1 bunch) fresh asparagus, trimmed
> 4 tablespoons olive oil
> ¼ cup bread cubes cut from stale bread
> 2 garlic cloves
> 12 almonds, shelled and peeled
> Several threads of saffron
> 2 teaspoons sherry vinegar
> ¾ cup extra virgin olive oil, such as DaVero
> Kosher salt
> Black pepper in a mill

Preheat the oven to 475°F. Place the asparagus on a baking sheet in a single layer, toss with 1 tablespoon of the olive oil, season with salt and pepper, and roast until tender, about 7 minutes for thin stalks, 12 to 15 minutes for very thick stalks. Remove from the oven and arrange on a serving platter.

Meanwhile, heat the remaining 3 tablespoons of olive oil in a medium sauté pan set over medium heat. Add the bread cubes, garlic, and almonds, and sauté, stirring continuously, until the bread is golden brown. Add the saffron, stir, and remove from the heat. Transfer the bread, garlic, and almonds to a large mortar or suribachi, add the vinegar, and grind to a paste using a wooden pestle. Slowly whisk in the extra virgin olive oil to form a thick emulsion. Taste, season with salt and pepper, spoon the mixture over the asparagus, and serve immediately.

To drink: Dry Creek Dry Chenin Blanc—B. T.

Roasted Asparagus with Black Raspberry Vinaigrette

Serves 4 to 6

This is another recipe that survived by request, specifically that of my daughter Nicolle, who loves it. The original version called for the asparagus to be steamed or boiled, techniques I no longer use with the spring vegetable. Roasting is far easier and produces much better results. There are two brief seasons when you can make this dish: in June, when the first summer raspberries coincide with the last of spring's asparagus, and October, when a bumper crop of asparagus can be paired with fall's berries.

> 1 ½ *pounds asparagus, tough stems snapped off*
> 1 *tablespoon olive oil*
> *Kosher salt*
> *Black pepper in a mill*
>
> BLACK RASPBERRY VINAIGRETTE
> 3 *tablespoons Kozlowski Farms black raspberry vinegar*
> 1 *garlic clove, minced*
> *Pinch of ground clove*
> *Pinch of sugar*
> *Kosher salt*

Black pepper in a mill
½ cup extra virgin olive oil

❀

2 cups fresh red raspberries

Preheat the oven to 475°F.

Place the asparagus on a baking sheet, drizzle with the olive oil, and then toss lightly with your fingers until the spears are all coated with a bit of oil. Season with salt and several turns of black pepper, and roast until the asparagus is just tender, about 7 to 8 minutes for thin spears, about 12 minutes for thicker ones.

In a small bowl, mix together the raspberry vinegar, garlic, ground cloves, and sugar. Season with salt and several turns of black pepper, and then stir in the olive oil. Taste and correct the seasoning.

Arrange the asparagus on a large serving platter, spoon the vinaigrette over, and then top with the raspberries. Serve immediately, or cover and chill for 1 to 2 hours before serving.

To drink: Kunde Sauvignon Blanc—B. T.; Crane Canyon Cellars 1998 White Crane—B. T.

Beets with Walnuts, Olives & Feta

Serves 4 to 6

I've always combined beets with Roquefort or blue cheese, but recently tried feta, which is delightful with sweet beets. This dish is excellent as an accompaniment to a simple pasta or roasted chicken.

3 tablespoons fresh lemon juice
1 shallot, minced
2 pounds beets, roasted until tender and peeled
Zest of 1 lemon, minced
2 tablespoons minced fresh Italian parsley
2 tablespoons minced fresh cilantro
1 tablespoon minced fresh mint

½ teaspoon ground coriander

Kosher salt

Black pepper in a mill

⅓ to ½ cup extra virgin olive oil

½ cup toasted walnut pieces

¼ cup oil-cured black olives, pitted and halved

3 ounces feta cheese, preferably Redwood Hill Farm goat feta, cut in ¼-inch cubes

Combine the lemon juice and shallot in a medium bowl and set aside for 15 minutes.

Cut the beets into wedges (quarters if small beets, sixths if larger), place in a salad bowl, and toss with the lemon zest. Add the parsley, cilantro, mint, and coriander to the lemon and shallot mixture and season with a generous pinch of salt and several turns of black pepper. Whisk in ⅓ cup olive oil, taste, and add the remaining oil if necessary for proper balance. Pour the dressing over the beets, toss lightly, add the walnuts, olives, and feta, toss again, and serve.

To drink: Clos du Bois Pinot Noir

Cardoon Gratin

Serves 4 to 6

"What's wrong with your car?" asked my friend Jerry Hertz, who is a musician and teacher from Sebastopol, when I said I was off in search of cardoons. I'm still not sure if he was kidding. Cardoons are unfamiliar to most Americans, but they are delicious; the plant itself is easy to grow, provided you protect it from gophers. Cardoons are related to artichokes, but we eat a different part of the plant, the stalk rather than the flower. Long and silvery with soft, delicate spikes, a cardoon resembles space-age celery. I first learned of them in the mid-1980s when the late Louie Traverso urged me to include them in my *bagna cauda*, if I could find some, he added. He was right, of course; the cardoon is the most traditional of all the vegetables in the Italian meal that resembles *le grand aïoli*. I couldn't find them then, but now they appear each spring at our local farmers' markets, most of them grown by Larry Tristano of Triple T Farms in Santa Rosa. Cardoons are also grown in Provence, where cardoon gratin is often served during the Christmas season. Today, cardoons are also showing up on restaurant menus and are available in many markets.

14 small cardoon stalks (enough to make about 8 cups trimmed)

2 cups half-and-half

2 cups chicken stock

2 tablespoons butter

Kosher salt

Black pepper in a mill

3 ounces Parmigiano-Reggiano cheese, grated

1 cup fresh bread crumbs

2 tablespoons minced fresh Italian parsley

Butter the inside of an earthenware dish and preheat the oven to 375°F. Trim the cardoons, removing any tough strings, and cut them into 2- or 3-inch lengths. Boil them in salted water until tender, refresh and cool in ice water, and drain thoroughly. Meanwhile, combine the half-and-half and stock in a medium saucepan, set over medium heat, and simmer until reduced by one-third. Remove from the heat. Place the cardoons in an even layer in the earthenware dish. Break the butter into small pieces and scatter it over the cardoons, then pour the hot stock mixture over. Season with salt and pepper, and spread the cheese over the top. Mix together the bread crumbs and parsley and spread on top of the cheese. Bake until the dish is hot and bubbly and the top lightly browned. Remove from the oven and serve immediately.

To drink: Seghesio Pinot Gris—P. R.

Haricots Verts with Cherry Tomato Vinaigrette

Serves 4 to 6

Haricots verts are tiny green beans, not much bigger than a pencil lead. "I have to pick them twice a day or they grow too large," a local farmer explained in describing the difficulty of the crop. Still, they are so tender and delicious that they're worth both the effort and the high price they command ($10 a pound, or more). A good substitute is the increasingly available Chinese long bean, blanched until barely tender and cut into 3-inch lengths.

CHERRY TOMATO VINAIGRETTE

1 garlic clove, minced

1 small shallot, minced

2 tablespoons white wine or champagne vinegar

¾ cup small cherry tomatoes, quartered

4 tablespoons extra virgin olive oil

Kosher salt

Black pepper in a mill

6 to 8 basil leaves, cut into very thin strips

1 tablespoon kosher salt

8 ounces haricots verts

Basil sprigs, for garnish

Combine the garlic and shallot in a small bowl, cover with the vinegar, and set aside for 20 minutes. In a medium bowl, combine the cherry tomatoes, olive oil, and the vinegar mixture. Taste, season with salt and pepper, and add the sliced basil.

Fill a medium pot with water, bring it to a boil, add the tablespoon of kosher salt, and blanch the green beans for 60 seconds (longer for larger beans and long beans, until the beans are tender but retain a hint of resistance). Drain, rinse, and drain again. Put in a serving bowl.

Pour the vinaigrette over the green beans, garnish with basil sprigs, and serve immediately.

Celery Root & Potato Purée

Serves 4

Celery root is another vegetable that has been overlooked for several decades but is slowly becoming available once again. A good thing, too; it's great. It is one of the more interesting crops during the lean winter months, when Cliff Silva of Ma & Pa's Garden in Sebastopol offers it at the farmers' market. Serve this savory purée in place of mashed potatoes.

> *2 pounds potatoes, scrubbed and cut into 1-inch pieces*
> *1 pound trimmed celery root, cut into 1-inch pieces*
> *6 garlic cloves*
> *¾ cup half-and-half*
> *2 tablespoons butter*
> *2 tablespoons minced fresh Italian parsley*
> *1 teaspoon kosher salt, plus more to taste*
> *Black pepper in a mill*
> *2 ounces Dry Jack cheese, grated (about ½ cup)*

Place the potatoes, celery root, and garlic in a medium saucepan, add water to cover, and bring to a boil over high heat. When the water boils, reduce the heat to medium-low and simmer until the celery root and potatoes are tender when pierced with a fork. Drain thoroughly.

Press the potatoes, celery root, and garlic through a potato ricer. (If you do not have a ricer, find the garlic cloves, remove their skins, and then mash the vegetables into a purée using a hand-held potato masher.)

Heat the half-and-half and butter together over medium heat until the butter is melted. Using a wooden spoon, whip the potato mixture with the half-and-half. Add the parsley, salt, several turns of black pepper, and the cheese, and mix thoroughly. Taste, correct the seasoning, and serve immediately.

Oven-Roasted Peppers

Serves 6 to 8

Today, everyone is familiar with peppers roasted over an
open flame or hot coals. After the skins are blackened, the
peppers are steamed in a covered bowl or plastic or paper bag,
and then their skins are peeled or rubbed off. It's a messy job, but it's
how most of us do it. Years ago, I watched a chef do it the French way and it's a
method I've frequently used since then. There are several benefits to roasting peppers in this way; the flesh never burns, for one thing, and it's nowhere near as messy.
As is the case with many French techniques, it's a bit more elegant.

> 8 to 10 large red, yellow, or orange bell peppers
> Olive oil
> Kosher salt
> Black pepper in a mill

Preheat the oven to 375°F. Use a paring knife to remove the stem and seed core
of each pepper and to cut each pepper in half lengthwise. Place the peppers on a
large baking sheet, drizzle with a little olive oil, and toss to coat with the olive oil.
Arrange the peppers, cut-side down, in a single layer on the sheet and bake until
the skins blister (they do not need to turn black), about 15 to 20 minutes. Remove
from the oven, let cool, and use your fingers or a sharp paring knife to pull off the
skins. Cut each half in half again, lengthwise, arrange on a large platter, and season
with salt and pepper.

Variation: Peel and slice 6 or 7 garlic cloves and toss with the peppers, along with
2 tablespoons red wine vinegar.

Baked Cherry Tomatoes

Serves 6 to 8

Cherry tomatoes are among the first of the season's tomatoes to ripen, and the vigorous plants produce a crop throughout the season if the weather cooperates. A
backyard gardener can end up with a daunting abundance of cherry tomatoes. This
recipe uses a lot, and there are so many variations that it will serve you as long as
you have plenty of tomatoes. The primary recipe is for a simple side dish; for other
serving suggestions, see the variations that follow.

1 quart (4 cups) cherry tomatoes, stemmed and halved
10 to 12 garlic cloves, peeled
¼ cup extra virgin olive oil
Juice of 1 lemon
Kosher salt
Black pepper in a mill

Preheat the oven to 350°F. Put the tomatoes in a glass baking dish, add the garlic cloves, and toss together. Pour the olive oil and lemon juice over the tomatoes, season with salt and several turns of black pepper, and toss again. Bake for 25 minutes, until the garlic is tender. Let cool for 5 minutes, taste, correct the seasoning, and serve immediately as a side dish.

VARIATIONS

To serve as an appetizer, spoon the cooked tomatoes over an 8-ounce log of goat cheese and serve with toasted baguette slices.

To make a sauce for pasta, add 3 anchovy fillets to the tomatoes before baking them. Boil 1 pound (dry weight) spaghetti and when it is cooked toss it with the cooked tomatoes and top with ½ cup (2 ounces) grated Dry Jack cheese.

Stir 3 tablespoons of Pistou (page 127) or homemade pesto into the cooked tomatoes.

Add 2 minced serranos to the tomatoes before baking them; add 3 tablespoons minced cilantro to the cooked tomatoes and serve as a side dish with Mexican food.

Johanna's Hungarian Sweet Peppers

Serves 4 to 6

Johanna Monroe of Dry Creek Peach and Produce had been telling me about her stuffed peppers for months, so I was very pleased when the recipe appeared via my fax machine. Although you can use any sweet peppers in this recipe, try it with Hungarian peppers for the best results.

6 Hungarian sweet peppers or other large sweet peppers
Kosher salt
Black pepper in a mill
3 ounces sharp cheddar cheese, cut in strips

Preheat the oven to 350°F. Use a sharp paring knife to remove the stems and seed pods of the peppers; rinse them under cool water and dry thoroughly. Season the inside of each pepper with salt and pepper, set them in a single layer in a glass baking dish, and bake until completely tender but not mushy, about 45 minutes. Remove from the oven and carefully (so as not to burn your fingers) slip strips of cheese into the peppers. Return to the oven and cook until the cheese is completely melted, about 2 to 3 minutes. Remove from the oven and serve immediately as an appetizer or side dish.

Provençal Ragout of Sunchokes

Serves 4 to 6

Nancy Skall of Middleton Gardens, an organic farm on the edge of Dry Creek Valley just outside Healdsburg, grows excellent sunchokes (commonly called Jerusalem artichokes), as do several other organic farmers in Sonoma County. A relative of sunflowers, sunchokes have a pleasantly nutty, earthy taste. When cooked in olive oil as they are here, they are a classic dish of Provence. Cook them in butter instead, and you'll have a traditional dish of Brittany.

> 4 tablespoons olive oil
> 1½ pounds sunchokes (Jerusalem artichokes), scrubbed and thinly sliced
> 4 garlic cloves, minced
> ¾ teaspoon kosher salt
> Black pepper in a mill
> 1 tablespoon minced Italian parsley

Heat the oil in a medium frying pan set over medium-high heat. Add the sunchokes and garlic and sauté, stirring constantly, for 1 minute. Season with salt and pepper. Reduce the heat to medium-low, cover, and cook slowly for 10 minutes, until the chokes are tender but not mushy when pierced with a fork. Uncover, increase the heat to high, and cook for 5 to 7 minutes more, shaking the pan frequently, until the sunchokes begin to brown just slightly.

Remove from the heat and serve immediately.

Bernadette's Zucchini Blossoms Stuffed with Polenta

Serves 4 to 6

Dempsey's Restaurant & Brewery, a lively pub with some of the best food in the county, has several signature dishes, including these remarkably good zucchini blossoms.

> 3 cups Bernadette's Creamy Polenta (page 166), at room temperature
> 3 ounces chèvre, such as chabis
> ¼ cup (1 ounce) golden raisins
> 1 tablespoon minced Italian parsley
> ¼ cup (1 ounce) grated Dry Jack, Bellwether Carmody, or aged Asiago
> 2 cloves minced garlic
> Kosher salt
> Black pepper in a mill
> 18 medium zucchini blossoms
> ½ cup buttermilk
> 3 tablespoons all-purpose flour
> 3 tablespoons cornmeal
> ¼ teaspoon cayenne pepper
> ½ cup mild olive oil

In a medium bowl, combine the polenta, chèvre, raisins, parsley, Dry Jack, and garlic. Taste and correct the seasoning with salt and pepper, if necessary. Cover with plastic wrap and chill until firm, at least 1 hour.

Fill a medium bowl with tap water and gently submerge each zucchini blossom; dry the blossoms on a tea towel. Fill each blossom with about 2½ tablespoons of the polenta filling, squeeze the end of the flower together, and roll gently to form an oblong shape, like a small football. Set the filled blossoms on a sheet pan in a single layer.

Put the buttermilk in a small bowl. In a medium bowl, combine the flour, corn-meal, and cayenne and season with salt and pepper. Heat half of the olive oil in a heavy sauté pan. Turn each filled blossom in the buttermilk, roll it in the flour mixture, and fry it, turning frequently, until it is evenly browned, about 5 minutes total cooking time. Work in batches, being sure not to crowd the pan; add more of the oil as necessary. Drain the cooked blossoms on absorbent paper. When all of the blossoms have been cooked, serve them immediately.

To drink: White Oaks Meyers Limited Reserve Chardonnay—P. R.

CHAPTER 7

Salads

THE BEST SALAD IS, TO MY PALATE, THE SIMPLEST—utterly fresh greens, a kiss
of salt, a hint of olive and vinegar, maybe a little black pepper—it's all delicious vir-
tuousness, the perfect conclusion to a meal. It hardly needs a recipe, but I've offered
one just in case you've felt obliged to imitate the typical restaurant salad in which
too many competing elements—wedges of out-of-season tomatoes, raw mushrooms,
carrot coins, a torrent of heavy dressing—collapse the lettuce. Wild greens—
increasingly available in Sonoma County, as well as elsewhere—present wonderful
possibilities, and specialty growers are offering all sorts of vintage greens, too, those
revived heirloom greens our grandparents used to grow.

   Composed salads have their place, as main courses at lunch or dinner, occasionally even at breakfast when the garden presents an irresistible opportunity. But
rather than being all jumbled together, the ingredients should be arranged with a
bit more care, so that their textures and flavors interact thoughtfully, intentionally.

Simple Green Salad

Serves 4

The Italian word for salad, *insalata*, actually means that which is salted. This recipe for the most basic of all salads begins in the Italian tradition of applying salt first, before olive oil or anything else is added. Once you get used to doing it this way, you'll never want to return to other methods; it's simple and the results are exactly what you want, perfectly seasoned greens with just a whisper of other flavors.

6 cups mesclun
Kosher salt
2 tablespoons extra virgin olive oil
2 teaspoons medium-acid red wine vinegar
Black pepper in a mill

Place the mesclun in a large salad bowl. Immediately before serving, sprinkle the greens lightly with kosher salt and toss to distribute the salt evenly. Drizzle the olive oil over the greens, toss lightly, drizzle the vinegar over, toss again, grind black pepper over the greens, toss once more, and serve immediately.

Miner's Lettuce Salad

Serves 4 to 6

Craig Strattman, the chef at Chalk Hill Estate Vineyards & Winery, has a large organic garden at the winery and he incorporates wild native species in his harvest. Even though miner's lettuce grows wild throughout North America, you can always sow seeds to get it started in your yard if you're not blessed with it naturally. Nasturtiums, too, are very easy to grow at home, either in the garden or in a planter box. Harvest the smaller of the leaves, and if you're in a colorful mood, garnish your salad with a few of the flowers.

MUSTARD VINAIGRETTE
1 hard-cooked egg yolk
1 tablespoon Dijon mustard
2 garlic cloves, minced
1 tablespoon lemon juice
1 tablespoon sherry vinegar

Kosher salt

Black pepper in a mill

½ cup extra virgin olive oil

❧

6 handfuls (about 6 cups) young miner's lettuce, washed and dried

2 handfuls (about 2 cups) small to medium nasturtium leaves

In a medium bowl, use a fork to mash the egg yolk. Add the mustard and garlic and mix into a thick paste. Whisk in the lemon juice and vinegar, taste, and season with salt and pepper. Whisk in the olive oil, making a smooth emulsion. Pass the dressing through a strainer and set it aside.

In a large bowl, toss the miner's lettuce and nasturtium leaves together, sprinkle them lightly with salt and pepper, and toss again. Add about half of the dressing and toss gently to coat each leaf. If the greens seem a little dry, add more dressing and toss again. Divide among individual plates and serve immediately.

Hearts of Butter Lettuce with Bellwether Blue Cheese & Meyer Lemon Vinaigrette

Serves 4

Although Sonoma County is not a major citrus producing region, there are microclimates here and there where lemon and orange trees, including Meyer lemons and blood oranges, thrive. The Meyer lemon, a mild, slightly sweet-tasting fruit with a thin skin, was introduced into California in 1908 by Frank Meyer, who brought the tree from Beijing. You can occasionally find  Meyer lemons at local stores and farmers' markets, and they have become increasingly available nationally, too. If you don't have Meyer lemons, use whatever lemons you do have (they'll probably be the Eureka variety), but add a little more olive oil if the dressing is too tart. If you can get our Bellwether Blue, use it; if not, imported Gorgonzola will work just fine.

MEYER LEMON VINAIGRETTE

1 Meyer lemon

1 garlic clove

1 tablespoon snipped fresh chives

¼ teaspoon kosher salt

⅓ cup extra virgin olive oil

Black pepper in a mill

※

3 medium heads of green or red butter lettuce, thoroughly rinsed and dried

1 small torpedo onion, thinly sliced

2 ounces Bellwether Blue, Maytag Blue, or imported Gorgonzola

Use a zester or vegetable peeler to remove the zest of the lemon; if using a peeler, mince the zest. Set the zest aside. Use a sharp paring knife to cut away all of the white rind. Cut the lemon in half and remove any seeds. Place the lemon in the work bowl of a food processor, add the garlic, chives, and salt, and pulse several times. Add the olive oil and several turns of black pepper and pulse again, until the dressing is evenly mixed. Transfer to a small bowl and set aside.

Remove the large outer leaves of the lettuce and set aside for another purpose. Carefully break apart the remaining leaves and hearts of lettuce and place them in a large salad bowl. Separate the round slices of onions into rings, reserve several for garnish, and add the rest to the bowl of lettuce. Add the vinaigrette and toss gently but thoroughly. Add the cheese and several turns of black pepper, toss, and divide among individual plates.

Warm Spinach Salad

Serves 4 to 6

Over the years I have received many requests for a recipe for a classic spinach salad. This one is about as close as I'll probably get; portobello mushrooms provide the depth of flavor usually contributed by bacon. Vegetarians can enjoy this version without making adjustments; baco-vegetarians will know exactly what to do.

> 3 tablespoons olive oil
> 1 small portobello mushroom, minced
> 3 garlic cloves, minced
> Kosher salt
> Black pepper in a mill
> 2 tablespoons sherry vinegar
> Juice of 1 lemon
> ¾ pound baby spinach, rinsed and dried
> 1 small red onion, thinly sliced (about ½ cup slices)
> 4 hard-cooked eggs, peeled and quartered
> 4 ounces feta cheese, crumbled
> 3 tablespoons heavy cream
> 12 thin baguette slices, toasted
> ½ cup Easy Olive Tapenade (page 269)
> 6 tablespoons extra virgin olive oil

Heat the olive oil in a medium sauté pan set over medium-low heat, add the diced portobello, and sauté until it is limp and has released its liquid. Continue to cook until the liquid is evaporated, stirring frequently to prevent burning. Add the garlic and sauté for 2 minutes more. Season with salt and pepper, add the vinegar and lemon juice, and remove from the heat.

Place the spinach in a large bowl, add the red onion and eggs, and toss together gently. In a small bowl, mix together the feta, cream, and several turns of black pepper and spread a little of the mixture on each of the toasted baguette slices. Top with a little tapenade and set aside.

Return the sauté pan with the portobello mixture to medium-low heat, add the extra virgin olive oil, heat through, and immediately pour over the salad. Toss quickly and gently, and divide among individual plates. Add two or three of the tapenade toasts to each portion and serve immediately.

To drink: Pezzi King Sauvignon Blanc—P. R.

Raspberry Coleslaw with Black Raspberry Mayonnaise

Serves 6 to 8

Most raspberry vinegars in the marketplace are made using red raspberries; most are also fairly high in acid, between 6 and 7 percent. I developed this recipe to highlight the low-acid black raspberry vinegar made by Kozlowski Farms. It is rich and full-bodied, yet not a shock to the palate because it contains only 4.5 percent acetic acid, which allows the taste of the raspberries to dominate.

BLACK RASPBERRY MAYONNAISE

2 egg yolks

1 teaspoon raspberry mustard (see Kozlowski Farms, Resources, page 295) or Dijon mustard

Kosher salt

White pepper in a mill

¾ cup olive oil

½ cup crème fraîche or sour cream

6 tablespoons Kozlowski Farms black raspberry vinegar

2 tablespoons lemon juice, or more to taste

¼ cup sugar, plus more to taste

1 tablespoon cumin

Black pepper in a mill

❧

1 medium red cabbage, shredded

1 small red onion, minced

¼ cup chopped Italian parsley

1 pint fresh raspberries

Sprigs of Italian parsley

First, make the mayonnaise. In a medium bowl, whisk together the egg yolks and mustard, add a generous pinch of salt and several turns of white pepper, and whisk again. Begin to add the olive oil a few drops at a time, whisking between additions. Continue to whisk until all of the oil has been incorporated and the emulsion is very thick. Add the crème fraîche (or sour cream), the vinegar, and the lemon juice and whisk until smooth. Add the sugar, cumin, several turns of black pepper, and a teaspoon of kosher salt and whisk thoroughly. Taste and correct the seasoning, adding more salt if the sauce seems a little flat and a pinch of sugar if it is too tart. Set the dressing aside.

In a large bowl, toss together the cabbage, onion, and parsley. Pour the dressing over the cabbage mixture and toss gently but thoroughly. Add the raspberries, toss very gently, and serve immediately, garnished with sprigs of Italian parsley.

Fall Greens with Grilled Figs & Bacon Vinaigrette

Serves 4

From the late summer through fall, local figs are abundant, many of them from old orchards. A tree in the garden of Alexander Valley Vineyards bears both white and black figs, the trunks of two trees having woven themselves together more than a hundred years ago.

6 fresh figs
3 ounces Teleme
3 strips of bacon, fried until not quite crisp, drained

BACON VINAIGRETTE
1 small shallot, minced
3 tablespoons white wine vinegar
4 strips of bacon, diced

⅓ cup extra virgin olive oil

3 tablespoons minced fresh Italian parsley

✻

6 cups fall salad mix

Kosher salt

Black pepper in a mill

Prepare a charcoal fire in an outdoor grill or heat a stove-top grill.

Use a paring knife to make a lengthwise slit in each fig and press a small amount of Teleme into each slit. Cut the bacon slices in half and wrap each filled fig with a strip, using a toothpick to secure the bacon. Cover the filled figs with a tea towel and set them aside. Put the shallot in a small bowl, pour the vinegar over it, and set it aside for 15 minutes.

Meanwhile, fry the diced bacon in a small sauté pan until it is crisp. Using a slotted spoon, transfer it to absorbent paper. Drain off and discard all but 3 tablespoons of the bacon fat, add the shallot and vinegar mixture, the olive oil, and the parsley, and heat through. Remove from the heat immediately and stir in the bacon.

Grill the figs, turning them frequently, until the bacon is crisp and the cheese heated through, about 5 to 6 minutes; do not overcook or the cheese will ooze out onto the grill.

Place the salad greens in a large salad bowl, sprinkle with salt, and toss lightly. Pour the dressing over the greens, toss thoroughly, and season with black pepper. Divide the greens among individual plates, top each serving with a fig, and serve immediately.

To drink: Dumol 1998 Chardonnay—P. R.

Almond-Crusted Feta
with Grilled Grapes & Frisée

Serves 4 to 6

When I first tried this sensational salad at Mariposa, a tiny restaurant in downtown Windsor, I was intrigued by the idea of grilling grapes. The hot but not melted feta makes for a great combination with the fruit. It is admittedly a lot of trouble to build a charcoal or wood fire to use for just 3 or 4 minutes, so you might want to make this salad when you're using the grill for other things as well. If you have a wood-burning oven, you can roast the grapes in a dry pan instead of grilling them; they'll pick up a wonderfully smoky flavor. The recipe for the vinaigrette comes from my friend Andrew, who at 4 and 5 years old had one of the most developed palates of anyone I've ever met. Because of his love of both lettuce and of all things sour, he often insists on making the vinaigrette when he's at my house for dinner, and he almost always makes it at home, too. He's 9 years old now, and is more opinionated about which vinegar to use, and how much, than ever.

> 8 ounces Redwood Hill Farm raw goat feta, in one piece, chilled
> 4 ounces whole almonds, shelled and peeled
> Kosher salt
> Black pepper in a mill
> 1 teaspoon fresh Italian parsley, minced
> 1 teaspoon fresh snipped chives
> 1 teaspoon fresh thyme leaves, minced
> 2 egg yolks, beaten
> 2 teaspoons all-purpose flour
> 4 ounces Red Flame grapes, all stems removed
> 2 teaspoons plus ¼ cup mild-flavored olive oil
> 1 pound frisée or other hearty salad green
> Andrew's Balsamic Vinaigrette (recipe follows)

Chill the feta in the coldest part of the refrigerator. Preheat the oven to 375°F. Put the almonds in a heavy, ovenproof pan that holds them in a single layer; season with salt and pepper and roast, stirring occasionally, until they are golden brown (when their aroma develops, they are nearly done). Let cool, set aside half of the almonds, and use a heavy, sharp knife to mince the remaining almonds with the parsley, chives, and half the thyme. Set the mixture aside. In a medium bowl, whisk together the egg yolks and flour; set aside.

Set the feta on your work surface and use a sharp knife to cut it into ¼-inch slices. Brush one side of each slice with the egg yolk mixture, sprinkle with some of the almond mixture, and use your fingers to press the almonds gently into the cheese. Set the coated cheese slices on a plate, cover with plastic wrap, and refrigerate.

Forty-five minutes before assembling the salad, prepare a small charcoal or wood fire in an outdoor grill. Wash the grapes, dry them on a tea towel, and cut each grape in half. Put them in a medium bowl, drizzle with the 2 teaspoons of olive oil, add the remaining ½ teaspoon of thyme, season with salt and pepper, toss, and set aside.

Hold a wire strainer with a long handle over the coals and pour the grapes into it, shaking the strainer to scatter the olive oil and any collected moisture over the coals, which will spark flames. Be careful not to burn yourself, but continue shaking the grapes until they are just barely charred and are heated through, about 3 to 4 minutes, depending on the heat of the coals. Set them aside.

Put the greens, remaining whole almonds, and grilled grapes in a large bowl, drizzle the vinaigrette over, and toss together gently. Divide among individual plates, being sure that each serving includes both grapes and almonds.

Pour the remaining ¼ cup olive oil into a medium-sized heavy sauté pan and set it over medium-high heat. Remove the feta from the refrigerator, carefully set each piece, crust-side down, in the sauté pan, and sauté until the crust is golden brown, about 30 to 45 seconds. You must work very quickly so that the nuts do not burn and the cheese does not melt into the pan. Do not crowd the cheese and work in batches if necessary; you will be sautéing only one side of each piece. Use a solid metal spatula to transfer the cheese to the salad, turning each slice so that the crust is face up. Serve immediately.

ANDREW'S BALSAMIC VINAIGRETTE

2 teaspoons minced shallots

1 garlic clove, minced

2 tablespoons Vinaigre de Banyuls or sherry vinegar

1 tablespoon balsamic vinegar

Squeeze of lemon juice

Kosher salt

Black pepper in a mill

⅓ cup extra virgin olive oil

Put the shallots and garlic in a small bowl, cover them with the vinegars, and set aside for a few minutes. Add a squeeze of lemon juice, season with salt and pepper, and whisk in the olive oil. Taste and correct the seasoning and the acid balance, adding a bit more vinegar or lemon juice for a more tart taste or adding a little more olive oil to soften the harshness of the vinegar.

To drink: Fanucci 1998 Trousseau Gris—P. R.

Sprout Salad with Avocados & Tahini Dressing

Serves 4 to 6

Since the late 1960s, alfalfa sprouts have been the supreme cliché of both vegetarian food and California cooking at its silliest, and for good reason—sprouts find their way into many places where they have absolutely no business. They don't belong in a salad niçoise, a taco, or in soup of any kind, yet I've fished mounds of alfalfa sprouts from all of those dishes more times than I can count. I admit to having a bit of an attitude about sprouts, but I also know that when they are used in the right way they are delicious. To my palate, less is more. Sprouts have an appealingly crunchy texture, and many have very good flavors that are best enjoyed without too much interference, as in this simple salad.

TAHINI DRESSING
¼ cup sesame tahini
2 tablespoons lemon juice, plus more to taste
1 garlic clove, pressed
Pinch of ground cumin
Pinch of chipotle powder
⅓ cup plain (unflavored) yogurt
Kosher salt
Black pepper in a mill

⁘

2 Hass avocados, halved, peeled, and seeded

4 cups mixed sprouts (see Note, below)

6 radishes, cut in thin julienne

1 carrot, peeled and cut in thin julienne

1 tablespoon white sesame seeds, toasted

4 lemon wedges

To make the dressing, whisk together the tahini, lemon juice, garlic, cumin, chipotle powder, and yogurt. Season with salt and pepper, taste, and correct the seasoning with more salt, pepper, or lemon juice. If necessary, thin with 2 or 3 tablespoons of water until the consistency is thin enough to fall from a spoon. Cover and refrigerate until ready to use.

Cut the avocados into ⅛-inch-thick lengthwise slices, arrange the slices on four individual salad plates, and season with salt and pepper. Top each avocado with some of the sprouts, spoon dressing over the sprouts, and scatter radishes and carrots on top. Sprinkle with sesame seeds, garnish with a lemon wedge, and serve immediately.

Note: R-Gang Sprouts in Healdsburg has been growing a variety of sprouts since 1987. Among their selections is a salad mix, a selection of several types of sprouted seeds. To ensure the sprouts you buy are fresh, look for brands, such as R-Gang, that include an expiration date on the package.

Carrot, Olive & Feta Salad

Serves 4 to 6

The sweetness of the carrots, saltiness of the olives and feta, and fragrance of the spices create an enticing harmony on the palate. I developed this recipe in the spring of 1999, shortly after my dear friend the renowned cheesemaker Steven Schack of Redwood Hill Farm goat dairy was diagnosed with cancer. When Steven called me with his difficult news, I turned, as I often do, to my kitchen for comfort. I thought of him as I let my imagination be guided by his good cheeses; several wonderful recipes resulted. Steven didn't make it; he died on August 5, 1999, but he lives on in his wonderful cheeses and in the hearts of all of us in Sonoma County. I tell myself he would have liked this salad.

2 pounds medium carrots, trimmed, peeled, and thinly sliced

1 teaspoon kosher salt, plus more to taste

¼ cup extra virgin olive oil

2 tablespoons fresh lemon juice

4 garlic cloves, minced

1½ teaspoons ground cumin

2 tablespoons minced fresh Italian parsley

2 tablespoons minced fresh cilantro

2 tablespoons minced fresh mint

4 ounces (about ½ cup) oil-cured black olives, diced

4 ounces feta cheese, diced

Black pepper in a mill

Steam the carrots over a small amount of water until they are tender when pierced with a fork, but not mushy, about 12 to 15 minutes. Set aside to cool to room temperature.

Sprinkle the salt over the carrots and toss lightly. Add the olive oil, lemon juice, garlic, cumin, parsley, cilantro, and mint and toss again, lightly but thoroughly. Add the olives and feta and toss again. Season with black pepper, taste, and correct the seasoning with more salt if necessary. Serve immediately, or store in the refrigerator, covered, for up to 2 days. Bring to room temperature before serving.

Farm Market Salad

Serves 4 to 6 as a main course, 6 to 8 as a first course

This salad was inspired by the wonderful heirloom tomatoes that Sonoma County farmers began growing and selling at local farmers' markets in the late 1980s. Although you can make it with any old store-bought tomato, you shouldn't. Search for great tomatoes with backyard flavor. The other ingredients—onions, cucumbers, peppers, and even the cheese—can be varied, depending on what is at hand. Quality should be the main consideration. By the way, confetti tomatoes are not a variety of tomato but a mix of various colors of cherry tomatoes sold in a single basket. There are several varieties of tomatoes that remain green when they are ripe, including green zebra, green grape, and evergreen.

3 red tomatoes, cored and sliced

3 orange tomatoes, cored and sliced

3 yellow tomatoes, cored and sliced

3 green ripe tomatoes, cored and sliced

2 young torpedo onions, thinly sliced

4 mild peppers, such as Anaheim, in various colors (red, orange, yellow, green),
   very thinly sliced

3 lemon cucumbers, thinly sliced

1 pint confetti tomatoes, halved

Kosher salt

⅓ cup DaVero olive oil or other best-quality, fruity olive oil

6 plump garlic cloves, or more to taste, peeled and cut in thin julienne

Several basil leaves, cut in thin julienne

Sel gris (see Note, below)

Black pepper in a mill

California Gold Dry Jack cheese, in one piece

Several small sprigs of red, yellow, and orange currant tomatoes

Arrange the sliced tomatoes in concentric circles on a large, flat serving platter, alternating colors. Tuck onion slices, pepper slices, and cucumber slices here and there among the tomatoes. Scatter the confetti tomatoes over the top and season with kosher salt. Drizzle with olive oil and scatter the garlic and basil over the tomatoes. Season with *sel gris* and several turns of black pepper. Use a vegetable peeler to make curls of Dry Jack and scatter them over the salad. Garnish with the sprigs of currant tomatoes and let rest for 10 to 15 minutes. Serve with hot bread alongside.

Note: *Sel gris* is the sea salt harvested from the north coast of France. It is also called Celtic Gray Sea Salt, which is the brand developed and sold by the Grain and Salt Society. These salty crystals, larger and harder than many other salts, contribute both flavor and texture to the salad.

Root Vegetable Salad

Serves 4 to 6

The delightful and refreshing crunchiness of this salad, and it's ever-so-slight spiciness, make it an ideal companion to rich Mexican dishes, such as Slow-Roasted Chipotle Pork (page 196) and Tacos Lengua (page 205). And remember, virtually all of my recipes are both flexible and forgiving; if you can't find, say, golden beets, use red ones; if you don't have chipotle powder, use a tiny bit of cayenne.

> 4 to 5 small Oregon Blue potatoes or other waxy-fleshed potatoes, peeled
> 1 tablespoon kosher salt, plus more to taste
> 6 ounces jícama, in one piece, peeled
> 2 carrots, peeled and cut in 2-inch lengths
> 10 radishes, preferably French Breakfast or Easter Egg
> 4 to 5 small golden beets, roasted until tender, cooled, and peeled
> ½ teaspoon chipotle powder
> Black pepper in a mill
> Zest of 1 orange
> Juice of 1 orange
> 3 tablespoons walnut oil
> 2 tablespoons walnut pieces, toasted and minced

Fill a medium-sized pot two-thirds full with water and bring to a boil over high heat. Cut the potatoes into matchstick-sized julienne, add the salt to the boiling water, and cook the potatoes until they are just tender, about 3 minutes. Drain in a colander, rinse gently in cool water, and drain thoroughly. Set them aside.

Cut the jícama, carrots, radishes, and beets into julienne roughly the same size as the potatoes. Toss all of the vegetables together in a wide, shallow serving bowl, sprinkle the chipotle powder over them, season with salt and pepper, and toss gently. In a small bowl, mix together the orange zest, orange juice, and walnut oil, season with salt and pepper, and pour over the vegetables. Toss gently, top with the walnuts, and serve immediately.

Russian Egg Potato Salad

Serves 8 to 10

Traces of the Russians who settled along the north coast of
Sonoma may be found all over the West County—there's the
Russian River, Moscow Road, Fort Ross, and the apple orchards
first planted by the immigrants. We don't, however, see much of a
Russian influence in the way we eat today; a friend gave me this recipe
many years ago and I've found variations in Russian cookbooks now and then,
but it was not, to my knowledge, common in Sonoma County during the Russian
period, partly because, I am assuming, the Russians never succeeded in growing
potatoes here. They blamed their failure on ground rats, those hungry subterranean
creatures we know today as the western pocket gopher. Some farmers have been
successful growing outstanding potatoes in the West County, though constant vig-
ilance is necessary if you want to do more than grow gopher food; Cliff Silva of Ma
& Pa's Garden always has stories about his prowess as a gopher hunter.

3 pounds waxy-fleshed potatoes

¾ cup Caraway Vinaigrette (page 262) or other red wine and herb vinaigrette

4 large carrots, peeled and diced

1 red onion, minced

1 bunch scallions, trimmed and thinly sliced

5 celery stalks, trimmed and diced

2 pounds fresh peas, shelled and blanched, or 2 cups frozen petite peas, thawed

¼ cup minced fresh Italian parsley

Kosher salt

Black pepper in a mill

¾ cup mayonnaise

½ cup sour cream

½ cup Dijon mustard

10 hard-cooked eggs, peeled

1 ounce black caviar, such as sevruga or osetra

Cook the potatoes in plenty of boiling water until they are tender but not mushy
when pierced with a fork. Let cool, and when they are easy to handle, peel them
and slice them thinly. Put the potatoes in a large bowl, pour the dressing over them,
and let marinate for 1 hour.

Meanwhile, put the diced carrots in a small saucepan, add an inch or so of water, cover, set over medium heat, and cook until the carrots are just tender, about 7 or 8 minutes. Drain and let cool to room temperature. Add the carrots, all but 1 tablespoon of the red onion, the scallions, celery, peas, and Italian parsley to the potatoes and toss together thoroughly. Season with salt and pepper and toss again.

In a small bowl, whisk together the mayonnaise, sour cream, and mustard; taste and season with salt and pepper. Reserve ½ cup of the mixture, pour the remainder over the vegetables, and fold the dressing into the salad. Taste and correct the seasoning.

Put the salad in a wide, shallow serving bowl. Cut each of the eggs in half lengthwise and arrange them attractively over the top of the salad. Top each egg with a spoonful of the reserved dressing, followed by a dollop of caviar. Sprinkle with the reserved minced onions and serve immediately.

To drink: Landmark 1998 Overlook Chardonnay

Sonoma Country-Style Greek Salad

Serves 6 to 8

In Greece, this salad is served year-round, but in the winter, cabbage is used instead of tomatoes, which are not available out of season.

> 6 heirloom slicing tomatoes, cored and cut into wedges
>
> 4 garlic cloves, minced
>
> Kosher salt
>
> Black pepper in a mill
>
> 1 small red onion, peeled and cut in half lengthwise
>
> 3 lemon cucumbers, peeled, halved, and seeded
>
> 2 Oven-Roasted Peppers (page 227), cut into lengthwise strips, or ¾ cup Garlic-Roasted Peppers (page 270)
>
> ½ cup minced fresh Italian parsley
>
> 8 ounces feta cheese, crumbled
>
> 1 tablespoon capers, rinsed
>
> ⅓ cup fruity extra virgin olive oil
>
> 2 tablespoons red wine vinegar

Juice of 1 lemon

½ cup Kalamata olives

2 tablespoons fresh Greek oregano leaves

½ teaspoon coarse sea salt, such as sel gris

Hot country-style bread, cut in thick slices

Arrange the tomatoes in a wide, shallow bowl, scatter the garlic on top, season with salt and pepper, and set aside for 30 minutes.

Cut both onion halves into very thin, crosswise slices and scatter them over the tomatoes. Cut the cucumbers crosswise into thin half moons, add them, along with the roasted pepper strips, to the tomatoes and onions, and toss very gently. Top the vegetables with the parsley, feta, and capers, drizzle the olive oil on top, and sprinkle the vinegar and lemon juice over everything. Add the olives, sprinkle the oregano and sea salt on top, and serve immediately with hot bread alongside.

Chickpea, Celery & Scallion Salad

Serves 4

It's so convenient to open a can of garbanzo beans, but you'll have much better results if you begin with dry beans. They don't take all that long to cook and are far better than canned beans.

8 ounces dried chickpeas (garbanzo beans)

4 ounces pennette or ditalini (salad-sized pasta tubes)

1 lemon

3 celery stalks, cut into small dice

6 scallions, white and green parts, trimmed and thinly sliced

3 ounces feta cheese, crumbled

⅓ cup extra virgin olive oil

1 tablespoon medium-acid red wine vinegar

Kosher salt

Black pepper in a mill

2 tablespoons minced fresh Italian parsley

Soak the chickpeas in water for several hours or overnight. Drain and rinse them, place them in a medium pot, cover them with water, and bring to a boil over high heat. Reduce the heat to medium-low and simmer until the chickpeas are completely tender, about 45 to 60 minutes, depending on the age and size of the pea. As they cook, skim off any foam that accumulates on the surface of the water. Drain and rinse the cooked chickpeas, place in a medium salad bowl, and let them cool to room temperature.

Cook the pasta in boiling salted water according to package directions until it is just tender; drain and rinse thoroughly. Add to the chickpeas.

Use a zester or a vegetable peeler to remove the zest from the lemon; if using a vegetable peeler, mince the zest. Squeeze the juice from the lemon and strain it to remove any seeds. Toss the zest, celery, scallions, and feta with the chickpeas. Add the olive oil, lemon juice, and vinegar, season with salt and pepper, and toss lightly. Taste, correct the seasoning, add the Italian parsley, and serve immediately.

Wild Rice, Portobello Mushroom, Blueberry & Walnut Salad

Serves 4 to 6

I almost always serve this earthy salad with duck, either mixed in with the grain, or alongside. They are all natural companions, not just on the plate but in the wild, too. Several varieties of wild rice are available in the United States (though the one I wrote about in *A Cook's Tour of Sonoma* is long gone); be sure to consult the instructions on the package for exact cooking times.

> *1 cup wild rice*
> *2 teaspoons kosher salt, plus more to taste*
> *1 shallot, minced*
> *3 tablespoons blueberry vinegar*
> *2 tablespoons olive oil*
> *1 large portobello mushroom (about 8 ounces), cleaned and diced*
> *2 teaspoons honey, warmed*
> *1 tablespoon snipped chives*
> *2 tablespoons minced Italian parsley*
> *Black pepper in a mill*
> *3 tablespoons unrefined walnut oil*

6 tablespoons mild extra virgin olive oil

1 cup fresh blueberries

½ cup walnut pieces, toasted and minced

Put the rice in a medium saucepan, add the 2 teaspoons of salt and 3 cups of water, and bring to a boil over high heat. Reduce the heat to low and simmer, covered, until the water is absorbed and the rice is tender, about 45 minutes. Remove from the heat and let stand for 10 minutes before uncovering. Turn the rice into a large salad bowl, fluff it with a fork, and set it aside to cool.

Put the shallot in a medium bowl, pour the blueberry vinegar over it, and set it aside.

Heat the olive oil in a medium sauté pan set over medium-low heat, add the diced mushroom, and sauté until the mushroom is tender and has released its liquid, about 15 minutes. Continue to sauté until the liquid has evaporated. Toss the mushroom with the wild rice.

Whisk the warm honey into the shallot and vinegar mixture, stir in the chives and parsley, and season with salt and pepper. Whisk in the walnut oil and olive oil, taste, and correct the seasoning. Pour the dressing over the rice and toss it thoroughly. Add the blueberries and walnuts, toss again, and let rest 15 minutes before serving. The salad will keep, covered, in the refrigerator for 3 or 4 days; bring it to room temperature before serving.

To drink: Pedroncelli 1998 Rosé of Zinfandel

VARIATIONS

Seasonal: When blueberries are not in season in your area, omit them, use sherry vinegar in place of the blueberry vinegar, and increase the walnuts to ¾ cup.

With duck: For a heartier salad, add 1 cup cooked and shredded duck meat.

Quinoa Salad with Corn, Currants & Avocado

Serves 4 to 6

Contrast is the key to this salad—the earthiness of quinoa against the sweet brightness of corn, the sweet chewiness of currants against the voluptuous smoothness of avocado, the icy refreshment of lime against the heat of chipotle.

½ teaspoon kosher salt, plus more to taste

2 teaspoons chile powder, such as Gebhardt's

1 cup domestic quinoa, thoroughly rinsed

½ cup dried currants

Boiling water

3 ears of corn, shucked

6 scallions, white and tender green parts, trimmed and thinly sliced

2 tablespoons minced fresh cilantro or Italian parsley

Juice of 2 limes

1 tablespoon sherry vinegar

Pinch of cayenne pepper or chipotle powder

Black pepper in a mill

⅓ cup extra virgin olive oil

2 to 3 avocados (half an avocado per serving), halved and peeled

Pour 1¾ cups water in a 1-quart saucepan, add the salt and 1 teaspoon of the chile powder, and bring to a boil over high heat. Stir in the quinoa, reduce the heat to low, and simmer, covered, for 12 to 15 minutes, until the water is absorbed and the grain tender and translucent. Remove from the heat and let rest, covered, for 5 minutes. Turn out the quinoa into a large salad bowl and fluff it with a fork. Set aside to cool to room temperature.

Put the currants in a small bowl, cover them with boiling water, and set them aside to soften.

Heat a stove-top grill over medium heat. Grill the corn, rotating it frequently, until it is evenly cooked, about 5 minutes. Let it cool until it is easy to handle, and then use a sharp knife to cut the kernels from the cob. Toss the corn, scallions, and cilantro with the quinoa. Drain the currants, add them to the salad, and toss again.

In a small bowl, mix together the lime juice, vinegar, remaining 1 teaspoon of chile powder, and pinch of cayenne or chipotle powder. Season with salt and pepper, and whisk in the olive oil. Pour the dressing over the salad and toss thoroughly. Taste and correct the seasoning.

Cut the avocados in thin, lengthwise slices, keeping the halves together. Set an avocado half on individual serving plates and press to spread it out like a fan. Season with a little salt and pepper, spoon some of the salad alongside each avocado fan, and serve immediately.

Sorrel Tabbouleh

Serves 6 to 8

The inspiration for this tangy tabbouleh comes from two sources, Jack McCarley of Green Man Farms in Healdsburg, and the author Paula Wolfert, who has a home in the town of Sonoma. Jack sells his produce at the Healdsburg farmers' market, and I'd been enjoying several of the things he grows for sometime before he called me one afternoon to ask if he could send me a bag of his sorrel. When I realized I had to prepare a very large batch of tabbouleh, I thought of Jack's sorrel and recalled a recipe of Paula's that called for a small amount of the lemony green. I played around until I came up with the right balance of seasonings to work with a version of tabbouleh that incorporated a substantial quantity of sorrel; it has become one of my favorite salads.

> 1 cup medium-grain bulgur
> ¼ cup fresh lemon juice
> 2 teaspoons kosher salt
> 1 teaspoon crushed black pepper
> ⅛ teaspoon chipotle powder, ground cayenne pepper, or Basque red pepper
> ⅛ teaspoon ground cloves
> ⅛ teaspoon ground cinnamon
> ¼ teaspoon nutmeg, preferably freshly grated
> ¼ cup extra virgin olive oil

> 1 bunch scallions (about 8 to 10), thinly sliced
> 1 cucumber, peeled, seeded, and diced
> ½ cup minced fresh Italian parsley
> ½ cup mint leaves, shredded
> 2 cups fresh sorrel leaves, shredded
> 1 or 2 red Roma tomatoes, peeled, seeded, and diced

Place the bulgur in a strainer or colander, shake out any dust, rinse it under cool water, and set the strainer with the grain in it in a large bowl. Cover with water and set aside for 10 minutes. Drain off the water, place the bulgur in a tea towel, and twist to squeeze out excess moisture. Return the bulgur to the bowl.

In a small bowl, mix together the lemon juice, salt, pepper, chipotle powder (or cayenne or Basque pepper), cloves, cinnamon, and nutmeg and stir until the salt is dissolved. Whisk in the olive oil and pour the dressing over the bulgur. Scatter the scallions over the surface of the bulgur, followed by the cucumber, parsley, and mint and ending with the sorrel. Top with the tomatoes, cover tightly with plastic wrap, and refrigerate for several hours, or overnight, before serving.

To serve, toss the tabbouleh so that the ingredients are evenly mixed. Taste, correct the balance of salt and pepper, and serve. Tabbouleh will keep, refrigerated, for 2 or 3 days. Serve it cold or at room temperature.

Leftovers: Cut pita breads in half, toast them until they are hot but not crisp, and fill them with the leftover salad. Top with Tahini Dressing (page 242) or a generous spoonful of Feta Olive Salad (below).

Feta Olive Salad

Serves 4 to 6

This simple salad, tangy from feta and fragrant from citrus zest, is very flexible. You can use any olives you like, omit the tomatoes, use scallions instead of red onions, and use just one of the herbs if four seem to be too much trouble. Just don't change the key ingredients, good feta, garlic, and citrus zest; they form the foundation of the salad's flavor. Serve it as a first course or a side dish.

> 1 pound feta, preferably Redwood Hill Farm's goat feta, crumbled
> Half a small red onion, diced
> 3 garlic cloves, minced

Zest of 1 lemon, minced

Zest of 1 orange, minced

1 cup very small cherry tomatoes, halved (optional; see Note, below)

½ cup green olives, pitted and sliced

½ cup Kalamata olives, pitted and sliced

⅓ cup extra virgin olive oil

2 tablespoons minced fresh Italian parsley

1 tablespoon minced fresh cilantro (optional)

2 teaspoons minced fresh oregano

1 teaspoon minced fresh mint

Black pepper in a mill

Several large romaine or butter lettuce leaves

Place the feta in a large shallow bowl, add the onion, garlic, lemon zest, orange zest, cherry tomatoes, if using, green olives, and black olives. Toss lightly but thoroughly. Drizzle the olive oil over the salad and toss again. Add the fresh herbs, toss, and add several turns of black pepper. Arrange the lettuce leaves on one large or several individual plates and spoon the feta salad on top. Serve immediately.

Note: Use the tomatoes only when they are in season locally; otherwise, omit them.

Pasta, Shrimp & Pea Salad

Serves 4 to 6

The unrefined corn oil produced by Spectrum Naturals of Petaluma is a revelation. It is full-flavored and rich with the taste of fresh corn, qualities that are lost in cooking. The oil should be used in small quantities as a flavoring agent. The oil is highly unstable, which means it will go rancid quickly. Use it within two or three months of purchasing it, and if you sense a slight tingly, bitter taste on the tip of your tongue, you should return it to the store where you purchased it.

½ cup plus 1 tablespoon warm water

⅓ cup raisins or currants

Pinch of saffron threads

12 ounces seme di melone, orzo, or other seed-shaped pasta

⅓ cup unrefined corn oil

2 to 3 tablespoons unseasoned rice vinegar

1 tablespoon fresh lime juice (from half a lime)

Pinch of sugar

Kosher salt

Black pepper in a mill

8 ounces cooked and peeled bay shrimp

1 pound fresh shelling peas, shelled (about ½ cup shelled)

2 tablespoons minced fresh cilantro

1 tablespoon minced fresh mint

1 lime, cut in wedges, for garnish

In a small bowl, combine the ½ cup water and the raisins; set aside. In a second small bowl, combine the 1 tablespoon warm water and saffron threads; set aside. Cook the pasta in boiling salted water until it is just done, drain it, rinse it in cool water, drain it thoroughly, and place it in a medium bowl.

Mix together the corn oil, 2 tablespoons of rice vinegar, lime juice, sugar, and saffron and water mixture. Taste, add the remaining 1 tablespoon of vinegar for more tartness, season with salt and pepper, and pour over the pasta. Toss lightly. Drain the raisins and add them to the salad, along with the shrimp, peas, cilantro, and mint. Toss again, taste, and correct the seasoning. Garnish with lime wedges and serve immediately.

Grilled Salmon Salad with Lemon Vinaigrette

Serves 4

Although excellent mesclun is easy to find these days, as it has become increasingly popular, inferior versions have come along. Look for organic mixes that include a wide variety of very young lettuces, herbs, and flowers. If you have questions about a particular mix, use your sense of smell—mesclun, or any salad mix, should smell bright and fresh and mildly grassy, not unlike a summer afternoon in a garden.

of the blueberry

—— with salt and pep-

—— removing fat and any dark

—— spinner or on a tea towel, place
—— of olive oil. Arrange on a serving

—— th salt, pepper, and the remaining cloves.
—— ns of olive oil until they are soft and trans-
—— vers and sauté quickly, about 1½ minutes on
—— the pan with a slotted spoon and place them in

—— emaining vinegar. Pour the liquid over the chicken liv-
—— the warm livers on top of the spinach and drizzle with
—— s and juice from the livers combined.

—— berries decoratively over the salad and garnish with the quail
—— through the shell; don't attempt to shell them).

—— e vinaigrette on the side.

—— Gallo of Sonoma Cabernet Sauvignon—B. T.; Frick Cinsault Rosé—P. R.

Zest of 1 lemon, minced
4 wild king salmon fillets, about 6 ounces each
Kosher salt
Black pepper in a mill
Olive oil
6 to 8 cups fresh mesclun, or other high-quality salad mix
¼ cup O brand olive oil (see Resources, page 295)
Juice of 1 lemon
1 tablespoon minced Italian parsley
1 lemon, cut in wedges

Rub a little of the lemon zest into the top of each salmon fillet, and then season the fillets on both sides with salt and pepper. Brush a stove-top grill or ridged cast-iron pan very lightly with olive oil, set it over medium-high heat, and when it is hot, grill the salmon fillets, skin-side up, for 6 minutes, rotating them after about 2 minutes to mark them. Turn them skin-side down and continue to grill until they are cooked through, about 6 minutes more for 1¼-inch-thick fillets, and less if they are thinner.

Meanwhile, place the greens in a large bowl, sprinkle about ½ teaspoon salt over them, and toss lightly. Drizzle about half of the olive oil over, toss again, add half the lemon juice and several turns of black pepper, and toss one more time. Divide the dressed greens among 4 serving plates. In a small bowl, mix together the remaining olive oil and lemon juice, add the Italian parsley, and season with salt and pepper. When the salmon is done, place a fillet on top of each portion of greens, and drizzle dressing over it. Garnish with a wedge of lemon and serve immediately.

To drink: Sapphire Hill Chardonnay—B. T.

Winter Jewel Salad with Lamb

Serves 4

This elegant salad is a perfect main course on a night before a holiday that features a heavy meal, or perhaps the night after. Vegetarians can simply omit the lamb and have a lovely first course. There are many untended persimmon trees in Sonoma County, and the fruit hangs long after the leaves have fallen. On a foggy night, they glisten like winter jewels, one of the most bea[ti]ful sights of the season. In Cloverdale and Sonoma there are p[o] which need hot, dry summers. When the weather cooperates, [] are outstanding; in a cool year, they may never ripen.

> *1 or 2 medium pomegranates*
> *Pomegranate Vinaigrette (recipe follows)*
> *8 small loin lamb chops, boned and trimmed of fat*
> *Kosher salt*
> *Black pepper in a mill*
> *¼ cup pomegranate concentrate (also called pomegr[]*
> *¼ cup warm water*
> *1 large bunch of arugula (about 6 to 8 ounces)*
> *2 Fuyu persimmons, stem ends removed and thinl[]*
> *2 firm-ripe Hass avocados, peeled, seeded, and c[]*

Cut the pomegranates in half, remove the seeds [] Extract the juice from ½ cup of the seeds by pla[] at a time, in a strainer or sieve, and pressing out [] the back of a heavy spoon, or place the seeds [] plastic blade and pulse several times until the [] seeds. Set the juice aside to use in the vinaig[] arately. Make the pomegranate vinaigrette.

Preheat a stove-top grill or a broiler. Season the lamb on both si[] pepper. Cook the lamb until it is just rare (or medium-rare), about 5 to 7 m[] per side depending on the thickness of the meat. Mix together the pomegranate concentrate and warm water and, during the last few minutes of cooking, brush the lamb with the mixture several times. Transfer the cooked lamb to a plate, brush with the remainder of the mixture, and keep warm.

⅓ cup olive oil, plus more for frying
3 to 4 tablespoons blueberry vinegar
1 teaspoon ground cloves
Pinch of sugar
Kosher salt
Black pepper in a mill
¾ pound chicken livers
¼ pound baby spinach
3 shallots, minced
1 cup fresh blueberries
8 soft-boiled quail eggs

In a small bowl, mix together the ⅓ cup olive oil, 2 tablespoons vinegar, ½ teaspoon of the cloves, and the pinch of sugar. Seaso[] per and set aside.

Rinse the livers in cool water, dry them, and trim them [] spots. Set them aside.

Rinse the spinach in cool water, dry it in a lettuc[] it in a large bowl, and toss it with 1 tablespoon [] platter or on individual plates.

Cut each liver into 4 pieces and season w[] Sauté the minced shallots in 2 tablespo[] parent, about 5 minutes. Remove the [] each side. Remove the livers from [] a mixing bowl.

Deglaze the pan with the [] ers and toss well. Arran[] the warm pan drippin[]

Sprinkle the blue[] eggs (cut in half[]

Serve with [] **To drink** []

To assemble the salad, place a handful of arugula on each of four serving plates. Arrange alternating slices of persimmon and avocado around the arugula. Season with several turns of black pepper and a bit of kosher salt Slice the lamb into thin, diagonal strips, and arrange several slices on top of each mound of arugula. Spoon some of the vinaigrette over each portion and then scatter pomegranate seeds on top. Serve immediately.

POMEGRANATE VINAIGRETTE
1 shallot, minced
2 tablespoons pomegranate vinegar
¼ cup fresh pomegranate juice
Pinch of granulated sugar
Kosher salt
⅓ to ½ cup mildly flavored extra virgin olive oil
Black pepper in a mill

Place the shallot in a medium bowl, cover it with the pomegranate vinegar, and let sit for 20 minutes or so. Stir in the pomegranate juice and pinch of sugar, season with salt, and whisk in the olive oil. Taste, season with several turns of black pepper, and set aside until ready to use.

To drink: Rutz Pinot Noir; Pedroncelli Zinfandel Rosé—B. T.

Blueberry & Chicken Liver Salad with Blueberry Vinaigrette

Serves 4

When I had a catering business, I made this salad all the time and everyone was always surprised by it, by the way the flavors work together so beautifully. Back then, I didn't pay a lot of attention to pairing the salad with wine, but I have since discovered that a rich, round cabernet sauvignon is a stunning complement. It's certainly not typical to serve a cab with a salad but, because of the blueberries and the succulent livers, it works beautifully. Really. Give it a try; just be sure not to use a cab with out-of-control tannins or you'll think I am crazy. If you can't find blueberry vinegar, black—not red—raspberry vinegar is a good substitute.

⅓ cup olive oil, plus more for frying

3 to 4 tablespoons blueberry vinegar

1 teaspoon ground cloves

Pinch of sugar

Kosher salt

Black pepper in a mill

¾ pound chicken livers

¼ pound baby spinach

3 shallots, minced

1 cup fresh blueberries

8 soft-boiled quail eggs

In a small bowl, mix together the ⅓ cup olive oil, 2 tablespoons of the blueberry vinegar, ½ teaspoon of the cloves, and the pinch of sugar. Season with salt and pepper and set aside.

Rinse the livers in cool water, dry them, and trim them, removing fat and any dark spots. Set them aside.

Rinse the spinach in cool water, dry it in a lettuce spinner or on a tea towel, place it in a large bowl, and toss it with 1 tablespoon of olive oil. Arrange on a serving platter or on individual plates.

Cut each liver into 4 pieces and season with salt, pepper, and the remaining cloves. Sauté the minced shallots in 2 tablespoons of olive oil until they are soft and transparent, about 5 minutes. Add the livers and sauté quickly, about 1½ minutes on each side. Remove the livers from the pan with a slotted spoon and place them in a mixing bowl.

Deglaze the pan with the remaining vinegar. Pour the liquid over the chicken livers and toss well. Arrange the warm livers on top of the spinach and drizzle with the warm pan drippings and juice from the livers combined.

Sprinkle the blueberries decoratively over the salad and garnish with the quail eggs (cut in half through the shell; don't attempt to shell them).

Serve with the vinaigrette on the side.

To drink: Gallo of Sonoma Cabernet Sauvignon—B. T.; Frick Cinsault Rosé—P. R.

Zest of 1 lemon, minced

4 wild king salmon fillets, about 6 ounces each

Kosher salt

Black pepper in a mill

Olive oil

6 to 8 cups fresh mesclun, or other high-quality salad mix

¼ cup O brand olive oil (see Resources, page 295)

Juice of 1 lemon

1 tablespoon minced Italian parsley

1 lemon, cut in wedges

Rub a little of the lemon zest into the top of each salmon fillet, and then season the fillets on both sides with salt and pepper. Brush a stove-top grill or ridged cast-iron pan very lightly with olive oil, set it over medium-high heat, and when it is hot, grill the salmon fillets, skin-side up, for 6 minutes, rotating them after about 2 minutes to mark them. Turn them skin-side down and continue to grill until they are cooked through, about 6 minutes more for 1¼-inch-thick fillets, and less if they are thinner.

Meanwhile, place the greens in a large bowl, sprinkle about ½ teaspoon salt over them, and toss lightly. Drizzle about half of the olive oil over, toss again, add half the lemon juice and several turns of black pepper, and toss one more time. Divide the dressed greens among 4 serving plates. In a small bowl, mix together the remaining olive oil and lemon juice, add the Italian parsley, and season with salt and pepper. When the salmon is done, place a fillet on top of each portion of greens, and drizzle dressing over it. Garnish with a wedge of lemon and serve immediately.

To drink: Sapphire Hill Chardonnay—B. T.

Winter Jewel Salad with Lamb

Serves 4

This elegant salad is a perfect main course on a night before a
holiday that features a heavy meal, or perhaps the night after.
Vegetarians can simply omit the lamb and have a lovely first
course. There are many untended persimmon trees in Sonoma
County, and the fruit hangs long after the leaves have fallen. On
a foggy night, they glisten like winter jewels, one of the most beautiful sights of the season. In Cloverdale and Sonoma there are pomegranate trees,
which need hot, dry summers. When the weather cooperates, local pomegranates
are outstanding; in a cool year, they may never ripen.

> 1 or 2 medium pomegranates
> Pomegranate Vinaigrette (recipe follows)
> 8 small loin lamb chops, boned and trimmed of fat
> Kosher salt
> Black pepper in a mill
> ¼ cup pomegranate concentrate (also called pomegranate molasses)
> ¼ cup warm water
> 1 large bunch of arugula (about 6 to 8 ounces)
> 2 Fuyu persimmons, stem ends removed and thinly sliced
> 2 firm-ripe Hass avocados, peeled, seeded, and cut into ¼-inch-thick slices

Cut the pomegranates in half, remove the seeds, and discard the skins and rinds.
Extract the juice from ½ cup of the seeds by placing the seeds, about a tablespoon
at a time, in a strainer or sieve, and pressing out the juice using a wooden pestle or
the back of a heavy spoon, or place the seeds in a food processor fitted with the
plastic blade and pulse several times until the juice is released; then strain out the
seeds. Set the juice aside to use in the vinaigrette; set the unjuiced seeds aside separately. Make the pomegranate vinaigrette.

Preheat a stove-top grill or a broiler. Season the lamb on both sides with salt and
pepper. Cook the lamb until it is just rare (or medium-rare), about 5 to 7 minutes
per side depending on the thickness of the meat. Mix together the pomegranate
concentrate and warm water and, during the last few minutes of cooking, brush
the lamb with the mixture several times. Transfer the cooked lamb to a plate, brush
with the remainder of the mixture, and keep warm.

CHAPTER 8

Condiments & Sauces

THINK OF A CONDIMENT AS A CULINARY PUNCTUATION MARK, a small but essential element in the grammar of cuisine. A condiment can be as simple and basic as salt, as humble as a shake of Tabasco or a squirt of ketchup, as complex as a slowly cooked chutney, as exotic and refined as beluga caviar. Condiments and sauces add flavor, flourish, and style to the foods they join on the plate, and our menus would be sadly diminished without their unique contribution.

Chipotle Oil

Makes 1 pint

Many pizza parlors have bottles of olive oil with
crushed red pepper available on each table for customers to
drizzle over pizza. Use this smoky oil in the same way, or in salsas and other sauces,
wherever a jolt of heat is wanted.

>   4 chipotles, preferably from Tierra Vegetables
>   2 cups Spectrum Naturals unrefined corn oil or mildly flavored olive oil

Use a sharp knife to make two lengthwise slits in each chipotle. Put the chipotles in a jar, pour the corn oil or olive oil over them, close the jar with its lid, and store in a cool, dark cupboard for 2 weeks. Use the oil without straining it, adding fresh oil with each use. If you have used unrefined corn oil, it will keep at full flavor for 1 to 2 months. Olive oil will last 3 to 4 months.

Caraway Vinaigrette

Makes about ¾ cup

I developed this vinaigrette specifically for Russian Egg Potato Salad, but soon discovered that it was equally inviting on sliced cooked beets and as a dip for hot rye bread. If you love the flavor of caraway seeds, as I do, you'll think of other great uses, too.

>   1 small red shallot, minced
>   2 garlic cloves, crushed and minced
>   ¾ teaspoon caraway seed, toasted and crushed
>   2 tablespoons red wine vinegar
>   Juice of 1 lemon
>   2 teaspoons minced fresh Italian parsley
>   1 teaspoon minced fresh oregano
>   1 teaspoon minced fresh thyme
>   1 teaspoon celery seed
>   Kosher salt
>   Black pepper in a mill
>   ½ cup extra virgin olive oil

In a small bowl, mix together the shallot, garlic, and caraway seed, pour the vinegar and lemon juice over the mixture, and let it sit for 20 minutes. Mix in the parsley, oregano, thyme, and celery seed, season with salt and pepper, and whisk in the olive oil. Taste and correct the acid balance with more vinegar or more oil and the seasoning with more salt or pepper as necessary. Use the dressing within 2 days.

French Herb Vinaigrette

Makes about ¾ cup

Tarragon, a key flavor in this dish, has an aggressive flavor reminiscent of licorice and should be used with restraint so that it does not overpower other elements.

> 1 small red shallot, minced
> 1 garlic clove, crushed and minced
> 3 tablespoons champagne vinegar or Vinaigre de Banyuls
> 1 teaspoon mustard flour (dry mustard, such as Colman's)
> ¾ teaspoon herbes de Provence
> ½ teaspoon minced fresh tarragon leaves
> Kosher salt
> Black pepper in a mill
> ½ cup extra virgin olive oil

In a small bowl, mix together the shallot and garlic, pour the vinegar and lemon juice over them, and let the mixture sit for 20 minutes. Mix in the mustard flour, *herbes de Provence*, and tarragon. Season with salt and pepper and whisk in the olive oil. Taste and correct the acid balance with more vinegar or more oil and the seasoning with more salt or pepper as necessary. Use the dressing within 2 days.

Aioli

Makes about 1 cup

Aioli is a versatile sauce and very easy to make by hand once you get the hang of it. You can make good versions in a blender or food processor, but they lack the voluptuousness and intensity of those made in a mortar and pestle or a similar device. I use a suribachi, a Japanese mortar and pestle. In the rigid porcelain bowl the garlic breaks down more quickly than it will on the smooth surface of a standard mortar. For the best aïoli, you must use good juicy garlic that has not begun to sprout.

> 6 to 8 garlic cloves, peeled
> Kosher salt
> 1 extra-large egg yolk
> ¾ cup extra virgin olive oil, such as DaVero
> White pepper in a mill
> 1 to 2 teaspoons hot water, if needed
> Half a lemon, if needed

Put the garlic cloves in a suribachi and use a wooden pestle to crush them. Sprinkle the garlic with salt and grind the garlic, crushing it against the bowl to break up the larger pieces, until it is nearly liquified. Add the egg yolk and mix it with the garlic until a thick paste is formed. Begin to add the olive oil a few drops at a time, mixing thoroughly after each addition and continuing until all of the oil has been added. Taste the aioli, season with salt and pepper, and if it seems overly stiff, mix in a little hot water to thin it just slightly. Taste it again, and if you notice any bitterness, squeeze in a few drops of lemon juice and mix it thoroughly. Taste again and add a little more lemon juice if the sauce needs further correcting. Cover the bowl and refrigerate for at least 30 minutes before using. This aioli will keep 2 to 3 days, but is at its best the day it is made.

Yogurt-Mint Sauce

Makes about ¾ cup

This sweet-hot sauce, inspired by the cuisine of Thailand, is excellent as a condiment (admittedly, a slightly unorthodox condiment) with both
Curried Onions with Sausage Stuffing (page 214), as well
as with the Thai Dolmas (page 104) for which it was
developed.

⅛ cup dried, unsweetened coconut or ⅛ cup
    fresh coconut, minced

2 tablespoons hot water

¼ cup fresh mint leaves

¼ cup fresh cilantro leaves

1 serrano chile, stemmed but not seeded

1 teaspoon minced fresh dill

2 tablespoons lime juice

1 teaspoon sugar

Pinch of kosher salt

¾ cup plain (unflavored) yogurt

Black pepper in a mill

If you are using dried coconut, place it in a small bowl, pour the hot water over it, and set it aside for 15 minutes. Put the dried coconut and any liquid, or the fresh coconut, in the work bowl of a food processor, along with the mint leaves, cilantro leaves, serrano, and dill, and pulse several times. Add the lime juice, sugar, and salt, pulse, add the yogurt, and pulse until smooth. Transfer to a small bowl and season with black pepper. Serve immediately or refrigerate, covered, until ready to serve.

Garlic & Cilantro Sauce

Makes about 1¼ cups

You can use this sauce as a topping for any spicy soup made with tomatoes or pota-toes; it is great on tacos, alongside grilled or roasted chicken and pork, spooned over Queso Fundido (page 109), or as a dip for shrimp or prawns.

> *12 garlic cloves, minced*
> *2 serrano chiles, stemmed and minced*
> *2 bunches (about 4 cups) cilantro leaves, minced*
> *Juice of 3 limes (about ½ cup)*
> *1 teaspoon kosher salt*
> *Black pepper in a mill*
> *⅓ cup extra virgin olive oil*

In a medium bowl, toss together the garlic, serranos, and cilantro. Stir in the lime juice and salt, season with black pepper, and stir in the olive oil. Taste, correct the seasoning, and let rest 30 minutes before using. The sauce will keep, covered, in the refrigerator for 2 to 3 days.

Anticipation Salsa

Makes about 4 cups

The best salsa is made with dense-fleshed tomatoes at their peak of ripeness, just before they become too soft. But as you wait for backyard or farm market toma-toes to ripen, you can make a very decent salsa using the season's first cherry toma-toes. If you slice the tomatoes small enough, you can use this salsa with chips. If you cheat and cut them in half instead of into quarters, you'll have something perfectly suitable for tacos, quesadillas, and grilled seafood, but a bit large to work on a chip.

3 cups very small cherry tomatoes (of various colors, if available)

1 to 2 jalapeño chiles, stems removed

1 small red onion, diced

2 garlic cloves, minced

2 tablespoons fresh lime juice

¼ cup extra virgin olive oil

2 tablespoons minced fresh cilantro

Kosher salt

Black pepper in a mill

If the tomatoes are indeed tiny, cut them in half; otherwise, cut them in quarters, and place them in a medium bowl. Mince the jalapeños; for a mild salsa, remove and discard the seeds first. Add the jalapeños, onion, and garlic to the tomatoes and toss lightly. Stir in the lime juice, olive oil, cilantro, a teaspoon of salt, and several turns of black pepper. Taste the salsa and correct the seasoning, adding a little more lime juice and a little more salt if the salsa doesn't seem balanced. Let rest 15 minutes before serving. This salsa will keep in the refrigerator for 2 to 3 days.

Chèvre Sauce

Makes about 1½ cups

Extraordinarily simple and easy to make, this sauce is actually quite elegant and versatile. You can use it in place of béchamel in lasagne and moussaka, in place of Alfredo sauce with fettuccine, or you can spoon over grilled vegetables such as eggplant and zucchini.

2 teaspoons butter

1 shallot, minced

Kosher salt

2 cups half-and-half

5 ounces chabis or other young chèvre

Black pepper in a mill

2 tablespoons minced fresh Italian parsley

Melt the butter in a medium saucepan set over medium-low heat and, when it is foamy, add the shallot and sauté until it is soft and transparent, about 6 to 7 minutes. Season with salt, add the half-and-half, increase the heat to medium high, and simmer until the cream is reduced by one-third, about 5 or 6 minutes. Reduce the heat to low, add the chabis, and stir until it is completely melted; do not let the sauce boil. Season generously with black pepper, add the parsley, taste, and correct the seasoning. Serve hot. This sauce may be cooled and stored in the refrigerator for 2 to 3 days. Reheat over very low heat before serving.

Roasted Garlic Cream Sauce with Fresh Thyme

Makes about 2 cups

I particularly like this rich, flavorful sauce with fresh pasta made with either pumpkin or sage and cut into fettuccine so that the sauce clings to it. It is also outstanding with chicken.

> 1 garlic bulb, loose outer skins removed
> 3 tablespoons olive oil
> 3 cups half-and-half
> 3 sprigs of fresh thyme
> Kosher salt
> Black pepper in a mill

Preheat the oven to 350°. Put the garlic bulb in a small oven-proof container, add the olive oil and ¼ cup water, cover the container tightly with a lid or aluminum foil, and roast until the garlic is very soft, about 45 to 60 minutes, depending of the age of the garlic. Remove from the oven, set the garlic in a small dish, and let it cool. Remove the pulp from the roasted garlic by carefully pulling the cloves from their root and squeezing out th pulp; mash the pulp with a fork.

Put the half-and-half and thyme in a medium-sized heavy saucepan set over medium heat, bring to a boil, and simmer until it is reduced by half, about 10 minutes. Remove and discard the thyme, whisk in the garlic purée, and heat through. Season with salt and several turns of black pepper. Taste, correct the seasoning, and use immediately or cool, refrigerate for up to 2 days, and reheat before serving.

Easy Olive Tapenade

Makes about 1 cup

You can make this tapenade using almost any olive, including the mixed olives sold at the olive bars common in upscale markets these days. If you select the individual olives yourself, try a mix of Kalamatas, picholines, cracked green, and California black. Salted capers are available in good delis and markets.

>   8 ounces mixed olives, pitted and minced
>   1 tablespoon salted capers, rinsed and dried
>   3 garlic cloves, minced
>   1 tablespoon minced fresh Italian parsley
>   1 tablespoon minced fresh basil
>   1 minced anchovy fillet
>   2 to 3 tablespoons extra virgin olive oil
>   2 teaspoons minced lemon zest
>   Black pepper in a mill

In a small bowl, toss together the olives, capers, and garlic. Add the parsley, basil, anchovy, oil, and lemon zest. Mix together, season generously with black pepper, and set aside for 30 minutes before serving. The tapenade will keep in the refrigerator for a day or two, after which time its flavors will deteriorate.

Mary's Red Onion Marmalade

Makes about 2½ cups

When onions are cooked slowly for a long time, their natural sugars are released and begin to caramelize. Some recipes take a shortcut by calling for quick cooking and the addition of sugar, but it is impossible to achieve the delicious depth of flavor that slow-cooked onions have. Mary Evely, the chef at Simi Winery and author of the lovely book *Vintner's Table* (Simi Winery, 1997), adds wine and vinegar to balance the onion's sweetness so that it is more wine friendly.

>   4 tablespoons unsalted butter
>   6 large red onions, very thinly sliced
>   3 cups cabernet sauvignon or other hearty red wine
>   3 tablespoons balsamic vinegar

3 tablespoons crème de cassis (blackcurrant liqueur)
Kosher salt
Freshly ground black pepper

Melt the butter in a large, heavy sauté pan set over low heat, add the onions, and sauté, stirring occasionally, until they are very soft and sweet, about 1 hour. Increase the heat to high, add the wine, vinegar, and crème de cassis, bring to a boil, reduce the heat to medium-low, and simmer until the liquid has been completely absorbed by the onions. Season with salt and pepper and set aside to cool to room temperature. Serve immediately, or refrigerate for up to 10 days.

Garlic-Roasted Peppers

Makes about 1 pint

If you're used to roasting peppers on top of the stove until their skins turn black, try this method to see how you like the results. It takes a little longer, but it preserves more of the pepper's flavor. With the stove-top method, there is a tendency to overcook the peppers a bit and parts of them always end up mushy.

4 or 5 serrano or jalapeño chiles, stemmed, seeded, and cut in half
4 large red bell peppers, stemmed, seed, and cut in half
1 garlic bulb, cloves separated, peeled, and minced
¼ cup extra virgin olive oil

Preheat the oven to 400°F. Layer the chiles, bell peppers, garlic, and olive oil in a large, shallow baking dish and bake for 45 minutes or until the peppers are very soft. Cool to room temperature, peel off the thin skin on the peppers, place in a glass jar, pour the olive oil and any pan drippings over the top, and store in the refrigerator, covered, until ready to use. They will keep for between 7 and 10 days.

Gravenstein Chutney

Makes about 1 quart

Gravenstein apples are not crucial to the success of this
chutney, but they are the ones I prefer to use because they
have such good, true apple flavor. Use whatever apples you
have and be sure to taste and adjust the amount of sugar and
vinegar in case your apples are more or less sweet than mine.

> *3 cups fruity red wine, such as Beaujolais, sangiovese, or zinfandel*
>
> *1 cup sugar*
>
> *4 whole cloves*
>
> *½ teaspoon grated nutmeg*
>
> *Juice of 1 lemon*
>
> *4 Gravenstein apples, peeled and diced*
>
> *½ cup red raspberry vinegar*
>
> *4 garlic cloves, minced*
>
> *1 serrano chile, minced*
>
> *1½-inch piece of fresh ginger, peeled and grated*
>
> *½ teaspoon crushed red pepper flakes*
>
> *4 cups diced fresh strawberries*
>
> *½ cup fresh cilantro leaves*

Combine the wine, ½ cup of the sugar, cloves, nutmeg, and lemon juice in a heavy,
nonreactive saucepan set over medium heat and stir until the sugar is dissolved. Add
the apples and simmer until they are tender but not mushy, about 10 minutes.
Remove from the heat and let the apples cool in the liquid. Drain, reserving the
liquid. Return the cooking liquid to the pot, set it over medium heat, and reduce
it until it forms a syrup. It will happen quickly when there is about ⅓ cup liquid
remaining. Remove it from the heat immediately or it will scorch.

Place the apples in a clean pot, add the remaining ½ cup sugar, the raspberry
vinegar, garlic, serrano, ginger, and pepper flakes, set over medium heat, and stir
until the sugar is dissolved. Simmer slowly for 10 minutes. Add in the syrup, the
strawberries, and the cilantro, stir, heat through, and remove from the heat. Chill
before serving; the chutney will keep, properly stored, for about 1 week.

Bonnie's Prune Chutney

Makes about 3 cups

From 1970 to about 1983, Louise Madden grew prunes on her ranch in upper Dry Creek Valley, near Lake Sonoma. A friend named Bonnie picked prunes each year, and when she returned the following year, she'd bring a few jars of her homemade prune chutney with her. Eventually, the Maddens replanted the orchard with grapes and Bonnie moved away; Louise Madden now gets her prunes from a neighbor and makes the chutney herself.

1 cup light brown sugar

1 cup granulated sugar

¾ cup apple cider vinegar

1½ to 2 tablespoons crushed red pepper flakes

2 teaspoons salt

2 teaspoons white mustard seeds

2 garlic cloves, thinly sliced

¼ cup onion, thinly sliced

½ cup candied ginger, thinly sliced

1 cup seedless golden raisins

3½ cups fresh prune plums, pitted

Combine the sugars, vinegar, red pepper flakes, salt, and mustard seeds in a medium nonreactive pot set over medium heat and stir until the sugar dissolves. Stir in the garlic, onion, ginger, raisins, and prune plums, reduce the heat to low, and simmer, stirring frequently, until the mixture thickens, about 1½ hours. Remove from the heat, let cool slightly, ladle into sterilized jars, and process in a boiling water bath for 7 minutes. Cool the jars on tea towels, check the seals, and store in a cool, dark cupboard for up to 1 year. Refrigerate after opening.

Pickled Dried Prunes

Makes 2 pints

Oral histories of Sonoma County contain countless references to pickled prunes, a dish that seemed to have been served at every gathering or meeting, as you would expect when prunes were a major crop here. There are a few of those old orchards left, but I know of just one that's being harvested. The last thing I bought from Malcolm Skall, who died while I worked on this book, was a bagful of his hand-picked, sun-dried prunes, which I used to test this recipe.

1 pound dried prunes, pitted
1 cup red wine vinegar or apple cider vinegar
1 cup sugar
1 teaspoon whole cloves
1 teaspoon whole black peppercorns
2-inch cinnamon stick
3 allspice berries

Rinse the prunes thoroughly, place them in a heavy saucepan, cover with water, set over medium heat, and bring to a boil. Reduce the heat to low and simmer for 10 minutes. Transfer to a colander to drain, saving the liquid. Combine the vinegar, sugar, cloves, peppercorns, cinnamon stick, allspice berries, and 1 cup of the cooking liquid in the saucepan, set over medium heat, and stir until the sugar is dissolved. Add the prunes, stir until the mixture boils, remove from the heat, and let the prunes cool to room temperature in the liquid. Return them to the heat, bring to a boil a second time, and ladle the hot prunes and their liquid into sterilized pint jars. Add the lids and rings to the jars, cool them, and use the prunes within 6 months. The prunes also may be stored, covered, in the refrigerator rather than in sealed jars.

Gravenstein Applesauce

Makes about 2 quarts

The Gravenstein apple harvest usually begins in late July, though it can be sooner or later, depending on the weather. Although you can make this applesauce with any apple, it is never better than when it is made with Sebastopol Gravensteins.

5 pounds Gravenstein apples, peeled, cored, and quartered,
    or a mix of available apples
2 cups medium-bodied red wine
2 cardamom pods
2-inch cinnamon stick
Sugar, to taste
Whole nutmeg

Slice the quartered apples ¼ inch thick; place them in a large, nonreactive saucepan, and add the wine. Tie the cardamom and cinnamon stick in a square of cheesecloth, add it to the pot (be certain that it is submerged in the liquid), and bring the wine to a boil over medium heat. Reduce the heat to low and simmer, partially covered, until the apples are very tender and begin to fall apart, about 15 to 20 minutes.

Remove and discard the spice bag. Use a slotted spoon to transfer the apples to a bowl, return the cooking liquid to the heat, and reduce it by two-thirds. Stir the reduced liquid into the apples. Taste the applesauce, and if it is tart, stir in some sugar, a tablespoon at a time, until it is sweet enough. Add several gratings of nutmeg, stir again, and if you have added sugar, return to low heat, stirring constantly, for 5 minutes. Serve warm, or cool to room temperature and refrigerate until chilled. Applesauce will keep in the refrigerator for about a week.

Gravenstein Apple Butter

Makes 4 pints

Making fruit butter seems rather old fashioned these days, but when you live in the midst of apple country it is an almost irresistible venture. It can seem to be a lot of trouble, but a small batch doesn't take long. Once you get the hang of it, you can easily double or triple the recipe. I make my apple butter using the hard honey cider made by Ace in the Hole cider company, located just a few miles from my home, but any apple cider will do.

> 3 cups hard apple cider, preferably honey cider
> 1 teaspoon whole white peppercorns
> 1 teaspoon whole black peppercorns
> 3 whole cloves
> 2 whole cardamom pods
> 1½-inch cinnamon stick
> 2-inch piece of vanilla bean
> Juice of 1 lemon
> 5 pounds Gravenstein apples
> 2 cups packed brown sugar, plus more to taste

Pour the cider in a large, heavy pot and set it over medium heat. Tie the spices and vanilla bean in a spice bag or a square of cheesecloth and add them to the cider. When the cider is hot, cover the pot and remove it from the heat.

While the spices steep in the cider, prepare the apples. Fill a large bowl half full with water, add the lemon juice, and set aside. Peel, core, and quarter the apples; hold the peeled apples in the lemon water bath to keep them from turning brown.

Drain the apples thoroughly, place them in the pot with the cider and spices, set over medium heat, and bring the cider to a boil. Reduce the heat to low and simmer, partially covered, until the apples are tender, about 15 to 20 minutes. Stir the apples now and then.

Strain the cooking liquid and reserve it; discard the spice bag, and press the cooked apples through a potato ricer. For a smoother butter, strain the apple purée through a fine strainer. Return the liquid to the cleaned pot, set over medium-low heat, stir in the brown sugar, and simmer, stirring continuously, until the sugar is dissolved. Stir in the apple purée, taste, and if the mixture is too tart, add more brown sugar, tasting after each ¼ cup addition.

Simmer, stirring frequently, until the butter is thick and all the juice has evaporated off. Meanwhile, sterilize four pint canning jars or eight half-pint canning jars. When it is done, ladle the hot apple butter into the jars, add the seals and lids, and process in a boiling water bath for 7 minutes. Set the jars on tea towels to cool, check the seals, label the butter with the date, and store in a cool, dark cupboard. Fruit butters will keep for at least a year.

Asian Pear Butter

Makes about 3 pints

Asian pears have the squat, stout shape of a true apple, an appearance that encourages the misconception that this fruit is some sort of hybrid between an apple and a pear. In fact it is a true pear, and several varieties are raised in various parts of the United States (there are about a hundred in Japan), including Sonoma County, where they ripen in late summer and fall, when there is often an abundance of them available for a song because many people are not certain what to do with them. I love the intense flavor of this butter, especially on buttery toast.

3 cups pear cider
1 tablespoon whole white peppercorns
1 tablespoon whole black peppercorns
2-inch piece of vanilla bean
Zest of 1 lemon, in wide strips
Juice of 1 lemon
7 pounds Asian pears
1 to 2 cups packed light brown sugar

Pour the pear cider in a large, heavy pot and set it over medium heat. Tie the peppercorns, vanilla bean, and lemon zest in a spice bag or a square of cheesecloth and add it to the cider. When the cider is hot, cover the pot and remove it from the heat.

While the spices steep in the cider, prepare the pears. Fill a large bowl half full with water, add the lemon juice, and set aside. Peel, core, and quarter the pears; hold the peeled pears in the lemon water bath to keep them from turning brown.

Drain the pears thoroughly, place them in the pot with the cider and spices, set over medium heat, and bring the cider to a boil. Reduce the heat to low and simmer, partially covered, until the pears are tender, about 25 minutes. Stir the pears now and then.

Preheat the oven to 275°F. Strain the cooking liquid and reserve it; discard the spice bag, press the cooked pears through a potato ricer, and strain the purée. Return the liquid to an ovenproof pot, set it over medium heat on the top of the stove, and simmer until it is reduced by two-thirds, about 15 minutes. Stir in the pear purée, taste it, and add as much of the brown sugar as necessary for appropriate sweetness. After the sugar is dissolved, transfer the pot to the oven and bake until it is thick and the juices have evaporated off; stir the butter every now and then to prevent its scorching. Spoon the butter into sterilized half-pint or pint jars, seal with rings and lids, and store in a cool, dark pantry until ready to use.

CHAPTER 9

Desserts

TO MY PALATE THE BEST DESSERTS ARE LIGHT AND BUOYANT, something that leaves me refreshed at the end of the meal. The easiest way to achieve this is to use fruits that are in season: pears, kiwi, grapefruit, tangerines, and persimmons in the winter, for example. In May, indulge in Bing cherries before their short season is over. During the heat of summer, nothing is more refreshing than a wedge of sweet watermelon or a perfectly ripened peach. To appreciate fruit in its own true time, you must avoid the imports from the Southern Hemisphere. That fruit must be harvested before it is ripe or it will rot before it completes its long journey. And an apricot will never taste as good in the chilly winter months, when those from South America are available, as it will on a warm June night. Certain occasions call for more elaborate desserts, but the same rules apply. If you are using fruit, for the best results be sure it is in season. Chocolate, of course, is suitable at any time at all.

Summer Fruit in Red Wine

Serves 4 to 6

When Bob Broderson was preparing to plant berries in the 1970s, he found the local sources for canes expensive and began looking for an alternative. One day he was driving near Guerneville, showing his wife where he'd grown up, when he spotted what he thought were raspberries. He stopped and approached the farmer, a man in his 80s, who offered to dig up some canes. As Broderson was leaving with his fortuitous gift, he asked what kind of berries they were.

"I don't know," the farmer said. "They're just Sonoma everberries." The name stuck and became the berries that built Bob's Berries reputation. The berries are similar to raspberries but darker red and very perishable. Bob died in May of 1997, and his daughter Ceclie Kraus now runs the family business. Over the years she has tried to discover the variety of her father's everberries but has never seen a similar one.

1 cup strawberries, washed, stemmed, and halved
1 cup Sonoma County everberries or raspberries
1 cup blackberries, rinsed and dried
4 Santa Rosa plums, cut into thick slices
¼ cup granulated sugar
2 to 3 white peaches, peeled and sliced
2 cups fruity red wine, such as Dry Creek Valley Zinfandel
8 to 10 mint leaves, cut in thin julienne
Mint leaves for garnish

In a medium bowl, toss together the berries and plums, sprinkle with the sugar, cover, and refrigerate for at least 1 hour or up to 3 hours. Place the peaches in a large bowl, pour the wine over them, cover, and refrigerate. To serve, add the berries, their juices, and the cut mint to the peaches, toss gently, and spoon into glass dessert dishes. Garnish with mint leaves and serve immediately.

Poached Apples with Maytag Blue Cheese

Serves 6

As I worked on this book, Liam Callahan of Bellwether Farms in Two Rock was experimenting with blue cheese. His wasn't quite ready for market, and so I used Maytag, a handcrafted farmstead cheese developed long before the renaissance in artisan cheese began in the mid-1980s. In fact, you could say that Fred Maytag inspired the renaissance, as his son Fritz Maytag did with the microbrewery movement. Fritz rescued Anchor Brewing Company and its steam beer from bankruptcy in the mid-1960s, and it was the success of Anchor Steam that inspired a new generation of beer makers. Maytag also makes premium gin and whisky at the brewery, and his estate atop Spring Mountain in St. Helena produces wine and olive oil. As this book goes to press, Bellwether Blue is finally ready for market.

> 6 large Fuji apples
> 1 bottle (750 ml) red wine, preferably a Rhône-style
> ⅔ cup sugar
> 1 cinnamon stick, 1 inch long
> 1 teaspoon white peppercorns
> 5 whole cloves
> 5 whole allspice berries
> Whole nutmeg
> 6 ounces Maytag Blue cheese
> 6 walnut halves, toasted
> 2 tablespoons unsalted butter
> ½ cup toasted walnuts, coarsely chopped

Preheat the oven to 350°F. Cut a slice off the stem end of each apple, fairly close to the top. Remove the apple cores, creating a cone-shaped hollow in the center of the apple; do not cut all the way through it.

Combine the wine, sugar, cinnamon, peppercorns, cloves, allspice, and several gratings of nutmeg in a heavy saucepan set over medium heat and stir until the sugar is dissolved. Add the apples and simmer over medium heat until they are almost but not quite tender, about 20 minutes.

Transfer the apples to a baking dish. Fill the cavity of each apple with some of the cheese and top with a walnut half. Bake until the apples are completely tender and the cheese hot and bubbly, about 10 minutes. Meanwhile, strain the poaching liquid, discard the spices, and over medium heat reduce the liquid by two-thirds. Remove the sauce from the heat and stir in the butter.

Set the apples on individual serving plates, spoon sauce and scatter walnuts over each apple, and serve immediately.

Spiced Apple Tart

Serves 6 to 8

We have the French to thank for thin-crusted apple tarts, which are among my favorite ways to use apples. My version defies French tradition by adding a spicy element, a dimension I enjoy in sweets. If you're horrified by the idea, you can easily omit the chipotle powder and use a less risqué jelly, such as one made of red wine, apples, or currants. I'd give this version a try first, though.

> 1 cup all-purpose flour
> ½ teaspoon plus ⅛ teaspoon kosher salt
> ½ cup (1 stick) unsalted butter, cut in pieces and chilled
> 3 to 4 tablespoons ice water
> Juice of 1 lemon
> 3 to 4 apples
> 3 tablespoons unsalted butter, melted
> 3 tablespoons sugar
> ½ teaspoon ground cinnamon
> ¼ teaspoon chipotle powder
> 3 tablespoons hot red pepper jelly, or other hot pepper jelly or jam, warmed

Place the flour and the ½ teaspoon of the salt in a medium bowl, add the butter, and use your fingers or a pastry cutter to work the butter into the flour so that it forms an evenly crumbly mixture, working quickly so that butter stays cold. Add 3 tablespoons of ice water and mix together quickly with your fingers or a fork. Do not overmix or overwork the dough. Gather it up into a ball, wrap it in plastic, and chill it for an hour.

Meanwhile, prepare the apples. Fill a medium bowl half full with water and add the lemon juice. Peel the apples, cut them in half through their cores, and use a sharp knife or melon baller to remove the cores and flower and stem ends. Drop the peeled apples into the acidulated water so that they do not brown. Cut the apples into lengthwise, ⅛-inch-thick slices and return them to the water.

Preheat the oven to 375°F. Roll out the dough on a floured work surface so that it forms a circle about ⅛ inch thick and 10 to 11 inches in diameter. Carefully transfer it to a baking sheet. Turn in the outer edge to form a ½-inch rim. Use the tines of a fork to prick the tart in several places.

Drain the apples, shaking them vigorously. Set them on a tea towel and pat them dry. Arrange a circle of apple slices, overlapping them slightly, near the outer rim of the dough. Continue adding apples in concentric circles that overlap one another slightly. Use a pastry brush to brush the apples and the outer rim of dough with the butter; use all of the butter. In a small bowl, combine the sugar, cinnamon, chipotle powder, and the remaining ⅛ teaspoon of salt and sprinkle the mixture over the apples. Bake until the apples are cooked and the crust is golden brown, about 40 to 45 minutes. Transfer to a rack and cool for 5 minutes. Set the tart on a serving plate, brush the top of it with the hot pepper jelly, cut into wedges, and serve immediately.

Kathleen's Apple Peach Compote

Makes about 5 pints

Kathleen Berman is the dessert chef at Mixx, the restaurant she co-owns with her husband, the chef Dan Berman. Through Dan's work with Select Sonoma County and the Redwood Empire Restaurant Association and their use of local farm products at the restaurant, they have been enthusiastic supporters of Sonoma County agriculture.

> *Juice of 1 lemon*
> *1 pound Gravenstein apples*
> *1 cup sugar*
> *½ cup spiced rum, such as Captain Morgan Original Spiced Rum*
> *1 pound Henry peaches, peeled and sliced*
> *½ cup toasted pine nuts*
> *½ teaspoon ground cinnamon*

Fill a bowl two-thirds full with water and add the lemon juice. Peel the apples, cut them in quarters, and remove their cores. As you peel each apple, drop it into the lemon water bath so that it does not brown. After all the apples have been cored, cut them into ⅛-inch-thick slices and return them to the bowl of acidulated water.

In a large, heavy saucepan, combine the sugar and ¼ cup water (do not stir it) and set over high heat; simmer until all of the sugar is dissolved and the mixture begins to thicken slightly. Reduce the heat to low. Drain the apples thoroughly, dry them on a tea towel, and very carefully add them to the syrup. Simmer, stirring frequently, until the apples soften slightly. Heat the rum in a small saucepan set over medium-low heat, pour it over the apple mixture, and carefully ignite it with a match. The mixture will flame, then die down as the alcohol is consumed by the fire.

Fold in the peaches and pine nuts and simmer for 5 minutes more, until the compote comes together but the fruits are not mushy. If the apples or peaches seem a little too firm, cook for 5 minutes more. Remove from the heat, add the cinnamon, and stir gently. Spoon into dessert bowls and serve immediately. The compote will keep, properly refrigerated, for up to two weeks.

Green Valley Farms' Blueberry Pie

Serves 6 to 8

Bruce Goetz of Green Valley Farms says the secret to this pie, which is sold at the farm, is the combination of cooked and raw berries. Green Valley Farm is located not far from Kozlowski Farms in the heart of the Green Valley viticultural area. Bruce Goetz's family acquired the farm in 1940 and in 1942 planted nineteen acres of blueberries, the first commercial blueberry farm in California. For years, they grew raspberries and other berries, too, but the vines were destroyed by intense storms in 1983. The blueberries survived. Unlike raspberry vines, which have a life span of just four to five years, blueberry trees have a life expectancy of forty-five years. Today, Goetz farms just seven acres, and many of the original trees are still producing.

> ¼ cup (½ stick) butter
> 6 cups blueberries
> 4½ tablespoons fresh lemon juice
> 3 tablespoons flour, plus more as needed
> ¼ teaspoon salt

¾ cup granulated sugar

¾ cup brown sugar

One 10-inch pie shell, baked

Melt the butter in a large saucepan set over medium-low heat. Add 3 cups of the blueberries and lemon juice and continue to cook, stirring frequently, until the blueberries release their juice. Stir in the flour, salt, and sugars, and simmer until the mixture thickens, about 8 to 10 minutes. If it does not thicken sufficiently, make a slurry of 1 tablespoon flour and a little of the cooking liquid and stir it into the mixture.

Remove the blueberry mixture from the heat and let cool to room temperature. Fold in the remaining 3 cups of blueberries, pour into the baked pie shell, and let rest at least 15 minutes before serving. Cut into wedges and serve neat, or with crème fraîche, fresh whipped cream, or ice cream.

Vanilla Peach Grunt

Serves 4 to 6

When John Ash shared his recipe for Blackberry Grunt with me, he explained that the name refers to the sound the berries make as they simmer on the stove. Sounds like a story your grandma might tell perhaps as an object lesson to cure you of pretentious recipe titles. John may be known all over the United States and much of the rest of the world as one of the pioneers of wine-country cuisine, but his heart seems to be firmly rooted in good old American cooking. He mentions his grandma more than almost anyone I know. Peaches, by the way, make a similar sound to blackberries, though it is perhaps pitched a bit higher. For John's version of grunt, consult the variation at the end of this recipe.

6 to 8 ripe yellow peaches, peeled and sliced

⅓ cup plus 2 tablespoons sugar, plus more to taste

¼ cup white wine such as viognier

3-inch piece of vanilla bean

1 cup all-purpose flour

1 teaspoon baking powder

½ teaspoon baking soda

⅛ teaspoon salt

2 tablespoons unsalted butter, melted

½ cup buttermilk, plus more as needed

2 tablespoons sugar mixed with 1 teaspoon cinnamon

Combine the peaches, the ⅓ cup of sugar, white wine, and vanilla bean in a medium-size deep skillet, taste the mixture, and if it is too tart, add more sugar, a tablespoon at a time, until it tastes right. Bring to a boil over medium heat, reduce the heat to low, and simmer for 10 minutes, until the peaches are tender and juicy.

While the peaches cook make the dumpling dough. In a mixing bowl, stir together the flour, 2 tablespoons of sugar, baking powder, baking soda, and salt. Stir in the melted butter. Add enough of the buttermilk to form a soft, sticky dough that is slightly wetter than a biscuit dough.

Use tongs to remove and discard the vanilla bean. Use a large soup spoon to form small dumplings of dough and set them on top of the simmering peaches. Sprinkle the dumplings with the cinnamon sugar. Cover the skillet with a lid or a sheet of aluminum foil and steam the mixture over medium-low heat until the dumplings are set and the surface is dry when touched with a fingertip, about 15 minutes.

Spoon the warm grunt into wide bowls and serve immediately.

VARIATIONS

If you prefer a slightly toasty crust, preheat an oven broiler while the grunt steams. Remove the lid when the grunt is cooked and set the skillet under the broiler for 4 to 5 minutes, until the dumplings just begin to turn golden brown.

For blackberry grunt, combine 6 cups fresh blackberries with ¾ cup sugar, ⅓ cup red wine, and 1 tablespoon minced lemon zest. Continue as directed in the main recipe. Serve with sweetened whipped cream or ice cream.

Crescenza with Apple Peach Compote & Honey

Serves 4

In many ways, Sonoma County cuisine is a cuisine of possibility. With its remarkable agricultural bounty as inspiration, it is possible simply to gather up what is in season and prepare a wonderful meal without ever consulting or testing a recipe. This lush dessert, from Dan and Kathleen Berman of Mixx Restaurant in Santa Rosa, is just such a dish, the quintessential Sonoma County dessert, Dan says. It sprung to life during a dinner for members of Select Sonoma County, an agricultural marketing organization. Dan confesses that it was not tested beforehand. It simply came together, inspired by ingredients that had been donated by various members: cheese from Bellwether Farms, apples from Kozlowski Farms, peaches from Dry Creek Peach & Produce, berries from Middleton Gardens, mint from Wine Country Cuisine, and honey from DaVero, their first batch. The figs arrived at the beginning of the dinner, a gift from Condra Easley of Renaissance Bakery. When the kitchen crew tasted the dish, everyone simply said, "Wow!" and out it went to the dinner guests.

> *8 ounces Bellwether Crescenza, cut in 4 equal pieces*
> *4 to 6 tablespoons Kathleen's Apple Peach Compote (page 281)*
> *¾ cup blackberries*
> *2 figs, cut into crosswise slices (rounds)*
> *4 tablespoons honey*
> *Zest of half a lemon, cut in thin julienne*
> *4 small mint sprigs*

Set a square of cheese on individual dessert plates and top each piece of cheese with a generous spoonful of compote. Arrange several blackberries on top of the compote, and set several slices of figs next to the cheese. Drizzle honey over everything, garnish with a few strips of lemon zest and a mint sprig, and serve immediately.

Variation: For an old-fashioned version of this dish, replace the compote with Pickled Dried Prunes (page 272) spooned over the cheese, drizzle with honey, and serve with gingersnaps.

White Peach Galettes

Serves 6 to 8

My friend John Kramer is one of the best home cooks I know, but he's afraid of dough. In trying to give him both advice and the courage to try again, I developed this way of explaining the technique. I added a few safeguards, too, such as chilling the mixing bowl and using a food processor to mix the flour and butter, a helpful technique if you happen to have warm hands. If you have no problem making short crust, feel free to use your own method. If you've had trouble, perhaps this method will work for you. I make these galettes using the exquisite white peaches grown by Dry Creek Peach & Produce; Arctic Gems, which ripen in the middle of summer, are my favorite of the several varieties they grow.

> 2 cups all-purpose flour
> ½ teaspoon kosher salt
> 4 teaspoons sugar
> 1 cup (2 sticks) unsalted butter, cut into pieces and chilled
> ½ cup ice water
> 6 to 7 ripe white peaches, such as Arctic Gem
> Juice of 1 lemon
> 3 tablespoons butter, melted
> 2 tablespoons coarse sugar, such as turbinado

Chill a medium metal mixing bowl. Put the flour, salt, and 2 teaspoons of the sugar in the work bowl of a food processor and pulse briefly. Continue to pulse as you drop a few pieces of butter at time through the opening in the lid, working quickly so that the butter stays cold. The mixture is ready when it resembles coarse crumbs; this should take less than 30 seconds. Remove the chilled bowl from the refrigerator; quickly dump the dough into the bowl, using a rubber spatula to scrape out any that sticks to the container. Stretch a large piece of plastic wrap on your work surface. Drizzle about two-thirds of the water over the dough and quickly press the dough together, adding more water wherever it seems too dry and crumbly. Do not mix the dough; press it together. Carefully dump it onto the plastic wrap and lift both ends of the wrap to press the dough together; set the ends down and pull together the sides of the wrap, again pressing the dough into itself. Pull the plastic wrap around the dough, making a ball. Refrigerate it for 1 to 1½ hours.

Shortly before the dough is fully chilled, peel the peaches, cut them into ⅛-inch-thick slices, put them in a wide shallow bowl, and drizzle with the lemon juice. Set them aside while you roll out the galettes.

Line 2 baking sheets with parchment. Preheat the oven to 400°F. Sprinkle a work surface generously with flour.

Cut the chilled dough into eight equal pieces; return four of the pieces to the refrigerator. Use the palm of your hand to flatten one piece of dough into a flat circle. Using a rolling pin, roll it into a 6-inch circle that is about ⅛ inch thick. Set the circle on the parchment; continue until you have made four circles. Set the baking sheet with the circles of dough in the refrigerator and shape the four remaining pieces of dough into circles.

To fill the galettes, divide the peaches among the dough circles, leaving a 2-inch margin. Fold the dough gently up and over the fruit so that it forms a 1-inch pocket; pleat the edges as you fold them. Sprinkle the fruit with some of the remaining 2 teaspoons of sugar, brush the edges of the dough with butter, and sprinkle the coarse sugar on top.

Bake until the pastry is golden brown and the fruit is hot and bubbly, about 30 to 35 minutes. Let the galettes cool on a rack; serve them warm or at room temperature.

Strawberry Rhubarb Cobbler

Serves 8

This homey dessert is easy to make and requires very little last-minute attention. Put it in the oven when you first sit down, remove it when you serve the salad, and let it cool while you linger over conversation. If any is left over, serve it for breakfast.

> *4 cups strawberries, stemmed and sliced ¼ inch thick*
> *1 pound rhubarb, wash, peeled, and cut into ½-inch pieces*
> *1¼ cups sugar, plus more to taste and for the dough*

1 teaspoon vanilla extract

1 ¾ cups all-purpose flour

1 tablespoon baking powder

¼ teaspoon salt

6 tablespoons (¾ stick) butter, chilled and cut into ½-inch cubes,
   plus more for the baking dish

¾ cup milk

In a large bowl, combine the strawberries, rhubarb, ¾ cup of the sugar, and the vanilla extract, and toss lightly. Cover and set aside for 1 hour. Taste the juices that have collected, and if they are too tart, add an additional ¼ cup sugar. Set aside.

Preheat the oven to 350°F. To make the topping, mix together the flour, ½ cup sugar, baking powder, and salt. Add the butter and, using your fingers or a pastry blender, cut the butter into the flour until the mixture resembles coarse crumbs. Add the milk and stir very quickly to blend; do not overmix.

Butter a 9- by 13-inch glass baking dish, and pour the fruit mixture into it, shaking to spread the fruit evenly. Top with the batter, using a spatula to spread it over the surface of the fruit as best you can (it will smooth out while baking). Sprinkle 1 tablespoon of sugar over the top and bake for 45 minutes, or until the crust is golden brown and the fruit hot and bubbly. Remove from the oven and let rest 10 to 15 minutes before serving neat or with vanilla ice cream.

Russian River Vineyards Cheesecake with Green Valley Blueberry Sauce

Serves 10 to 12

Christine Topolos, who runs the restaurant at Russian River Vineyards, shared her cheesecake with me when I was writing the first edition of this book. It remains my favorite cheesecake recipe and I offer it here, unchanged. I have embellished it with blueberry sauce, which can be omitted if you prefer your cheesecake neat (as I often do). The sauce can also be used over ice cream or as a sauce for the Summer Chocolate Roll (page 292).

BLUEBERRY SAUCE

2 cups fresh blueberries

¼ cup orange juice

½ teaspoon ground cloves

½ cup dessert wine, such as black muscat

CHEESECAKE

1½ cups crushed graham crackers

1 cup plus 2 tablespoons sugar

½ cup butter, melted

12 ounces old-fashioned cream cheese, at room temperature

3 teaspoons vanilla extract

4 large eggs, beaten

1½ cups sour cream

First, make the sauce. Put the blueberries, orange juice, and cloves in the work bowl of a food processor or blender and pulse until smooth. Strain into a clean bowl, stir in the wine, taste, and adjust the consistency and flavor. If the berries are a little tart, add a tablespoon or two of granulated sugar to boost the flavor. If the sauce seems a bit too thick, thin it with a little water or more wine. Chill the sauce until ready to serve.

Preheat the oven to 325°F. Toss together the graham cracker crumbs and ½ cup of the sugar in a medium bowl, drizzle the butter over it, and mix thoroughly. Press the mixture firmly into the bottom and ¾ inch up the sides of an 8-inch springform pan. Bake for 10 minutes and set aside to cool.

In a medium bowl, beat together the cream cheese, ½ cup of the remaining sugar, and 2 teaspoons of the vanilla. Fold in the eggs and mix thoroughly. Pour the mixture into the crumb crust and bake until the center is just set, about 40 minutes.

Meanwhile, combine the sour cream, the remaining 2 tablespoons of sugar, and remaining 1 teaspoon of vanilla in a small bowl. Spread it over the cheesecake, return to the oven, and bake for 10 minutes more. Remove from the oven, let cool to room temperature, cover, and chill thoroughly. To serve, spoon sauce onto individual dessert plates, cut the cheesecake into wedges, set a wedge on top of the sauce, and serve immediately.

Carmen's Wine Cake

Serves 8 to 10

Carmen Kozlowski of Kozlowski Farms is an enthusiastic cook who has developed many of the recipes that are now staples in their line-up of products. This cake is one of her most recent new recipes. I like it with fresh berries alongside.

1 cup butter, at room temperature

2 cups sugar

4 eggs

3 cups all-purpose flour

2 teaspoons baking soda

2 teaspoons baking powder

1 ½ teaspoons freshly grated nutmeg

1 cup California cream sherry

½ cup Gravenstein Applesauce (page 273) or other applesauce

¾ cup water

¼ cup powdered sugar

Preheat the oven to 350°F. In a large bowl, mix together the butter, sugar, and eggs until smooth and very creamy. In a separate bowl, sift together the flour, baking soda, baking powder, and nutmeg. In a third bowl, combine the sherry and apple-sauce with ¾ cup water.

Using a rubber spatula or wooden spoon, add one-third of the dry ingredients to the butter mixture, followed by one-third of the sherry mixture. Continue adding in thirds, alternating between dry and liquid ingredients. Pour the mixture into a Bundt pan and bake for 45 to 50 minutes or until golden brown. Invert the cake onto a rack and when it has cooled to room temperature, dust with powdered sugar.

Colleen's Olive Oil Cake

Serves 8 to 10

Colleen McGlynn, who along with her husband Ridgely Evers, produces DaVero Olive Oil and DaVero Honey, often serves this cake as one of a entire tableful of desserts at their annual olive oil luncheon. It's yummy on its own and is also great accompanied by Kathleen's Apple Peach Compote (page 281).

6 ounces almonds, toasted

2 small oranges

1 lemon

4 eggs

½ teaspoon kosher salt

1½ cups sugar

1 cup all-purpose flour

1 tablespoon baking powder

⅔ cup extra virgin olive oil

2 tablespoons powdered sugar

Place the almonds in the work bowl of a food processor and pulse until pulverized. Transfer to a small bowl and set aside. Place the oranges and lemon in a medium saucepan, cover them with water, and bring to a boil over medium heat. Reduce the heat to medium-low and simmer for 30 minutes. Drain and cool them. Cut the oranges and lemon in half, scoop out and discard the lemon pulp and any orange seeds, and place in the work bowl of a food processor. Pulse until the fruit is finely minced.

Preheat the oven to 350°F. Beat the eggs until they are foamy, add the salt, whisk thoroughly, and add the sugar gradually, whisking continuously. Sift together the flour and baking powder and add it to the egg mixture. Using a rubber spatula, quickly blend in the olive oil, chopped fruit, and pulverized almonds. Do not overmix.

Pour the mixture into a 10-inch springform pan for 50 to 60 minutes, until the sides begin to pull away and the middle of the cake is set. Remove from the oven, let cool, and dust with powdered sugar before serving.

Summer Chocolate Roll

Serves 8 to 10

I had planned to exclude this recipe; in fact, it was already on the cutting room floor, so to speak. I made so many of these cakes in the early 1990s when I still worked as a chef that I never wanted to see one again. But then I ran into Maile Arnold, a landscaper who lives in Sebastopol and is an enthusiastic fan of the first edition of this book. When I told her of the revision, the first thing she said was, "You're not taking out the Summer Chocolate Roll, are you?" When I told her indeed I was, she offered an impassioned argument for keeping it, so here it is, with just a couple of changes.

CAKE

1 tablespoon butter, at room temperature

4 eggs, separated

½ cup powdered sugar, sifted

1 teaspoon vanilla extract

4 tablespoons cocoa, sifted

1 teaspoon instant espresso powder

1 tablespoon cake flour

¼ teaspoon cream of tartar

2 tablespoons granulated sugar

FILLING AND SAUCE

12 ounces fromage blanc

1 teaspoon vanilla extract

4 tablespoons superfine granulated sugar

1 pint fresh raspberries

2 white nectarines or peaches

2 tablespoons framboise liqueur

Juice of 1 lemon

Nasturtium and borage blossoms

First, prepare the cake. Butter the inside of a 9- by 13-inch cake pan, line it with parchment paper, and butter the parchment paper. Preheat the oven to 325°F.

Beat the egg yolks until they are light and lemon colored. Gradually sift in the sugar, beat until creamy, and mix in the vanilla. Sift in the cocoa and fold to mix well. Fold in the espresso and the cake flour. Using an electric mixer, beat the egg whites and add the cream of tartar when they reach soft peaks. Fold the egg whites into the batter, spread it in the cake pan, and bake for 20 to 25 minutes, until set. Cool on a rack for 5 minutes, remove the cake from the pan, and set it on a large piece of parchment on which you have sprinkled a couple of tablespoons of granulated sugar. Set it aside.

In a medium bowl, mix together the fromage blanc, vanilla, and 2 tablespoons of the superfine sugar. Fold in ¾ cup of the raspberries and set the mixture aside. Peel and slice the nectarines and set them aside. Spread the fromage blanc and raspberry mixture over the surface of the cake and spread the nectarines on top. Carefully, using the parchment to help, roll the cake lengthwise. Set on a platter and cover.

To make the sauce, purée the remaining raspberries with the remaining 2 tablespoons sugar, the framboise, and the lemon juice. Refrigerate the cake and the sauce until ready to serve.

To serve, spoon some of the sauce in the center of individual plates and agitate the plate to spread the sauce evenly. Cut the cake into ¾-inch-thick slices and set them on top of the sauce. Top with a small spoonful of sauce, garnish with blossoms, and serve immediately.

Blood & Chocolate Tart

Serves 6 to 8

Although blood peaches have not become as easy to find as blood oranges are, you can find them at farmers' markets now and then. Orchard Farms in Sebastopol has them in late summer. They must be peeled; their thick, fuzzy skin is not a tasty thing to eat. But inside, the reddish purple peach is beautiful and has a rich, spicy flavor that is perfect in a tart and ideal paired with chocolate.

TART CRUST
¼ cup whole wheat pastry flour
¾ cup all-purpose flour, plus more as needed
½ teaspoon kosher salt
½ cup (1 stick) unsalted butter, cut in pieces and chilled
3 to 4 tablespoons ice water

FILLING

5 or 6 blood peaches

1 ½ ounces bittersweet chocolate, preferably Scharffen Berger, chopped

3 egg yolks, beaten

1 teaspoon vanilla extract

½ cup sugar

5 tablespoons unsalted butter, melted

2-ounce piece bittersweet chocolate, preferably Scharffen Berger

Mint sprigs, for garnish

To make the crust, place the flours and salt in the work bowl of a food processor and pulse briefly. Continue to pulse as you drop the butter, a few pieces of butter at time, through the opening in the lid, working quickly so that the butter stays cold. The mixture is ready when it resembles coarse crumbs; this should take less than 30 seconds. Transfer to a medium bowl, make a well in the center, add 3 table-spoons of water, and mix quickly with your fingers. If the dough does not hold together, sprinkle the remaining 1 tablespoon of water over it, gather it into a ball, and wrap it in plastic wrap. Chill for 1 to 2 hours.

Peel the peaches; the skin should come off easily. Cut them in half, remove the stones, and cut into ⅛-inch-thick slices. Cover them with a tea towel and set them aside.

Sprinkle a work surface generously with flour and roll out the dough to form a 12-inch circle. Fit the dough into a 10-inch tart pan with a removable bottom. Preheat the oven to 375°F. Fill the bottom of a double-boiler half full with water and bring to boil over high heat. Reduce the heat to low and, when the water is simmering, set the top of the double boiler over it. Add the chopped chocolate and remove the entire double boiler from the heat. When the chocolate is just melted, use a pastry brush to paint the surface of the tart shell with it, working quickly and gently.

Beginning at the outer edge of the tart, arrange the peaches in overlapping con-centric circles on top of the chocolate.

Beat the egg yolks until they are creamy and pale in color. Add the vanilla and sugar and mix thoroughly. Whisk in the melted butter, pour the mixture over the peaches, and gently jostle the tart pan to spread it evenly. Bake the tart until the crust is golden brown, about 40 minutes. Let rest 15 minutes. Remove the tart pan ring, cut the tart into slices, and set each slice on an individual dessert plate. Grate some chocolate over each slice, garnish with a mint sprig, and serve immediately.

PART III

Appendices

Resources

Farmers' Markets

Healdsburg Farmers' Market
Vine & North Streets
707-431-1956
Saturdays, May—November
9—noon

Town Plaza
707-431-1956
Tuesdays, June—October
4—6:30

Oakmont Farmers' Market
Oakmont Drive & White Oak, Santa Rosa
707-538-7023
Saturdays
9—noon

Petaluma Farmers' Market
Walnut Avenue & Petaluma
Boulevard South, Walnut Park
707-762-0344
Saturdays, May—October
2—5

Santa Rosa Downtown Farmers' Market
Fourth & B Streets
707-524-2123
Wednesdays, June—August
5—8:30

Santa Rosa Original Certified Market
Veterans' Memorial Building
1351 Maple Street, east parking lot
707-538-7023
Wednesdays & Saturdays, rain or shine
8:30—noon

Sebastopol Farm Market
Downtown Plaza
McKinley Street, near Main
707-522-9305
Sundays, April—November
10—1:30

Sonoma Valley Farm Market
Depot Park
707-538-7023
Fridays
9—noon

Sonoma Plaza
707-538-7023
Tuesdays, April—October
5:30 until dusk

Fresh Produce

Chester Aaron
P.O. Box 388
Occidental, CA 95465
Mail order, garlic seed

Andersen's Organics
4588 Bodega Avenue
Petaluma, CA 94952
707-773-1740
Farm stand, seasonal

Dry Creek Peach & Produce
2179 Yoakim Bridge Road
Healdsburg, CA 95448
707-433-7016
Farm stand, farmers' markets

Gourmet Mushrooms Inc.
P.O. Box 391
Sebastopol, CA 95473
707-823-1743
Mail order

Green Valley Farm
9345 Ross Station Road
Sebastopol, CA 95472
707-887-7496
Farm stand, mail order

Grossi Farms
6652 Petaluma Hill Road
Santa Rosa, CA 95404
707-664-1602
Farm stand

Petaluma Mushroom Farm
782 Thompson Lane
Petaluma, CA 94952
707-762-1280
Retail, wholesale

Point Arena Mushrooms
707-882-2772
Farmers' markets, mail order

Red Barn Store at Oak Hill Farm
15101 Sonoma Hwy
Glen Ellen, CA 95442
707-996-6643
Farm stand, seasonal

Sunshine Farms
   26653 River Road
   Cloverdale, CA 95425
   707-894-3984
   Specialty garlic, organic produce
   Mail order, farmers' markets

Tierra Vegetables
   13684 Chalk Hill Road
   Healdsburg, CA 95448
   707-837-8366
   www.tierravegetables.com
   Smoked peppers (chipotles), produce
   Farmers' markets, mail order, CSA

Westside Farms
   7097 Westside Road
   Healdsburg, CA 95448
   707-431-1432
   Farm stand, seasonal

Dairy, Seafood, Poultry, Meat

Bellwether Farms
   888-527-8606, 707-763-0993
   www.bellwethercheese.com
   Sheep's milk and Jersey milk cheeses
   Mail order

C. K. Lamb
   11100 Los Amigos Road
   Healdsburg, CA 95448
   707-431-8161
   Wholesale

Carniceria Contreras
   1401 Todd Road
   Santa Rosa, CA 95407
   707-585-2308
   Meat, including cabrito
   Retail, wholesale

Laura Chenel Chevre
   4310 Fremont Drive
   Sonoma, CA 95476
   707-996-4477
   Fresh and aged goat cheeses
   Mail order through Williams-Sonoma catalog;
   wholesale

Clover-Stornetta Farms
   91 Lakeville Road
   Petaluma, CA 94952
   707-778-8448
   Tours

The Crab Pot
   1750 Highway 1
   Bodega Bay, CA 94923
   707-875-9970

Gourmet Goat
   17190 Bodega Highway
   Bodega, CA 94922
   707-876-9686
   Retail outlet for Bodega Goat Cheese

Hog Island Shellfish Co.
   P.O. Box 829
   Marshall, CA 94940
   415-663-9218
   Retail sales; picnic area

Lucas Wharf
   595 Highway 1
   Bodega Bay, CA 94923
   707-875-3571 *wholesale*
   707-875-3562 *retail*
   Local seafood

Marin French Cheese Company
   7500 Red Hill Road
   Petaluma, CA 94952
   707-762-0430
   On-site retail, picnic grounds, mail order

Martindale's Meats & Deli
   5280 Aero Drive
   Santa Rosa, CA 95403
   707-545-0531
   Retail, wholesale

Joe Matos Cheese Factory
   3669 Llano Road
   Santa Rosa, CA 95407
   707-584-5283
   On-site retail, mail order

Niman Ranch
   1025 East 12th Street
   Oakland, CA 94606
   510-808-0330
   www.nimanranch.com
   Premium beef, lamb, pork

Paisano Brothers Fisheries
   1820 Westshore Road
   Bodega Bay, CA 94923
   707-875-3576
   Local seafood, retail and wholesale

Panizzera Meat Co.
   3903 Main Street
   Occidental, CA 95465
   707-874-1854
   Retail

Petaluma Poultry
   2700 Lakeville Highway
   Petaluma, CA 94952
   707-763-1904
   Rocky & Rosie chickens, wholesale

Piotrkowski Smoked Poultry
   1285 Skillman Lane
   Petaluma, CA 94952
   707-778-8482
   Mail order, wholesale

Redwood Hill Farms Goat Dairy
   10855 Occidental Road
   Sebastopol, CA 95472
   707-823-8250
   Mail order, wholesale

Sonoma Cheese Factory
2 East Spain Street
Sonoma, CA 95476
800-535-2855, 707-996-1000
www.sonomacheese.com
Mail order, tours

Sonoma Foie Gras
4333 Lovell Valley Road
Sonoma, CA 95476
707-938-1229
Foie gras and Muscovy duck

Sonoma Poultry Company
P.O. Box 140
Penngrove, CA 94951
707-795-3797
Liberty Duck

Sonoma Sausage Factory
414 First Street East, Suite 5 *(office)*
Sonoma, CA 95476
707-938-1215
Wholesale; retail facility planned for summer 2000

Spring Hill Jersey Cheese Factory
4235 Spring Hill Road
Petaluma, CA 94952
707-762-3446
Home of Peter's Pumpkin Patch, Georgia's potatoes, produce, cheese Farmers' markets

Vella Cheese Company
315 Second Street East
Sonoma, CA 95476
800-848-0505, 707-938-3232
www.vellacheese.com
Mail order, tours

Willie Bird Turkeys
5350 Sebastopol Road
Santa Rosa, CA 95407
707-545-2832
www.williebird.com
Mail order, retail

Willowside Meats
3421 Guerneville Road
Santa Rosa, CA 95401
707-546-8404
Housemade sausages, customer processing of seafood, meat, and game

Bread

Alvarado Street Bakery
500 Martin Avenue
Rohnert Park, CA 94928
707-585-3293

Artisan Bakers
750 West Napa Street
Sonoma, CA 95476
707-939-1765

Basque Boulangerie
460 First Street East
Sonoma, CA 95476
707-935-7687

Bennett Valley Bread & Pastry
2755 Yulupa Avenue
Santa Rosa, CA 95405
707-575-9345

Brother Juniper's Bakery
463 Sebastopol Avenue
Santa Rosa, CA 95401
707-542-6546

Costeaux French Bakery
417 Healdsburg Avenue
Healdsburg, CA 95448
707-433-1913

Downtown Bakery & Creamery
308 Center
Healdsburg, CA 95448
707-431-2719

Lotus Bakery
3336 Industrial Drive
Santa Rosa, CA 95403
707-526-1520

Santa Rosa Bread Company
1021 Hahman Drive
Santa Rosa, CA 95405
707-577-0021

Alan Scott
Ovencrafters Wood-Fired Ovens
5600 Marshall-Petaluma Road
Marshall, CA 94940
415-663-9010
co-author of The Bread Builder *(Ten Speed Press)*

Village Bakery
7225 Healdsburg Avenue
Sebastopol, CA 95472
707-829-8101

Wild Flour Bread
140 Bohemian Highway
Freestone, CA 95472
707-874-2938

Producers

Adamson's Happy Haven Ranch
1480 Sperring Road
Sonoma, CA 95476
707-996-5121
Mail order, farmers' markets

Bohemian Foods
P.O. Box 231
Occidental, CA 95465
888-287-8356, 707-874-1663
Larry's Bohemian Pepper Sauces (formerly Bustelo's)

Da Vero Extra Virgin Olive Oil
See Toscano-Sonoma

Sonoma Moment
411 Foss
Healdsburg, CA 95448
707-433-5896
Oils, vinegars

Timber Crest Farms
4791 Dry Creek Road
Healdsburg, CA 95448
707-433-8251
www.timbercrest.com
Dried tomatoes, fruits, nuts, condiments
Mail order, tours

Toscano-Sonoma
1195 Westside Road
Healdsburg, CA 95448
707-431-8000
www.davero.com
DaVero Extra Virgin Olive Oil, estate honey

Markets

Anstead's
102 Healdsburg Avenue
Healdsburg, CA 95448
707-431-0530

Fiesta Market
550 Gravenstein Highway North
Sebastopol, CA 95472
707-823-9735

Imwalle Gardens
685 West Third Street
Santa Rosa, CA 95401
707-546-0279
Founded in 1886; fresh produce, plant starts,
cut flowers, seeds, retail and wholesale

Jimtown Store
6706 Highway 128
Healdsburg, CA 95448
707-433-1212
Antiques, vintage toys, wine, deli

Lepe's Tienda
7365 Healdsburg Avenue
Sebastopol, CA 95472
707-829-9175

Lolita's Market
451 Lakeville Highway
Petaluma, CA 94952
707-766-8929

Oakville Grocery
124 Matheson
Healdsburg, CA 95448
707-433-3200

Oliver's Market
546 East Cotati Avenue
Cotati, CA 94931
707-795-9501

560 Montecito Center
Santa Rosa, CA 95409
707-537-7123

Pacific Market
1465 Town & Country Drive
Santa Rosa, CA 95404
707-546-3663

Traverso's Gourmet Foods & Wines
Third & B Streets
Santa Rosa, CA 95401
707-542-2530

Distributors

Sonoma Organics
1120 Barlow Lane
Sebastopol, CA 95472
707-829-8200
Richard Robinson, wholesale

Nurseries & Garden Shops

Absolute Home & Garden
2227 Gravenstein Highway South
Sebastopol, CA 95472
707-823-5039
Garden statuary, fountains, classes

California Carnivores
7020 Trenton-Healdsburg Road
Forestville, CA 95436
707-838-1630

Chalk Hill Clematis Nursery
707-433-8416
www.chalkhillclematis.com
Mail order clematis vines, also estate olive oil
and traditional balsamic vinegar

Enchanted Gardens
4315 Miles Avenue
Forestville, CA 95436
707-568-0912

Garden Valley Ranch & Nursery
498 Pepper Road
Petaluma, CA 94952
707-795-0919

The Gardener
516 Dry Creek Road
Healdsburg, CA 95448
707-431-1063

Hallberg Butterfly Gardens
8687 Oak Grove Road
Sebastopol, CA 95472
707-823-3420
Plants to attract butterflies and other wildlife,
classes; tours, call ahead

Miniature Plant Kingdom
4125 Harrison Grade Road
Sebastopol, CA 95472
707-874-2233

Mom's Head Garden
4153 Langner Avenue
Santa Rosa, CA 95407
707-585-8575
Tours, sales, classes; seasonal

The Nursery at Emerisa's Gardens
555 Irwin Lane
Santa Rosa, CA 95401
707-525-9644
Outstanding selection of perennials

Petite Plaisance
P.O. Box 386
Valley Ford, CA 94972
707-876-3496
www.sonic.net/orchids
Rare orchids, open by appointment, call ahead for address

Sonoma County Antique Apple Nursery
4395 Westside Road
Healdsburg, CA 95448
707-433-6420
Catalog

Western Hills Rare Plants
16250 Coleman Valley Road
Occidental, CA 95465
707-874-3731
Retail nursery

Wishing Well Nursery
306 Bohemian Highway
Freestone, CA 95472
707-823-3710

Ya-Ka-Ama Native Plants Nursery
6215 Eastside Road
Forestville, CA 95436
707-887-1586
Native plants, education center, gift shop of Native American arts, crafts, and jewelry

Cooking Classes & Education

Ramekins Culinary School
450 West Spain Street
Sonoma, CA 95476
707-933-0450
www.ramekins.com
Culinary classes for consumers, culinary tours

Taylor Maid Farms
P.O. Box 14
Occidental, CA 95465
707-824-9110
Organic coffee, tea, herbs, tours, classes

Occidental Arts & Ecology Center
Dave Henson, Director
15290 Coleman Valley Road
Occidental, CA 95465
707-874-1557
www.oaec.org
Organic farm and residential educational center, biannual plant sales, membership

Wild About Mushrooms
P.O. Box 1088
Forestville, CA 95436
707-887-1888
Information, tours, classes

Organizations

Alexander Valley Winegrowers Association
707-431-2894

California North Coast Grape Growers Association
707-578-8331

California Olive Oil Council
19229 Sonoma Highway, #264
Sonoma, CA 95476
www.cooc.com

Hispanic Chamber of Commerce of Sonoma County
2435 Professional Drive
Santa Rosa, CA 95403
707-526-7744

North Bay Italian Cultural Foundation
1275 Fourth Street, #241
Santa Rosa, CA 95404
707-522-9448

Rhone Rangers
707-939-8014

Russian River Valley Winegrowers Association
707-546-3276

Russian River Wine Road Inc.
707-433-4335

Select Sonoma County
5000 Roberts Lake Drive
Rohnert Park, CA 94928
707-586-2233
www.sonomagrown.com
Agricultural marketing organization

Sonoma County Farmlands Group
707-576-0162

Sonoma County Farm Trails
PO Box 6032
Santa Rosa, CA 95406
800-207-9464, 707-571-8288
www.farmtrails.org

Sonoma County Grape Growers Association
5000 Roberts Lake Road, Suite A
Rohnert Park, CA 94928
707-527-0200

Sonoma County Herb Association
707-522-8500

Sonoma County Wineries Association
5000 Roberts Lake Drive
Rohnert Park, CA 94928
707-586-3795
www.sonomawine.com

Sonoma Land Trust
1122 Sonoma Avenue
Santa Rosa, CA 95405
707-526-6930
slt@sonic.net

Sonoma Provence Exchange
P.O. Box 4954
Santa Rosa, CA 95402
sonprov@metro.net
707-576-1434

Sonoma Valley Vintners & Growers
707-935-0803

Wine BRATS
707-545-3539

Winegrowers of Dry Creek Valley
707-433-3031

Tourism & Visitor Information

Armstrong Redwoods Visitor Center
17000 Armstrong Woods Road
Guerneville, CA 95446
707-869-2958

Bodega Bay Area Visitors Center
850 Highway 1
Bodega Bay, CA 94923
707-875-3866
www.bodegabay.org

California Welcome Center
5000 Roberts Lake Road
Rohnert Park, CA 94928
707-586-3795
www.sonomawine.com
*Tourist info, maps, wine tastings & sales, Select
Sonoma County information*

Jenner Visitors Center
10439 Highway 1
Jenner, CA 95450
707-865-9433

Petaluma Visitors Program
799 Baywood Drive
Petaluma, CA 94952
707-769-0429
www.petaluma.org

Russian River Region Visitors Bureau
14034 Armstrong Woods Road
Guerneville, CA 95446
707-869-9212
www.sonoma.com/rusriver

Santa Rosa Convention & Visitors Bureau
9 Fourth Street
Santa Rosa, CA 95401
707-577-8674
www.visitsantarosa.com

**Sebastopol Area Chamber of Commerce
Visitor Center**
265 South Main Street
Sebastopol, CA 95472
707-823-3032
www.sebastopol.org

Sonoma County Tourism Program
520 Mendocino Avenue, Suite 210
Santa Rosa, CA 95401
707-565-5383
www.sonomacounty.com

Sonoma Valley Visitors Bureau
453 First Street East
Sonoma, CA 95476
707-996-1090, 707-935-1111 *(events
hotline)*
www.sonomavalley.com

A Vine Line Tours
5513 Highway 12
Sebastopol, CA 95472
707-829-7234
vineline@sonic.net
*Suzanne Reda
Tours of Sonoma County in Spanish*

Additional Informational Websites

www.gosonoma.com
www.sonomagrown.com
www.sonomazone.com
www.winecountry.com

Restaurants, Bars & Pubs

Ace in the Hole Cider Co.
3100 Gravenstein Highway North
Sebastopol, CA 95472
707-829-1223

Dempsey's Restaurant & Brewery
50 East Washington Street
Petaluma, CA 94952
707-765-9694

The Farmhouse Inn
7871 River Road
Forestville, CA 95436
707-887-3300

Healdsburg Charcuterie
335 Healdsburg Avenue
Healdsburg, CA 95448
707-431-7213

Juanita Juanita
19114 Arnold Drive
Sonoma, CA 95476
707-935-3981

La Salette Restaurant
18625 Highway 12
Sonoma, CA 95476
707-938-1927

Lucy's Cafe
110 N. Main Street
Sebastopol, CA 95472
707-829-9713
Restaurant and bakery

Mariposa Restaurant
275 Windsor River Road
Windsor, CA 95492
707-838-0162

Papa's Taverna
5688 Lakeville Highway
Petaluma, CA 94952
707-769-8545

Powerhouse Brewing Co.
268 Petaluma Avenue
Sebastopol, CA 95472
707-829-9171

Santi
21047 Geyserville Avenue
Geyserville, CA 95441
707-857-1790

Stormy's Tavern
6650 Bloomfield Road
Bloomfield, CA 94952
707-795-9127

Taqueria Santa Rosa
1950 Mendocino Avenue
Santa Rosa, CA 95401
707-528-7956

Tea & Tarot English Tea Room
(at the Antique Society)
2661 Gravenstein Highway South
Sebastopol, CA 95472
707-823-3882

Volpi's Speakeasy
122 Washington Street
Petaluma, CA 94952
707-765-0695

Water Street Bistro
111 Petaluma Boulevard, Suite 106
Petaluma, CA 94952
707-763-9563

Bookstores & Cookware Stores

Copperfield's Books
650 Fourth Street
Santa Rosa, CA 95404
707-545-5326

140 Kentucky
Petaluma, CA 94952
707-778-3898

2316 Montgomery Drive
Santa Rosa, CA 95405
707-578-8938

210 Coddingtown Mall
Santa Rosa, CA 95401
707-575-0550

138 North Main Street
Sebastopol, CA 95472
707-823-2618

Levin & Co Books
306 Center
Healdsburg, CA 95448
707-433-1118

Jack London Bookstore & Research Center
14300 Arnold Drive
Glen Ellen, CA 95442
707-996-2888

McCoy's Cookware
2759 Fourth Street
Santa Rosa, CA 95405
707-526-3856

North Light Books
530 East Cotati Avenue
Cotati, CA 94931
707-792-9755

Readers Books
127 East Napa Street
Sonoma, CA 95476
707-939-1779

Robin's Nest
116 East Napa Street
Sonoma, CA 95476
707-996-4169
Kitchenware

Robinson & Co
108 Matheson
Healdsburg, CA 95448
707-433-7116
Kitchenware

Sign of the Bear
435 First Street West
Sonoma, CA 95476
707-996-3722
Kitchenware

Sonoma Bookends
201 West Napa Street
Sonoma, CA 95476
707-938-5926

Toyon Books
104 Matheson
Healdsburg, CA 95448
707-433-9270

Treehorn Books
625 Fourth Street
Santa Rosa, CA 95401
707-525-1782

Special Destinations

Aerostate Hot Air Balloon Rides
P.O. Box 2082
Healdsburg, CA 95448
707-433-3777

Armstrong Woods Trail Rides & Pack Station
17000 Armstrong Woods Road
Guerneville, CA 95446
707-887-2939
www.metro.net/ayers
Horseback tours

California Rivers Paddle Sports
10070 Old Redwood Highway
Windsor, CA 95492
707-838-8919

Fort Ross
Highway 1 & Fort Ross Road
707-847-3286
Open daily, 10–4:30

General Mariano Vallejo's Home
Corner of West Spain & West Third Streets,
⅔ mile northwest of the town plaza
Sonoma, CA 95476
707-938-9559
Open daily, 10–5

Isis Oasis Lodge
20889 Geyserville Avenue
Geyserville, CA 95441
707-857-3524
Unique accommodations, wild animal preserve

Jack London State Park
2400 London Ranch Road
Glen Ellen, CA 95442
707-938-5216

Kruse Rhododendron Preserves
Highway 1, 20 miles north of Jenner
707-847-3286

Luther Burbank Home & Gardens
Santa Rosa & Sonoma Avenues
Santa Rosa, CA 95401
707-524-5445

Luther Burbank's Gold Ridge Experiment Farm
7781 Bodega Avenue
Sebastopol, CA 95472
707-829-6711
Docent and self-guided tours; please call ahead

The Olive Press
14301 Arnold Drive
Glen Ellen, CA 95442
707-939-8900
Cooperative olive mill, retail sales

Pepperwood
3450 Franz Valley Road
Santa Rosa, CA 95404
707-542-2080
Observatory

Pet-A-Llama Ranch
5505 Lone Pine Road
Sebastopol, CA 95472
707-823-9395

Petaluma Adobe
3325 Adobe Road at Casa Grande Road
Petaluma, CA 94952
707-762-4871

Peter's Pumpkin Patch
See Spring Hill Jersey Cheese Factory

Ragle Ranch Park
Ragle Road, 1 mile north of
Bodega Highway
Sebastopol, CA 95472
707-527-2041

Safari West
3115 Porter Creek Road
Santa Rosa, CA 95404
707-579-2551
Wild animal preserve, tours

Salt Point State Park
6 miles north of Fort Ross on Highway 1,
between Timber Cove & Kruse Ranch Road
707-865-2391, 707-847-3221

Train Town Railroad Rides
20264 Broadway
Sonoma, CA 95476
707-938-3912

Trowbridge Canoe Trips
707-433-7248

Wine Bars

Family Winery Tasting Room
9200 Scenic Highway 12
Kenwood, CA 95452
707-833-5504
Daily, 1–6
*Wineries: Asuncia Winery, Deerfield Ranch
Winery, Mayo Family Wineries, Nelson Estate,
Noel, Sable Ridge*

Sebastopol Fine Wine Company
6932 Sebastopol Avenue
Sebastopol, CA 95472
707-829-9378

Twisted Vines
16 Kentucky
Petaluma, CA 94952
707-766-8162
Wine bar, retail sales, restaurant

The Wine Exchange of Sonoma
452 First Street East
Sonoma, CA 95476
707-938-1794

The Wine Room
9575 Sonoma Highway
Kenwood, CA 95452
707-833-6131
www.the-wine-room.com
Daily, 11–5
*Wineries: Kaz Vineyards, Smother Brothers
Winery, Cale Cellars, Castle Vineyards,
Adler Fels, Moondance Cellars*

A Few Favorite Places

Michael Anthony
227 North Main Street
Sebastopol, CA 95472
707-823-7204
Customer western boot maker

Art for Living
14301 Arnold Drive
Glen Ellen, CA 95442
707-935-2310

KRCB-FM
5850 Labath Avenue
Rohnert Park, CA 94928
707-585-6284 *(studio line)*
Sonoma County's community radio station,
91.1 and 90.9 FM

Last Record Store
739 Fourth Street
Santa Rosa, CA 95404
707-525-1963
CDs and tapes

802 Fourth Street
Santa Rosa, CA 95404
707-528-2350
Vinyl

Milagros
414 First Street East
Sonoma, CA 95476
707-939-0834
Mexican folk art

The Quicksilver Mine Co
154 North Main Street
Sebastopol, CA 95472
707-829-2416

Wineries

The Wineries of Alexander Valley

Alexander Valley Vineyards
8644 Highway 128
Healdsburg, CA 95448
707-433-7209
www.avv.com
Daily, 10–5, picnic facilities
Chardonnay, Chenin Blanc, Gewürztraminer,
Pinot Noir, Merlot, Cabernet Sauvignon,
Zinfandel, Syrah, Cabernet Franc, Red Meritage
Est. 1975, 80,000 cases annually

Arbios Cellars
4145 Shadow Lane, #426
Santa Rosa, CA 95405
707-539-5641
By appointment
Cabernet Sauvignon
Est. 1993, 2,500 cases annually

Bandiera Winery
155 Cherry Creek Road
Cloverdale, CA 95425
707-894-4295
Sauvignon Blanc, Chardonnay, White Zinfandel,
Cabernet Sauvignon
Est. 1937, 100,000 cases annually

Canyon Road Cellars
19550 Geyserville Road
Geyserville, CA 95441
707-857-3417
www.canyonroadwinery.com
Daily, 9–5
Sauvignon Blanc, Chardonnay, Merlot
Est. 1908, 100,000 cases annually

Chateau Souverain
400 Souverain Road
Geyserville, CA 95441
707-433-8281
www.chateausouverain.com
Daily, 10–5, restaurant
Sauvignon Blanc, Chardonnay, Merlot, Chenin
Blanc, Zinfandel
Est. 1973, 120,000 cases annually

Chauffe-Eau Cellars
24401 Chianti Road
Geyserville, CA 95441
707-857-3722
By appointment
Chenin Blanc, Chardonnay, Syrah
2,000 cases annually

Clos du Bois Wines, Inc.
19410 Geyserville Avenue
Geyserville, CA 95441
707-857-3100
www.closdubois.com
10–4:30
Sauvignon Blanc, Chardonnay, Pinot Noir,
Merlot, Temperanillo, Shiraz, Cabernet
Sauvignon, Zinfandel, Late Harvest Semillon
Est. 1974, 1,000,000 cases annually

DeLorimier Winery
2001 Highway 128
Geyserville, CA 95441
800-546-7718, 707-857-2000
www.delorimierwinery.com
Friday–Monday, 10–5:30
Chardonnay, Late Harvest Sauvignon Blanc,
Red Meritage
Est. 1985, 10,000 cases annually

Estancia Estate
P.O. Box 407
Rutherford, CA 94573
707-963-7111
www.estanciaestates.com
*Chardonnay, Pinot Noir, Merlot, Cabernet
Sauvignon, Red Meritage, Duo
Est. 1986, 130,000 cases annually*

Field Stone Winery
10075 Highway 128
Healdsburg, CA 95448
707-433-7266
www.fieldstonewinery.com
*Daily, 10–5
Viognier, Chardonnay, Merlot, Chenin Blanc,
Petite Sirah, Sauvignon Blanc, Chardonnay,
Gewürztraminer, Chenin Blanc, Sangiovese
Est. 1977, 10,000 cases annually*

Geyser Peak Winery
22281 Chianti Road
Geyserville, CA 95441
800-255-9463, 707-857-9400
www.geyserpeakwinery.com
*Daily, 10–5
Sauvignon Blanc, Chardonnay, Johannisberg
Riesling, Gewürztraminer, Merlot, Cabernet
Sauvignon, Shiraz, Zinfandel, Cabernet Franc,
Petite Sirah, Petite Verdot, Red Meritage,
Sparkling Wine, Late Harvest Riesling
Est. 1880, 275,000 cases annually*

Goldschmidt Vineyards
152 Piper Street
Healdsburg, CA 95448
707-433-2061
*Cabernet Sauvignon
Est. 1998, 1,500 cases annually*

Hafner Vineyard
P.O. Box 1038
Healdsburg, CA 95448
707-433-4606
hafnervinyd@aol.com
*Chardonnay, Cabernet Sauvignon
Est. 1982, 14,000 cases annually*

Hanna Winery
9280 Highway 128
Healdsburg, CA 95448
707-431-4310

2nd tasting location:
5345 Occidental Road
Santa Rosa, CA 95401
707-575-3371
*Daily, 10–4, picnic facilities
Sauvignon Blanc, Chardonnay, Chenin Blanc,
Pinot Noir, Merlot, Zinfandel
Est. 1985, 14,000 cases annually*

Hart's Desire Winery
25094 Asti Road
Cloverdale, CA 95425
707-579-1687
*Chenin Blanc, Chardonnay, Zinfandel
Est. 1991, 1,300 cases annually*

Johnson's Alexander Valley Wines
8333 Highway 128
Healdsburg, CA 95448
707-433-2319
*Daily, 10–5
Chenin Blanc, Chardonnay, Johannisberg
Riesling, White Zinfandel, Pinot Noir, Zinfandel
Est. 1974, 3,000 cases annually*

Jordan Winery
P.O. Box 878
Healdsburg, CA 95448
707-431-5250
*By appointment
Chardonnay, Cabernet Sauvignon
Est. 1976, 75,000 cases annually*

Marietta Cellars
2295 Chianti Road
Geyserville, CA 95441
707-433-2747
*Cabernet Sauvignon, Syrah, Zinfandel
Est. 1978, 40,000 cases annually*

Murphy-Goode Estate Winery
4001 Highway 128
Geyserville, CA 95441
707-431-7644
*Daily, 10:30–4:30
Fumé Blanc, Chenin Blanc, Chardonnay, Pinot
Blanc, Gewürztraminer, Merlot, Zinfandel
Est. 1985, 100,000 cases annually*

Pastori Winery
23189 Geyserville Avenue
Cloverdale, CA 95425
707-857-3418
*Daily, 9–5
Chenin Blanc, Chardonnay, White Zinfandel,
Zinfandel
Est. 1975, 1,500 cases annually*

Sausal Winery
7370 Highway 128
Healdsburg, CA 95488
707-433-2285
*Daily, 10–4
Chenin Blanc, Zinfandel, Sangiovese
Est. 1973, 15,000 cases annually*

Silver Oak Cellars
24625 Chianti Road
Geyserville, CA 95441
707-857-3562
www.silveroak.com
*By appointment
Cabernet Sauvignon
Est. 1973, 25,000 cases annually*

Simi Winery
  16275 Healdsburg Avenue
  Healdsburg, CA 95448
  707-433-6981
  www.simiwinery.com
  Daily, 10–4:30, picnic facilities
  Sauvignon Blanc, Chardonnay, Pinot Noir,
  Chenin Blanc, Zinfandel, Rosé of Cabernet
  Sauvignon, Muscat Canelli
  Est. 1876, 180,000 cases annually

Sommer Vineyards
  5110 Highway 128
  Geyserville, CA 95441
  707-433-1944
  Daily, 10–5
  Chardonnay, Zinfandel, Late Harvest Zinfandel,
  Carignane
  Est. 1982, 6,000 cases annually

Stonestreet Winery
  4611 Thomas Road
  Healdsburg, CA 95448
  707-433-9000, 707-544-4000
  Chenin Blanc, Chardonnay, Gewürztraminer,
  Pinot Noir, Merlot, Red Meritage
  Est. 1989

Trentadue Winery
  19170 Geyserville Avenue
  Geyserville, CA 95441
  707-433-3104
  www.trentadue.com
  Daily, 11–4, picnic facilities
  Chenin Blanc, Merlot, Sangiovese,
  Zinfandel, Port
  Est. 1969, 9,000 cases annually

Wattle Creek Winery
  25510 River Road
  Cloverdale, CA 95425
  707-894-5166
  Sauvignon Blanc, Chenin Blanc, Chardonnay,
  Shiraz
  Est. 1994, 6,000 cases annually

White Oak Vineyards & Winery
  7505 Highway 128
  Healdsburg, CA 95448
  707-433-8429
  www.whiteoakwines.com
  Daily, 11–5, picnic facilities
  Sauvignon Blanc, Chardonnay, Merlot, Cabernet
  Franc, Zinfandel
  Est. 1981, 7,000 cases annually

The Wineries of Sonoma Carneros

Cline Cellars
  24737 Arnold Drive
  Sonoma, CA 95476
  707-935-4310
  www.clinecellars.com
  Daily, 10–6
  Marsanne, Viognier, Syrah, Carignane,
  Mourvedre, Zinfandel, Rhône-style blends
  Est. 1989, 125,000 cases annually

Gloria Ferrer Champagne Caves
  2355 Highway 121
  Sonoma, CA 95476
  707-996-7256
  www.gloriaferrer.com
  Daily, 10:30–5:30, picnic & event facilities
  Sparkling Wine, Chardonnay, Pinot Noir
  Est. 1986, 80,000 cases annually

Homewood Winery
  23120 Barndale Road
  Sonoma, CA 95476
  707-996-6353
  Weekends by appointment
  Chardonnay, Zinfandel, Cabernet Sauvignon
  Est. 1988, 3,000 cases annually

MacRostie Winery
  17246 Woodland Avenue
  Sonoma, CA 95476
  707-996-4480
  By appointment
  Chardonnay, Pinot Noir, Merlot
  Est. 1988, 8,000 cases annually

Richardson Vineyards
  2711 Knob Hill Road
  Sonoma, CA 95476
  707-938-2610
  Pinot Noir, Merlot, Cabernet Sauvignon, Syrah,
  Zinfandel
  Est. 1986, 3,000 cases annually

Roche Winery
  28700 Arnold Drive
  Sonoma, CA 95476
  707-935-7115
  www.rochewinery.com
  Daily: summer, 10–6, winter, 10–5
  Chardonnay, Pinot Noir, Pinot Noir Sec, Merlot,
  Muscat Canelli, Tamarix
  Est. 1988, 6,500 cases annually

Schug Carneros Estate Winery
  602 Bonneau Road
  Sonoma, CA 95476
  800-966-9365, 707-939-9363
  www.schugwinery.com
  Daily, 10–5, petanque, caves, special events
  Sauvignon Blanc, Chardonnay, Chenin Blanc,
  Pinot Noir, Merlot, Sparkling Wine
  Est. 1991, 20,000 cases annually

Sonoma Creek Winery & Vineyards
23355 Millerick Road
Sonoma, CA 95476
707-938-3031
www.sonomacreek.com
Weekends, April–October, 11–4
Chardonnay, Gewürztraminer, Pinot Noir,
Merlot, Cabernet Sauvignon
Est. 1988, 10,000 cases annually

Tantalus
19320 Orange Avenue
Sonoma, CA 95476
707-938-8509
Chenin Blanc, Sauvignon Blanc, Merlot, Syrah
Est. 1988, 1,800 cases annually

Viansa Winery and Marketplace
25200 Arnold Drive
Sonoma, CA 95476
707-935-4700
www.viansa.com
Daily, 10–5
Italian varietals & blends
Est. 1988, 30,000 cases annually

The Wineries of Chalk Hill

Chalk Hill Estate
10300 Chalk Hill Road
Healdsburg, CA 95448
707-838-4306
By appointment
Sauvignon Blanc, Chardonnay, Pinot Gris,
Merlot, Cabernet Sauvignon
Est. 1972, 75,000 cases annually

The Wineries of Dry Creek

Alderbrook Winery
2306 Magnolia Drive
Healdsburg, CA 95448
707-433-9154
www.alderbrook.com
Daily, 10–5
Sauvignon Blanc, Chardonnay, Gewürztraminer,
Pinot Noir, Zinfandel, Port, Viognier, Chenin
Blanc, Merlot
Est. 1981, 40,000 cases annually

Amphora
5540 West Dry Creek Road
Healdsburg, CA 95448
707-431-7767
rhutchwine@aol.com
Zinfandel, Petite Sirah, Syrah
Est. 1997, 600 cases annually

Armida Winery
2201 Westside Road
Healdsburg, CA 95448
707-433-2222
Daily, 11–5, picnic facilities
Zinfandel, Chardonnay, Pinot Noir, Merlot
Est. 1989, 9,000 cases annually

Bradford Mountain Winery
1440 Grove Street
Healdsburg, CA 95448
707-433-7499
www.bradfordmountain.com
Cabernet Sauvignon, Zinfandel
Est. 1998, 12,000 cases annually

Brogan Cellars
3232 Dry Creek Road
Healdsburg, CA 95448
707-473-0211
Sauvignon Blanc, Chardonnay, Pinot Noir,
Zinfandel
Est. 1998, 550 cases annually

Chateau Diana
6195 Dry Creek Road
Healdsburg, CA 95448
707-433-6992
White Zinfandel, Chardonnay
Est. 1981

David Coffaro Vineyard & Winery
7485 Dry Creek Road
Geyserville, CA 95441
707-433-9715
www.coffaro.com
By appointment
Sauvignon Blanc, Carignane, Petite Sirah,
Zinfandel
Est. 1994, 3,500 cases annually

Collier Falls Vineyard
9931 West Dry Creek Road
Healdsburg, CA 95448
707-433-7373
By appointment
Cabernet Sauvignon, Zinfandel
Est. 1997, 1,000 cases annually

Deux Amis Wines
1960 Dry Creek Road
Healdsburg, CA 95452
707-431-7945
Petite Sirah, Zinfandel
Est. 1987, 1,800 cases annually

Domaine Danica
3554 Round Barn Boulevard, Suite 204
Santa Rosa, CA 95403
707-573-3100
ron@domainedanica.com
Zinfandel, Merlot
Est. 1998, 1,000 cases annually

Dry Creek Vineyards
3770 Lambert Bridge Road
Healdsburg, CA 95448
707-433-1000
www.drycreekvineyards.com
Daily, 10:30–4:30
Chenin Blanc, Chardonnay, Reserve Chardonnay,
Fumé Blanc, Reserve Fumé Blanc, Chenin Blanc,
Merlot, Zinfandel, Red Meritage
Est. 1972, 100,000 cases annually

Duxoup Wine Works
707-433-5195
Syrah, Charbono, Rhône-Style Blends
Est. 1981, 2,000 cases annually

Everett Ridge Vineyard and Winery
435 West Dry Creek Road
Healdsburg, CA 95448
707-433-1637
www.everettridge.com
Daily, 11–4:30
Sauvignon Blanc, Chenin Blanc, Merlot,
Chardonnay, Zinfandel, Syrah
Est. 1996, 4,000 cases annually

Ferrari-Carano Vineyard and Winery
8761 Dry Creek Road
Healdsburg, CA 95448
707-433-6700
www.ferraricarano.com
Daily, 10–5
Fumé Blanc, Chardonnay, Cabernet Sauvignon,
Merlot, Zinfandel, Siena, Syrah, Tresor,
El Dorado Gold
Villa Fiori Label: Chenin Blanc, Muscat Canelli
Est. 1987, 88,000 cases annually

Forchini Vineyards and Winery
5141 Dry Creek Road
Healdsburg, CA 95448
707-431-8886
www.forchini.com
By appointment, picnic facilities
Zinfandel, Pinot Noir, Paradiso, Rosato,
Cabernet Sauvignon
Est. 1996, 3,000 cases annually

Frick Winery
23072 Walling Road
Geyserville, CA 95441
707-857-3205
www.frickwinery.com
Call for tasting hours
Syrah, Viognier, Cinsault, Cinsault Rosé, Merlot
Est. 1976, 2,200 cases annually

J. Fritz Cellars
24691 Dutcher Creek Road
Cloverdale, CA 95425
707-894-3389
Daily: summer, 10:30–4:30, winter, 10:30–4
Sauvignon Blanc, Late Harvest Sauvignon
Blanc, Chardonnay, Zinfandel, Late Harvest
Zinfandel, Merlot, Cabernet Sauvignon
Est. 1979, 30,000 cases annually

Gallo of Sonoma
3387 Dry Creek Road
Healdsburg, CA 95448
707-433-4849
Not open to the public
Chardonnay, Merlot, Pinot Noir, Zinfandel,
Chenin Blanc, Cabernet Sauvignon
Est. 1933

Hawley Wines
P.O. Box 1831
Healdsburg, CA 95448
707-431-2705
jhwines@aol.com
By appointment
Merlot, Viognier
Est. 1995, 10,000 cases annually

Lake Sonoma Winery
9990 Dry Creek Road
Geyserville, CA 95441
707-431-1550
Daily, 11–5
Chardonnay, Zinfandel, Sauvignon Blanc,
Cabernet Sauvignon
Est. 1986, 3,500 cases annually

Lambert Bridge Winery
4085 West Dry Creek Road
Healdsburg, CA 95448
800-975-0555
www.lambertbridge.com
Daily, 10:30–4:30, picnic facilities
Merlot, Chardonnay, Sauvignon Blanc,
Zinfandel, Petite Sirah, Viognier, Rhône-Style
Blend
Est. 1975, 18,000 cases annually

Mazzocco Vineyards
1400 Lytton Springs Road
Healdsburg, CA 95448
707-433-9035
www.mazzocco.com
Daily, 10–4:30
Chardonnay, Zinfandel, Merlot, Cabernet
Sauvignon
Est. 1985, 15,000 cases annually

McCray Ridge
1960 Dry Creek Road
Healdsburg, CA 95448
707-433-2932
By appointment
Merlot, Cabernet Sauvignon,
Est. 1995, 800 cases annually

The Meeker Vineyard
21035 Geyserville Avenue
Geyserville, CA 95441
707-431-2148
cmmeek@aol.com
(temporary facility, new winery under
construction in Dry Creek Valley)
Chardonnay, Cabernet Sauvignon, Merlot, Petite
Sirah, Carignane, Zinfandel, Four Kings
Est. 1984, 5,000 cases annually

Michel-Schlumberger Benchland Wine Estate
  4155 Wine Creek Road
  Healdsburg, CA 95448
  707-433-7427
  www.michel-schlumberger.com
  Daily, 11–2
  Chardonnay, Merlot, Syrah, Pinot Blanc,
  Cabernet Sauvignon
  Est. 1983, 12,000 cases annually

Mill Creek Vineyards and Winery
  1401 Westside Road
  Healdsburg, CA 95448
  707-431-2121
  www.mcvonline.com
  Daily, 10–5, picnic facilities
  Chardonnay, Gewürztraminer, Sauvignon Blanc,
  Merlot, Cabernet Sauvignon, Rosé, Zinfandel
  Est. 1974, 15,000 cases annually

Robert Mueller Cellars
  120 Foss Creek Circle
  Healdsburg, CA 95448
  707-431-1353
  By appointment
  Chardonnay, Pinot Noir
  Est. 1991, 3,200 cases annually

Nalle Winery
  2383 Dry Creek Road
  Healdsburg, CA 95448
  707-433-1040
  By appointment
  Riesling, Gewürztraminer, Zinfandel
  Est. 1984, 2,500 cases annually

Optima Wine Center
  498 Mourvedrerris Lane
  Healdsburg, CA 95448
  707-431-7018
  By appointment
  Chardonnay, Pinot Noir, Cabernet Sauvignon
  Est. 1985, 3,500 cases annually

Pedroncelli Winery
  1220 Canyon Road
  Geyserville, CA 95441
  800-836-3894, 707-857-3531
  www.pedroncelli.com
  Daily, 10–5
  Fumé Blanc, Chardonnay, White Zinfandel, ZR,
  Pinot Noir, Merlot, Cabernet Sauvignon, Port
  Est. 1927, 85,000 cases annually

Peterson Winery
  1040 Lytton Springs Road
  Healdsburg, CA 95448
  707-431-7568
  petersonwinery@juno.com
  By appointment
  Zinfandel, Cabernet Sauvignon, Chardonnay,
  Merlot, Carignane, Pinot Noir
  Est. 1985, 4,500 cases annually

Pezzi-King Winery & Vineyard
  3805 Lambert Bridge Road
  Healdsburg, CA 95448
  707-569-1400
  www.pezziking.com
  Daily, 10–4:30, picnic facilities
  Fumé Blanc, Chardonnay, Merlot, Zinfandel,
  Syrah
  Est. 1995, 29,000 cases annually

Preston of Dry Creek
  9282 West Dry Creek Road
  Healdsburg, CA 95448
  707-433-3372
  www.prestonvineyards.com
  Weekdays, 12–4, weekends, 11–4:30
  Picnic facilities, petanque and bocce ball
  courts, bakery
  Rhône-Style Blends, Semillon, Viognier, Barbera,
  Syrah, Rosé, Zinfandel, Muscato Curioso
  Est. 1974, 30,000 cases annually

Quivira Vineyards
  4900 West Dry Creek Road
  Healdsburg, CA 95448
  707-431-8333
  www.quivirawine.com
  Daily, 11–5
  Sauvignon Blanc, Zinfandel, RSB
  Est. 1983, 20,000 cases annually

A. Rafanelli Winery
  4685 West Dry Creek Road
  Healdsburg, CA 95448
  707-433-1385
  By appointment
  Zinfandel, Cabernet Sauvignon
  Est. 1911, 10,000 cases annually

Ridge
  650 Lytton Springs Road
  Healdsburg, CA 95448
  707-433-7721
  www.ridgewine.com
  Friday–Monday, 11–4
  Zinfandel
  Est. 1964, 6,500 cases annually

Seghesio Winery
  14730 Grove Street
  Healdsburg, CA 95448
  707-433-3579
  www.seghesio@wco.com
  Daily, 10–4:30
  Picnic facilities
  Zinfandel, Sangiovese, Pinot Noir, Pinot Grigio
  Est. 1895, 50,000 cases annually

Selby Winery
  5 Fitch Street
  Healdsburg, CA 95448
  707-431-1703
  Daily, 11–5
  Chardonnay, Syrah, Zinfandel, Pinot Noir,
  Merlot
  Est. 1992, 4,000 cases annually

Philip Staley Vineyards & Winery
1657 Dry Creek Road
Healdsburg, CA 95448
707-763-6717
Mourvedre, Syrah, Grenache, Zinfandel
Est. 1993, 6,500 cases annually

William Talty Vineyards
7129 Dry Creek Road
Healdsburg, CA 95448
707-431-0276
By appointment
Zinfandel
Est. 1997, 175 cases annually

F. Teldeschi Winery
3555 Dry Creek Road
Healdsburg, CA 95448
707-433-6626
www.winecoco.com
Weekends, 11–5, or by appointment
Zinfandel, Petite Sirah, Zinfandel, Port,
White Zinfandel
Est. 1946, 2,000 cases annually

Unti Vineyard
4202 Dry Creek Road
Healdsburg, CA 95448
707-433-5590
www.untivineyards.com
By appointment, picnic facilities
Syrah, Zinfandel, Sangiovese
Est. 1998, 3,000 cases annually

Windsor Vineyards
308B Center Street
Healdsburg, CA 95448
707-433-2822
www.windsorvineyards.com
Weekdays, 10–5, weekends, 10–6
Cabernet Sauvignon, Carignane, Chardonnay,
Fumé Blanc, Gewürztraminer, Rosé, Semillon,
Zinfandel, Red Meritage, Sparkling Wine, Port,
Sherry
Est. 1959, 200,000 cases annually

Yoakim Bridge
7209 Dry Creek Road
Healdsburg, CA 95448
707-433-8511
By appointment
Zinfandel
Est. 1996, 1,000 cases annually

The Wineries of Green Valley

Gan Eden Wines (Yayin Corporation)
4950 Ross Road
Sebastopol, CA 95472
707-829-5686
Chardonnay, Sauvignon Blanc, Semillon, Pinot
Noir, Gewürztraminer, Cabernet Sauvignon
Est. 1985, 15,000 cases annually

Iron Horse Ranch & Vineyards
9786 Ross Station Road
Sebastopol, CA 95472
707-887-2913
www.ironhorsevineyards.com
Daily, 10–3:30
Sparkling Wine, Fumé Blanc, Chardonnay, Pinot
Noir, Sangiovese, Rosé, Cabernet Sauvignon
Est. 1976, 40,000 cases annually

Marimar Torres Estate
11400 Graton Road
Sebastopol, CA 95472
707-823-4365
Weekdays by appointment
Chardonnay, Pinot Noir
Est. 1989, 11,000 cases annually

Eric Ross Winery
P.O. Box 2156
San Anselmo, CA 94979
707-874-3046
Zinfandel, Merlot, Chardonnay, Pinot Noir, Port
Est. 1993, 2,000 cases annually

Scherrer
4940 Ross Road
Sebastopol, CA 95472
707-824-1933
Chardonnay, Cabernet Sauvignon, Zinfandel
Est. 1991, 2,400 cases annually

Taft Street Winery
2040 Barlow Lane
Sebastopol, CA 95472
707-823-2049
Wednesday–Sunday, 11–4
Chardonnay, Sauvignon Blanc, Pinot Noir,
Zinfandel, Merlot, Cabernet Sauvignon
Est. 1982, 65,000 cases annually

Topolos at Russian River Vineyards
5700 Gravenstein Highway North
Forestville, CA 95436
707-887-1575
www.topolos.com
Daily, 11–5:30
Chardonnay, Zinfandel, Alicante Boushet,
Sauvignon Blanc, Chardonnay, Sparkling Wine,
Sherry, Pinot Noir, Zinfandel, Petite Sirah,
Rhône-Style Blend, Carignane, Charbono
Est. 1963, 20,000 cases annually

The Wineries of Russian River Valley

Acorn Winery
P.O. Box 2061
Healdsburg, CA 95448
707-433-6440
By appointment
Cinsault, Zinfandel, Sangiovese, Dolcetto
Est. 1996, 1,000 cases annually

Albini Family Vineyards
886 Jensen Lane
Windsor, CA 95492
707-838-9249
Open to the public one day a year
Merlot
Est. 1990, 500 cases annually

Barefoot Cellars
420 Aviation Boulevard #106
Santa Rosa, CA 95403
800-750-8828, 707-524-8010
www.barefootwine.com
Chenin Blanc, Merlot, Zinfandel, Chardonnay,
Sauvignon Blanc, sparkling wine
Est. 1986, 125,000 cases annually

Battaglini Winery
2948 Piner Road
Santa Rosa, CA 95403
650-588-4171
By appointment
Zinfandel, Petite Sirah, Chardonnay
Est. 1995, 1,000 cases annually

Belvedere Winery
4035 Westside Road
Healdsburg, CA 95448
800-433-8296, 707-433-8236
www.belvederewinery.com
Daily, 10–4:30

2nd tasting room:
250 Center Street
Healdsburg, CA 95448
Daily, 10–5
Syrah, Gewürztraminer, Pinot Noir, Zinfandel,
Merlot, Cabernet Sauvignon
Est. 1979, 70,000 cases annually

Blackstone Winery
9060 Graton Road
Graton, CA 95444
707-824-2401
mike@blackstone-winery.com
Daily, 11–5, picnic facilities
Chardonnay, Merlot
Est. 1990, 200,000 cases annually

Christopher Creek Winery
641 Limerick Lane
Healdsburg, CA 95448
707-433-2001
Friday–Monday, 11–5
Chardonnay, Syrah, Petite Sirah
1974, 4,000 cases annually

Davis Bynum Winery
8075 Westside Road
Healdsburg, CA 95448
707-433-5852
www.davisbynum.com
Daily, 10–5, picnic facilities, lodging
Merlot, Fumé Blanc, Chardonnay,
Gewürztraminer, Pinot Noir, Merlot, Chenin
Blanc, Zinfandel
Est. 1965, 24,000 cases annually

Dehlinger Winery
6300 Guerneville Road
Sebastopol, CA 95472
707-823-2378
Not open to the public
Syrah, Chardonnay, Pinot Noir, Cabernet
Sauvignon, Chardonnay
Est. 1975, 8,000 cases annually

De Loach Vineyards
1791 Olivet Road
Santa Rosa, CA 95401
707-526-9111
www.deloachvineyards.com
Daily, 10–4:30
Chardonnay, Petite Sirah, Pinot Noir, Merlot,
Cabernet Sauvignon, Zinfandel,
Gewürztraminer, Late Harvest Gewürztraminer,
Fumé Blanc, Sauvignon Blanc, White Zinfandel
Est. 1975, 175,000 cases annually

De Natale Vineyards
11020 Eastside Road
Healdsburg, CA 95448
707-431-8460
By appointment
Chardonnay, Sauvignon Blanc, Pinot Noir,
Sangiovese, Cabernet Sauvignon
Est. 1988, 1,000 cases annually

Domaine St. George Winery
1141 Grant Avenue
Healdsburg, CA 95448
707-433-5508
www.comstgeo.com
Monday–Friday, 10–4
Cabernet Sauvignon, Merlot, Chardonnay,
Sauvignon Blanc, White Zinfandel
Est. 1973, 300,000 cases annually

Gary Farrell Wines
10701 Westside Road
Healdsburg, CA 95448
707-433-6616
www.garyfarrell.com
Call for tasting hours

2nd tasting room:
250 Center Street
Healdsburg, CA 95448
Daily, 10–5
Pinot Noir, Zinfandel, Chardonnay, Merlot,
Cabernet Sauvignon
Est. 1982, 25,000 cases annually

Foppiano Vineyards
12707 Old Redwood Highway
Healdsburg, CA 95448
707-433-7272
www.foppiano.com
Daily, 10–4:30
Cabernet Sauvignon, Petite Sirah, Pinot Noir,
Merlot, Sauvignon Blanc, Chardonnay,
Zinfandel
Est. 1896, 150,000 cases annually

Paul Hobbs Cellars
3355 Gravenstein Highway North
Sebastopol, CA 95472
707-824-9879
By appointment
Chardonnay, Pinot Noir, Merlot, Cabernet
Sauvignon
Est. 1991, 7,000 cases annually

Hop Kiln Winery
6050 Westside Road
Healdsburg, CA 95448
707-433-6491
Daily, 10–5
Chardonnay, Valdiquie, Late Harvest Zinfandel,
Chenin Blanc, Zinfandel, Red Meritage
Est. 1975, 10,000 cases annually

J Wine Company
11447 Old Redwood Highway
Healdsburg, CA 95448
707-431-5400
Wednesday–Sunday, 11–5, tasting fee
Sparkling Wine, Pinot Noir
Est. 1987, 30,000 cases annually

Kendall-Jackson Wine Center
5007 Fulton Road (at Highway 101)
Fulton, CA 95439
707-571-8100
www.kj.com
Daily, 10–5
Chardonnay, Pinot Noir, Sauvignon Blanc,
Viognier, Gewürztraminer, Johannisberg
Riesling, Merlot, Muscat Canelli, Pinot Noir,
Semillon, Zinfandel
Est. 1982, 1 million cases annually

Kistler Vineyards
4707 Vine Hill Road
Sebastopol, CA 95472
707-823-560
Not open to the public
Chardonnay, Pinot Noir
Est. 1978, 18,000 cases annually

Korbel Champagne Cellars
13250 River Road
Guerneville, CA 95446
707-824-7000
www.korbel.com
Daily, 10–3
Sparkling Wine, Chardonnay, Chenin Blanc,
Barbera Armstrong Ridge Label: Sparkling Wine
Est. 1882, 1.45 million cases annually

La Crema
4940 Ross Road
Occidental, CA 95465
707-571-1504
Chardonnay, Pinot Noir
Est. 1979, 50,000 cases annually

Limerick Lane Cellars
1023 Limerick Lane
Healdsburg, CA 95448
707-433-9211
Friday–Monday, 10–5
Also by appointment
Zinfandel, Syrah
Est. 1986, 5,000 cases annually

Lynmar Winery at Quail Hill Ranch
P.O. Box 742
Sebastopol, CA 95473
707-829-3374
www.lynmarwinery.com
Pinot Noir, Chardonnay
Est. 1982, 5,000 cases annually

Mark West Winery & Vineyard
7010 Trenton Healdsburg Road
Forestville, CA 95436
707-544-4813
Daily: summer, 10–4:30, winter, 11–4
Chardonnay, Gewürztraminer, Pinot Noir
Est. 1976, 40,000 cases annually

Martinelli Vineyards
3360 River Road
Windsor, CA 95495
707-525-0570
Daily, 10–5
Sauvignon Blanc, Chardonnay, Gewürztraminer,
Pinot Noir, Zinfandel, Muscat of Alexandria
Est. 1985, 5,000 cases annually

Martini & Prati Winery
2191 Laguna Road
Santa Rosa, CA 95401
800-955-9585, 707-823-2404
www.martiniprati.com
Daily: June-October, 10–5, November–May,
11–4
Sangiovese, Barbera, Pinot Blanc, Muscat
Canelli, Zinfandel, Port
Fountain Grove Label: Chardonnay, Cabernet
Sauvignon, Sauvignon Blanc, Pinot Noir,
Merlot, Red Meritage, Viognier
Est. 1902, 20,000 cases annually

Mietz Cellars
602 Limerick Lane
Healdsburg, CA 95448
707-433-7103
By appointment
Merlot, Zinfandel
Est. 1989, 3,000 cases annually

Paradise Ridge
4545 Thomas Lake Harris Drive
Santa Rosa, CA 95403
707-528-9463
Daily, 11–6, picnic facilities
Chardonnay, Sauvignon Blanc, Cabernet
Sauvignon, Merlot, Sparkling Wine
Est. 1994

Porter Creek Vineyards
8735 Westside Road
Healdsburg, CA 95448
707-433-6321
Daily, 10:30–4:30
Chardonnay, Pinot Noir
Est. 1982, 2,500 cases annually

Rabbit Ridge Winery & Vineyards
3291 Westside Road
Healdsburg, CA 95448
707-431-7128
Daily, 11–5
Sauvignon Blanc, Chardonnay, Zinfandel, White Meritage, Pinot Noir, Sangiovese, Merlot, Syrah, Carignane, Barbera, Zinfandel, Rhône-Style Blend
Est. 1981, 150,000 cases annually

J. Rochioli Vineyards and Winery
6192 Westside Road
Healdsburg, CA 95448
707-433-2305
Daily, 10–5
Sauvignon Blanc, Chardonnay, Pinot Noir, Cabernet Sauvignon, Zinfandel
Est. 1982, 10,000 cases annually

Rutz Cellars
P.O. Box 1420, 3637 Frei Road
Sebastopol, CA 95473
707-823-0373
By appointment
Chardonnay, Pinot Noir
Est. 1993

Sapphire Hill
P.O. Box 634
Windsor, CA 95492
707-838-3245
Chardonnay
Est. 1989, 1,350 cases annually

Sebastopol Vineyards at Dutton Ranch
8757 Green Valley Road
Sebastopol, CA 95472
707-829-9463
Friday–Sunday, 11–4
Chardonnay, Pinot Noir
Est. 1995, 4,000 cases annually

Thomas Sellards Winery
6400 Sequoia Circle
Sebastopol, CA 95472
707-823-8293
Not open to public
Chardonnay, Pinot Noir
Est. 1980, 1,000 cases annually

Rodney Strong Vineyards
11455 Old Redwood Highway
Healdsburg, CA 95448
707-431-1533
www.rodneystrong.com
Daily, 10–5
Sauvignon Blanc, Chardonnay, Pinot Noir, Cabernet Sauvignon, Zinfandel, Merlot
Est. 1959, 400,000 cases annually

Joseph Swan Vineyards
2916 Laguna Road
Forestville, CA 95436
707-573-3747
Weekends, 11–4:30
Chardonnay, Pinot Noir, Syrah, White Meritage, Pinot Noir, Cabernet Sauvignon, Zinfandel, Mourvedre, Rhône-Style Blends
Est. 1968, 4,500 cases annually

Tarius Wines
980 Airway Court, Suite C
Santa Rosa, CA 95403
707-566-8007
Pinot Noir, Zinfandel
Est. 1996, 2,500 cases annually

Toad Hollow Vineyards
4024 Westside Road
Healdsburg, CA 95448
707-431-1441
By appointment
Chardonnay, Pinot Noir, Zinfandel, Pinot Noir Rosé, Merlot
Est. 1994, 40,000 cases annually

Villa Pompei
5700 River Road
Santa Rosa, CA 95401
707-545-5899
www.pompeiwinery.com
Weekends, 10–5, picnic facilities
Pinot Noir, Sangiovese, Zinfandel
Est. 1992, 2,000 cases annually

Williams & Selyem Winery
6575 Westside Road
Healdsburg, CA 95448
707-433-6425
By appointment
Chardonnay, Pinot Noir
Est. 1981, 7,000 cases annually

The Wineries of Sonoma Coast

Annapolis Winery
26055 Soda Springs Road
Annapolis, CA 95412
707-886-5460
Daily, 12–5, special events
Sauvignon Blanc, Gewürztraminer, Cabernet Sauvignon, Zinfandel
Est. 1989, 2,500 cases annually

Flowers Vineyard & Winery
28500 Sea View Road
Cazadero, CA 95421
707-847-3661
www.flowerswinery.com
Pinot Noir, Chardonnay, Perennial
Est. 1994, 7,000 cases annually

Keller Estate
5875 Lakeville Highway
Petaluma, CA 95452
707-765-2117
Chardonnay, Pinot Noir
Est. 1995, 2,000 cases annually

Sonoma-Cutrer Vineyards
4401 Slusser Road
Windsor, CA 95492
707-528-1181
www.sonomacutrer.com
By appointment
Chardonnay
Est. 1972, 100,000 cases annually

Wild Hog Vineyard
P.O. Box 189
Cazadero, CA 95421
707-847-3687
By appointment
Pinot Noir, Zinfandel, Nebbiolo, Dolcetto
Est. 1990, 2,500 cases annually

The Wineries of Sonoma Mountain

Benziger Family Winery
1883 London Ranch Road
Glen Ellen, CA 95442
707-935-3000
www.benziger.com
Daily, 10–5
Tribute Red, Tribute White, Sparkling Wine,
Pinot Noir, Zinfandel, Merlot, Cabernet
Sauvignon, Muscat Canelli
Est. 1980, 130,000 cases annually

Coturri Winery
P.O. Box 386
Glen Ellen, CA 95442
707-525-9126
www.coturriwinery.com
Zinfandel, Merlot, Cabernet Sauvignon, Pinot
Noir, Albarello
Est. 1979, 3,500 cases annually

Laurel Glen Vineyard
P.O. Box 548
Glen Ellen, CA 95442
707-526-3914
www.wineaccess.com\laurelglen
Cabernet Sauvignon
Other labels: Counterpoint, Quintana, Terra
Rosa, REDS
Est. 1981, 70,000 cases annually

The Wineries of Sonoma Valley

Arrowood Vineyards & Winery
4347 Sonoma Highway
Glen Ellen, CA 95442
707-938-5170
www.arrowoodvineyards.com
Daily, 10–4:30
Viognier, Chardonnay, Cabernet Sauvignon,
Merlot, Mal, Syrah, Pinot Blanc, Late Harvest
Riesling
Domaine Grand Archer Label: Cabernet
Sauvignon, Merlot, Chardonnay
Est. 1986, 27,000 cases annually

Bartholomew Park Winery
1000 Vineyard Lane
Sonoma, CA 95476
707-935-9511
www.bartholomewparkwinery.com
Daily, 10–4:30, special events
Chardonnay, Pinot Noir, Merlot, Cabernet
Sauvignon
Est. 1994, 4,200 cases annually

Buena Vista Winery
18000 Old Winery Road
Sonoma, CA 95476
707-938-1266
Daily, 10:30–4
Chardonnay, Gewürztraminer, Sauvignon Blanc,
Pinot Noir, Merlot, Cabernet Sauvignon
Est. 1857, 250,000 cases annually

Candelle of Sonoma
P.O. Box 2167, 15449 Arnold Drive
Glen Ellen, CA 95442
707-938-5862
Chardonnay, Cabernet Sauvignon
Est. 1986, 2,000 cases annually

Carmenet Vineyard
1700 Moon Mountain Drive
Sonoma, CA 95476
707-996-5870
By appointment
Red Meritage, Cabernet Franc, Cabernet
Sauvignon, White Meritage, Chardonnay
Est. 1982, 30,000 cases annually

Chateau St. Jean
8555 Sonoma Highway
Kenwood, CA 95452
707-833-4134
www.chateaustjean.com
Daily, 10–4:30, picnic grounds
Chardonnay, Fumé Blanc, Rosé, Gewürztraminer,
Pinot Noir, Late Harvest Riesling, Pinot Blanc,
Viognier, Merlot, Cabernet Sauvignon
Est. 1974, 250,000 cases annually

B. R. Cohn Winery
15140 Sonoma Highway
Glen Ellen, CA 95442
800-330-4064, 707-938-4064
www.brcohn.com
Daily, 10–5, picnic facilities
Cabernet Sauvignon, Pinot Noir, Chardonnay
Est. 1984, 25,000 cases annually

Crane Canyon Cellars
4727 Szeehan Lane
Santa Rosa, CA 95404
707-575-3075
www.cranecanyon.com
By appointment
Pinot Noir, Zinfandel, White Crane (blend of
Viognier and Gewürztraminer), Rosé
Est. 1993, 1,000 cases annually

Fallenleaf Winery
3370 White Alder
Sonoma, CA 95476
650-348-5621
Chardonnay, Sauvignon Blanc, Merlot
Est. 1982, 3,500 cases annually

Fisher Vineyards
6200 St. Helena Road
Santa Rosa, CA 95404
707-539-7511
fishervineyards@metro.net
By appointment
Cabernet Sauvignon, Merlot, Chardonnay
Est. 1979, 10,000 cases annually

Glen Ellen Tasting Room and History Center
14301 Arnold Drive
Glen Ellen, CA 95442
707-939-6277
Daily, 10–5, history center, picnic facilities
Chardonnay, Sauvignon Blanc, White Zinfandel,
Cabernet Sauvignon, Merlot, Pinot Noir
Est. 1980, 3 million cases annually

Gundlach-Bundschu Winery
P.O. Box 1, 2000 Denmark Street
Sonoma, CA 95487
707-938-5277
www.gunbun.com
Daily, 11–4:30
Sonoma White, Sonoma Red, Chardonnay,
Gewürztraminer, Kleinberger, Rosé, Pinot Noir,
Merlot, Cabernet Franc, Chenin Blanc,
Zinfandel
Est. 1858, 50,000 cases annually

Hanzell Vineyards
18596 Lomita Avenue
Sonoma, CA 95476
707-996-3860
www.hanzell.com
By appointment
Chardonnay, Pinot Noir
Est. 1957, 3,000 cases annually

Kenwood Vineyards
9592 Sonoma Highway
Kenwood, CA 95452
707-833-5891
Daily, 10–4:30
Merlot, Sauvignon Blanc, Chardonnay, Pinot
Noir, Zinfandel, Merlot, Cabernet Sauvignon
Est. 1970, 350,000 cases annually

Kunde Estate Winery
10155 Sonoma Highway
Kenwood, CA 95452
707-833-5501
www.kunde.com
Daily, 11–5, picnic facilities
Chardonnay, Sauvignon Blanc, Merlot,
Zinfandel, Chenin Blanc, Viognier, Syrah
Est. 1989, 100,000 cases annually

Landmark Vineyards
101 Adobe Canyon Road
Kenwood, CA 95492
707-833-0053
www.landmarkwine.com
Daily, 10–4:30, lodging
Chardonnay, Pinot Noir
Est. 1974, 20,000 cases annually

Ledson Winery & Vineyards
7335 Highway 12
Santa Rosa, CA 95401
707-833-2330
Daily, 10–5
Merlot, Sauvignon Blanc, Chardonnay, Rosé,
Muscat, Michele's Cuvee
Est. 1998, 7,500 cases annually

Matanzas Creek Winery
6097 Bennett Valley Road
Santa Rosa, CA 95405
800-590-6464, 707-528-6464
www.matanzascreek.com
Daily, 10–4:30
Sauvignon Blanc, Chardonnay, Merlot
Est. 1978, 31,000 cases annually

Ravenswood Winery
18701 Gehricke Road
Sonoma, CA 95476
800-NO-WIMPY, 707-938-1960
www.ravenwood-wine.com
Daily, 10–4:30
Merlot, Zinfandel, Cabernet Sauvignon, Red
Meritage, Chardonnay
Est. 1976, 185,000 cases annually

Robert Hunter Winery
15655 Arnold Drive
Sonoma, CA 95476
707-996-3056
By appointment
Sparkling Wine
Est. 1975, 600 cases annually

Robert Stemmler Winery
18000 Old Winery Road
Sonoma, CA 95476
800-926-1266, 707-526-1917
www.robertstemmlerwinery.com
Daily, 10:30—5
Pinot Noir
Est. 1982, 3,500 cases annually

Sebastiani Vineyards
389 Fourth Street East
Sonoma, CA 95476
707-938-5532
www.sebastiani.com
Daily, 10—5 (closed for renovations until 2001)
Chardonnay, Merlot, Cabernet Sauvignon,
Zinfandel, Barbera
Est. 1904, 5 million cases annually

St. Francis Winery & Vineyards
8450 Sonoma Highway
Kenwood, CA 95452
707-543-7713, 707-833-4666
www.stfranciswine.com
Daily, 10—4:30
Chardonnay, Merlot, Cabernet Sauvignon,
Zinfandel
Est. 1979, 225,000 cases annually

Stone Creek Wine
9380 Sonoma Highway
Kenwood, CA 95452
707-833-5070
www.stonecreekwines.com
Daily, 10:30—5
Cabernet Sauvignon, Fumé Blanc, Chardonnay,
Gewürztraminer, White Zinfandel, Merlot
Est. 1982, 250,000 cases annually

Valley of the Moon Winery
777 Madrone Road
Glen Ellen, CA 95442
707-996-6941
www.valleyofthemoonwinery.com
Daily 10—4:30, picnic grounds
Sparkling Wine, Pinot Blanc, Chardonnay,
Sangiovese, Zinfandel, Syrah, Red Meritage
Est. 1941, 35,000 cases annually

Wellington Vineyards
P.O. Box 568, 11600 Dunbar Road
Glen Ellen, CA 95442
707-939-0708
www.wellingtonvineyards.com
Daily, 11—5
Chardonnay, Viognier, Sauvignon Blanc,
Zinfandel, Syrah, Merlot, Cabernet Sauvignon,
Port, Rhône-Style Blend
Est. 1979, 6,000 cases annually

No AVA

Golden Creek Vineyard
4480 Wallace Road
Santa Rosa, CA 95404
707-538-2350
Merlot, Chenin Blanc, Shiraz
Est. 1983, 1,500 cases annually

Siduri Wines
980 Airway Court, Suite C
Santa Rosa, CA 95403
707-578-3882
Pinot Noir
Est. 1994

Bibliography

Agriculture & History

Dawson, Arthur. *From Arrowhead Mountain to Yulupa: The Stories Behind Sonoma Valley Place Names*. Glen Ellen, CA: Kulupi Publishing, 1998.

Hansen, Harvey J., and Jeanne Thurlow Miller. *Wild Oats in Eden: Sonoma County in the 19th Century*. Santa Rosa, CA.: Historia, 1962.

Heig, Adair. *History of Petaluma: A California River Town*. Petaluma, CA: Scottwall Associates, 1982.

Illustrated Atlas of Sonoma County. Reynolds and Proctor, 1877.

LeBaron, Gaye, Dee Blackman, Joann Mitchell, and Harvey Hansen. *Santa Rosa: A Nineteenth Century Town*. Santa Rosa, CA: Clarity Publishing Services, 1985.

LeBaron, Gaye, & Joann Mitchell. *Santa Rosa: A Twentieth-Century Town*. Santa Rosa, CA: Historia, Ltd., 1993.

Wilson, Simone. *Sonoma County: The River of Time*. Chatsworth, CA: Windsor Publications, Inc., 1990.

Guidebooks

Anstruther, Richard, ed. *Everyday Favorites of Sonoma County*. Sebastopol, CA: High Gain Press, 1998.

Burton, Jack. *Sonoma Picnic*. Mendocino, CA: Bored Feet Press, 2000.

Cusick, Heidi. *Sonoma: The Ultimate Winery Guide*. San Francisco, CA: Chronicle Books, 1995.

Doerper, John. *Wine Country: California's Napa & Sonoma Valleys*. Oakland, CA: Compass American Guides, Inc., 1996.

Fish, Tim, and Peg Melnik. *The Napa & Sonoma Guide Book*. 2nd. Stockbridge, MA: Berkshire House, 1995.

Graham, Jerry, and Catherine Graham. *Jerry Graham's Bay Area Backroads*. New York: Harper & Row, 1988.

Lorentezen, Bob. *The Hiker's Hip Pocket Guide to Sonoma County*. Mendocino, CA: Bored Feet, 1995.

Ter Sarkissoff, Rita, and Michel Ter Sarkissoff. *The Guide to Sonoma County Nurseries*. Sebastopol, CA: Spring Hill Press, 1997.

Sonoma County Authors

Aaron, Chester. *Garlic Is Life*. Berkeley, CA: Ten Speed Press, 1996.

————. *The Great Garlic Book*. Berkeley, CA: Ten Speed Press, 1997.

Ash, John, and Sid Goldstein. *American Game Cooking*. Reading, MA: Aris Books/Addison-Wesley Publishing, 1991.

————. *From the Earth to the Table*. New York: Dutton, 1994.

Bundschu, Jeff, John Sebastiani, and Mike Sangiacomo. *The Wine Brats' Guide to Living, with Wine*. New York: St. Martin's Griffin, 1999.

Burch, Byron. *Brewing Quality Beers*. Fulton, CA: Jody Books, 1986.

Chenel, Laura, and Linda Siegfried. *American Country Cheese*. Reading, MA: Aris Books/Addison-Wesley, 1989.

————. *Chèvre! The Goat Cheese Cookbook*. Reading, MA: Aris Books/Addison-Wesley, 1990.

Evely, Mary. *Vintner's Table Cookbook*. Healdsburg, CA: Simi Winery, 1998.

Fisher, M. F. K. *As They Were*. New York: Alfred A. Knopf, 1982.

Florence, Jack W., Sr. *A Noble Heritage: The Wines and Vineyards of Dry Creek Valley*. Healdsburg, CA: Wine Growers of Dry Creek Valley, 1993.

————. *Legacy of a Village: Italian Swiss Colony and the People of Asti, California*. Phoenix, AZ: Raymond Court Press, 1999.

Kensler, Chuck, ed. *Lip-Smacking Comfort Food . . . A Culinary Legacy of West Sonoma County*. Sebastopol, CA: Burbank Activity Center, 1998.

Kourik, Robert, and Coralie Castle. *Cooking from the Gourmet's Garden*. Santa Rosa, CA: The Cole Group, 1994.

————. *The Lavender Garden*. San Francisco, CA: Chronicle Books, 1998.

Luebbermann, Mimi. *Terrific Tomatoes*. San Francisco, CA: Chronicle Books, 1994.

————. *Paydirt: How to Raise and Sell Herbs and Produce for Serious Cash*. Revised. Roseville, CA: Prima Publishing, 1997.

————. *Little Potted Gardens, Homegrown Fruit*: San Francisco, CA: Chronicle Books, 1998.

Matanzas Creek Winery. *Fragrant Harvest: Lavender Recipes from Celebrity Chefs*. Santa Rosa, CA: Matanzas Creek Winery, 1998.

Otis, Johnny. *Red Beans & Rice and Other Rock 'n' Roll Recipes*. San Francisco, CA: Pomegranate Artbooks, 1997.

Perdue, Lewis. *The French Paradox and Beyond*. Sonoma, CA: Renaissance Publishing, 1992.

————. *The Wrath of Grapes: The coming Wine Industry Shake-out and How to Take Advantage of It*. New York: Spike, 1999.

Sterling, Joy. *Vintage Feasting*. New York: Pocket Books, 1996.

About Sonoma County Food & Wine

Bynum, Lindley. *California Wines: How to Enjoy Them*. Los Angeles, CA: Home H. Boelter Lithography, 1955.

Chirich, Nancy. *Life with Wine*. Oakland, CA: Ed-it Productions, 1984.

Darlington, David. *Angels' Visits: An Inquiry into the Mystery of Zinfandel*. New York: Henry Holt, 1991.

Francisco, Cathleen. *Pinot Noir: A Reference Guide to California and Oregon Pinot Noir*. Sonoma, CA: Wine Key Publications, 1998.

————. *Zinfandel: A Reference Guide*. Sonoma, CA: Wine Key Publications, 1997.

Halm, Meesha, and Dayna Macy. *Savoring the Wine Country*. San Francisco, CA: CollinsPublishers, 1995.

Hill, Amie, ed. *Gopher Soup for Six*. Sebastopol, CA: Sonoma West Publishers, 1999.

Jordan, Michele Anna. *California Home Cooking*. Boston, MA: Harvard Common Press, 1997.

Lorenzo, Henry R. *The Berry Cookbook*. San Francisco. CA: Easy Banana Productions, 1984.

Lorenzo, Jake. *Cold Surveillance: The Jake Lorenzo Wine Columns*. Vineberg, CA: Wine Patrol Press, 1993.

Moorehead, E. D., ed. *Sonoma County . . . Its Bounty*. Petaluma, CA: Privately printed, 1997.

Morse, Kitty. *The California Farm Cookbook*. Gretna, LA: Pelican Publishing, 1994.

Peninou, Ernest P. *History of the Sonoma Viticultural District*. Santa Rosa, CA: Nomis Press, 1998.

Waters, Alice. *The Chez Panisse Menu Cookbook*. New York: Random House, 1982.

Index

Note: Page numbers in **bold** indicate recipes.

and shiitake kebabs, **208**
   steak (market or ribeye), with Gorgonzola
      butter, **207**
beekeeping, 24–26
beet(s), 166
   golden, 166, 174, 246
   risotto, **174**
   with walnuts, olives, and feta, **222**
Behr, Edward, 43
bell peppers. *See* peppers, bell
Bellwether Farms, 11–12, 78, 279, 285
Benedetti, Dante (Dan), 5, 6
Benedetti family, 21
Benedetti, Gene, 5, 6
Bennett Valley Bread and Pastry, 43
Benzinger Family Winery, 61
Bergen, Lea, 211
Berglund, Rod, 60–61
Beringer Wine Estates, 60
Berman, Kathleen and Dan, 281, 285
Bernstein, Laura and Allan, 188
Bertino (poacher and illicit-wine maker), 57
beurre noisette, **111**
Bice, Jennifer, 7
Birds, The, 71, 75
blackberries, 278, 284, 285
blueberry(ies)
   and chicken liver salad, **259**
   pie, **282**
   sauce, **288**
   wild rice, and portobello salad, **251**
boar, wild, 24
Bodega Bay, fish from, 14–15
Bodega Goat Cheese, 13, 71
bones, to smoke, 129
Born Again Barrels, 90
bread
   artisan, 40–44, 85
   lamb loaf in, 202
   Mexican cheese, **135**
   see also bruschetta; croutons; sandwiches; toasts
bread crumbs, fresh, to make, 220
bread pudding, savory Italian, **46**
Brocco, Karen, 73
Broderson, Bob, 278
Brother Juniper's Bakery, 42, 43
bruschetta, **99**
Buena Vista Winery, 65, 79
Buffo, Linda, 16
bulgur, 253
Bundschu family, 62, 79
Burbank, Luther, 1–3, 45, 73, 145, 164, 177

Bureau of Alcohol, Tobacco and Firearms, 58
Burrell, Bernadette and Peter, 166
butter
   apple, 144, **274**
   brown *(beurre noisette),* **111**
   garlic and anchovy, for crudités, 113
   Gorgonzola, **207**
   pear, **275**
buttermilk, 230, 284
Byce, Lyman, 15
Bynum, Davis, 57, 58

C

cabbage, 138, 237
cactus paddles. *See* nopales
Caggiano Company, 23, 212, 213
Caggiano, Richard, 23, 212, 213
cake (*see also* chocolate roll)
   olive oil, **291**
   wine, **290**
caldo verde, **128**
California Carnivores (nursery), 72
California Cooperative Creamery, 4
California Olive Oil Council, 47
California Olive Oil Festival, 84
California School of Herbal Studies, 38
California Visitors Center, 92
California Wine Winners, 50
Callahan family, 11–12, 279
calzone
   shell bean and chard, **153**
   winter squash and feta, **152**
Campbell, Bruce, 21–22, 204
Campbell family, 21
Campbell, Patrick, 60, 61
candles, beeswax, 26
Cannard, Bob, 137
Canyon Road winery, 78
capers, salted, 269
caraway vinaigrette, 247, **262**
cardoon gratin, **223**
Carmenet Vineyard, 62
Carneros. *See* Los Carneros
Carniceria Contreras, 87
Carpenter, Stan, 14, 84
carrot(s), 246, 247
   olive, and feta salad, **243**
cassis. *See* liqueur, blackcurrant
caviar, as garnish, 142, 247
celery, 247
chickpea and scallion salad, **249**
celery root, 124

M

feta, almond-crusted, with grilled grapes and
frisée, **240**
feta and olive, **254**
Greek, **248**
green, **233**
with grilled figs and bacon vinaigrette, **238**
miner's lettuce, **233**
pasta, with shrimp and peas, **255**
persimmon and pomegranate, with lamb, **258**
quinoa, with corn, currants, and avocado, **252**
root vegetable, **246**
salmon, grilled, with lemon vinaigrette, **256**
spinach, warm, **236**
sprout and avocado, with tahini dressing, **242**
tabbouleh, **253**
tomato and vegetable, **244**
wild rice, portobello, blueberry, and walnut,
250
salad greens, 138, 240, 259
fall, with grilled figs and bacon vinaigrette, 190,
238
with lambs tongue vinaigrette, 204
with linguine, **157**
see also arugula; frisée; mesclun
Salmon, Patti and Javier, 13
Salom, Marcello, 47
salsa, 100
cherry tomato, **266**
corn, **184**
salt, 13, 99, 149, 245
salt marshes, 64
Salt Point State Park, 78
sandwiches
farm market panino, **137**
pan bagnat, **40**
radish and chive, **136**
salmon and tapenade, **39**
toasted, with Teleme, tapenade, and soppressata,
39
San Francisco, farmers' market, 29
Sangiacomo, Mike, 62
Sangiacomo vineyards, 65
San Raphael, farmers' market, 29
Santa Rosa: A Nineteenth-Century Town (LeBaron), 45
Santa Rosa, farmers' markets in, 13, 28, 38, 116,
137
Santa Rosa Bread Company, 44
Santos Berryessa, José de los, 59
Sartori, Ralph, 4
sassafras. *See* filé powder
sauce
aioli, **264**
blueberry, **289**
canned tomato, 202
chèvre, 114, 166, **267**

for crudités, 113
garlic and cilantro, **266**
garlic cream, **268**
harissa, **107**
pistou, **127**
raspberry, **292**
rémoulade, Meyer lemon, **181**
romesco, for crudités, 113
skordalia, **101**
tomato
Greek, **202**
and ricotta, uncooked, **158**
walnut gremolata, **132**
yogurt-mint, 104, **265**
sausages
andouille, 21, 155, 192, 211
British banger, 23
Cajun, 23
chicken, 22, 212
chicken-apple, 22–23, 214
chorizo, 23, 110, 185, 195
with chicken livers and spaghetti, **162**
Hawaiian Portuguese, 22
Italian, 155
hot, with spinach and spaghetti, **212**
kielbasa, 23, 192
linguiça, 23, 128, 163
Louisiana-style hot, 23
making, 22–23
merguez, 106, **107**
Polish, 23
Sicilian, and lentil stew, **213**
smoked garlic, 23
Swedish-style potato, 23
scallions (spring onions), 104, 110, 254
and cheese toasts, **134**
chickpea and celery salad, **249**
Schack, Steven, 7, 243
Scharffen Berger chocolate, 294
Schug Carneros Estate, 65
Scott, Alan, 200
Sebastiani family, 38, 62, 65
Sebastiani Vineyards, 63
Sebastopol, 14, 84–86, 87
Sebastopol Fine Wine Company, 85
seed-saving, programs for, 94
Seghesio, Eduardo, 53
Seghesio Winery, 53, 55
Select Sonoma County, 91, 92, 121, 281, 285
sel gris, 99, 245
Selyem, Ed, 57
Seppi, Nancy and Carl, 42
Shainsky, Allen, 17
sheep farming, 22, 92

Swiss chard, 161
    and bean calzone, **153**

T
tabbouleh, sorrel, **253**
tacos lengua, 201, **205,** 246
tahini dressing, **242**
tamales, nopales, **115**
Tancer, Forrest, 59
Tang, Raymond, 85–86
tapenade, olive, 139, 236, **269**
Taqueria Santa Rosa, 86
tart
    blood peach and chocolate, **293**
    spiced apple, **280**
    tomato custard, **47**
Tasting on the Plaza (wine store), 74
Taverna Santi, 78
Taylor Maid Farms, 93, 135
Tea & Tarot (tea room), 85
teachers, rules for, 52
Teitel, Martin, 18
Teldeschi Winery, 55
Teller, Otto and Ann, 92
Ter Sarkissoff, Rita and Michael, 69
Thai dolmas, **104**
Theis, Rick, 97, 200
Thomas, Rich, 55
Thompson, Robert, 28, 87
Thornton, Paul, 14, 84
Tierra Vegetables, 30, 124, 131, 184, 196, 262
Tiller, Larry, 29, 30
Timber Crest Farms, 32
Timm, Betsy, 121
toasts, 111, 142, 200, 228, 236, 237
    cheese and scallion, **134**
    small, **103**
    see also croutons
Tomales Bay Foods, 11
tomato(es), 110, 119, 138
    Brandywine, 147, 149
    canned, 164, 167, 202, 212, 213
    Celebrity, 33
    cherry, 100, 158, 160, 209, 255
        baked, **227**
        salsa, **266**
        vinaigrette, **225**
    confetti, 160, 244, 245
    currant, 245
    custard tart, **47**
    Evergreen, 244
    galette, **149**
    Green Grape, 244

green ripe, 121, 244
Green Zebra, 244
heirloom, 31–32, 147, 149, 244, 248
Northern Lights, 147, 149
plum. *See* tomato(es) Roma
Roma (plum), 127, 184, 212, 254
salad, 244, **248**
sauce, Greek, **202**
sun-dried, 32
Sungold, 29
uncooked, and ricotta, with pasta, **158**
Topolos, Christine, 288
Topolos Winery at Russian River Vineyards, 72
topping, for cobbler, 288
tortilla, potato and nopales, **45**
tortillas, 86, 109, 196, 205
tour(s)
    antiquing, 84–86
    gardeners', 69–73
    history, 79, 81
    Provençal Sonoma, 81–84
    wild Sonoma, 74–78
    winery, in Spanish, 87
Train Town, 88
Traverso family, 51, 76–77, 97, 223
Traverso's market, 51, 76–77, 97
Trentadue Winery, 78
triangles, wild mushroom, **114**
Triple T Ranch & Farm, 112, 223
Tripp, Egmont, 32–33
Tristano, Larry, 223
Truxaw, Evie, 184
turkey(s), 19, 21
    gumbo, **191**
    risotto with cooked, **175**
    smoked, 20, 21
Twele, Gerhard, 22
Twisted Vine (wine shop), 81

U–V
Vallejo, General Mariano Guadalupe, 49–50, 79, 81
vegetables
    for crudités, 112
    root, salad of, **246**
    sandwich of various, **137**
    see also individual kinds
Vella Cheese Company, 9, 79
Vella family, 8–9, 19, 161
Viansa Winery and Marketplace, 65
Vigne, Loreon, 74
Village Bakery, 41, 44, 139
vinaigrette (*see also* dressing, salad)
    bacon, **238**
    balsamic, **241**

black raspberry, **221**
blueberry, **259**
caraway, 247, **262**
cherry tomato, 111, **225**
French herb, **263**
Meyer lemon, **235**
mustard, **233**
of poached lamb tongue, **204**
pomegranate, **259**
vinegar, fruit, 35
black raspberry, 221, 237, 259
blueberry, 250, 259, 260
pomegranate, 259
raspberry, 271
Vine Line Tour, A, 87
vineyards, 65
see also wines, vineyard-designated
Vintner's Table (Evely), 269
visiting, 68–70, 92
see also tours
viticultural areas, 51–67
Viviani, David, 8
Volpi's Speakeasy, 81

W

Wallach, Jad, 44
walnut(s), 135, 171, 174, 223, 246, 251, 279
gremolata, **132**
Waltenspiel, Ruth and Ronald, 32
Ward, Richard, 65
Warm Springs Farm, 29
watercress, 31, 138
watermelon, Moon and Stars, 35
Waters, Alice, 10
Water Street Bistro, 79
Watson, Larry and Susan, 31
Weber, Ed and Kathleen, 41
Weber, Linda, 41
Webvan, 207, 211
Wente Brothers, 56
Western Hills Rare Plants, 71–72
Westside Farms, 88
White House Chef Cookbook (Verdon), 198
White Oak Vineyards, 231
Wild About Mushrooms, 38, 78
Wild Flour Bakery, 41, 44, 71
Wild Hog Vineyard, 66
wild rice, portobello, blueberry, and walnut salad,
250
Williams & Selyem Winery, 57
Williams, Burt, 57
Willie Bird Turkeys, 21

Willowside Meats, 23, 106
Wine X Magazine, 50, 62, 97
wine
Estate Bottled, 52, 66, 67
in recipes, 190
applesauce, **273**
apples poached in, **279**
chutney, **271**
curried stuffed onions, **214**
mussels and herbs, **180**
peach grunt, **283**
red onion marmalade, **269**
stewed quail, **167**
summer fruit in, **278**
wine cake, **290**
recommendations, 51, 97
see also under individual recipes
in Sonoma County, 49–51
vineyard-designated, 57, 59, 62
see also American Viticultural Areas; tours,
winery; wine library
Wine Brats, 38, 62
Wine Brats' Guide to Living, with Wine, 62
wine cake, **290**
Wine Country Cuisine, 285
wine library, 64, 84
Wine Shop, The, 51, 74, 97
Wise, Chuck, 14
Wishing Well Nursery, 71
Wolfert, Paula, 253
Woodhull, Joan, 35, 85
World Cup of Baking, 40–41

X–Z

yogurt, 7, 104, 106, 215, 242
and mint sauce, **265**
zucchini, 127
blossoms, polenta-stuffed, 166, **230**
and potato stew, with andouille, **211**

Michele Anna Jordan, an awarding-winning writer and chef,
is the author of thirteen books on food and wine, including
Salt & Pepper (1999). She is a columnist for the *Santa Rosa Press Democrat*
and North Bay restaurant critic for the *San Francisco Chronicle*. Her
articles appear in numerous publications, including *San Francisco Magazine,*
Wine Enthusiast, Bon Appetit, and *food.com.* She has two daughters,
and lives, with her two cats and a 1954 Seeburg jukebox,
in Sonoma County, where she hosts two weekly radio shows.